PATRICK BLACKETT

Frontispiece: Bust of Patrick Blackett, which now hangs in Imperial college, by Epstein (*Source*: Blackett family)

PATRICK BLACKETT

Sailor, Scientist and Socialist

Edited by
PETER HORE

With a Foreword by
TAM DALYELL

FRANK CASS
LONDON • PORTLAND, OR

First published in 2003 in Great Britain by
FRANK CASS PUBLISHERS
Crown House, 47 Chase Side, Southgate
London N14 5BP

and in the United States of America by
FRANK CASS PUBLISHERS
c/o ISBS, 5824 N.E. Hassalo Street
Portland, Oregon, 97213-3644

Website: www.frankcass.com

British Library Cataloguing in Publication Data

Patrick Blackett: sailor, scientist and socialist
1. Blackett, P. M. S. (Patrick Maynard Stuart), Baron Blackett, 1897–1974 2. Great Britain. Royal Navy
3. Scientists – England – Biography 4. Socialists – England – Biography
I. Hore, Peter
359′.0092

ISBN 0-7146-5317-9 (cloth)

Library of Congress Cataloging-in-Publication Data

Patrick Blackett: sailor, scientist, and socialist / edited by Peter Hore; with a foreword by Tam Dalyell
p. cm.
Includes bibliographical references and index.
ISBN 0-7146-5317-9 (cloth)
1. Blackett, P. M. S. (Patrick Maynard Stuart), Baron Blackett, 1897–1974. 2. Physicists–Great Britain–Biography. 3. Great Britain. Navy–Officers–Biography. 4. World War, 1939–1945–Science. 5. Operations research. I. Hore, Peter.

QC16.B59 P37 2002
530′.092–dc21
[B]

2002067626

Typeset by Frank Cass Publishers Ltd, Southgate, London.
Printed in Great Britain by MPG Books Ltd, Victoria Square, Bodmin, Cornwall

Contents

Illustrations

Between pages 142 and 143

Foreword

Patrick Maynard Stuart Blackett was, quite simply, the most personally formidable man for whom I have ever worked – or, indeed, whom I ever met, at close quarters. And, others, now passed on, would have said exactly the same. It was not simply that he was a Fellow of the Royal Society – when he became President, he mellowed a fraction, but only a fraction.

It was not simply that he was a considerable physicist and a Nobel prize winner: in the course of 40 years as a Member of the British House of Commons, I have come into contact, as an officer of the Parliamentary and Scientific Committee and a politician interested in science policy, with 23 Nobel prize winners. Twenty-two did not daunt me in the way that Pat Blackett daunted me. And he had a capacity to daunt, even the heavyweights of international science. As a young MP, asked to lunch at their club, the Athenaeum, by Sir Howard Florey, FRS, and Sir Lindon Brown, FRS, I had told them that the then Leader of the Opposition, Harold Wilson, had told me that he wanted me to work directly on science policy, to Professor Blackett. Two pretty formidable scientists, themselves, they glanced at each other knowingly, and chimed with a wry smile, laconically, 'We hope that you emerge, alive!'

However, if I found Blackett somewhat nerve-wracking, my wife, Kathleen, did not. His impeccable, naval good manners, combined with an ever-present seriousness of purpose, deeply impressed her. Other women, to whom I have talked about Blackett, would not dissent.

The other 'young man' who was told by Wilson that he should work to Blackett, in 1963, was the Labour Parliamentary candidate for the Buckingham constituency, Captain Robert Maxwell, MC. In Blackett's presence, I observed that Maxwell behaved himself. He managed to bite his tongue rather than offering the bombastic opinions with which he tended to shower the rest of us. Indeed, Blackett brought out the brilliant, imaginative, constructive best in Maxwell. For example, it was for Blackett, in 1963, that Maxwell produced his potentially seminal paper, to the Labour Party Standing Conference on the Sciences, of which I was Honorary Secretary, on

'The Potential of Using Public Purchasing for the Development and Enhancement of British Science'. In return, Blackett took the view that any harm in Maxwell was heavily outweighed by the good, energetic and creative. How do you suppose that so many British scientists, Phillips, Robinson and a list of others, would have got their learned papers published so quickly had it not been for Pergamon and Bob Maxwell? And, when I muttered to Blackett about some Maxwell enormity, the tart, clipped reply came back, 'Remember, Tam, Bob Maxwell won an MC, and you didn't!' It is necessarily an 'if' of History, but my feeling is that if Blackett had been around, somehow Maxwell would have remained 'on the rails', and the whole story of the Maxwell empire might have been different.

A crucial ingredient in the dominating presence, that was Blackett, was his life-long naval officer-ness. Even the Cabinet minister, diarist and Oxford don, philosopher Richard Crossman, felt he was on the quarterdeck. 'Always remember', he warned me, when he was in charge of Labour Party science policy in 1963, 'that Pat commanded a battery of guns on the battleship HMS *Barham*, at the Battle of Jutland, as a teenager!'

It is wholly appropriate that the initiative and implementation of this volume should come not from an academic, not from a physicist, still less from a politician, but from another naval officer, Peter Hore.

Tam Dalyell, MP
House of Commons
November 2001

Acknowledgements

Patrick Stuart Maynard Blackett has been described as one of the greatest scientists of the twentieth century. Even the briefest research easily reveals that, spanning most of the twentieth century, Blackett's scientific achievements were prodigious, that he was the most gifted of experimental physicists in an extraordinary age, the father of three distinct scientific disciplines, and a hero to many. In addition, in one world war he saw active service in some of the most arduous campaigns at sea, and in another his personal efforts were war-winning. Later Blackett had influenced the development of science and defence policy, in several countries, notably Britain and India. In awarding Blackett the Nobel prize in physics for his outstanding achievement in this science, it was the quality of his work which was judged, not the value of the man. According to Benedetti and Benedetti writing in 1948, great science is produced by whole men: men who are great in the human and humanistic sense, not only for their intellectual ability, but also for their remarkable personalities; men who are interested in all aspects of the world in which they live, who participate and leave a trace in more than one field. Patrick Blackett was one of these great, whole men.

Always anxious to give others credit when this was due, on several occasions Blackett paid tribute to the education which he had received while in the Royal Navy. Yet the Navy has ignored Blackett. For example, a naval historian writing about the period after 1918, when the Navy sent its young officers to be civilised after four years of brutal war, managed to do so without mentioning that one of those young men was a Nobel prize winner and President of the Royal Society. And while the physics laboratory at Imperial College is known as the Blackett Laboratory, there is no ship named after Patrick Blackett, not even a research vessel, no laboratory or workshop in the Royal Navy named for him, and hardly a trace of Blackett at his alma mater, about which he was so complimentary, the Royal Naval College, Dartmouth.

On the other hand, there are numerous articles about Blackett, scattered over an astonishing spectrum of professional journals – reflecting, of course, the wide impact which this great man had in many different spheres of human activity. However, it is a conundrum that, apart from Professor Sir Bernard Lovell's biographical memoir of Blackett, no biography exists. Thus in 1998, as Head of Defence Studies for the Royal Navy, I set up a conference at Cambridge to mark the centenary of Blackett's birth. Some of the papers given at that conference are reproduced here, and others, when their authors heard of my interest, have been added.

For their many and various contributions I would like to thank, on behalf of all the contributors to this book, Blackett's son, Nicolas Blackett, and his daughter, Giovanna Bloor, and also his nephew, John Milner. Warm thanks are due too to the following individuals: Itty Abraham, Richard Aldrich, Chris Bayley, Barton Bernstein, Lt Gen. M.L. Chibber, Sandra Cummings, Pat Duffy, Francis Everitt, Andrew Lambert, Norman Lawrie, Doug McLean, Marc Milner, Robert Nye, Ashok Parthasarthi, George Perkovich, Jonathan Rosenhead, Mary Sampson, Roger Sarty, Shiv Visvanathan, Lady Wilson, Jenny Wraight and Ben Zachariah.

These organisations, in Australia, Britain, India and North America, have been helpful in giving access to archives and other documents as well as permission to publish, and this is gratefully acknowledged: the Admiralty Library, the American Institute of Physics, the National Science Foundation, the *Naval Review*, the Regenstein Library of the University of Chicago, the Royal Society, and the Thomas Hart and Mary Jones Horning Endowment; likewise the Cavendish Laboratory, Churchill College, Corpus Christi College and Magdalene College, all of Cambridge.

Some previously published documents have been extensively relied upon. These are: Sir Bernard Lovell, *P.M.S. Blackett – A Biographical Memoir* (London: The Royal Society, 1976), Robert Anderson, *Notes and Records of the Royal Society*, Vol. 53, Nos 2, 3 (1999), Robert Anderson, *Nucleus and Nation: Scientists, International Networks, and Power in India* (forthcoming), and Mary-Jo Nye, 'A Physicist in the Corridors of Power: P.M.S. Blackett's Opposition to Atomic Weapons Following the War', *Physics in Perspective* (1999). They are warmly thanked for permission to republish.

On a personal level I wish to thank Geoff Sloan, who first pointed out to me the opportunity of Blackett's centenary, Nicolas Blackett, Paul Sutcliffe and latterly Tam Dalyell: these four people sustained me and encouraged me in the project to publish a book about Patrick Blackett. I wish especially to thank Nicolas Blackett, whose courage in the face of great illness has been an inspiration to me. Sadly, Nicolas died in April 2002, before this book could be published. And, of course, I wish to thank the authors themselves who have contributed their energy and their knowledge in writing about Patrick Blackett's life and times, and Tam Dalyell for agreeing to write the foreword.

So, what follows is an attempt to explain the Navy's influence on Blackett, and his influence on the higher realms of military operations and national strategy. It is necessarily a team effort because, quite simply, there is currently no one with the knowledge of naval and air operations, science and politics who could write the biography which Blackett deserves. These essays by specialists in their fields have been chosen to help make known more about Blackett's character and achievements, and to pay honour to a great man.

Meanwhile, Cambridge continues to help educate the Royal Navy's officers, and, for much of the time when this work was being researched, the Vice Chief of Defence Staff, the Chief of Defence Procurement, the Second Sea Lord, and the Controller of the Navy, all senior admirals, were Cambridge men.

Peter Hore
Rotherhithe
May 2002

1

Boy Blackett

Patrick Blackett[1]

The Blacketts came originally from Hamsterley, in Northumberland and were small farmers. My great-grandfather moved to London and his children were baptised in St Mary's Church, now Southwark Cathedral. My grandfather went into the Church and was vicar of St Andrew's, Croydon, at the time of his death. He married twice and had a large family. Two of his sons went into the Church, one as a missionary in India. My father became a reluctant stockbroker; his interests were literary and he had a great love of nature.

My mother's family descended from the Whitmores, Shropshire landowners, who represented Bridgnorth, a pocket borough, from the time of Charles I until 1870. They were all Tories but one, Wolryche Whitmore (1787–1858), who sat as a Whig at the same time as a Tory cousin. Wolryche had progressive views on reform, the repeal of the Corn Laws and slavery. His half-sister married Charles Babbage, and Wolryche helped Babbage in promoting the calculating machine. Wolryche's father, William, had been in the Navy and when retired developed his scientific interests and in 1810 tried to get the Admiralty interested in some invention to do with ship's pumps. William was my great-great-grandfather.[2] There was a tradition in the Maynard family too of service in the Navy and Army. My maternal grandfather was Major Charles Maynard of the Royal Artillery, who served in India at the time of what used to be called the Indian Mutiny. His brother William also spent many years in India as a tea-planter, so India and memories of India were part of the family background.

My family lived first in Kensington, where I was born, then in Kenley, and later Woking and Guildford, where I went to a small preparatory school, at the age of 9. In the spring of 1910 my parents entered me as a candidate for the Navy. I do not remember any strong wish to go into the Navy – nor any marked reluctance. However, my family background no doubt had some influence. The method of entry at that time was not only a written examination but also an interview, by a board of four admirals. There were many tales of these ordeals and of the unexpected questions which might be shot at one, such as, 'What was the number of your taxi?' or some other test of the applicant's memory. Luckily for me the first question I was asked was what did I know about Charles Rolls's flying machine, in which he had made the first double crossing of the Channel the day before my interview. I was an aeroplane enthusiast and proceeded to bore the admirals by telling them more than they wanted to know about Rolls and his machine.

A few weeks later I was told that I had been accepted as one of the 65 or so cadets to enter Osborne Naval College in September 1910. I was just under 13 years old. Two other groups, each with the same numbers, were admitted at four-month intervals, so making the total number of cadets entering each year around 200. Each group, or term, as they were called, spent two years at Osborne and then moved on to Dartmouth College for a further two years.

The education of naval cadets seemed to me to be good. It had a strong bias towards science and engineering, and this fitted in well with my interests and, of course, also with my future careers. Sailing in the Dart estuary was an attractive alternative to the usual field games and encouraged one to explore the countryside, especially the cliffs to the west of the river Dart. My father had a great love of nature and had encouraged my interest in birdwatching, and these cliffs and the sands and marshes below were full of birds, duck and waders, and reed warblers with their domed nests built on the high marsh stems. I remember that one day we found the nest of a kestrel and nearby a rock pigeon with its head cut right off, presumably by a kestrel or a peregrine. During the four and a half years at sea during the First World War, I renewed my interest in the ocean birds, albatross, penguins, petrels and others. I read much about the migration of birds and the first lecture I ever gave was on the migration of birds to the university physics undergraduate society. I never revisited the attractive coast of my Dartmouth days until the spring of 1943, when I took part in a practice military exercise in combined operations to test various landing vessels and weapons including some new types of rockets fired from landing craft over the beaches on to the hard land behind the marsh. The duck and waders about seemed to take no notice at all of the extremely noisy bombardment with guns and rockets.

Looking back on my four years at Osborne and Dartmouth I think we got a good education with emphasis on mathematics, science and engineering: this suited me very well and provided a good background for my scientific career after the war. What, of course, was different, compared with a public school, was the service environment, the wearing of uniform from the age of 13, the learning to salute, and the discipline and other naval rituals, which all emphasised the training for a professional sailor.

When war broke out in 1914 about 200 senior cadets at Dartmouth were allocated to one or other fighting ship. The sending of very young cadets to sea in fighting ships was a very old tradition but has long since been abandoned. Certainly the younger cadets were of little use on board a fighting ship but, of course, were as vulnerable as all the crew. In fact these young cadets suffered heavy casualties in the first months of the war when three old cruisers, the *Aboukir*, *Hogue* and *Cressy,* were torpedoed off the Dutch coast. I was one of ten or so who were appointed to HMS *Carnarvon*, one of the County class cruisers, but when we reached Devonport the *Carnarvon* had already left for the South Atlantic, so we were put on board HMS *Monmouth*, also destined for the south seas. On 13 September 1914, luckily for us, the *Carnarvon* and the *Monmouth* met when coaling in the Cape Verde Islands. I and all but one of the cadets in the *Monmouth* were transferred to the *Carnarvon.*

The *Monmouth* continued south passing through the Straits of Magellan and joined the heavy cruiser *Good Hope* off the coast of Chile. On 15 November off Coronel, the German battleships *Scharnhorst* and *Gneisenau* sank the *Good Hope* and the *Monmouth.* Five British survivors were picked up by the enemy ships.

After some weeks patrolling off the African coast, the *Carnarvon* also proceeded south, where she joined up with the British battle cruisers *Invincible* and *Inflexible* off the Brazilian coast and together with the light cruisers *Kent*, *Cornwall* and *Bristol* we all arrived at Port Stanley in the Falkland Islands on the evening of 8 December and started to coal ship in a hurry. Early the next morning the German Fleet came in sight but hurriedly withdrew when they saw the British battle cruisers in Port Stanley. The two fleets came into range in the early afternoon. The *Scharnhorst* and *Gneisenau* and two light cruisers, the *Leipzig* and the *Nuremberg*, were sunk. One light cruiser, the *Dresden*, escaped. The British ships suffered very little damage. Being the slowest ship of the squadron and lightly armed, the *Carnarvon* took only a small part in the battle.

Two years later, when I was 18½, I took part in the Battle of Jutland in the *Barham*, flagship of the Fifth Battle Squadron. The facts recorded in my diary of the battle were as known to me at the time and were not in all cases what the historians eventually decided did in fact happen. The literature on Jutland is, of course, immense and highly controversial.

The relevant pages of my daily diary, which I kept continuously during the first two years of the war, are as follows:

May 30th, 1916 [aged 18½]

We did ordinary instruction in the forenoon, and in the afternoon I again went into Edinburgh with R.M. Dick and we bought a very nice armchair for the gunroom, second-hand and quite cheap. I am writing this up four days late and my memory is somewhat confused. We marched through the Rosyth dockyard and I saw the basin and docks for the first time. They seem very fine. Some seaplanes were up from the *Engadine.* As we were waiting for the boat to come back in the evening we saw a well known signal flying and sure enough, when we were back in the ship we found we were raising steam. The *Engadine* went out first and later the 2nd and 1st battle cruiser squadrons. We came next and last, passing the bridge a few minutes before midnight. The night was lovely and it was my first watch. We imagined it was some raid we were out for.

May 31st

The day dawned glorious but with a slowly falling glass. When I got up I heard that the *Lion*, five miles ahead of us had sighted a submarine and the *Royalist* fired at it. During my forenoon watch we had several submarine scares, once when the *Lion* sighted one ahead of us. We could not see her, however. Some suspicious neutral trawlers were about as usual. Our station was five miles astern of the Battle Cruiser Squadrons. The latter were six in number, the *Lion*[3] and 1st BCS[4] in one line and the *Indefatigable* and *New Zealand* on their port beam. The *Australia* is in dock as is also the *Queen Elizabeth*. We went to Exercise Action in the forenoon to clear away and to get the cages loaded. I slept all the afternoon and just after tea, about 3.50 p.m. 'Action' was sounded. When we realised it was without the 'G': real action that is, we wondered what was up. Of course I could not find my Gieve [life belt][5] – I had put it in the gunroom five minutes before, but it had apparently vanished. We closed up and learnt that some light cruisers of the enemy had been sighted. Just before five o'clock we loaded and trained on a light cruiser – the first German ship I have seen since the Falkland Islands. At 4.57 p.m. we opened fire at about 18,000 yds. range. A few minutes earlier we had seen the flashes of the Battle Cruisers firing ahead of us. After two salvoes at the light cruiser, both of which failed to hit, we shifted target on to the 2nd German battle cruiser from the left, probably the *Seydlitz*. The visibility was not good but our shooting might have been much better. I saw a lot of misses for deflection. I could see through my periscope quite well at first, but later it got misty and was eventually smashed. We were firing on and off, when we could see, and for the first part were not being fired at. After a short time we passed a destroyer picking up survivors from an oily patch on the water. I had, of course, no idea what it was that had sunk but learnt later that it was the *Queen Mary*. I also saw one of our 'M'-class destroyers with her bow out of the water and very much down by the stern. I did not like it a bit when we began to be fired at, seeing the splashes a few yards short, all their shots falling very close together. The noise of them falling was just like our six inch guns going off. Things did not seem to be going very well then, but I was very cheered to see one beautiful straddle we made on one of the German Battle Cruisers, one of our shots bursting on the waterline armour. I saw the flash of it. We then fired four more salvoes rapid and straddled again. After this I saw an explosion aft. We then shifted target. About a quarter to six the British battle cruisers turned sixteen points to starboard and crossed our line of fire. About 6 p.m. we also turned and during it got a bad strafing from the German 3rd Division, their crack squadron. As the Battle Cruisers crossed in front of us I saw that there were only four instead of six, so knew they must have been badly strafed. I saw one of the *Lion*'s turrets out of action by a shell, also one of the *Princess Royal*'s.

About this time we got the cheering news that the Grand Fleet was coming up. We carried on firing at ranges varying from 24,000 yds. to, at the end, as little as 8000 yds. Most of the time we could see nothing but the flashes of their guns. These were very curious. The guns fired in succession beginning with the after gun, so that one saw a succession of flashes, not all at once, as with our director control, or haphazard as in individual control. It was very horrible seeing the flashes, then waiting for the salvoes to fall. They formed very small splashes of far lesser height than ours, and they caused practically no interference with our fire.

The terrible part of it was that we could not see them to reply, for they had the modern 'weather gauge' not of wind but of light. We were silhouetted against the bright western sky and they were merged in a great haze.

About this time we got our 'five minutes hate'. It really lasted much longer and was extraordinarily unpleasant. It is estimated that some five hundred 12-inch bricks were fired at the *Barham* and the rest of the squadron. How we survived with so very few hits I have no idea. Many people say that we were saved by one of the armoured cruiser squadrons. They got in front of us and made a very great smoke screen, which I believe was meant to shield themselves, but it effectively screened us and saved us from a far worse strafing. The terrible fate of the ships I did not see luckily. We do not quite know why Arbuthnot (R.A. Defence) got there at all.[6]

Soon after this the German destroyers attacked and met ours in the middle between the lines. One got through and about five torpedo tracks were seen from the ship, all of which we avoided, but one mouldy [torpedo] struck the *Marlborough.* This ship was three ahead of us in the line of the Grand Fleet, when deployed but she continued in the line after being hit. She had a ten degree list. Everyone was very relieved that the Grand Fleet had joined up, for it was exceedingly unpleasant alone. About this time we trained fore and aft and lined up. I went on top of the turret and saw the battle line extending miles into the mist. The German ships were not visible. We avoided more than one torpedo attack by submarine and the *Revenge,* two ships ahead claims to have rammed and sunk one. The 1st Battle Squadron was next ahead of us and did a good deal of shooting. The 4th ahead of them did less and the 2nd in the van practically none. If we had only another hour of daylight I think very few Germans would have got back. We tried to close them about 9 p.m. but had to draw off eventually owing to the gathering dark.

We were then allowed to leave our stations to get some supper. In order to get aft it was necessary to go along the mess deck. Many people did not know till then that we had been hit, but one realised it terribly then. There was an extraordinary reek of T.N.T. fumes, which mixed with the smell of disinfectant and blood was awful. Nearly all the killed, some twenty-four in number, were lying laid out on the deck, and many were terribly wounded, limbs being completely blown off and nearly all burnt. I then learned that the Padre and Paymaster had been killed in the Forward Medical Distributing station. When I got to the gun-room flat, I found the whole place completely wrecked. The gun-room and the Eng. Comm's cabin were merged into one and the flat outside riddled with holes. The after cabin was also in an appalling mess.

I got some food in the wardroom and then returned to my turret. As I was going there I saw a very violent action, some way off on our starboard beam. Some of our light cruisers had met and blown up a German one. Various actions continued all night, the flashes being very visible and one huge explosion being seen. The night was very trying, waiting closed up – trying to sleep in turns.

We expected to renew the action at dawn and had everything ready.

June 1st

Dawn was welcomed as an end to waiting. I had the morning watch and left my turret to go on to the bridge. The weather was thick and beastly. We were with the rest of the Grand Fleet and were steaming up and down, in order to try and keep the huns from returning to port. The battle cruiser suddenly appeared and then went off again. There were five, not six of them, the *Indomitable* and *Inflexible* having joined up. The German fleet had been reported S.W. of us. Until 2 a.m. we were in touch with them and small actions were going on. But after that we lost touch owing to the thick weather. We could only see about three miles. The battle cruisers reported sighting a Zep.[7] It was probably this that enabled them to escape.

We sighted nothing but a mine, which passed fairly close to us. About noon we turned round and made for Scapa, rather disappointed to have not finished the show off, but I must say longing to get into a defended harbour and sleep. For it had been a great strain, twenty-four hours at actions stations, and part of it, when we were under a very heavy fire without being able to reply, had been terrible.

I learnt at intervals of incidents in the fight which I had not seen: the blowing up of the three British battle cruisers after a very few salvoes, the terrible strafing the 1st armoured cruiser squadron got, ending in the *Defence* and *Black Prince* blowing up and sinking, and the *Warrior* blowing up aft and being taken in tow by the *Engadine*, but sinking eventually.

Several destroyer attacks were made and a lot of light cruiser and destroyer actions occurred between the lines. We sank one German destroyer by 6 inch fire – I think the one that torpedoed the *Marlborough*. A submarine was sighted close to the ship but disappeared on being fired at. The *Revenge* claims to have sunk one by ramming. As to the enemy losses it is very difficult to decide anything as we could see so little. But one 'Kaiser' class certainly blew up amidships and a battle cruiser or two very badly strafed indeed. One curious three funnelled ship was sunk, but what she was we do not know.

We had great hopes of good results from the night's actions, for we had seen one light cruiser given hell by ours and left a glowing mass.

We had several fires on board but they had been very quickly put out. The worst hit was forward. A shell, or rather two came in on the starboard glacis. They both burst on or near the mess deck. One, the forward of the two, wrecked the boys' mess deck and medical store, splinters smashing the starboard hydraulic pump and the telemotor in the lower conning tower. It was this hit which killed Mr. Blythe. The other shell hit the cordite in the forward end of the battery and then burst in the Forward Medical Distributing station causing many casualties. The irony of it lay in the fact that the sick bay, from where everyone had been removed, as it was unprotected, was entirely untouched. The cordite fire in the battery caused many serious burns and only escaped flashing down to the magazine by a miracle; a fragment did actually penetrate there, Lieut. Porter did very well in the battery, putting the fire out and rescuing the men. He got badly burnt.

We steamed back to Scapa with the Grand Fleet, the weather getting nasty as we went.

The *Valiant*, being uninjured, left us for Rosyth. The *Warspite*, who had been damaged in the engine room hauled out of the line and then went back to Rosyth. The *Marlborough* managed to get back to Immingham.

We arrived at Scapa about 12.30 a.m. on June 2nd and at once started to oil and get out empty cordite cases. The C. in C. and numerous other flag officers came on board to examine the damage and we heard we were to dock in Plymouth at once and had been allowed a month to repair and refit it.

At last we get a night in, we are still terribly tired.

Two minor episodes of the latter days of the war may be of interest. I was then sub-lieutenant on the destroyer *Sturgeon* based at Scapa Flow with the Grand Fleet. Unexpectedly, the *Sturgeon* was transferred to the Harwich force under command of Admiral Tyrwhitt. The *Sturgeon* arrived in Harwich harbour from Scapa late one evening and tied up to the first available buoy. At midnight the whole Harwich force was ordered to sea immediately. However, there had been no time for the *Sturgeon* to collect all the local Harwich force orders, so the *Sturgeon* attached herself on to the destroyer which happened to be just ahead of her in the jostling crowd of some 30 destroyers trying to get out of a narrow anchorage on a dark night as quickly as possible. At dawn the next morning the *Sturgeon* found herself stationed on the starboard bow of Tyrwhitt's flagship, whereas she should have been on the port bow. The flagship ordered the *Sturgeon* to take up her proper station. To do this as quickly as possible the *Sturgeon* went full speed across the admiral's bow without waiting for permission – a heinous offence in the protocol of pre-war days, but a protocol absurd in war. Just as the flagship was hoisting a signal reprimanding the *Sturgeon* for such a breach of protocol the *Sturgeon* hoisted the signal 'U-boat in sight on port bow' and then proceeded to sink the U-boat with depth charges – in sight of the whole Harwich force. This was, I believe, the first U-boat to be sunk by the Harwich destroyer force.[8] For this to have been done by a Grand Fleet destroyer in the first 12 hours of attachment to the Harwich force must have been very galling.

The *Sturgeon* became notorious a few months later by the outcome of a scrap off the Dutch coast. The Harwich force was making a raid to attack some light German forces believed to be minesweepers. Four destroyers, one of which was the *Sturgeon*, were sent ahead to investigate. It was soon realised that the enemy ships were not minesweepers but the latest and most powerful destroyers and that we and the enemy were closing in range at high speed, probably 50 knots. Commander [Admiral] Tyrwhitt, on his flagship, immediately ordered our four-destroyer group to alter course by 180 degrees towards the shelter of the whole Harwich force as fast as we could. The enemy opened fire just as we turned. The enemy's gun salvo was some 200 yards or less short of the *Sturgeon.* One shell from the second salvo hit the water a few feet from the starboard side of the *Sturgeon* and blew a large hole in the side of the engine room. This was superb gunnery, and far beyond the competence of the British destroyers: I knew because I was controlling our fire. Our engine room rapidly filled with water and the engine room staff, untouched, walked up the ladder on to the deck. Miraculously the turbines continued to work, though completely under water, for half an hour. The *Sturgeon* was towed back to the safety of the Harwich force at 20 knots with only a foot of freeboard aft. After half an hour the turbines had to be stopped, because seawater began to get into the boilers, which could become dangerous. Remarkably enough the electric dynamos also ran under water and so kept the lighting system etc. running normally, as did the main turbines. The *Sturgeon* was then towed home to Harwich. Since there was nothing else to do and only the after gun could train on the enemy I fired a few shots at the German ship, with no success.

By the standards of the Grand Fleet destroyers, the gunnery and torpedo training in much of the Harwich force seemed to me to be defective. For instance, at Scapa gunnery practice against towed targets was a serious affair and a full analysis was always made of the falls of shot by each destroyer. The analyses were sent to the squadron gunnery officer for assessment and criticism, when needed. When the *Sturgeon* arrived at Harwich we continued this essential practice. Much to my chagrin I found that the squadron gunnery officer took little interest in the fall shot analysis of the *Sturgeon* or any other destroyer.

A similar situation appeared with the torpedo armament. In the summer of 1918 with the end of war in sight, we were told that naval intelligence indicated the possibility of a massive raid on the Channel ports by a large part of the German High Sea Fleet. In preparation of this the Harwich force urgently practised the running of torpedoes against towed targets. The results were always disappointing. Many torpedoes ran incorrectly: some jumped out of the water, others went to the bottom and of those which kept their depth few ran straight to the target.

In the autumn of 1918 I began to think seriously about my future. As nearly as I can remember my reasoning was somewhat as follows: I enjoyed my four years at sea during the war, but I was very doubtful if I would enjoy peacetime Navy. There seemed to me to be two attitudes which I might take if I decided to stay in the Navy. I could treat the Navy as providing a pleasant way of life and an introduction to the best clubs around the globe, or I could take the technological problems of naval warfare very seriously and so become orientated towards fighting another war. As I put it to myself rather crudely: I enjoyed shooting at the enemy during the war – would I enjoy shooting at targets? I decided I would not. So I decided to resign from the Navy as soon as the war was over.

As far back as my youthful days I had always been orientated towards science and technology. I spent most of my free time at home making crystal sets, using galena or some other crystal, and picking up Morse signals from Poldhu and other early stations. On the roof of our house in Guildford I built a wireless set. This was taken away by the Post Office on the outbreak of war. I also made elastic-driven model aeroplanes, optical spectroscopes, induction coils, etc. All this was a useful prelude to my later research career. I was also greatly interested in the aeroplanes of those days and watched the early flights of Cody on Laffan's Plain.[9] I used to bicycle over to Brooklands, where the centre of the famous racetrack had become one of the best airfields in the country. I remember watching A.V. Roe flying his paper-covered triplane and landing nose down in the local sewage farm.[10] In December 1913 I persuaded F.S. Barnwell, chief pilot of the Vickers Co., to give me a five-minute flight around the airfield in his Farman type of biplane. There was no cabin at all and one sat in the open on an agricultural machinery seat holding on to two struts, one each side, and with a rotary engine spinning behind one.[11] My interest in flying continued during my naval period at sea. Some time in 1916 I applied to the Admiralty to be transferred from the RN to the RNAS[12] but the application was refused. An arrogant wisecrack was current in the Admiralty at that time: 'It takes six years to train a naval officer and six weeks to train a flying officer and we are not going to waste all that training.'

I started to read science textbooks during the last months of the war in Harwich harbour and started to look for possible jobs. By the

Armistice in 1918 I was in touch with London University and also with the well-known instrument firm Barr & Stroud, which made all the naval rangefinders with which I was very familiar. While in the *Barham* in 1916, I, together with Sub-Lieutenant Bellars, invented a novel gunnery device. The Admiralty took out a secret patent for this but did not proceed to develop it – rightly, I think, because it would have taken too long. So it was reasonable for me to think of instrument firms as possibly supplying a suitable job for me if I could not get into a university.

However, soon after the Armistice and quite out of the blue, the Admiralty took a step which was to affect the future careers of very many young naval officers, including myself. The Admiralty sent some 400 junior officers to Cambridge for a six-month course of general lectures, with the object of instilling into us some general culture, which had been lacking among those who had been whisked away to sea in 1914, when very young. Thus it came about that, on 25 January 1919, I found myself at Magdalene College, Cambridge, in uniform. The first night in the college I met Kingsley Martin, back from an ambulance unit train on the Western Front. From his talk I realised how relatively comfortable the war at sea had been compared with the grim horrors of the Western Front. A few days later I wandered into the Cavendish Laboratory to see what a scientific laboratory was like. Three weeks later I resigned from the Navy and became an undergraduate student studying for Part 1 of the maths tripos, which I took in May 1919, getting a second class. In October I was accepted as a student of physics, taking Part 2 physics and getting a first in 1921. In 1921 I became a research student under Sir Ernest Rutherford.

Even without the far-sighted action of the Admiralty, I would surely have found a place in some university or technologically orientated firm. But to be deposited, so to speak, on the shores of Cambridge just as the Cavendish Laboratory was rising under Rutherford's inspired direction to great heights of eminence was luck indeed for me. So I owe much to the Royal Navy.

NOTES

1. Royal Society BLA/A11, a typescript of autobiographical reminiscences by Patrick Blackett (three versions of 'My Early Life'). Blackett made notes for an autobiography and drafted a small number of episodes, fortunately including

three versions of 'Naval Period' or 'Early Reminiscences'. In this chapter, by kind permission of his son, Dr Nicolas Blackett, the three versions have been fused.

2. PRO ADM 6/87. A William Whitmore 'who by certificate appears to be more than 22 years of age' was commissioned as lieutenant on 19 January 1771 and appointed to HMS *Alarm.* By 1771 Whitmore already had seven years' service at sea – so he may have gone to sea at an age even earlier than Patrick Blackett. He escapes the standard biographies of the period and so seems not to have been promoted further or ever to have been captain of a warship. According to Woodcroft's *Alphabetical Index of Patentees and Inventions*, between 1789 and 1810 a William Whitmore registered a variety of patents, including one for 'pumping ships and vessels underway, by means of wheels and other machinery, without manual labour' and, according to PRO ADM 12/146, on 10 June 1810 a William Whitmore wrote to the Navy Board 'respecting a plan for ... Movement of Ships in a Calm ... and for clearing their Water on springing dangerous Leaks ...': this seems to have been the same person and, if so, it is from his mother's side that P.M.S. Blackett received his gifts as an experimental engineer.
3. The flagship of Admiral Sir David Beatty, commanding the Battle Cruiser Fleet, consisting of the 1st and 2nd Battle Cruiser Squadrons and the 5th Battle Squadron. Blackett's ship, *Barham*, was flagship of the 5th Battle Squadron, commanded by Rear-Admiral Hugh Evans Thomas.
4. BCS = Battle Cruiser Squadron.
5. Which P.M.S.B. had purchased himself, life belts not then being standard, personal issue in the Royal Navy.
6. Rear-Admiral Sir Robert Arbuthnot, in HMS *Defence*, commanding the 1st Cruiser Squadron. According to Sir Julian Corbett, the official historian, shortly after this incident, *Defence* was hit by two heavy salvoes and disappeared in a roar of flame at 1820.
7. Zep = Zeppelin, a German airship.
8. However, the official history by Sir Henry Newbolt credits the sinking of UB54 on 11 March 1918 to HMS *Retriever* – of the Harwich destroyer force.
9. Samuel Franklin Cody was an American born in 1861. Cody became interested in aeronautical matters and, around 1900, began to experiment with kites. Early attempts to interest the British Army were unsuccessful, but by 1904 his success began to attract the Army's attention and Cody was employed by the War Office between 1905 and 1909. He built Britain's first military dirigible, the *Nulli Secundus*, and then built the first aeroplane to fly in Britain. The machine, based on the Wright brothers' latest model, made the first sustained flight in Britain on 16 October 1908. By 1909, the War Office had decided to discontinue work on aeroplanes but Cody continued with his own experiments at Laffan's Plain, Farnborough, until 1913 when he was killed in a flying accident. The editor is grateful to Dr Neil Young of the Imperial War Museum for these, and the following, notes about early aviators.
10. Alliot Verdon Roe, born 1877. After a short career in the Merchant Navy, Roe built and tested biplanes and triplanes from 1907 onwards; he also patented the aircraft control column. His first biplane flew between September 1907 and June 1908 at Brooklands. Roe also built two triplanes, the second, made from packing paper of yellow oiled cotton, under the railway arches near Lea Marshes. His flights in a triplane on 23 July 1909 can be regarded as the first all-British flight over British soil, by a British pilot in a British-built machine of British design, powered by a British engine. By 1910, Roe was back at

Brooklands flying his triplanes. Roe was a lifelong supporter of Oswald Moseley and thus an unlikely acquaintance of P.M.S. Blackett.

11. Frank Sowter Barnwell, born in 1880, was a Scottish-based automobile and maritime engineer who joined the British & Colonial Aeroplane Company in Bristol during 1911 as a draughtsman. He and his brother Harold had previously formed the Grampian Engineering & Motor Company of Stirling and begun the design and construction of their own aircraft. Barnwell rose to become chief designer of the (renamed) Bristol Aeroplane Company, producing the Bristol Scout, the Bristol Fighter, the Bulldog and the Blenheim. Barnwell learned to fly in order to test his own aircraft, and the Bristol Company had flying schools at Brooklands as well as at Larkhill on Salisbury Plain.
12. Royal Naval Air Service.

2

The Selborne Scheme: The Education of the Boy

Evan Davies

When the First World War began in August 1914, Patrick Blackett was near the end of his passing out examinations from Britannia Royal Naval College at Dartmouth. This was routine, and there was every expectation that Blackett would succeed in his career in the Navy, especially in one of the technical branches. Academically he had been a success at the naval colleges: when he moved from Osborne to Dartmouth, he had been second in his class of 71, and he was the top cadet at Dartmouth in the passing out examinations.[1] A successful officer in the Navy could look forward to good promotion and a steady career, if the previous years of the Navy were any guide.

Blackett was a member of the last class of naval cadets to go through the so-called 'Selborne Scheme' of training in its full form. The war disrupted the Scheme severely, and, although the Scheme continued until 1948, it never fully recovered. It had already lost its position as monopoly supplier of regular seaman and engineer officers for the Royal Navy: the so-called 'Special Entry Scheme', where cadets joined at 17, being instituted in 1913.

Since the 1880s the Royal Navy had been expanding, and in manpower the service grew by a factor of nearly three in the 30 years before the First World War. At least until the challenges of the German and American navies had been surmounted or proved unsurmountable, growth was likely to continue. The demand for officers was steadily rising, especially for officers with a technical bent, and so Patrick Blackett's prospects were good. He could expect to be a captain in about 1935, and, perhaps, an admiral in about 1948.

For eight and a half years Blackett wore the uniform of an officer (or trainee officer) of the Royal Navy, from the age of 13 to 22¼.

When he left the Navy his education was far from complete, but he was a man who had been through some enormously striking experiences. The aim of this chapter is to examine the nature of the naval college system within which the first four years of those experiences happened and to seek to show how it might have influenced him.

The reference books will tell you that Blackett was in the Royal Navy from September 1910, when he arrived at the Royal Naval College at Osborne in the Isle of Wight, until he resigned his commission in early 1919 and became an undergraduate at Magdalene College, Cambridge.[2] They are wrong. Cadets at Osborne and Dartmouth were not in the Royal Navy. From September 1910 to the end of July 1914, he was a schoolboy in two public schools which were run by the Royal Navy, and which existed to provide officers for the Royal Navy. It is not quite clear when Patrick Blackett was first in receipt of pay from the Navy: it was between 4 and 13 August 1914, certainly not later than 13 August.[3]

Blackett spent four years at the Royal Naval Colleges: six, 13-week terms from September 1910 to August 1912 at Osborne on the Isle of Wight, and a similar period at Dartmouth from September 1912 to August 1914.[4] These two schools were almost new: Osborne had opened in September 1903, and Dartmouth in September 1905. Neither was really complete.[5] Dartmouth had seen major building almost continuously since the site was levelled in 1898, and work to double the college in size began during Blackett's last term. They were strange establishments, for they were run by the Navy, along naval lines, with naval officers in command and providing the disciplinary framework as well as doing some of the instruction. On the other hand, the bulk of the teaching, and effective control of the academic syllabus were then in the hands of a group of, largely, civilian masters, led by a headmaster. The pupils' parents paid fees at the level of a good public school to have them educated in the only way which made them eligible to be regular executive or engineer officers in the Royal Navy.[6] The boys were called cadets, although they did not appear in the *Navy List* in that rating or in any other. They wore naval officers' uniforms with the badges of cadets, and were indoctrinated with the ethos of the Royal Navy. All were under an obligation to accept appointments as officers in the Navy should they pass out, and should they be offered one.[7] Generally the cadets believed that they were in the Navy. Indeed they seem to have assumed that the one shilling a week they were given as pocket money was naval pay. It was not: it was charged to their parents in the end-of-term bills. The Archer–Shee affair, which only ended in an Admiralty climbdown in July 1910, when Blackett was seeking to join, showed that cadets were not in the Navy.[8]

The Navy of 1910 was in the midst of a revolution, although the principal architect of change, Jacky Fisher, more properly Admiral of the Fleet John Arbuthnot, Baron Fisher of Kilverstone, had retired in January 1910. The two new colleges were a serious attempt by the Navy's most energetic leader of the era to address some of the problems, but it is important to realise that what Fisher sought and what Blackett received were not the same.

At the end of the nineteenth century, the Royal Navy faced a series of manpower problems. There were worries about the quality of officer education. In 1902, with the new Education Act, the subject of naval officer education began to appear in the public prints:

> It is an old and treasured saying that Waterloo was won on the playing fields of Eton. It is at least equally true that Colenso was lost in her classrooms. There is an uneasy feeling, which we all have come to acquire, that the short-comings of our army are mainly due to a defective system of education and training. After shutting our eyes to the trouble year after year we have come to feel that something must be done, and that quickly … [A]nyone in touch with the junior ranks of the service knows this to be a fact … The bare hint that a system, which somehow manages to turn out officers so good as it does, may be radically defective is treated as the hysteria of the alarmist. Those who know can only look on in hopeless impotence, and trust that when the naval Colenso comes it may be at a moment that is not vital.[9]

Julian Corbett wrote that, but his informant about conditions was Lieutenant Herbert Richmond. Critics of naval officer education are always having a go. While the article was in the press, Fisher, who was Commander-in-Chief of the Mediterranean Fleet, was told that he was to be the next Second Naval Lord, the head of personnel in the Navy. Lord Selborne, the First Lord of the Admiralty, told Fisher in a letter dated 9 February 1902, to which the ever-energetic Fisher replied with three memoranda dated 25 February 1902.[10] The first memorandum shows that Fisher was beginning to plan reforms of the Navy's educational system, but not necessarily for educational reasons.

Fisher's new scheme, always known as the Selborne Scheme, was announced at Christmas 1902, but had already run into a problem before publication. The new college at Dartmouth was intended to be a very handsome building but it was far too small. The new scheme called for 12 terms of 75 cadets. Dartmouth had been designed for about 280 cadets, that is for four terms of 70. The college would not be complete until the summer of 1904. Fisher needed the new scheme in effect at the earliest possible moment, which meant September 1903. So another college was extemporised while Dartmouth was enlarged to accommodate six terms and eventually opened in September 1905.[11] Osborne was a rush job. Various ideas had been considered in the autumn of 1902, including mooring an obsolete ironclad battleship, HMS *Sultan*, in the Medina River. However, Edward VII had given his mother's favourite house at Osborne to the nation, and Fisher's friend, Lord Esher, who was effectively in charge of deciding what to do with it, offered the stable block and some land by the Medina River as a site for the new college which Fisher needed. Between January 1903 and September 1903 enough was ready at Osborne to allow the college to open. Only enough accommodation then existed for the first term. The cadets lived in large huts, but the chapel, classrooms and so on were in the adapted stables. Building went on more or less continuously up until the time of Blackett's arrival. The plan was now that the cadets would spend six terms over two years at Osborne before going on to Dartmouth for a similar time.

The Selborne Scheme has been extensively misunderstood. Fisher was thought to be was doing two things: modernising officer education by introducing a more technical slant to its intellectual formation; and, second, trying to heal the social cleavage threatening the morale of the Navy. Neither is true. Fisher does not seem to have been interested in education. He was not concerned with producing young men who could tackle the problems of being a twentieth-century naval officer at a high level. Fisher, like most people who have had responsibility for basic officer training, was concerned with producing good watch-keeping officers with the self-confidence and capacity for decision in emergency. For Fisher, officership was about mental readiness for emergency action. Officership was not intellectual; it was improvisatory. He argued that:

> The deck officers have no longer what really was an all-absorbing task in becoming proficient in handling a ship under sail. Men's lives aloft were absolutely on the skill of the officer of the watch. A brace improperly touched with the men on the yards, the helm only touched the wrong way, a sudden shift of wind unprepared for by an inexperienced officer brought such odium that only the laziest and most thick-skinned felt compelled to be sailors and became so, and involved an alertness, a perpetual thinking of what to do that the readiness of resource was acquired almost insensibly, which has been the great characteristic of those who go to sea and has led to the expressive public nickname of the 'handyman'.[12]

Rather, in 1902 the Navy was seriously short of officers, and this was the core problem which Fisher was trying to address. Estimates could show the required number of officers and from this a calculation could be made of how many recruits would be needed to provide an officer corps of the required size. In 1902 the holding rank was lieutenant, or the equivalent in other branches, and lieutenants were rather more than half the Royal Navy's active seaman officer corps. In turn, the Navy's officer policy depended upon the Navy's function. If the expectation was more imperial policing, then the Navy needed enough officers for its existing ships. If the Navy was to perform a deterrent function, then some sort of reserve of officers who could bring forward the ships in reserve was also necessary, but there was no need to enlarge the active officer corps. However, if the future included a major mobilisation for a long war, then things would be very different.

In the eighteenth century access to the officer corps of the Royal Navy had been relatively open: a competent person, from almost any social origin, could achieve commissioned status. Entry was not under Admiralty control, and there was very little organised training or education for officers. Most officers learned their job by apprenticeship at sea and from a very young age. A problem for the Navy was that it emerged from each war with a large number of experienced officers whom it could not employ. The policy followed produced an apparent surplus of officers even for wartime requirements, and, because of the absence of a coherent retirement policy, an excess over any plausible peace requirement that was almost absurd. Even at the height of the Great War, in 1809, the Navy employed just under half of its 2,870 officers at sea. In 1813, the Royal Navy had 5,152 commissioned officers, all of them, by 1900 standards, military or executive branch officers. By 1816 this number had risen to 6,156. When demobilisation was complete, there was active employment for only about 10 per cent. This very wasteful officer policy was workable while there were frequent, large wars and nearly static technology. After 1815/16 the Navy possessed many officers who were an unemployable promotion block, so it then began a policy of under-recruitment.

By 1864 the Admiralty had seized control of entry to the officer corps, and created an officer training policy. The hulk, HMS *Britannia*, was a part of the seizure and the policy. *Britannia* was an improvement but flexibility had disappeared and the Navy had narrowed its recruiting base. After the end of the Great War in 1815/16, promotion from the lower deck of worthy ratings ceased, and the age range for recruiting officers also became very narrow. Only new branches, like engineering, were recruiting before 1864 for growth. Even there the Cooper–Key Committee, 1874/75, recommended that the establishment of engineers be reduced.

By 1871/72 there were about 3,500 officers on the estimates, although the *Navy List* gives over 3,800 commissioned officers on the active list. By 1884/85 the estimated number had fallen to about 2,650 but the 1884 officer corps was not comparable with that of 1815. In 1884 it included new branches, not commissioned in 1815, and the separate Masters' branch had been abolished in 1883. Engineers had arrived, and paymasters had developed from the old pursers. To compare properly, the totals must be roughly halved, to about 2,000 for 1871/72 and to 1,500 for 1884/85. By the early 1880s there were only a quarter as many military branch officers as there had been in 1815 and only just over half the number of military branch officers actively employed in the Navy in 1809.

The Navy, in 1884, had 56,950 all ranks and ratings as against 140,000 in 1809. So, apparently, the Navy possessed enough officers for peacetime. The ratio of executive officers to total manpower on the estimates was about 1:42, compared with the 1:48 for active officers in 1809. But the 1809 situation had depended upon a reserve of officers: in 1884 the Navy had almost no reserve of officers. There was the Coastguard, but its total strength, officers and men, was only about 4,000. There were retired officers who could come back, but, in an era of accelerating technical change, they were a diminishing asset. Anyway, the retired list depended upon a substantial active list as its only source of supply. There would be some useful officers, but not all that many. The Royal Naval Reserve had no officers above the rank of lieutenant, and only 196 lieutenants and sub-lieutenants all told.

However, the trend of naval technology had meant that the decline in the size of ships' companies in the years after 1860 was reversed from the late 1870s. Torpedoes, bigger guns, quick-firing guns, electrical installations and, later, wireless all made increasing demands for manpower. As engines grew, the amount of coal to be shovelled grew so the number of stokers rose, to a peak during the First World War. With engines came engineer officers, whose numbers would also rise.

Ships became less economical in their use of officers: the *Inflexible* of 1882 had only half as many ratings per seaman officer as *Minotaur* of 1868 or *Victory* of 1759 (in March 1882, when Jacky Fisher was her captain, she had six seaman lieutenants for a complement of 440). The arrival of weapons like the torpedo had resulted in a great multiplication of smaller ships, which meant more officers per rating. To use an example Fisher was fond of, HMS *Irresistible*, the newest battleship in the Royal Navy when he was appointed Second Naval Lord, had a complement of 780 and required six watch-keeping lieutenants, while HMS *Dwarf*, a Bramble class steel gunboat of 710 tons, launched in 1898, with a complement of 85 needed three.[13]

Notably, in former wars the major increase in the number of ships had been among the little ships that war made necessary. In the period 1793 to 1810, in nearly 16 years of war (and one of peace), the number of operational ships fit for the line of battle had grown by 11 (10 per cent) while the number of operational ships of fifth-rate or below had risen from 191 to 729 (nearly 300 per cent). The demand for officers also grew because the Navy grew so fast: from the estimates for 1884/85 to the last set of peacetime estimates, those for the financial year 1914/15, there was an increase in naval expenditure of 414 per cent. The total manpower of the Royal Navy increased by 165 per cent, and the number of naval personnel, as opposed to Royal Marines, Coastguard, pensioners, or persons under basic training ashore, increased by about 280 per cent. The number of the Navy's commissioned officers increased by only 113 per cent.

The calculation of how many cadets would be needed to produce the required number of lieutenants depended on two figures. The first figure was wastage rates: men quit for many reasons. The cadets of the 1860s and 1870s included one future field marshal (the future Earl French of Ypres) and one future king (the future King George V).[14] Officers failed courses, fell ill, died. The second figure was how long the average lieutenant would be a lieutenant. For the Selborne Scheme, the assumed wastage rate was 20 per cent, from joining to promotion to lieutenant, and a life expectancy as lieutenant of 14.42 years.[15]

A wastage rate of 20 per cent fits known examples, but the expectation that an officer would spend an average of 14.42 years in the rank of lieutenant was less plausible. The 14.42 years cannot be more than the time between promotion to lieutenant and promotion to commander. There were passed-over officers who might last 22 or 23 years on the lieutenants' list, but they must have been at least counterbalanced by those who left the service. In fact, in the years from 1882 to 1902, the seniority as lieutenants of officers promoted to commander varied between about 12.6 years and 11.1 years, declining over time. Using the Admiralty's own estimated wastage rate, 83.3 cadets, the average number per year for 1882–1902, each cohort would provide 66.6 lieutenants, and produce a lieutenants' list of 961 using the Admiralty multiplier, or, 800 using the 12-year assumption.

The inadequacy of the recruiting policy became obvious in the middle 1880s, when the fleet's expansion began. The average entry for the four years 1880–84 was nearly 63 cadets. The estimates claimed increased new cadets from 1883–84, but the number entered only rose significantly the following year. The last seven entries of the 1880s for which firm figures are available give an average of just over 109 cadets per year. The year 1886 was the first in which over 100 cadets were entered in *Britannia* after 1870. All classes in *Britannia* were over 60 strong from July 1891 to September 1904, and from 1897 onward there were three classes a year instead of two. So, by the end of the century the Navy was recruiting between 180 and 210 executive officer candidates per year, three times the number of the early 1880s.

Nonetheless, by 1902 the Navy was suffering from a serious shortage of officers. The estimates for 1902/3 called for 4,048 commissioned officers, with a ceiling of 1,500 executive branch lieutenants. There were, according to the *Navy List* for 1902, only 3,538 commissioned officers, fewer by over 400 than there had been in 1871 when the Navy only had half as many men on the books. There were 1,078 lieutenants (and 132 supplementary lieutenants). So the Selborne Scheme was produced at a time of officer shortage. Actually the measures taken meant the Royal Navy was hauling itself out of the officer shortage that underlay the Selborne Scheme before the scheme was invented. The lieutenants' list had reached the 1902 establishment of 1,500 by 1907, and the modified 1902 establishment of 1,800 by 1912, before any Selborne Scheme cadets would reach the lieutenants' list. But because the Navy continued to expand, and new officer-intensive devices like submarines were coming along, the shortage did not go away. The size of the new college at Dartmouth, dating from 1898, with a maximum output under the old scheme of around 180–210 cadets per year, limited the lieutenants' list to 2,016, a figure it would reach in about 1917. The Selborne Scheme, originally including all officers, would have added at least one-third to the requirement for ex-college officers, and the lieutenants' list of Selborne officers would not have reached completeness till about 1923–25.[16]

As far as Patrick Blackett was concerned he would have had to apply for a cadetship at Osborne, be selected for interview where he would have had to pass a medical examination, write a short essay and pass before an interview panel of senior naval officers, civilian academics and civil servants. When he passed that he would have had to take a non-competitive written educational examination. In his case this process would have occurred in the summer of 1910. The objectives of the interview and examination process were made very clear: the Navy wanted a definite type of boy whose characteristics were spelt out in Ewing's introduction to the report of the first committee:

> It appears, however, that the nature and intention of this examination is occasionally misunderstood, and that some parents make the mistake of supposing that the services of a crammer are necessary or desirable. It cannot be too plainly intimated to the parents of boys who are presented under the new Scheme that the Admiralty do not want candidates who have been specially prepared to pass an examination. They want boys who have had the advantage of natural mental and physical development under the usual conditions of a good preparatory school.[17]

This idea was expanded in *The Entry and Training of Naval Cadets* in 1914:

> What is the right sort of boy? To give a definite answer would be impossible; the boy's suitability often appears or develops as his training and work in the Navy goes on, and the only strict test of it is his career. But it may not be amiss to attempt some indication of the qualities likely to conduce to a boy's becoming a good officer, qualities which may be discernible before the boy is 13, when the question of his entry has to be decided. There is scope and need in the Navy for many types of men and varieties of talent, for the cultivated faculty of scientific thought and for the personal force that assures leadership. But whatever the variety of talent, a naval officer is a man of action. Accordingly that boy has the best chance that is resourceful, resolute, quick to decide, and ready to act on his decision. He must be no slacker, but keen to work and play. He should be sound alike in wind and limb and in the big and little principles of conduct. His life afloat with his brother officers and with the men will require him to be cheerful, unselfish, and considerate if he is to win repute as a good shipmate, and these qualities are essential to a leader. He should give promise of being responsive and observant, closely in touch with his surroundings, but master of himself. The boy of sensitive, poetic spirit, the ruminating young philosopher, the scholar whose whole heart is in his books, are types that have a real use in the world, but their proper place is not the Navy. A boy of the right sort will, within the limits natural to his age, show initiative and readiness for responsibility. He will be able to learn the secret of command through the discipline of obedience. If he is fond of an outdoor life, excels in sports, has a turn for practical mechanics, and does well in his studies, especially in mathematics, so much the better... It is advisable that the boy who is to be a candidate for Osborne should enjoy the full advantages of preparatory school ... Any special preparation for Osborne is to be deprecated, especially anything that savours of cramming.[18]

After a medical came an interview. Usually the interview committee had four members. An admiral who was, or had been, an Admiralty Board member, chaired all the first six committees. There was always a second naval officer, usually a captain or commander, with close associations with cadet training: on the first six committees two were at the time commanders of HMS *Britannia*, and all three captains and one of the commanders were or eventually became captains of one of the naval colleges. There was no one from the non-military branches. There was always a professional teacher: five of six were headmasters, and the odd one out was A.C. Benson who had been an assistant master at Eton and later became Master of Magdalene College, Cambridge. Finally there was a member of the First Lord's Private Office staff: four times, Vincent Baddeley, Deputy Secretary to the Admiralty in the 1930s.

The purpose of this system was to ensure open competition, and thus the formal practice of having to be nominated was done away with, or, rather, the interview was technically a preliminary to the award of a First Lord's nomination.[19] However, old systems, like old habits, die hard. In October 1903, Vincent Baddeley wrote:

> All boys who apply to the First Lord for nomination are invited to come before the Committee, except those who from their first communication are patently unsuitable – to these (& there are v. few of them) no form of application is sent at all.[20]

The issue of nomination was still causing confusion, even among the well informed in 1912. In theory, the interview was the preliminary test to a non-competitive examination, open to any boy who could get someone to apply on his behalf. Actually there was nearly always, in the Osborne period, an excess of qualified applicants over cadetships, and the Navy inevitably took those who did best.[21] Baddeley maintained the need for a weeding process subsequent to the interview in his evidence to the Custance Committee. In 1903, it was seen as a corrective to an interview committee which gave too much weight to character and too little to education.

In reality the competition was not all that open. Most children were simply not able to take advantage of the new system. Their parents lacked the financial resources to put them through the private educational system. Vincent Baddeley, for example, held that: 'The Committee's business is to register its verdict on the general suitability of the boys, and social fitness is certainly on the "counts".'[22] A.C. Benson is also clear:

> I may begin by stating what I believed it to be my duty to try to discover, by observation of the candidates, and by the questions

> which I addressed to them … In the first place I tried to observe the boy's physique, his character, his general bearing, his self-possession; and his *savoir faire*; moreover, I endeavoured to gauge what his social environment had been. I do not think that too great stress ought to be laid on this latter point. But I may say that I believe that there are two kinds of what, for want of a better word, I may call breeding; there is a real inferiority of tone which can hardly be disguised, even in a boy who has been brought up under favourable social influences, and there is also a superficial deficiency of manners, betraying itself in bearing and pronunciation, which could be eliminated under improved conditions. An inferior tone of breeding is not produced by nervousness, though it may be accentuated by it; and I considered it to be of high importance to endeavour to detect the presence of this inferiority of quality.

He then went on to argue that a worthwhile educational assessment was impossible, but he claimed that he could achieve a useful intellectual judgement:

> As to the educational side of the matter, it is of course evident that it is impossible in a few minutes to gauge a boy's attainments … therefore … I endeavoured to discover what the boy was best acquainted with, and then asked general and leading questions, the answers to which might show, in the first place, whether the boy had been thoroughly taught, and which, in the second place, might give the boy opportunity of putting into shape such knowledge as he possessed. It was very easy to see … whether he had memory, ability, and power of expression.[23]

The committees did use techniques for judging candidates other than simply listing parental occupations. Baddeley provided Napier with six sets of questions that a candidate might be asked. Clearly they were in use in the first set of interviews, as accounts of interviews make clear.[24] As the committees became more experienced, they moved a little from the script.[25] It is fairly easy to see that asking a 12-year-old what was the lowest London cab fare or how much a piece of luggage cost to carry in a cab, or what sort of animals or birds would be regarded as game in this country, or with what he should eat caper sauce, apple sauce or currant jelly, or how he should address a duchess, a king or a bishop could establish social background. The connection between that last question and the relative performance of clergymen's and doctors' sons is pretty obvious. He was to be asked other questions that more directly addressed general knowledge, like 'What are the chief agricultural crops grown in England?' though the landed interest might benefit from that one, or 'What are the principal railways of England?'. There are some imperialist questions, like asking for names of eight of England's colonies or six island colonies of the British Empire. Some are more directly naval: 'What is [*sic*] a lightship and a buoy and what are they used for?'[26]

Baddeley developed his idea of how the committee should approach its task of assessing a boy:

> One forms one's own opinion of the boy more by listening to his conversation to the other committee members than from his answers to oneself, & it is hard enough to keep a fair standard in assessing a boy when one's whole attention is devoted to him for 10 minutes. I fear it would be extraordinarily difficult to do so with 3 other conversations going on in the room at the same time … I believe the only way is to take the vote of the committee while all the members have their impressions fresh in their mind – i.e. immediately after he has left the room.[27]

The interview process demanded that the panels make judgements after a very short time with the boys. The 170 candidates interviewed in 1903 were seen in seven working days, at an average rate of about 24 a day. Baddeley clearly implies that the committee gave about ten minutes to each candidate, or about four hours of interviewing each day. There must have been time for deliberation between candidates: again Baddeley implies that. If this was confined to just five minutes per candidate, that means a six-hour interviewing day, exclusive of meal breaks. This calculation leaves no time for looking through the essays that the candidates wrote, or reading the headmasters' references. By June 1904, the members of the committee were taking the view that six solid days of interviewing at the rate of 26 candidates a day was too much, and Captain Sowerby argued in November 1904 that ten minutes was too short a time to make a satisfactory judgement.[28]

Of the 337 in 1903 and 1904, the fathers of 254 gave themselves under eight occupations: army officer, gentleman, merchant, clergyman, naval officer, doctor, lawyer and engineer. There was no general officer among the officer fathers, but there were four admirals. Only one candidate had a working-class father: he was a bricklayer, but the boy had been adopted into another family. The boy did not get in. All four sons of admirals passed into Osborne. Five candidates were not assigned marks but only one candidate passed without the formality of interview: his father was one of the admirals.[29] Sons of military branch naval officers had the best chance of passing, with, in the two successive years, 60 per cent and 88 per cent of such candidates entering Osborne. Sons of non-military branch naval officers had an 18 per cent chance of getting in. This put them in the second worst occupational category and looks like a deliberate policy to remove different social groups, rather than breaking barriers down. This sample shows how much the officer corps was drawn from the three learned professions plus the profession of arms. Of the 337 applicants, 163 (over 48 per cent) were drawn from these groups. However, the whole professional class was not equally acceptable. Doctors' sons did badly at 9 per cent. In 1903 the total failure of doctors' sons is attributable to the interview committee, not to the subsequent examination. Army officers' sons did about half as well as military branch naval officers while over half of clergymen's sons got in. All clergymen seem to have been Church of England. The titled aristocracy is almost completely absent, though the landed interest is strongly represented. Only one cadet entered Osborne who received a fail grade at the interview: he was a naval officer's son.

After the interview, candidates for Osborne had to pass an examination. This was a two-day series of written examinations. Some papers survive,[30] but for years after the First World War they were set by the Oxford and Cambridge Schools Examination Board. There were papers on English, English (*sic*) history, geography, French, arithmetic, algebra, geometry and Latin. In all the papers would have required about six hours in the examination room plus the French oral test. One part was combined history and geography, with a time of 90 minutes for both. History was traditional, the sort of questions parodied by Sellers and Yeoman in *1066 and All That*:

> 1. Write about three lines on any three of the following:
> The Roman Wall, the coming of Augustine, the Dandling [sic], the New Forest, Trial by Ordeal, the English Pale.

> 2. Would you have been on the side of –
> (a) Simon de Montfort or Henry III?
> (b) Richard III or Henry Tudor?
> (c) James Stuart (the Old Pretender) or George I?
>
> Answer any *one* and explain your reasons.
>
> 3. Write an account (not more than one page) of any *one* of the following:
> (a) Edward the Black Prince.
> (b) The Duke of Marlborough.
> (c) Robert Clive.
>
> 4. Show why and with what important results Nelson fought the battles of the Nile, Copenhagen, Trafalgar (about three lines each).[31]

Arithmetic included addition, multiplication and division, and there was conversion of units, questions on unitary method and tax calculations. Algebra included algebraic long division, simplification, finding of common multiples and the solution of simple and simultaneous, but not quadratic, equations. Geometry included constructions and proofs of some of the earlier theorems of Euclid. Each of the three maths exams lasted 90 minutes.

This system looks unconvincing as a way of predicting the performance, as adults, of boys of 12 or so. E. Lyttleton, Headmaster of Haileybury, and a member of the November 1904 committee, made exactly that point, and argued that the real test of the boys' suitability was the whole Osborne process:

> I came to the conclusion that … the work … was thoroughly satisfactory as a general test of the fitness of the candidates … Of course it is impossible to prophesy how a little boy will develop, but I have no doubt that for estimating the present all-round powers of a boy, this informal conversation, coupled with a paper test afterwards and the time at Osborne affords the best method of examination yet devised in England.[32]

Lyttleton is pointing up the dilemma on whose horns the Navy remained caught. The great majority of British naval officers thought early recruitment of potential naval officers essential, so the Navy was forced to assess for entry when the candidates were too far from delivery for the predictors to be any good anyway. On the other hand, the Navy could not grant an excess of cadetships over the likely requirement for officers and then have a high wastage rate. Few responsible parents would allow their sons to be put through a unique educational experience, to prepare only for the Navy, without a good chance of success. The Navy had to produce an effective selection procedure, but designing such a procedure is very difficult, especially in the case of making predictions about performance a long way in the future, which the Selborne Scheme's length of education and training made necessary:

> Typically predictive validity is measured using the registered characteristics of persons as predictors to forecast performance, measured by one or more criteria. The search and selection of criteria is difficult but very essential ... The validity of different ... criteria depends on the aim of the specific procedure, the predictors and criteria used, the target group, and the external conditions of the investigation. Regarding these aspects some general statements can be derived:
>
> (1) Short-term predictions (1–5) years are more reliable than long-term predictions.
> (2) Most of the procedures predict training performance better than job performance.[33]

The reports of the Interview Committees were confident that the system was achieving fair results, but fair has many meanings. If fair includes social justice, the claim is preposterous. If the Selborne Scheme sought to produce a socially united officer corps as the criterion for judgement, then the procedure was monstrous, but successful. It abolished the problem, by keeping out most strata of society. If the aim was an officer corps that was representative of society, with a career open to talent, then it must be condemned wholesale. The cadets were selected from a tiny minority. In that sense, the selection procedure was successful, for a military branch naval officer's idea of a gentleman was almost certainly someone like himself, and that is who was recruited. If fair means fair to the candidates as they presented themselves, that may be true. If fair means adequate as selectors of officers, that is hard to judge. The

Navy's leaders would have argued that social justice was not the Navy's business. Its job was to be efficient (and cheap). The fact that the Navy had therefore to restrict officer recruiting to those whose parents were able to subsidise the Navy by paying fees merely fulfilled one of the objectives set.

It could be argued that the selection procedure was unimportant, either because being a satisfactory naval officer is not all that difficult so it did not really matter what abilities as opposed to social qualities the officer had, or that the education and training given under the Selborne Scheme was so good that it could overcome all but the grossest deficiencies. The second may be true, for the period up to 1914. If either of those propositions is accepted, the exiguous interview process was satisfactory. The effort to publicise fairness was simply a smoke screen.

The real success or failure of the scheme can only be established by looking at the performance of the Royal Navy before and after the scheme's products came to be the core of the Navy's officer group. That is a very large question. It implies making an assessment of the relative performance of the Navy's officer corps before and after it came to be dominated by Selborne Scheme products. Broadly the Royal Navy fought the First World War with a *Britannia* Scheme regular military branch officer corps, and the Second World War with a post-1903 entry officer corps in the ranks below admiral (and some junior admirals from 1941 onwards too). An assessment of the relative performance of the officer corps in the two wars is fraught with difficulties. It may be impossible because the Navy's officer corps never came to be monopolised by Selborne Scheme officers. The first Selborne officers were just reaching fully trained status, which can be taken to be roughly defined as confirmed sub-lieutenants or lieutenants, when the First World War broke out. The September 1903 entry would, normally, have taken their sub-lieutenants' examinations in the summer of 1911 and become lieutenants in 1913, give or take any awards of seniority. It was not, therefore, until about 1918 that Osborne products became a majority of the Navy's lieutenants. By about 1919, they started beginning to be joined by Special Entry products. The neat patterns were much disrupted by accelerated promotions and an influx of officers from other sources, like the lower deck and wartime commissions from 1914 onwards.

Fisher also wanted to increase the amount of engineering education in basic officer training. A Fisher memorandum of

February 1902 is called 'The Engineer Question' although Fisher says in it that he is not addressing the grievances of engineers. However, Fisher did believe that he could deal with the problem of engineers coincidentally with solving the problem of officer development. To Fisher the great requirement of the officer for the Navy was the ability to deal with the unexpected or an emergency effectively. It was his belief that in former times the Navy's officers had acquired this readiness of resource through the repeated alarums and excursions of being officer of the watch in a sailing vessel. However, the arrival of engines had reduced seamanship to a routine activity so much that, and this proposition is a wonderful comment on the state of naval machinery at the start of the last century, the alarums now occurred in the engine room. It was also Fisher's claimed achievement that during his time in the Mediterranean Fleet command he had turned the squadron from being a 12-knot fleet with breakdowns to a 15-knot fleet without, having devoted unremitting attention to the problems of engineering and to boosting the morale of his engineers.

So Fisher's recommendation was that naval officers should have a large element of engineering education and practice: all officers should be trained and educated in common up to the rank of sub-lieutenant. He argued that all officers should have a full basic engineering training, and that the career paths should only diverge at lieutenant level, when an officer could specialise as a seaman, gunner, torpedo officer, instructor or engineer (or Royal Marine[34]). Then officers would come back together on a general list at the rank of commander.[35] There would be a need for a few to provide the senior specialist engineers, or senior Royal Marines, but everybody else could command ships and fleets.

This proposal was met with horror by the conservatives in and outside the service but was pushed through, with only detailed amendments. It would, in the end, as Fisher remarked, have solved the engineer problem. Of course, it would not have done so by raising the social and institutional status of the existing engineer officers, as they wanted, but by supplanting them, over the long term, with those who were of executive branch status.

Fisher always retained the view that the only way you could persuade someone to endure the life of a naval officer was to catch him young, and indoctrinate him early. Fisher never seems to have entertained the proposition that the Navy should leave general education to other agencies, and recruit potential officers as the

Army did at the ages 17 or 18. For this reason the Navy continued to recruit at the ages of 12 to 13, and condemned itself to an extraordinarily inflexible officer production system.[36] Nor did Fisher get as much engineering as he wanted. This was a sticking point in the discussions in the Admiralty in the autumn of 1902, and, in the end, an appeal was made to certain very distinguished practising and academic engineers and scientists. Fisher expected their support, but did not get it, for they wanted more general education, more of what would enhance their gentility. So, the Selborne Scheme only gave one-third of the cadets' time to engineering, but, compared to other public schools at this time, a third was a very high proportion.

In the event, Fisher, with the help of James Ewing, was able to put together a very effective academic and instructional staff for the new colleges at Osborne and Dartmouth. The first headmaster of Osborne, Cyril Ashford, had been senior science master at Harrow, and when, in 1905, Ashford moved on to Dartmouth, he was replaced by Charles Godfrey, a mathematics master from Winchester College.[37]

> The Naval Colleges are supplied with workshops and laboratories on a scale that public schools do not attempt, and much of the cadet's time is spent in learning principles and practice of engineering ... A modern warship is a mass of machines of extraordinary intricacy and variety. To deal with them intelligently, to direct to good purpose the work of the men who handle them, requires on the part of officers an understanding of mechanisms which is best got by an early training in the science of engineering ... The working week at Osborne is 38¾ hours ... and 43¾ at Dartmouth ... [A]bout one fourth of it is spent in manual work. Thus the [instructional] hours [each week] at Dartmouth include about nine hours spent in the workshops.[38]

Practical engineering was largely taught by naval personnel, and included drawing-office skills, lathework, casting, toolmaking, carpentry and so on. In addition there was classroom instruction in physics, and engineering as well. It is at the academic and workshop level that the Selborne Scheme succeeded. The education offered at Osborne and Dartmouth, especially before 1914, was in many ways unique in Britain for it gave to the cadets a grasp of maths, physics and engineering that was not available elsewhere in the public school system. Blackett, as well as the naval conditioning which he received, benefited from what was probably the most intensive physical science and engineering education available at secondary school level in Britain. His prowess as an experimenter, so much remarked on elsewhere, is a splendid vindication of exactly that readiness of resource which Fisher intended to instil in teenage boys. The problems of developing and making experimental apparatus must have seemed routine for Blackett. Whether his observations of the social experiment of Osborne and Dartmouth played any part in his developing socialist views is beyond the scope of this chapter.

In academic terms Blackett was a great success at the two colleges. In terms of those character traits, officer-like qualities, or the sporting abilities which the Navy prized so much, he excelled rather less. He did not engage the attention of the college magazine editors, and he was not sportsman enough to make any of the colleges' teams. However, the evidence is that he enjoyed sport, and was at least an acceptable rugby player.[39] It is, however, uncertain whether the game of cricket which he had to play on 4 August 1914 was a 'great bore' because he did not like cricket or because it was an interruption to the excitement of mobilisation and joining his first ship.[40]

NOTES

1. No examination results for his time at Osborne have come to light, but the cadets when they moved from Osborne to Dartmouth were listed in order of seniority in the *Britannia Magazine* for Christmas 1912. His record card in the headmaster's collection from BRNC Dartmouth survives. This gives his passing out place from Dartmouth in August 1914 as 1/71. This is an academic result. It does not include his mark for Former Service. With that taken into account, he appears to have been second to the King's Medal winner, J.R. Warburton.
2. He was born on 18 November 1897.
3. Blackett and his 11 contemporaries from Dartmouth all joined HMS *Carnarvon* on 13 August 1914. They were rated midshipmen from that day. It would appear that they joined HMS *Monmouth* at Devonport on 4 August as supernumeraries, and joined *Carnarvon* at St Vincent on 13 August.
4. He joined Osborne on 16 September 1910 and left on 3 August 1912. He joined Dartmouth on 20 September 1912 (*Britannia, Royal Naval College, Dartmouth: Admiralty Regulations and Captain's Orders*, London: HMSO, 1908, p. 27). The dates are also printed in the Colleges' 'Blue Lists', of which there is a complete set in the BRNC Library. I am grateful to the librarian for allowing me access to these and other documents.
5. The *Osborne Magazine* for Blackett's first term remarks that the expansion of the Captain's house was nearly complete. *Osborne Magazine*, Christmas (1910), p. 3.
6. The phrase is Jacky Fisher's.

7. In the years before the First World War, all cadets who passed out were offered places in the service. The Navy was expanding, and the requirement for officers was intense. However, in the immediate aftermath of the First World War, only about half of one passing out class was allowed to pass on into the Navy. Part of the reason why Blackett was able to leave the Navy so swiftly in 1919 was the dawning realisation in the Admiralty that the service had a gross oversupply of regular officers.
8. The Archer–Shee affair is better known to the general public through the play, *The Winslow Boy*.
9. Julian Corbett, 'Education in the Navy', *Monthly Review*, March (1902), p. 35.
10. A.J. Marder (ed.), *Fear God and Dread Nought*, Vol. 1 (London: Cape, 1953), p. 222. J. Hattendorf, R.J.B. Knight, A.W.H. Pearsall, N.A.M. Rodger and G. Till (eds), *British Naval Documents 1204–1960* (Aldershot: Navy Records Society, 1993), pp. 972–3.
11. The enlargement of Dartmouth involved building the accommodation for an extra two terms, so now the college could hold up to 420 cadets, but it could still only produce 210 per year. In other words the enlargement did not increase the number of officers the Navy could acquire; it merely made half of Fisher's new scheme possible.
12. Memorandum by Admiral Sir John Fisher accompanying a letter to Lord Selborne, 25 February 1902, Fisher papers, FISR 1/3, Churchill College, Cambridge. Printed in J Hattendorf *et al.* (eds), *British Naval Documents, 1204–1960*, document 512, pp. 972–4. The quotation is on p. 972.
13. The *Irresistible–Dwarf* example is used in the first progress report on the Selborne Scheme, April 1903, p. 9, Admiralty Print, Fisher-Crease Papers, Naval Historical Library.
14. The Royal Navy trained two future field marshals in the nineteenth century: the other was Sir Evelyn Wood.
15. The Selborne Scheme assumed 13 cadets would produce ten lieutenants and that 104 new lieutenants per annum would allow the maintenance of a lieutenants' list of 1,500 or that the lieutenants' list would be replaced every 14.42 years. The calculations are set out in the third progress report on the Selborne Scheme, Fisher-Crease Papers, Naval Historical Library.
16. The statement that the Selborne Scheme applied to all officers is a myth. Actually it did not. Paymasters were not included in the scheme. Neither were doctors or chaplains, although instructor officers were.
17. Command 1962 of 1903, pp. 3–4. Ewing signed this report on 4 January 1904.
18. *The Entry and Training of Naval Cadets*, prepared by the Director of Naval Education under the authority of the Lords Commissioners of the Admiralty, (London: HMSO, 1914), pp. 1–2 and 4.
19. Baddeley to Custance Committee, 2 July 1912, answer to question 4517, Education Committee, Minutes of Evidence, p. 169. Baddeley argued that the First Lord was entitled to enter anyone he liked, no matter what the committee and examination procedure suggested. Very often a naval officer's son had been squeezed in, although he was not really high enough in the committee's report. 'Q4517. An obvious example has not come to light, although of the 5 candidates admitted from the October–November 1903 interviews who were not assigned a mark by the committee, one was the son of a Captain Royal Navy.'
20. V. Baddeley to T.D.W. Napier, 19 October 1903, RNM 53/89/3. See also Baddeley's evidence to the Custance Committee. This discussion is very detailed, even if Baddeley was being fairly circumspect before a committee he

may have regarded as rather hostile given Custance's chairmanship. Baddeley was in charge of the entry of cadets from 1901 to 1910.

21. *The Entry and Training of Naval Cadets*, p. 2. In the old days boys who aspired to become naval cadets required a nomination from the First Lord of the Admiralty. The nominated candidates then competed for appointment, the number nominated being much in excess of the number of vacancies. Both these features were given up when the new scheme came into operation; there is now no nomination and no competitive examination.
22. Baddeley to Napier, 19 October 1903.
23. Cmnd 2540, pp. 8–9.
24. NMM Hamilton Papers HTN 247. A particularly interesting example is the letter written by the future Admiral Sir Louis H.K. Hamilton, apparently to a parent or, more likely, sibling. Undated but between 1 and 16 June 1903, on the day of his interview. Hamilton was a member of the first term to enter Osborne in September, and was the second Osborne cadet to reach flag rank. The interview committee sat for 11 days between 1 and 16 June 1903. New Scheme of Training, Selection of Candidates for Nomination as Cadets, Reports of members of the Interview Committees, Command Paper 1962 of 1904, pp. 3, 5. Another is to be found in Martyn Butt Sherwood, *Coston Gun* (London: Geoffrey Bles, 1946), pp. 7–9. Sherwood was interviewed in November 1914.
25. E. Lyttleton commenting on the committee of November 1904. Cmnd 2450, p. 11.
26. RNM 53/89/5.
27. Baddeley to Napier, 19 October 1903.
28. Comments by A.C. Benson, Captain Wemyss and Viscount Helmsley. Similar comments were made by Captain Sowerby in November 1904 and by Admirals Douglas and Fawkes and by Baddeley in February 1905, Cmnd 2450, pp. 9–13.
29. A.H. Lake merely has 'passed' scribbled against his name on one copy of the list, and is crossed through as if he did not attend in the other copy. In the remarks column is written (in the original clerkly hand) 'Lord W. Kerr will nominate'. Kerr was First Sea Lord in 1903.
30. In the writer's possession.
31. The above is a composite paper.
32. Cmnd Paper 1962 of 1904, p. 11.
33. Peter Braun, Dieter Wiegand and Herbert Ashenbrunner, 'The Assessment of Complex Skills and of Personality Characteristics in Military Services', in Reuven Gal and A. David Mangelsdorff (eds), *Handbook of Military Psychology* (Chichester: Wiley, 1991), p. 38.
34. This idea did not last long: the Royal Marines had escaped before Fisher left the Admiralty in January 1910.
35. This would have been a much more genuine general list than the so-called one introduced by AFO 1/56 in 1956.
36. Indeed the Selborne Scheme made it more protracted and inflexible. Now it would be at least 7½ years from recruitment to complement billet. By 1913, the failure of the Selborne Scheme was already accepted in that it was not capable of producing enough officers fast enough. In that year a Special Entry Scheme recruiting at 17–18 was set up to run in parallel.
37. Godfrey's name was still well known to schoolboys of my generation. Certainly to someone as mathematically ungifted as the present writer, the need to consult four-figure tables with the names of Godfrey and Sissons

on the outside kept the name green. He was a prolific writer of mathematical textbooks.

38. See *Admiralty: The Entry and Training of Naval Cadets*, pp. 3–4, 15.
39. See his diary entry for 20 November 1915. I am very grateful for access to this fascinating document, of which I have been lent a typed copy by the Hon. N.M. Blackett via Captain Peter Hore, RN.
40. The phrase appears in his diary for that day.

3

One of Fisher's Revolutions: The Education of the Navy

Geoff Sloan

Patrick Blackett was the beneficiary of a revolutionary scheme of education in which the Royal Navy inspired by yet another of Fisher's revolutions led the way. Ironically, at the beginning of the twenty-first century Admiral 'Jacky' Fisher still represents something of a paradox to naval historians, and an inspirational totem pole figure to the officer corps of the Royal Navy. Historians still praise and curse him. His sparkling naval career and his far-reaching reforms are viewed as being sublime. Yet the abject failure of the amphibious landings at Gallipoli during the First World War hangs over his reputation like a black storm cloud. Few serving officers today fully appreciate his far-reaching impact on their service. Perhaps through half-remembered lectures on naval history given at Dartmouth, the fact that he was responsible for the de-commissioning of 154 ships will come to the mind of some. More will remember the launch of HMS *Dreadnought* in December 1906, and the revolutionary impact that this design of ship had throughout the world. Regretfully, only a handful of officers know of the percussive impact that Jacky Fisher had upon education in the Royal Navy prior to the Great War.

Today we are all familiar with the links that have been made between education and economic prosperity. The Labour government since its election in 1997 has continually stressed the economic utility of raising educational standards. This relationship has been underlined by statistics which confirm a correlation between levels of education and prosperity. Fisher saw a similar synergy between education and fighting power. Although he was inclined to talk about what we would call today operational capability in frothy phrases such as 'think in oceans and sink on sight', his vision of the role of education was clear. In terms of the trinity of components that make up fighting power – the conceptual, the physical and the moral – Fisher saw all three dimensions being enhanced by education. It can be suggested that this will always be the critical yardstick of any scheme of service education.

If Fisher was clear about what he hoped to achieve via the mechanism of education, this raises the question about his approach to naval reform in general. It can be argued that Fisher had a unique approach to the problems of naval reform, and throughout his periods in the offices of Second and then First Sea Lord he continually brought in outside expertise to help him overcome the internal opposition to his various reforms. With respect to naval education he relied mainly on three men. The first was Sir John Colomb, who was an ex-Royal Marine and a prominent writer on defence. Interestingly, he had been advocating the idea of a common entry for all officers into the Royal Navy and Royal Marines for nearly 20 years.[1] The second important influence was Sir Julian Corbett, the naval historian. Corbett's article on 'Education in the Navy'[2] was published eight months before Fisher's memorandum of December 1902. There is evidence that Corbett benefited from collaboration with a Lieutenant H.W. Richmond[3] and the broad features of Corbett's article were actually incorporated into the scheme of education Jacky Fisher developed. However, the last and most dramatic example of this was the appointment of Sir Alfred Ewing, an engineer by profession, to a post newly created by Fisher, the Director of Naval Education. Ewing, prior to this appointment, had been Professor of Mechanical Engineering at Cambridge University. It is important to note that Ewing was much more than a mere academic: 'Ten years in Cambridge had been sufficient to classify him as a reformer, a teacher, organiser, and one who possessed the necessary make-up of an educationalist.'[4] What Ewing brought to the teaching of the new scheme of service education was the belief that engineering, which made up one-third of the syllabus, should have a large practical dimension to it, and included an emphasis on experimental work. Patrick Blackett's reputation as an experimenter was a product of this scheme of education that Ewing helped to devise. Ewing continued to supervise the work of naval education until 1916 while he also directed the preparation of several textbooks for young officers. It says much for Fisher's ability to attract men of real academic ability that, in May 1916, Ewing was offered the principalship and vice-chancellorship of Edinburgh University. It was a post he held until 1929, and under his leadership the university passed through an unparalleled period of development and expansion. It was these three men, John Colomb, Julian Corbett and Alfred Ewing, who provided much of the intellectual momentum that Fisher was to utilise to great effect.

There is no doubt that most writers regard Fisher as one of the most important British admirals of the twentieth century, and as his biographer, the distinguished Ruddock F. Mackay, says about him:

> It is quite true that Fisher already contrasted, with his particular array of formidable if potentially disturbing qualities, with his most gifted contemporaries. Some of the latter possessed at least equal knowledge and judgement in technical matters; and some of them were better endowed with qualities of leadership, or with tactical and strategic flair; and were therefore more likely to succeed as fleet commanders. But Fisher not only scored heavily in the technical field and possessed powers of leadership well above average in many respects. He also possessed unrivalled drive and energy, a capacity for ruthless action, and a hatred of anyone or anything standing in the way of his schemes for rationalization.[5]

Yet it was the manner in which Fisher went about his reforms that left such a turbulent wake behind him:

> In the course of his long career Fisher exerted a profound influence on all the fleets of the world, and transformed his own from a complacent instrument of Empire into the modern fighting force that won, or at least did not lose, the First World War. Thus he permanently affected all our histories. He did it with a contempt for the past, a ruthlessness, a disrespect for convention and a capacity for intrigue which made him innumerable enemies.[6]

Many revolutions have been credited to Fisher, and the one we are concerned with here is the scheme named after the then First Lord of the Admiralty, Lord Selborne. Fisher's role in the scheme was certainly unique, and, as was his wont, he drew upon important outside expertise. However, the role of the First Lord of the

Admiralty, must not be overlooked. In May 1901 Selborne wrote to the then First Sea Lord, Lord Walter Kerr, and succinctly put forward a number of cogent arguments as to why the Royal Navy had to end the distinction between the executive and engineering officers on board ships:

> I think that it is a very bad thing for the Navy that so large a body of its officers should be growing up in a different atmosphere of tradition and aspiration to that of the executive officers. This is the evil. I can only see one remedy. The abolition of the distinction between the engineer and the executive officer. Not by a sudden and mischievous fusion such as the Americans have recently effected, but by providing that in the future all officers whether engineer or executive should enter the Navy at the same age and under the same conditions, should up to a certain point be trained in the same way, and that then a sufficient number of them should specialise in engineering in exactly the same way neither more or less, as specialisation now exists among the executive officers of the Navy in gunnery and torpedo work.[7]

In addition to cogently setting out the nature of the problem that had to be addressed, Selborne was also willing to give the necessary bureaucratic impetus to these proposals or reforms: 'The scheme would have to be very carefully thought out in all its bearings, and by officers in whose wisdom the Board would place implicit reliance.'[8] Fisher at the time of this exchange was still Commander-in-Chief of the Mediterranean Fleet. However, by the end of 1902 Fisher had become Second Sea Lord, and the alliance between him and Selborne had become close and intimate. It was driven forward by Fisher's approach in ensuring that no one would get in the way of his proposed reforms:

> We have got out a skeleton of the whole scheme ... We have had some bad 'quarters of an hour' in reconciling conflicting views and interests, but I feel assured of success, only we must trample on anyone who gets in our way![9]

The 'New Scheme' or 'Selborne Scheme' was published on Christmas Day 1902. It was one of the most radical reforms of the Fisher era. The starting point of the revolution was the desire to sustain what was good and build on what had changed as a consequence of technology change:

> In the old days it sufficed if a naval officer was a seaman. Now he must be a seaman, a gunner, or engineer and a man of science as well … In dealing with this question the Board have been always conscious of the supreme importance of preserving to the Naval Officer his unmistakable naval character. This character is developed from the early training in responsibility, the powers of self-reliance thereby engendered and the essential unity of the Service.

Fisher argued that the best kind of naval officer is a product of more than just character:

> The highest type of naval officer is that wherein great professional knowledge is added to force of character. The danger within the Navy itself is lest insufficient importance should be attached to the results of study, and lest the value of what is called the practical character should be placed higher than it deserves. It is true that no student will ever become a victorious leader unless he is also a practical seaman and has the power of influencing men; but it is also true that no seaman, however practical, will be fit to rise beyond a certain rank unless he has thought out the problems of his calling as a student and has omitted no opportunity of acquiring the knowledge that makes up the science of his profession.[10]

Driving this vision was the concept of the unity of the service. This would be facilitated by ensuring that the changes proposed, although far-reaching and sweeping, were in the pursuance of a defined end state.

The following radical changes were proposed. First, the officers for the executive and engineering branches of the Navy, including the Royal Marines, would all enter the new naval college at Osborne between the ages of 12 and 13. Furthermore, all cadets would remain on the same scheme until they were aged between 19 and 20. It was only at that point that they would then be separated into the three branches. The target that Fisher was trying to hit was very clearly articulated: 'The result aimed at is … community of knowledge and lifelong community of sentiment. The only machinery which can produce this result is early companionship and community of instruction.'[11]

Naval historians have often been misleading about the Selborne Scheme.[12] The impression has been given that it was exclusively concerned with initial officer training and the period of time they served at sea up to the rank of sub-lieutenant. This is simply not the case. For example, one of the forgotten dimensions of the scheme was the proposed introduction of a promotion exam from the rank of lieutenant to commander (the rank of lieutenant commander was not introduced until 1914). This exam would be applied to officers in both the executive branch and the engineering branch of the Royal Navy. The Royal Marines would be treated slightly differently. Fisher even went so far as to outline the syllabus for this promotion exam. It would consist of the following subjects:

- court martial procedure;
- international law;
- knowledge of British and foreign warships, guns and torpedoes;
- naval history;
- signals;
- strategy;
- tactics and battle formations.

The engineer branch later would undertake specialist courses at the Naval Engineering College at Keyham and Greenwich. These arrangements would facilitate a parity of progression:

> By these arrangements Sub-Lieutenants of the Engineer branch will obtain their step in rank at the same age as the Sub-Lieutenants of the Executive Branch and they will enjoy the same opportunities of accelerated promotions and according to the classifications they receive at their previous examinations.

The Royal Marines would receive specialist training at the headquarters of their division or the depot for two years after having completed final exams as a sub-lieutenants. Interestingly they would have the opportunity to qualify as gunnery and torpedo lieutenants. The aim of this was clear: 'The future Royal Marines Officer will thus become available for keeping watch at sea and for general Executive duties on board ship up to and including the rank of

Captain of Marines.'[13] It was in this way that the Selborne Scheme would deliver the essential unity of the service that Fisher had so clearly identified. The cost, if there was one, was a lengthening of the training pipeline:

> The Cadet now takes about four and a half years to become an acting Sub Lieutenant; under the new system he will become fitted for the general services of the fleet in seven years, while the Engineer and Royal Marine Officer will require about two years more for their special professional instruction.[14]

Yet what was achieved was the clearly stated aim of a single system of supply, entry and training. This scheme would facilitate the ultimate goal of community of knowledge and sentiment.

It is interesting to note that Fisher's desire for 'unity of the service' did not stop with the officer corps of the Royal Navy and Royal Marines. The Selborne Scheme also addressed the service education of warrant officers, petty officers and men. Reference is made by Fisher to the 47 years that had elapsed since the beginning of continuous service in the Navy (1857). Fisher acknowledged the 'splendid fighting qualities and the daring seamanship of the sailor of by-gone days'. Yet he stressed the benefits of modern employment practices: 'To-day the manning of the Fleet can be organized with mathematical precision and every well-behaved man can rely on continuous employment followed by provision for old age.'[15] The memorandum then goes on to argue that the Navy had now become to the men what it always was to the officers – a profession and a devotion of a lifetime. As a consequence of these changes, there was now a corresponding need on behalf the part of the Board of Admiralty to ensure that their training and education were fully adapted to the work they had to perform. The Selborne Scheme enunciated four recommendations to enable these stated objectives to be met. They would include the following: first, the Masted Training Squadron would be abolished; second, specialisation was to become both continuous and systematic; third, the housing of men in barracks, then a new departure for the Royal Navy, would be organised in such a way as to gain maximum advantage for the Navy and the men; finally, the lines upon which the gunnery and torpedo schools should be developed were set out. The forming of shore establishments also became a confirmed policy. Fisher also argued that radical changes were needed in the rank structure if the supply of engine room artificers was to be maintained. To this end it was proposed to create the rank of 'boy artificers'. They would enter the Navy between the ages of 14 and 16 years and serve a two-year apprenticeship.[16] They would then serve for 12 years continuously from the age of 18.

Another radical aspect of the Selborne Scheme as far as ratings were concerned was the re-introduction of a procedure whereby warrant officers could be promoted to the rank of lieutenant. This avenue of promotion had existed in the Royal Navy up until the end of the Napoleonic Wars.[17] It has been suggested that this innovation was a product of lobbying by lower deck societies:

> From 1890 onwards the Warrant Officer's Society lobbied for regular commissions for its members, and in 1903 the campaign met with some success when 100 Chief Warrant Officers were elevated to Lieutenant. Jacky Fisher, then Second Sea Lord, was responsible for this departure.[18]

However, the important point is that Fisher opened up, in peacetime, the first mechanism for sailors to obtain commissioned rank, given the social attitudes and structures that pertained at the time, yet another aspect of revolution and one which was to have profound consequences for the social composition of the officer corps of the Royal Navy.

Yet one more important aspect of the Selborne Scheme was the penultimate paragraph where Fisher succinctly summed up the key opportunities that he saw the scheme presenting:

> The cardinal feature of the scheme was the homogeneous training of Executive Engineer and Marine Officers. The policy of the Board is to create a body of young officers who at the moment of mobilization for war will be equally available for all the general duties of the Fleet and to consolidate into one harmonious whole, the fighting officers of the Navy.[19]

If the Selborne Scheme represented a campaign plan for revolution in service education, this raises the question of how the revolution would be implemented. The answer to this question lies in an appreciation of the high academic calibre of the men Fisher recruited into the Navy to teach on the Selborne Scheme. The two key teachers were Sir Cyril Ashford and Charles Godfrey.

Cyril Ashford (later Sir) had been the senior science master at Harrow. He started his career in the Navy by being appointed the first headmaster at Osborne in October 1903. From the beginning of this appointment there was no doubt that he was conscious of the unique educational scheme that was beginning to unfold both at Osborne and Dartmouth: 'I have no hesitation in saying that the broader education now given will increase the officer's control over his men and his power of getting the best work out of the subordinate engine-room artificers.'[20] Charles Godfrey had been senior mathematics master at Winchester. When Ashford moved to Dartmouth to be the first headmaster in September 1905 Godfrey moved into the post of headmaster at Osborne. He was a gifted mathematician and prolific writer of textbooks.[21] It is no exaggeration to say that, as a result, Patrick Blackett received during his time at Dartmouth what was probably the best secondary technical education available in the United Kingdom.

It is also important to appreciate that from the inception of both Osborne and Dartmouth there was in each a naval staff and a staff of civilian masters, as they were then called. When Dartmouth opened in September 1905 there were 13 naval officers commanded by Captain W.E. Goodenough, and 11 masters. The 'professorial staff', as they were called in the 'Blue Lists',[22] expanded rapidly at both Osborne and Dartmouth. By 1905 there was a total of 34 teaching staff at Osborne and they were organised into five academic departments.[23] Dartmouth had started off with just 11 teaching staff under Ashford in September 1905. However, by January 1908 there was a total of 30 staff organised into five departments.[24]

Yet the success of the Selborne Scheme was dependeant on more than the appointment of a high-calibre academic staff. Success also rested on the harmony that was created between the civilian and naval staff of the new colleges. Anyone familiar with initial service education in the Royal Navy at the end of the twentieth century will know only too well the dominance of a culture described, perhaps unfairly, as 'one output, two aspects'. What is interesting about the Selborne Scheme is the apparent absence of this culture. Furthermore, it was something that both Ewing and Fisher in their own ways did much to facilitate. Initially there was an awareness of the problems that could arise between the academic and naval perspectives:

> at the outset Ewing recognised that friendly co-operation at Osborne between the newly appointed civilian staff under Ashford and the naval staff under Wemyss was absolutely essential. Fortunately the Admiralty had shown great wisdom in their choice, so any anxiety there may have been was quickly set at rest.[25]

If the Selborne Scheme was Napoleonic in its audacity, it was also Cromwellian in its thoroughness and understanding of what this scheme of service education was to deliver:

> The first and main consideration is that the Cadets' Training Establishment differs fundamentally (and must so differ) from any other kind of existing school, because the primary purpose of a Naval officers' education differs so entirely from that of any shore school. This primary purpose is to cultivate the following qualities in the cadets to fit them to be efficient sea officers:
>
> 1. The habit of command.
> 2. The habit of self-reliance.
> 3. The habit of fertility of resource.
> 4. The habit of fearlessness of responsibility.[26]

What was revolutionary was the process whereby these qualities were to be acquired. The demise of the sailing vessel meant the numerous alarms and emergencies of being officer of the watch in these vessels were no longer available. Instead, engineering education and practice was perceived as the new mechanism to facilitate these qualities. Yet it is important to stress that when the details of the Selborne Scheme were published engineering represented only one-third of the curriculum. In addition, it was the method of instruction that really set Fisher's scheme apart. It contained a large element of what educationalists today would call resourced-based student-centred learning:

> It has been fully admitted by the best authorities on the education of Engineers that the practice of attending workshops in the summer, and colleges in the winter months is the most effective

> method of instruction. But we go further in the Osborne training establishment for there we shall have the alternations daily, by having study in the forenoon, and practical sea-going work in the vessels or else in the workshops, in the afternoon. We may compare our system to listening to a lecture as to (a) how a thing should be done only; and (b) in addition, doing it – the one is an effort of memory, the other is the result of experience. We must therefore select our teaching staff with these above-mentioned two main purposes in view, and we must arrange our course of Education accordingly.'[27]

There is also evidence to suggest that the Board of Admiralty were concerned to have a real input from outside the Navy: 'The Board consider it essential, before arriving at a decision with regard to the future "curriculum" to consult the best representatives of the Educational and Scientific world.'[28]

Despite the clearly articulated aims of the Selborne Scheme and the revolutionary and modern dimensions that it contained, it is important to understand the close supervision that the scheme required from Admiral Fisher himself and the constant criticism that it attracted from within the Navy. An illustration of the former is given by Fisher in his autobiography. It was clear that being Second Sea Lord in London was too geographically removed to ensure successful implementation of the new scheme: 'More than that he [Lord Selborne] benevolently spared me from the Admiralty to become Commander-in-Chief at Portsmouth, to see that the scheme was carried out.'[29] Fisher also presided over the Admiralty Interview Board that selected cadets for his new scheme. There was also the necessity of using Ewing as a weapon of propaganda to sell the new scheme:

> elsewhere Fisher had many critics. Accordingly, he asked Ewing to visit the Royal Naval College at Portsmouth and, on behalf of the Admiralty, explain to all Naval Officers at that port the new scheme of training. The point that Ewing particularly wished to rub in hard was that up to the present there had been nothing but destructive criticism which in itself was futile … The scene in the lecture room at Portsmouth was remarkable. Every Admiral, Captain and Commander in the port was present, and all lieutenants who could be spared formed part of the tense audience. When Ewing closed with the words: 'The new scheme has come to stay', he threw a

> glance towards the reputed author of certain articles which had appeared in Blackwood [a current affairs magazine].[30]

But he had explained the scheme – and, moreover, explained it in language so lucid and intelligible to the ordinary listener, that no questions were put to him on points of principle.

Having examined the origins, objectives and mechanisms of the Selborne Scheme, it is now imperative to draw up an audit of success for Fisher's New Scheme. The first point that can be made is that the stated aim of creating a community of knowledge and sentiment to enhance the unity of the service did not survive to the end of the 1920s. The first to break ranks were the Royal Marines. By 1907 all Royal Marine cadets had left Dartmouth. It had taken the personal intervention of King Edward VII as commandant colonel to achieve this. From 1907 to the present the Royal Marines have been responsible for the training of their officer corps. The second attack on the Fisher concept of the community of knowledge and sentiment came in November 1925. The move has often been referred to as the 'Great Betrayal' by naval engineers. The motive of the then First Sea Lord David Beatty was simple. It represented a sustained attempt by the executive branch to enact, at a time of declining defence budgets, a restrictive practice agreement. With an Order in Council the principle of the Selborne Scheme received a massive frontal attack. This move by Beatty resulted in the officer corps of the Navy being divided into no less than 12 categories, seven of which were commissioned and five being warrant officers.[31] This replaced the five branches of military (containing both executive and engineer officers), medical, accountant, naval instructor and artisan which had been established by an Order in Council in 1915: 'The order's purpose was clearly to revert the engineer from the military branch to his old position where he could never succeed to the command of ships or operational units.'[32] Thus by 1925 the Selborne Scheme was still in place at Dartmouth but its original functions had been seriously eroded. Thirdly, with respect to the Selborne Scheme itself there were a number of changes in the inter-war period that are worthy of note. First, in 1927 the new headmaster, Eric Kempson,[33] who had taken over from Sir Cyril Ashford who had retired, made the first important change. He introduced a scheme that became known as the Alpha Classes. This was the streaming of the intellectually able cadets to enable them to undertake a more demanding curriculum. To facilitate these classes he also undertook an expansion of the library facilities. The second change came in 1937, when the then captain, Freddie Dalrymple-Hamilton, introduced a house system to the college. There were to be five houses plus a new entry house.[34] This replaced the horizontal scheme of 11 terms of instruction each named after a famous admiral which the cadets moved through in sequence.

It is also interesting to note that on the eve of the Second World War the original ethos of co-operation between academic and naval staff that Ewing had identified in 1905 as being essential was in robust health. The Board of Education report on the college in 1938 stated: 'The happy spirit of fruitful co-operation between naval and civilian members of the staff has now become traditional.'[35]

Fisher's scheme survived the turmoil of the Second World War by being suspended, for the duration. During the conflict, shorter courses of six months were rapidly introduced, first at Dartmouth and then at Eaton Hall in Cheshire. The end of the war, and the election of the Labour Party to government marked the beginning of the end of Jacky Fisher's scheme. There were two important changes that brought about its demise. First, there was the political decision to introduce free tuition, board and lodging, thus broadening the social composition of the officer corps of the Royal Navy. The second change was the introduction of a 16-year-old entry scheme which would entail a course of six terms' duration instead of 11. The Selborne Scheme, in one form or another, had survived generations, the last entry arriving at Dartmouth in May 1949, and finally passing out of the college in 1953. Fisher's vision had lasted 48 years.

This longevity was a remarkable testament to the radical philosophy of education that had underpinned it from the beginning. In essence this was the idea that education as opposed to training could produce not only knowledge of a particular subject, but it also could produce certain generic abilities which were centred around leadership. It can be argued that the Selborne Scheme was at least 85 years ahead of its time. In Britain, in both secondary and university education, since the beginning of the 1990s the aim has been not just to develop the knowledge of particular subject areas, but to infuse the student with transferable skills. These have been listed as: 'independent research and data interpretation, informed criticism and analysis, selection and interpretation of evidence, prioritising tasks, working as part of a team.'[36] Furthermore, the integration of these skills within curricula has become a priority in higher education learning.[37] Fisher's scheme of service education had both intended and unintended consequences.

Having looked at the evolutions of the scheme between 1905 and 1949, it is important to examine briefly two unintended consequences. The first was the inception of signals' intelligence during the First World War. Sir Alfred Ewing was approached, on 4 August 1914, by Admiral Oliver, then Director of Naval Intelligence, who showed him a number of German cipher telegrams – intercepted wireless messages which had been picked up by naval listening stations. Ewing agreed to examine the material to see if he could decipher the messages. Soon the number of messages reaching his private office in the Admiralty reached 2,000 per day. To cope with this flood of messages Ewing needed additional help. He turned to the institutions he had helped to create for a solution to his problem – the naval colleges at Osborne and Dartmouth. It was from the mathematics and modern languages departments of the two colleges that the first wave of recruits started to arrive at Room 40.[38] The identity of these masters has often been obscured. However, the Blue Lists of both Dartmouth and Osborne reveal their names and the date of their recruitment. The legend that was used to disguise the work of Room 40 was 'serving at Admiralty'. The first recruits were William H. Anstie and Denis Bond who were recruited in September 1914. In September 1915 A.G. Denniston was recruited. Denniston was never to return to Osborne. After the war he was to become the first head of the government code and cipher school, and when the Second World War started he was, until 1942, the head of Bletchley Park, which worked on the breaking of the German Enigma ciphers. In May 1916 E.C.J. Green was recruited, and finally R.P. Keigwin in May 1918. The contribution that Room 40 made to the British war effort is now regarded as one of the great force multipliers of this conflict.[39]

The second unintended consequence of the Selborne Scheme was one that has lasted to the present. It concerns the promotion of selected ratings into the officer corps of the Royal Navy. The scheme that Fisher initiated in 1902 has undergone a number of different configurations. It is currently referred to as the 'Senior Upper Yardman Course'. It has resulted in about 30 per cent of the officer corps of the Royal Navy today originally coming from the lower deck. This figure certainly has no comparison in either the British Army or the Royal Air Force.

In conclusion, it can be argued that although the profile of the officer cadets entering Dartmouth has radically changed since 1905, there are a number of core ideas which are still of relevance today. [40] First, in an era of increasingly joint warfare, there is still a need for the creation of a community of knowledge and a lifelong community of sentiment at the level of initial officer training and education. This can still only be produced by what Fisher described as a community of instruction. Second, with the emphasis now placed on joint staff training for the British armed forces, there is a need for the Royal Navy finally to implement Fisher's proposal of 1902 and institute promotion exams from the rank of lieutenant to lieutenant commander. This would put the Royal Navy on a par with the other two armed forces, and represents a more systematic way of selecting future senior officers for higher appointments in the service. Third, there is still the need for an officer, if he is to become an effective leader, to think out the problems of his profession as a student. The continuing relevance of this view has been echoed in the post-Second World War era by Field Marshal Slim. Writing in 1956 he stated: 'Preparation for war is an expensive and burdensome business, yet there is one important part of it that costs little – study.'[41] Jacky Fisher would have concurred with this view. To his credit, he constructed a scheme of naval education which did much more than that. It ultimately helped to increase the operational capability of the Royal Navy for 48 years to ensure that it survived both the inertia of peace, and the trauma and violence of war.

Finally, there is no doubt that Patrick Blackett remains intellectually the most distinguished product of what was for its time a revolutionary scheme of service education.

NOTES

1. See *The Times*, 2 January 1903, p. 8.
2. J. Corbett, 'Education in the Navy', *Monthly Review*, March (1902), pp. 10–25.
3. Later to be Admiral Professor Sir Herbert Richmond.
4. A.W. Ewing, *The Man of Room 40: The Life of Sir Alfred Ewing* (London: Hutchinson, London, 1939), p. 131.
5. R.F. Mackay, *Fisher of Kilverstone* (Oxford: Clarendon Press, 1973), p. 105.
6. J. Morris, *Fisher's Face* (London: Penguin Books, 1995), p. 12.

7. Lord Selborne to Lord Walter Kerr, 2 May 1901, from D. George Boyce, *The Crisis of British Power* (London: Historians' Press, 1990), p. 119.
8. Ibid., p. 119.
9. Ibid., pp. 151–2.
10. Memorandum on the Entry, Training and Employment of Officers and Men of the Royal Navy and of the Royal Marines, Command Paper 1385 (London: HMSO, 1902), p. 3.
11. Ibid., p. 4.
12. One example of this is S.W.C. Pack, *Britannia at Dartmouth* (London: Alvin Redman, 1966), pp. 147–60.
13. Memorandum on Entry, Training and Employment, p. 7.
14. Ibid., p. 7.
15. Ibid., p. 9.
16. Ibid., p. 11. However, the facility was to be extended to a limited number of specialisations: 'The Board have long been anxious to see their way to promote a certain proportion of Gunners, Boatswains and Carpenters to the commission ranks.'
17. The last commissions from the lower deck had been in 1818. In the next 84 years only four sailors were commissioned from the ranks.
18. A. Carew, *The Lower Deck of the Royal Navy* (Manchester: Manchester University Press, 1981), p. 47.
19. Memorandum on Entry, Training and Employment, p. 11.
20. Remarks by Cyril Ashford, headmaster of RN College, Osborne. Taken from Pack, *Britannia at Dartmouth*, p. 154.
21. He was the elder brother of Admiral Jack Godfrey who was Director of Naval Intelligence during the Second World War.
22. The Blue Lists contain the complete lists of all cadets and masters who served at the two naval colleges from 1903 to 1922. From 1922 they were published just for Dartmouth. A complete set is currently held by the library at Britannia Royal Naval College, Dartmouth.
23. These were as follows: history and English, science, geography, modern languages and mathematics.
24. These were as follows: science, modern languages, mathematics, history and English, and navigation. (Navigation was headed by the Revd William Hall, BA, chaplain and naval instructor.)
25. Ewing, *The Man of Room 40*, pp. 145–6.
26. The Third Addendum Appendix (Z), p. IX.
27. Ibid., p. 3.
28. Financial Secretary H.O. Arnold-Forster to Professor Perry, 9 December 1902.
29. J. Fisher, *Memories* (London: Hodder & Stoughton, 1919) p. 245.
30. Ewing, *The Man of Room 40*, pp. 152–3.
31. The 12 categories were as follows: executive, engineer, medical, dental, accountant, instructor, chaplains, shipwright, ordnance, electrical, schoolmasters and wardmasters.
32. G. Penn, HMS *Thunderer* (Hampshire: K. Mason, 1984), p. 73.
33. Kempson had been head of the science department at Rugby and had previously taught at Dartmouth between 1905 and 1911.
34. The houses were named Hawke, St Vincent, Grenville, Blake, Exmouth and Drake (new entry).
35. See Pack, *Britannia at Dartmouth*, p. 232.
36. Political Studies Association of the United Kingdom, *Studying Politics* (Newcastle upon Tyne: Political Studies Association of the United Kingdom, 1998), p. 12.

37. See *The Bulletin of the Quality Assurance Agency for Higher Education*, No. 6 (November 1999), p. 4.
38. The origins of the name came from the room that was assigned to Ewing's expanding staff in the old building of the Admiralty.
39. See C. Andrew, *Secret Service* (London: Sceptre Books, 1986), pp. 138–94.
40. The average age is 24, and 85 per cent are graduates.
41. W. Slim, *Defeat into Victory* (London: Cassell, 1956), p. 535.

4

Blackett at Sea

Peter Hore

In notes for his autobiography Patrick Blackett gives his service in the Royal Navy as 1914 to 1919, but if his time at the naval colleges of Osborne and Dartmouth is included, Blackett spent nearly ten years in uniform between the ages of 13 and 22.[1] Nearly a decade of imbibing naval tradition, the finest education which the land had to offer, and five years of arduous warfare at sea helped to form his character and influenced him throughout his life.

As Davies and Sloan have shown, at Osborne and more particularly at Dartmouth Blackett benefited from a revolution in naval education which had for its godparents, the politician Lord Selborne, Admiral Sir John Fisher, the lawyer turned historian and strategist Julian S. Corbett, and the precocious Lieutenant (later Admiral Sir) Herbert Richmond. The scheme of education known in history as the Fisher–Selborne was intended to inculcate a 'readiness of resource', and it included a large element of engineering skills and practice. The academics who were recruited to teach at Dartmouth were some of the finest in Britain, while skilled naval ratings delivered hands-on engineering training. In consequence, Blackett, who was evidently born with a strong practical bent, received the most intensive and probably the best education in physical science and engineering available at that period at any secondary school in Britain. Specific detail about Cadet Blackett is scant: the headmaster's record card at Dartmouth is undated and contains only the information of his place – top – in the end-of-term examinations. About seven years later, however, someone has noted on the reverse of the card: 'Retired during Camb course. Took Math Trip at 2 months notice and got senior [unreadable] In 1921 got 1st class Nat

Sci Trip part II and elected to Charles Kingsley Bye Fellowship at Magdal Coll.'[2]

However, 50 years later his former divisional officer at Dartmouth wrote to Blackett to congratulate him on the award of the Order of Merit. Quoting from the notes which he had kept of the cadets in his immediate charge, Captain Lord Alastair Graham recalled: 'Games: does not shine. Remarks on character: Clever, quiet and nice', and in fourth term, 'Works and does well, and should turn out well'.[3] Other, visual, information comes to us through Blackett's own photograph album. The professional photographs in the album are clearly chosen for their quality and clarity, almost as though Blackett was setting himself a standard. Blackett's own photographs from Osborne and Dartmouth, from sea during the First World War, and after the war are unique: there is a certain inevitability that some of them were taken with a camera which Blackett built himself and used over a number of years, and many were developed by him in makeshift laboratories in the ships in which he served.

On Saturday, 1 August 1914 Blackett had taken the first of his passing out examinations and was looking forward to going home on leave on the 5th.[4] The cadets had been given their dormant appointments to various ships, but he was beginning 'to think that the mobilisation stunt was really over'. Then he and his friends were ordered to mobilise: reading his diary (not his log which has yet to be found) one can sense his glee. When the order reached him, he was not revising for further examinations but indulging in one of his great life-long loves, sailing on the river. That was at 4 p.m. The cadets lived out of their sea chests, large wooden boxes measuring about three feet by two feet by two feet, so packing was merely a question of closing the lid. At 9 p.m. the cadets had left the college and crossed the river to the railway station; at 11 p.m. their train left Kingswear and they arrived at Jago's Mansions (as the naval barracks at Devonport was nicknamed) by 1 a.m., Sunday, 2 August. They slept on the floor of the wardroom (that is, the officers' mess). There was nothing for the boys to do on a very wet day in Devonport, though they were impressed that the war could cause the church service they were sent to to be halted half-way through. They wandered around the dockyard and admired the ships, Blackett noting what beautiful ships *Warspite* and *Aurora* were. He already knew of his appointment to the cruiser

HMS *Carnarvon* and was expecting to be sent by train to Chatham in Kent to join her. On Monday the remaining exam papers, in electricity and navigation, reached them and they completed the papers in Keyham College, sitting and writing on the lids of their chests. Under these circumstances, Blackett passed first out of 71 cadets.

Twelve of these 16-year-old cadets took passage to the Azores in the cruiser HMS *Monmouth*, in order to join *Carnarvon* and to begin their training at sea under war conditions.[5] *Monmouth*, which was delayed in dockyard hands, nearly did not make this rendezvous: if she had not, the cadets might have remained on board and all been killed when she was sunk by the Germans at the Battle of Coronel on 1 November 1914. Both Blackett and his friend Royer Dick recognised their luck.[6] It is said in the Blackett family that this chance event profoundly impressed Patrick with a sense of his having been preserved for another destiny. On 1 September 1914 in HMS *Carnarvon*, all 12 cadets were promoted midshipman with seniority backdated to the day they had joined, 13 August 1914.[7] The new midshipmen with two sub-lieutenants and two junior paymasters were put together into their own gunroom mess. A few days later the mess bought a monkey and christened it 'Kaiser Bill'.

Carnarvon was the flagship of Admiral Stoddart, commanding the 5th Cruiser Squadron, comprising the flagship and HM Ships *Cornwall*, *Cumberland* and *Monmouth*. Manning his ship from the so-called third fleet or reserve, Stoddart got his squadron away piecemeal, being the first to leave himself on 31 July, two days after the warning telegram for war. In the English Channel he met the German cruiser *Strassburg* (*sic*) hurrying home; the two ships passed without saluting. Stoddart's station was between Cape Verde and the Canaries, with his principal coaling station at Sierra Leone, and his instructions were to protect British trade in preference to attacking the enemy: 'interference with unarmed merchant ships not carrying contraband [is] of minor importance … [Such vessels are to be sent in with a prize crew] or in extreme cases they may be sunk.' His forces were thinly stretched, and were further reduced when he was ordered to provide escorts for French troop convoys from north and west Africa, and the *Monmouth* was sent to reinforce Admiral Cradock in the West Indies, who was, in turn, ordered to the South Atlantic. Although there was much movement of ships there was little action of the sort that boys, brought up on the *Sea Kings of Britain*, were hoping for.[8] The cruiser *Highflyer* on her way south to reinforce Stoddart found and sank the German commerce raider *Kaiser Wilhelm*, and several German merchant ships were captured at sea, one of which, *Turbantia*, was loaded with German gold and reservists. Many more German ships took refuge in Spanish and Portuguese ports, where the British persuaded the authorities to remove their wireless installations. It was remarkable how quickly German merchant traffic was brought to a halt, while British commerce, which was also very vulnerable, continued without much hindrance. In the words of the official historian, 'the wonder is they [the Germans] did not cause more mischief than they did … the impotence of the Germans while their chance lasted is remarkable'.[9]

Carnarvon herself captured a German steamer of 5,900 tons, the *President Woermann* on 23 August, but otherwise the patrols were uneventful. 'Nothing doing' appears several times in Blackett's diary and once he recorded that 'the ship is getting very annoyed with the Admiral for not doing more'. He was jealous when another ship of the squadron, *Cumberland*, was sent to the Cameroons.[10] Quite soon Blackett began to make notes about the flora and fauna he saw at sea and ashore. He also showed the poetic side of his character, writing the first of several similar entries, one of a whole five lines, about 'the most perfect sunset I think it would be possible to see'. Blackett had a boyish preoccupation with food and, despite a great quantity of stores taken from a German prize, wrote 'as usual no jam or butter for tea only dry and heavy cakes'. It was several days before he reported that the food was better, though there was still not enough. He received his first mail six weeks after leaving England, and was clearly disappointed that there were no letters from his family. He was, however, already a subscriber to the magazine *Flight* and received several copies. His interest in flying was evident: his photo album contains several pictures of early aeroplanes and he was delighted to meet a flyer in the English Club at Freetown who had flown 'with Cody and other well known pilots' and who was able to lend him more copies of *Flight*. He also met the bishop who 'knows Uncle Charlie Scott Moncreiff quite well' and he took tea with the chief justice who 'has taken a house quite close to us'.

Carnarvon's patrols seemed, at least in the eyes of 16-year-old Midshipman Blackett, to have been rather ineffectual: certainly they were boring for a youngster itching for action. Admiral Stoddart did have a huge area to patrol and few forces; nevertheless, he failed to communicate, to at least one youthful strategist, his sense of purpose. At last, there was relief from boredom when, on 15 October 1915, *Carnarvon* left her station for the South Atlantic to reconnoitre the coast of South America in search of the German raider *Karlsruhe*. Even there, after a rumour of the German being near, Blackett wrote, 'everybody in the ship [was] furious about not going after her'. However, war and the prospect of battle did not interrupt the crossing-the-line ceremony, with a visit by King Neptune and his court including the doctor and Neptune's policemen. There was more relief on 10 November when the admiral and his staff and a great deal of gear were shifted into the *Defence*, and on the same day Blackett saw the Southern Cross for the first time. His seventeenth birthday on 18 November 1914 passed unremarked in his diary.

Meanwhile, the German China squadron, composed of modern cruisers, under Admiral von Spee, had entered the south-west Pacific and was raiding British commerce there. The British Admiralty had divided its forces, exposing Admiral Cradock, giving him conflicting orders and a mixed squadron of elderly ships. Off Coronel on 1 November 1914 these ill-matched squadrons clashed. Von Spee, whose two largest ships, *Scharnhorst* and *Gneisenau*, were crack gunnery ships, was inshore of Cradock and had the advantage of calmer water, the outlines of his ships being obscured against the coast and the smoke from his guns, drifting towards the British, making spotting the fall of shot difficult for Cradock's ships. Held at long range, the silhouettes of the British ships were sharply defined against the setting sun. In the growing darkness the Germans were almost invisible to the British, even when the heavy seas and spray did not wash their sights. Cradock and his flagship, *Good Hope*, were lost; so too was the *Monmouth*. Blackett recorded this event laconically in his diary on 5 November: 'We heard news of the Pacific action and the loss of the Monmouth.'

This blow to British prestige 'let loose all the latent energy and resource of the oldest and most powerful of the navies'.[11] All available cruisers were ordered to concentrate on Stoddart's command in the River Plate. The news set off a flurry of activity in *Carnarvon*, which nevertheless occasioned more criticism from the diarist on 12 November: 'the ship's company chipping off the paint from the casemates and cutting up woodwork to be burnt, all of which should have been done long ago'. *Carnarvon* must have presented an odd picture, with her casemates and funnels stripped of paint, the upperworks painted light grey and the hull dark grey. Incredibly, after nearly four months of the war, only on 23 November did she conduct firings against a towed target and using full service charges. Judging by Blackett's diary, the *Carnarvon* does not seem to have been a ship 'furnished in warlike sort'.

From Britain, two of the latest and fastest battle cruisers, *Inflexible* and *Invincible*, were detached from the Grand Fleet and hurried south under the command of Admiral Sturdee. Sturdee had remarkable orders: an almost free hand, and, as Commander-in-Chief South Atlantic and Pacific, the largest command yet entrusted to a single admiral in modern times.[12] The British force concentrated at the Abrolhos Islands, nominally Brazilian but freely used by the Royal Navy as an anchorage and place of rendezvous, and then steamed on southwards on 28 November, with the ships formed in a scouting line at 12-mile intervals. Reaching the Falkland Islands on 7 December, they began at once to coal, *Carnarvon* taking in 1,400 tons of coal from the Admiralty collier *Trelawny* between 2 p.m. and 4 a.m. the next morning; 'the best coaling we have done yet', recorded Blackett, though he was in command of the steam pinnace that day and cheerfully recorded: 'I did several trips ashore and so did not have to coal.'

By chance, von Spee was planning a descent on the Falklands for the next morning: the surprise was mutual, but the horror, when the tall tripod masts of the battle cruisers were identified, entirely on the German side. There ensued a day-long series of chases and individual ship actions with heavy loss of life on the German side and from which only the light cruiser *Dresden* and a small collier escaped. The British loss was slight.

At general quarters, Blackett was supposed to be in the after 7.5-inch magazine, but he seems to have been aft on the upper deck for some considerable time during the chase of the two heaviest Germans ships, and took photographs. 'At first [the shooting] of the battle cruisers was very bad but it improved at the end', he recorded; and later 'our [*Carnarvon*'s] shooting was quite good and we did a lot of damage' and hits were scored at 10,550 yards. They picked up 40 survivors from the *Gneisenau*.

With the Battle of the Falklands, and the destruction of other German raiders elsewhere in the world, 'in little more than four months the command of the outer seas had been won, and [the Royal Navy] was free to throw practically [its] whole weight into the main theatre'.[13] Britannia assuredly ruled the waves and, perhaps, may even, like others, have believed that the war would be over by Christmas. There was certainly an air of insouciance about the subsequent cruise of the *Carnarvon*. Her search of the south-eastern and southern seaboards of Argentina and Chile for the escaped German cruiser *Dresden* was the subject of more implicit criticism by the diarist of the admiral's effectiveness and efficiency. It did not help that Christmas Day 1914 was spent coaling, or that the officers' fishing trip on New Year's Day to supplement their diet was unsuccessful.[14]

For a while after the battle, entries about bathing, cricket, boat expeditions, photography and observations of wild life dominate Blackett's diary. Scores of birds, fishes and flowers are named in the diary, and he was unusually sensitive and observant, including writing about one dawn: 'took the morning watch and it was one of the most beautiful days which I have seen'. During the year he had on a couple of occasions taken to his bed, but the causes are not given. Considering there were so many midshipmen with him in *Carnarvon*, Blackett seems to have volunteered for a disproportionately large number of duties as coxswain of various boats: he evidently enjoyed boat driving and was rather good at it. One suspects that he may also have enjoyed the opportunity this gave him to be alone – 'the loneliness of command'. On various jaunts ashore, his principal companions were Dick and Penney, but he also mentions Fowle, Graham, Hamilton, Johnson and Warburton. For example, on 17 May in Quebec, he went 'ashore with Dick … made some purchases, had tea, wandered about the town and saw … the Johnson–Willard fight film and the theatre'. He bought photographic materials as far afield as Rio de Janeiro and Montreal. Clearly, too, Blackett was now well supported from home: on 16 February 1915 at Montevideo 'we received a huge mail … there were lots of parcels and I got my whites [these had been pursuing him around the South Atlantic for over six months] and a coat and lots of other things including a Christmas pudding', and on 10 May at Halifax 'the best and biggest mail we have had. I got a new cap some warm clothes etc and lots of letters and parcels.'[15]

The leisurely and uneventful patrols of the Pacific and the South Atlantic were halted on 22 February when the *Carnarvon* grounded and was holed off the Abrolhos Islands. The damage was extensive and Blackett observed the emergency repairs in great detail, knowledge which was to stand him in good stead at the end of the war. Temporary repairs at Rio took several weeks and then *Carnarvon* was sent to Montreal for docking. It was intended to make the 3,400-mile passage from Rio to Bermuda in one stage and on one coaling, but in the event she coaled at Pernambuco and Barbados. On 28 April 1915, in the West Indies, Blackett became navigating officer's assistant, and from then onwards there are increasing references to the stars, to physical phenomenon and, off Canada, to the aurora borealis, an augury perhaps of his studies later in astrophysics. In Quebec, a Miss Macpherson seems to have caught Blackett's eye: shades of Nelson, who had fallen in love in Quebec with Mary Simpson.

Carnarvon's midshipmen, however, were sent home on board the White Star liner *Megantic*, sailing on 12 June 1915, and here at last was food, glorious food: 'the catering is wonderful, as good as any crack hotel ... and remember that the Government is paying for it all!' Arriving in Plymouth on 21 June, he caught the 12.30 London express, 'arriving punctually at 4.45', which, considering the trainloads of troops which were passed on the way, is an achievement which the railways could scarcely better 90 years later. After ten months away from England, Blackett celebrated by doing what generations of naval officers have done before: he visited his tailors and outfitters, Gieves, before going home to the village of Fleet in Hampshire. Thus ended the first phase of his first war.

For his next ship, on 19 August 1915, he joined the brand-new, fast, oil-fired, battleship HMS *Barham*.[16] Of the rivalry between the Grand Fleet at Scapa Flow and the Battle Cruiser Fleet at Rosyth; of the distrust between the former's commander, Jellicoe, and the battle cruisers' commander, Beatty; still less of the disputed nature of victory at the Battle of Jutland, Blackett wrote nothing – and this, despite *Barham* being the flagship of Evans-Thomas, the commander of the Third 'Fast' Battle Squadron, which played a controversial role at Jutland.[17] However, anyone who might think that life in the Grand Fleet was spent idly at its moorings during the Great War will have such ideas dispelled by the vivid picture which Blackett paints of life in *Barham* preparing for a decisive engagement in the North Sea.

Barham was a crack ship, commanded by Captain Craig, a leading gunnery expert in the Royal Navy. Orders were given out and stations at action allocated in the first few days of the ship's company joining in Glasgow. There were anti-collision drills, damage control was practised, and hands went to emergency stations before leaving harbour (unlike the *Carnarvon* where emergency stations were practised only *after* she was badly holed on the Abrolhos Rocks). There was physical training for the men and drills for gunnery, fuelling (3,000 tons) and coaling ('but a few tons for auxiliary purposes ... I hope coalling [*sic*] of the Carnarvon ... will be the last I shall ever do'). Waiting at Liverpool, there were trainloads of ammunition which took four days to embark, each 15-inch shell weighing over 17 hundredweight, and they worked from 6 a.m. to midnight. The midshipmen also had to compete against the 6-inch guns crews at loading drill and they came second, achieving 20 rounds in 74.2 seconds. Later, Blackett's right 15-inch gun of 'A' turret eventually achieved 16 rounds in 7 minutes and 52 seconds. The young officers of the gunroom also found time to buy furniture and a gramophone and records for their mess. And, by way of compensation, there was sightseeing at the new cathedral, restaurants, theatre, and even Arnold Bennett's *Helen of the High Hand* in repertory. There was also a spell in September 1915 when Blackett was able to take leave on three weekends running with his parents and sister, Molly, who were at Thorpe, and where he was also able to enjoy some 'ripping' trout fishing. Once at sea again *Barham* had to be cleaned and the great guns, their turrets and directors had to be tested and aligned.

At Scapa Flow, the Barhams continued to work and play hard.[18] The ship's routine frequently started during the morning watch (4 to 8 a.m.): there were more loading drills, and more tests, range taking, and director firing – 'Gunnery counts before all else'. But there were also torpedo firings, boat running in harbour and station keeping at sea, 'PZs' or manoeuvres at sea, and tabletop manoeuvres with brass models on the admiral's table in harbour. There were lectures and lessons which started at 9.30 in the evening, but the day, when not at sea overnight, usually finished before midnight. During one practice anchoring Blackett got a wire round his foot and was lucky not to be crippled: the injury hampered him for several weeks. Throughout, the weather was appalling: it snowed and it rained and it blew. On 11 November the barometer fell to the lowest young Blackett had ever seen; at other times Scapa Flow was just one sheet of foam. It was many months before he was able to record 'it is very nice feeling the heat of the sun again'. Blackett continued to gaze enviously at aeroplanes, made friends with 'Hunter our Eng Sub' and was fascinated to learn how 'all the wonderful gadgets in the Transmitting Station worked'.[19] Various term mates from Dartmouth, whom Blackett had not seen for many months, borrowed skiffs and visited each other's ships and caught up with the news. Ashore there was running and rugby, as well as picnics 'with the usual sloe gin on the heather'. On Sunday nights after dinner there was dancing in the flat (open space) outside the gunroom. There were 'staid dances [all-male, of course] interpolated with drinks' and on Christmas night 1915 'two sets of simultaneous sets of lancers [who charged each other and] which inevitably degenerated in a fight and scrum'. On the same night 'the great stunt was singing the headlines and ads of the *Daily Mail* to various well known tunes'.

Blackett seems to have read voraciously, if indiscriminately, and in one entry mentions 'we have had a very nice lot of books given to the mess by some people in Liverpool'. He found *The Tenedos Times*, which one of the ships had brought from the Dardanelles, wonderfully decorated and coloured, and 'screamingly funny'. He also read Conan Doyle and 'my favourite' Kipling, and other titles listed include *Whispers from the Fleet* by Percy Cradock and *Ordeal by Battle* by Frederick Oliver Scott.[20] Though one has to question his literary judgement when he wrote of one book, 'very interesting ... the basis and foundation of the Navy ... there is no other book in the world upon which so much depends'. The book was *King's Regulations and Admiralty Instructions.* Blackett still had the book on birds which he had acquired in *Carnarvon* and was now an acknowledged expert, so that all sorts of injured birds or corpses were brought to him for recognition.

He was also still under training. With the whole ship as his classroom, Blackett set to work to prepare for his next examinations, and soon found an outlet for his extraordinary genius as an inventor and designer. Between November 1915 and May 1916, Blackett and Lieutenant Edward Bellars designed a new and more accurate instrument for measuring rate of change of bearing, essential if ships under helm were to be able to compute a firing solution for the guns.[21] The Admiralty were sufficiently impressed to grant Blackett and Bellars a secret patent. Though the gadget was never brought into service, John Brooks has shown how it became a forerunner of the Mark XIV bombsight, which enabled aircraft to drop bombs accurately (or rather less inaccurately) without the need to fly straight and level, and which was adopted by the RAF and USAF in the Second World War. (The background and history to Blackett's invention of a secret gadget and his experiences at Jutland are told by John Brooks in Chapter 5.)

After Jutland, *Barham* was sent to Devonport for repairs where, 'the military and civilian population ... lined the front and cheered us [and] all ships cheered too' and the ship's company were given three weeks' leave, after which Blackett and his friends prepared for their oral and written examinations. Modestly, Blackett reported in his diary that he 'did quite well and the final list of marks was nearly that in which we left Dartmouth', that is, he was top again. Afterwards *Barham*'s navigator tried to teach Blackett mathematics, but on 6 October he wrote, 'I worked at maths by myself. Generally I can learn more by myself than with the [navigator] though he is very willing to teach me'. *Barham* remained based in Rosyth and the new Mrs Bellars and Dick's sister Nancy were at hand to join in some of the innocent pleasures there: 'we had a big and giggly lunch ... and then had a most delightful time playing tennis and lazing'.[22] On 30 September they celebrated their promotion to sub-lieutenants 'with a very riotous supper with fizz and afterwards excellent [still all-male] dancing'.

It was time to move on and he was 'exceedingly pleased' to be appointed as first lieutenant of a patrol boat, *P17*, on the Dover patrol.[23] Taking the train to London he crammed into one day a visit to Gieves to collect his mail, a visit to Elliotts' the instrument makers in Westminster to talk to Mr Elphinstone about the Hun teaser, lunch with his mother (using Gieves again as the rendezvous), and some shopping including 'books at one of the glorious second hand shops in Charing Cross Lane'.

On board *P17*, the turnover lasted just four hours and Blackett could not have familiarised himself with his new ship when, without warning and in the earliest hours of the morning, she was sent to sea. The diary which so far had been kept daily (though frequently, it seems, written up in retrospect) suddenly flags. No longer under training, and now as second in command of a patrol boat operating in the English Channel, he was clearly much busier and had less time for himself. But there is another reason, as Blackett himself made clear after a gap of nearly a month in the diary, just after his nineteenth birthday:

> I have given up trying to keep this book daily as I have very little time, secondly because it is not worth the effort. Since I last wrote, we have had a little good and a great amount of bad weather.

Unfortunately the log of *P17* has not been kept, but it is likely that Blackett found the anti-submarine patrols and convoy duties between the south coast of England and France monotonous and he was more uncomfortable in the short, lumpy seas than he cared to admit. On the other hand, there was plenty of opportunity to spot planes as well as birds: 'I shall never cease to delight in watching flying.' While on stand-off in Granville he also managed a visit to the Royal Naval Air Service field there to see an old friend, Acland, and tried to cadge a joy ride. However, by 26 March 1917 he was still trying to make up his mind whether or not to apply for a transfer to flying training.

The most notable incident of Blackett's time in *P17* is his claim to have attacked a German U-boat. No such incident is described in the official naval history of the war or in a contemporary summary of events kept by the Admiralty, though there was a U-boat sunk on the same day in a remarkably similar incident by the destroyer *Talisman* off Berwick.[24] *P17* was off Dover. However, Blackett's account is so full of circumstantial details that it seems likely to be true. Here in Blackett's own words is the story:

> *May 25th [1917].* I was sleeping lightly between a first & morning [his watches on the bridge, 2000 to midnight and 0400 to 0800], when a distinct noise of the helm hard over woke me. I slipped off my bunk & put on sea boots, then realising that we had increased speed, walked on deck. There I first noticed the funnel sparking, so guessed we had gone on quickly. When I reached the bridge (I had a sweater but no coat on) I saw a man bending over the starboard depth charge release handle, so at once knew what was up. I said to the Captain 'Is it really a Hun, this time?' but the reply was inaudible or possibly not given. Anyhow, 'Safety pins out' to the man at the handle release, answered the question. I went to the port

> gear and took out the pin. My eyes, not being yet accustomed to the dark, did not spot the submarine, until I saw her bow sticking out of the water some half cable on our starboard quarter. The starboard charge was let go. Nothing happened for a bit, so that I almost feared a dud, but then a shake and a crash dispelled my fear. I then noticed some smoke hiding the position of the sub, & said to the Captain that she was making smoke. A little later I realised that it was smoke from the charge. So it cannot have been far off. We then turned, zigzagged & swept with searchlight, but all to no effect. She was down & whether damaged or not we do not know. She had been sighted steering south about a mile on our starboard bow. We went full steam to ram. But when at 3 cables off she dived. Just as we crossed the track her bow appeared on our starboard beam, whereas she dived when on our port beam. So we must have missed her stern which was down by inches. Probably the depth charge exploded within 100 feet of her. So there is a chance that some damage was done. It is sickening to have missed by so little. The time was 2.10 GMT & the day was beginning to lighten. We searched the whole area, between the [Realge] & the French coast, but saw no signs. If only we had an explosive sweep to help the search!

However, the diary upon which this story depends was becoming more and more spasmodic. Blackett was on course (that is, at school) in July, and on 11 July 1917 he joined the brand-new *Sturgeon*, again as first lieutenant.[25] What entries there are increasingly reflect his moods and intellectual curiosity rather than the routine of life in a destroyer in the Grand Fleet. There was one entry between May and August, which had needed the restorative effect of a vigorous sail in the ship's whaler ('the mizzen unshipped and two reefs in the main and fore'). On 30 September he had required the stimulation of near drowning, when, after *Sturgeon* had broken down in a gale and was struggling to pass a tow, he narrowly avoided being swept off the rolling deck into the sea. Blackett, who always liked a good 'cag',[26] was curious about the new ship's doctor, a non-practising Jew, and his literary tastes were once more on display when he recommended to the doctor a poem, *The Hound of Heaven*, of mystical religiosity by an obscure English poet, Francis Thompson. What attracted Blackett to this poem, whether it was the poem's rich language or its sexual undertones, is not known.

Two other actions, the sinking of a submarine and a surface gun action with a superior force of German destroyers, are described by Blackett in his autobiographical chapter, as is his reasoning for wanting to leave the Navy after the war.

Blackett described the Admiralty's idea of sending young men to Cambridge to be civilised after the horrors of the war as 'out of the blue'. In fact it was not quite so, for at the end of the previous Great War, 1793–1815, the Admiralty had sent young officers on half-pay to the Revd Professor James Inman at the Royal Naval Academy, Portsmouth 'to obtain the scientific education which had been denied to them while they were at sea'. It is just possible that some twentieth-century clerk had looked up the precedent, particularly as both the nineteenth- and twentieth-century schemes were originally intended only for the study of science and mathematics.

For Acting Lieutenant Patrick Blackett, Cambridge was a godsend, and he experienced something like a Pauline conversion. On his very first night in Magdalene, by the light of the candles in the hall, he met Kingsley Martin and Geoffrey Webb.[27] This was, as the Magdalene College journal puts it:

> No slight conjunction for three men with such varied and outstanding careers ahead of them. They soon became well-seasoned, lifelong friends ... It was an extraordinary time for Cambridge when people knew to an uncommon degree what they were there for and were also well furnished with impelling experience. But still his new associates were exceptional: Kingsley Martin, brimming over with news, views, great causes and political science; and Geoffrey Webb, who had gone through 1917–19 before the mast, being torpedoed and the rest of it.[28]

Having decided to resign, there was no real resistance by the Admiralty. Years later his then commanding officer, Commander H.E. Piggott, recalled that he personally could not further Blackett's plans to resign because this 'would mean depriving the Service of one who would be likely to prove one of her brightest Senior Officers'.[29] Nevertheless, by March Blackett was in plain clothes. In the Magdalene photograph that term he appeared ostentatiously standing in the front row, as though making a statement, and he did not go to the Cambridge naval ball. Years later it was Piggott who took the initiative to write to him, just as later Graham would do. It was as if Blackett was trying to close the book on his naval service. Sadly, there is no evidence of any contact with his former friends, except Royer Dick, the only other exception being his attendance at the fiftieth anniversary of the Battle of the Falklands.[30]

However, there is no doubt that the Navy had influenced Blackett.

> I really do owe a lot to my early naval training, both on the educational side and as giving one a big experience of life quite young. So I owe a real debt to you and your other colleagues at Osborne and Dartmouth.[31]

Answering a question as to whether the Royal Navy had helped to form his habit of mind, he replied:

> I enjoyed my time at sea, I liked the Navy, I liked the life, but I was realistic enough to think that it would be very boring going back to a peacetime Navy, so I got out ... Some of my staff at my various universities ... said that I ran a department like a captain runs a ship.[32]

It is for ever a what-if of history, however, as to what would have happened had Blackett stayed in the Royal Navy, applied his mind and taken 'the technological problems of naval warfare very seriously' between the wars, and risen to command in the Second World War. Indeed so, but ten years in uniform had left a deep mark on Blackett, which many were to recognise, and he several times paid handsome tribute to the education and opportunities he had received from the Navy. [33] In 1919 no one could guess that two decades later he would receive another commission from the Lords Commissioners of the Admiralty.

NOTES

1. For the role and a description of these two colleges see: Michael Partridge, *The Royal Naval College Osborne, a History 1903–21* (Trowbridge: Sutton Publishing, 1999) and E.L. Davies, and E.J. Grove, *The Royal Naval College Dartmouth, 75 Years in Pictures* (Trowbridge: Gieves & Hawkes, 1980).
2. The author acknowledges the help of Dr Geoff Sloan for this research.
3. Royal Society BLA/A10, Graham to Blackett, letter dated 23 November 1967.
4. All dates and quotations in this chapter, unless otherwise noted, are taken from Blackett's diary, which is retained by his son, Nicolas Blackett, who has

transcribed this diary, and copies are in the possession of the author, deposited at the Admiralty Library, Royal Naval Museum, Portsmouth, and the National Maritime Museum, Greenwich.

5. Besides Blackett, the others in order of passing out were: Royer M. Dick, Arthur C. Jeff, Patrick C.M. Penney, John R. Warburton, Malise S. Graham, John C.E.A. Johnson, Reginald G. Fowle, Stephen P. Broughton, Christopher J.M. Hamilton, Raymond Mandley and Lionel H. Peppe.
6. Later Rear-Admiral Royer Mylius Dick, CB, CBE, DSC (1897–1991). Dick accompanied Blackett to *Carnarvon*, *Barham* and to Magdalene College; he was the only one of Blackett's contemporaries who served on in the Royal Navy after the 1920s. His papers, which corroborate Blackett's diary, are deposited at the National Maritime Museum, Greenwich. Royer Dick's first name is frequently, but erroneously, given as Roger.
7. They improvised their new badges of rank, white patches on the lapels of their jackets, out of flannel, but they only had their heavy blue uniforms to wear even in the tropics.
8. Geoffrey Callender, *Sea Kings of Britain* (London: Longmans Green, 1909). This was the standard text at Osborne, and took an inspirational view of British naval history.
9. Julian Corbett, *The [Official] History of the Great War, Naval Operations to the Battle of the Falklands, December 1914* (London: Longmans Green, 1920), Vol. I, pp. 42–3.
10. Where Captain Fuller and an impromptu force conducted a timeless series of operations on the rivers and coasts which Hoste, or indeed any other of Nelson's contemporaries, would have recognised.
11. Corbett, *The [Official] History of the Great War*, p. 365.
12. Sturdee, until he was given this special command, was Chief of Staff to Admiral Jellicoe commanding the British Grand Fleet of Grand Fleet of Battle. When they left Britain, both battle cruisers still had some dockyard mateys working on board.
13. Corbett, *The [Official] History of the Great War*, p. 436. These are the concluding words of Corbett's first volume of the three he wrote about the official history of the war.
14. NMM MSS/91/006 Tape 1 Side 1, 8 July 1986. According to Dick the staple food was corned beef, and they were made to drink a pint of lime juice every day. Fishing was therefore important to a variation of diet.
15. He had also received a Gieves life-saving waistcoat, on 21 March 1915 at Rio de Janeiro.
16. One of the last British Dreadnoughts to be built (in 1914), 27,500 tons, 8 × 15-inch and 12 × 6-inch guns. Her relatively small complement of 1,000 men was possible because of her oil-fired boilers.
17. Andrew Gordon, *The Rules of the Game: Jutland and British Naval Command* (London: John Murray, 1996). Gordon's analysis is the best and most recent dealing with the issues which surround Jutland.
18. On 5 October 1915 Blackett noted: 'It is curious to think that in this area of a few square miles is concentrated the force on which the safety of Europe depends.'
19. A room below the waterline from which primitive analogue computers controlled the guns.
20. Percy Cradock, *Whispers from the Fleet* (Portsmouth, London: J. Griffin, 1907). A book which had contributed enormously to Cradock's popularity in the Fleet and the sense of his loss at Coronel. Blackett wrote on 5 March 1914, 'It is a

fascinating book and teaches a great amount of Seamanship. What a loss it was of Cradock at Coronel. He seems to have been an extraordinarily good man at everything.' Frederick Scott Oliver, *Ordeal by Battle* (London: Macmillan, 1914). On 8 October Blackett wrote, '[Finished reading] ... the best and most valuable book written lately and deserving to be read by every man in the British Nation.'

21. The 'Hun teaser' or secret gadget.
22. Bellars had married on 16 June 1916 while on leave after the Battle of Jutland: a ceremony which Blackett did not attend. Fifty years later Nancy telegrammed Blackett: 'Having since we were both seventeen considered you one of the really great ones of our time I rejoice in your high honour.'
23. One of a class of patrol boats built under an Emergency War Programme to relieve larger ships of patrol and escort duties: they were intended to be as small as possible consistent with sea-keeping qualities: 1 × 4-inch gun, 2 × 14-inch torpedo tubes and 2 depth charge throwers; they had strengthened bows for ramming and were 613 tons, oil-fired and 50 to 54 in complement.
24. The author is grateful to the late David Brown, then head of the Naval Historical Branch for this information. Letter to the author dated 21 May 1998.
25. One of 34 'R' class destroyers, *Sturgeon* was newly launched in 1917. She was 1,065 tons, had 3 × 4-inch and 4 × 21-inch torpedo tubes, was oil-fired, and had a complement of 82. Her captain was Lt Cdr Coombs and she formed part of the 10th Destroyer Flotilla.
26. A word Blackett frequently used in his diary, and contemporary slang for anything from a vigorous discussion to a bout of energetic and competitive dancing.
27. Blackett always said that this was 25 January 1919, though his appointment was dated 15 January and other sources say it was 19 February. Martin was a conscientious objector, a socialist, a philanderer, and editor of *New Statesman.* Webb had arrived at Magdalene a term earlier, 'in old grey flannel trousers, a blue seaman's Jersey and with all his possessions in a sailor's canvas bag', as his British Academy obituary puts it. Webb also had a parrot whose nautical language (and neighbour's complaints) drew from his tutor the remark that: 'Mr Webb, I must ask you to keep your bird under better control. Otherwise, I will consult the Dean whether it is to be regarded as a gramophone or a dog.'
28. RS BLA/A10. Carbon copy of original typescript of the published Magdalene College journal.
29. RS BLA/A10. Piggott to Blackett, letter dated 25 February 1957.
30. RS BLA/F81, G17 and H56. Nor did he have contact with Mountbatten, who, though junior by a term or so at Osborne and Dartmouth, had been at Cambridge with him, and with whom he later shared a strong interest in India. However, between 1965 and 1970 Mountbatten courted Blackett and their correspondences graduated to first names.
31. RS BLA/A10. Blackett to Piggott, letter dated 28 February 1957.
32. RS BLA/A32. Typescript of an interview by Brian Connell for Anglia TV, 1971. The National Film Archive, London, has a copy of the tape of this interview.
33. RS BLA/A79. For Blackett's seventieth birthday, Magda Polanyi specially chose a card 'for a bookish naval man'.

5

The Midshipman and the Secret Gadget

John Brooks

After his adventures in the South Atlantic, Midshipman Blackett returned to serve in home waters. He was again fortunate in his next posting, to the new fast battleship *Barham*. He joined her on 19 August 1915 at Clydebank and was immediately assigned his action station in A turret. After her trials, on 2 October his new ship joined her sister ships *Queen Elizabeth* and *Warspite* with the Grand Fleet at Scapa Flow,[1] where she became the flagship of the Fifth Battle Squadron (5BS), commanded by Rear-Admiral Hugh Evan-Thomas.[2] Blackett soon found that, in *Barham*, 'Gunnery counts before all else for obvious reasons'.[3] Before the war, her captain, Arthur Craig, had been Experimental Commander in *Excellent* and Assistant Director of Naval Ordnance, and he had also commanded *Orion*, one of the Fleet's crack gunnery ships.[4] Gunnery drills began as soon as the trials had been completed and thereafter were conducted, in one form or another, almost daily. Once at Scapa, *Barham* was able to take full advantage of the protected Flow for sub-calibre firing and other exercises. Full-calibre firings were conducted in the open sea. On 16 November 1915, 'fire was opened on a towed battle practice target at a range of 10,000 yards. The turrets fired by individual and did good shooting … After we did director firing at a range of about 14,000 yards.' On 31 January 1916, *Barham* and *Canada* fired as a pair with full charges at a range of 17,000 yards, though, owing to a number of mishaps (Blackett's A turret alone fired all eight rounds), they were not as successful as *Warspite* and *Queen Elizabeth*, which 'strafed the target'. The diary records another shoot on 20 March when 'We fired six rounds a turret, two in main and four in local control. The range was 9,000 yards and the shooting was not at all bad.'[5]

With his interests in birds and working the ship's boats, life in Scapa Flow seems to have suited Blackett well, while the usual routine was broken by exercises and the occasional sortie by the Grand Fleet. On 22 November 1915, the midshipmen began a new instruction scheme leading to their examination for sub-lieutenant. They received lectures in seamanship, navigation, signalling, gunnery and torpedo work. For engineering (including hydraulics), the ship herself was their classroom and they were expected to produce a large number of sketches, a discipline which the young Blackett did not always appreciate.[6] Even before the new scheme, he recorded (for 17 November): 'I spent the forenoon looking into the mysteries of the T.S. [the Transmitting Station from which the ship's gunnery was controlled] and learning how all the wonderful gadgets worked.'

It was not long, however, before he came to appreciate that some of the devices were less than perfect. On 12 January 1916, he recorded that 'we had a great cag in the T.S. room to do with the Control system': and, on the 19th: 'Most of the afternoon was spent cagging about a new gadget to do with gunnery.'[7] On 3 March, 'in the evening Bellars & I had a great cag on the subject of bearing plot instruments', and, on Sunday 30 April, 'the Gunnery Lieutenant had a long cag with Bellars and myself about our instrument, and I spent the afternoon rigging up a knock up show in Bellars' cabin'. By 17 May, 'The drawings and description of Bellars' and my invention have gone into the Captain, but he has not said anything about it yet.' However, greater events then intervened and the diary next recounts Blackett's experiences of the Battle of Jutland, in which the 5BS would be heavily engaged, though not in their usual place in the British order of battle.

THE BATTLE OF JUTLAND

In a regatta held on 11 May 1916, Blackett rowed in one of *Barham*'s gigs, which came a good second. The following Monday:

> *May 15th.* At 10.0am the C. in C. came on board to distribute the prizes for the Regatta ... The usual speeches were made at the end, the C in C's being very notable. He said he had been unable to see the races, as he had been obliged to go down to Rosyth on business that might concern us. This appears to confirm the generally accepted rumour that we are going to Rosyth at the end of this week.

The 5BS actually sailed on the 21st, mooring in the Forth the following day, after which the *Queen Elizabeth* prepared to enter dock. On the same afternoon, the Third Battle Cruiser Squadron (*Invincible*, *Inflexible* and *Indomitable*) departed for Scapa Flow.[8] The four remaining fast battleships were, for the moment, to be attached to the Battle Cruiser Fleet (BCF) under the command of Vice-Admiral Sir David Beatty, who had been pressing for this exchange since February 1916. He believed, though wrongly on both counts, that his German counterpart, Vice-Admiral Franz von Hipper, commanding the First Scouting Group, would soon be reinforced by the new battle cruiser *Hindenburg*, and that she would be armed with 15-inch guns. Beatty also feared that the First Scouting Group (1SG) 'will probably be supported by a proportion of the High Sea Fleet in any future ventures'. Jellicoe initially refused but, on 14 April, Beatty proposed that in early May the Third Battle Cruiser Squadron (3BCS) should go to Scapa to calibrate their guns and adjust the new directors in *Inflexible* and *Indomitable*, before some much-needed firing practice. Then, on 7 May, he renewed his request that the 5BS should take their place, with the additional justification that *Australia*, damaged in a collision in fog with *New Zealand*, would not return from Devonport until 10 June.[9] As Jellicoe confided to the 5BS in his speech of the 15th, the exchange was agreed at Rosyth, when he and Beatty met the First Sea Lord, Admiral Sir Henry Jackson, on the 12th. Thus, at last, Beatty had under his command the most powerful battleships in service anywhere in the world. Yet he did not bother to meet Evan-Thomas or even to favour him with a copy of the Battle Cruiser Fleet Oders, so Evan-Thomas was given no insights into the battle cruisers' action doctrine, which was so much freer than that to which he was accustomed in the Grand Fleet.[10]

While in the Forth, so different from bleak and isolated Scapa Flow, Blackett and his fellow midshipmen were able to make the most of the pleasures available ashore. But, on 30 May,

> As we were waiting for the boat back in the evening, we saw a well known signal flying and sure enough, when we were back in the ship, we found that we were raising steam. The 'Engadine' [seaplane carrier] went out first and later the 2nd and then the 1st battle cruiser squadron. We came next and last, passing the bridge just before midnight [BST] … We imagined it was some raid we were out for.

Half an hour earlier, the squadrons of the Grand Fleet had left their anchorages in Scapa Flow and the Moray Firth. These opening British moves leading to the battle off Jutland the next day were ordered by the Admiralty after a marked increase in wireless traffic indicated that the German battle fleet was preparing to put to sea. The German plan was to advance northwards from the Jade and the Elbe to the entrance to the Skagerrak, with Hipper's 1SG acting as bait ahead of the main High Sea Fleet (HSF) under the command of Vice-Admiral Reinhard Scheer; it was hoped that submarines already in position off the British bases would sink some ships as they came out and that, subsequently, the whole German force might intercept and destroy British squadrons detached from the main Grand Fleet. It was no part of this plan that the British should already be well out to sea when Hipper left the Jade at 1 a.m. on 31 May, the squadrons of the HSF following at 2.30 a.m.[11] Only one of the waiting submarines succeeded in firing torpedoes (to no effect) while none provided any useful information on the number of British ships at sea or their courses. In fact, Beatty's force was heading eastwards towards a position due west of the Jutland Bank. Once this had been reached at about 2.30 p.m., his ships would turn north towards a rendezvous with the Grand Fleet some 70 miles further to the north-north-west. Initially, Beatty and Jellicoe had little cause to believe that they would not meet as planned; owing to the now notorious misunderstanding between Captain Thomas Jackson (director of operations) and the intelligence staff of Room 40, the Admiralty signalled at 12.30 p.m. that, an hour before, the German flagship was still in the Jade.[12]

In *Barham*, the morning passed without serious incident:

> *May 31st.* The day dawned glorious but with a slowly falling glass … During my forenoon watch we had several submarine scares … Some suspicious neutral trawlers were about as usual. Our station was five miles astern of the BCs … We went to Exercise Action in the forenoon to clear away and get cages loaded. I slept all the afternoon and just after tea, about [2].50 p.m. 'Action' was sounded … We closed up and learnt that some light cruisers of the enemy had been sighted.

At sunrise, Beatty had stationed the four available ships of the 5BS (*Barham* leading *Valiant*, *Warspite* and *Malaya*) on the port quarter of his battle cruisers at a distance of five miles. His flagship, *Lion*, led the First Battle Cruiser Squadron (*Princess Royal* followed by *Queen Mary* and *Tiger*); the Second Battle Cruiser Squadron (*New Zealand* and *Indefatigable*) were three miles off *Lion*'s port beam. At 4.28 a.m., *Tiger* was ordered to 'repeat all signals between Admiral and 5th B.S.' The method was not specified but by searchlight must have been meant; at a distance of five miles it was difficult if not impossible to read flag signals. Beatty continued eastwards. At 1.30 p.m., to prepare for the coming port turn towards the rendezvous, he made repositioning signals, by flags, which, while preserving their previous distances, now stationed the 5BS and the Second Battle Cruiser Squadron (2BCS) respectively north-north-west and east-north-east of *Lion*; also, the scouting line of light cruisers was ordered to reform on a line east-north-east. Andrew Gordon argues convincingly that these dispositions show that Beatty had no thought for an imminent meeting with the enemy, but that he was focused solely on the anticipated meeting with the Grand Fleet. However, they left his most powerful, though slowest, capital ships, the 5BS, well separated from the battle cruisers and in the opposite direction from that in which the enemy was most likely to be sighted and pursued.[13]

Beatty's force continued the normal routine of zigzagging until 2.08,[14] when *Lion* used flags to order destroyers to 'Take position as submarine screen when course is altered to north by east.' After seven minutes, the general signal, applicable to all squadrons, was made by searchlight: 'Alter course, leading ships together, the rest in succession to north by east.' At the same nominal time, searchlight was also used to order the 5BS: 'When we turn to northward, look out for advanced cruisers of Grand Fleet.' Finally, at 2.17, Evan-Thomas repeated the change-of-course order to the 5BS by means of flags. While these stately evolutions, controlled by an appropriate combination of flag and searchlight signals, were in progress, *Galatea*, in forming Beatty's new cruiser line, had been heading south-east. Times from signal logs must be treated as approximate only, but, at about 2.20, she transmitted the wireless message: 'Urgent. Two cruisers, probably hostile, in sight bearing east-south-east, course unknown.'[15] The process of encoding, transmitting, decoding and delivering wireless signals was by no means rapid, but the message must have been received by *Lion* before 2.25, when destroyers were ordered to 'Take position as submarine screen when course is altered to south-south-east.' As prior to the previous course change, the flagship waited seven minutes before, at 2.32, making the general signal: 'Alter course, leading ships together, the rest in succession to south-south-east.' However, unlike the signals for the earlier turn, both were made only by flags.

Blackett's diary establishes that *Galatea*'s wireless message was also received by *Barham*. However, Evan-Thomas's next orders to the 5BS were: '2.32 … Flags. Alter course together two points to port. 2.35 … Sem[aphore]. Length of line is 12 cables instead of nine. Take up appointed station.' Thus, after 2.32, the 5BS was on an almost opposite course to the battle cruisers as the latter turned about amidst clouds of dense funnel smoke; Captain Craig's report stated that they 'were out of sight for some time'. According to the *Official Despatches*, Evan-Thomas did not order the 5BS to turn about to south-south-east until 2.40,[16] though the navigational data indicate that *Barham*'s helm was put over at 2.38.[17] Thus the distance between the battle cruisers and the 5BS had now increased from five to some nine or ten miles.

The question of responsibility for this increase became a matter of bitter controversy after the Great War.[18] Evan-Thomas was aware of the presence of a pair of enemy ships, but his orders were to look out for the approaching Grand Fleet and he had no reason to think that, to deal with two light cruisers, Beatty's other forces needed the support of the 5BS. Thus if, as Gordon concludes in his comprehensive study, *Lion*'s executive signal was illegible from *Barham*, it was a reasonable assumption that it was the expected order to resume zigzagging: hence the two-point turn.[19] The matter then turns on whether, after 2.32, Evan-Thomas received either of the signals referring to course south-south-east, that is, the 2.25 informative signal for the destroyers or the 2.32 executive, and, if he did, when. *Barham*'s signal at 2.35 fussing about station keeping suggests that, even then, the rear-admiral was still intent on his progress northwards. And, according to his nephew:

> my uncle to the end of his life was quite certain *that NO executive signal was received by* Barham *at this time, and that no 'informative signal' giving any clue to the battle-cruiser movements was ever reported to him on the bridge.*

When the controversy was raised in Parliament in 1927, not long before Beatty stepped down as First Sea Lord, the First Lord, William Bridgeman, stated:

> the [destroyer restationing] signal is in the signal log of HMS *Barham* as received at 2.30 p.m., by searchlight from *Lion* … The executive signal to turn is recorded in *Barham*'s signal log as received at 2.37 p.m. by flags, from *Lion*, the text being as follows: – 'alter course, leaders together, remainder in succession, to SSE, speed 22 knots'. I may add that between these two times the *Barham* signalled to her own destroyers: 'take up station for screening on altering course to SSE'. The signal is timed at 2.34 p.m. in the log of HMS *Fearless*, senior officer of the flotilla.

However, this answer is trebly questionable. Firstly, it was based on information from the Naval Historical Branch, which had always been blatantly pro-Beatty, and which subsequently destroyed the Jutland fair signal logs.[20] Secondly, the executive signal allegedly received from *Lion* is worded identically to the flag signal made by *Barham* to the 5BS, supposedly at 2.40; *Lion* had ordered 22 knots in a separate signal timed at 2.33. And, thirdly, smoke and the growing separation of the flagships would have made it impossible for a flag signal from *Lion* to have been read from *Barham* at 2.37. If the executive signal ever reached *Barham*, it can only have been by searchlight repeat, for which there does not seem to be any definite evidence. Particularly in view of another instance of the record of Jutland being falsified to fit Beatty's version of events,[21] Evan-Thomas's carefully worded declaration is the most believable. His signal at 2.35 indicates that he then still had no indication of Beatty's intentions. While *Barham* never received the executive signal for course south-south-east, she may have relayed the destroyer signal but, even so, it was not reported to the bridge. Thus, after 2.35, when, despite smoke interference, it was becoming apparent that the battle cruisers were turning about, Evan-Thomas had to decide what to do without any prior guidance or clear orders. He probably did hesitate for a few minutes,[22] but that hardly justifies the savage criticism that he subsequently received. As Gordon says: 'the onus would not have devolved upon Evan-Thomas's initiative if *Lion*'s signalling had been conducted professionally and in accordance with Grand Fleet Battle Orders'.[23] *Lion*'s signallers had seven minutes to hoist the signal for course south-south-east and to make sure that it was acknowledged by *Barham*, if necessary after a searchlight repeat. Their failure to do so, and Beatty's to make sure that Evan-Thomas knew his intentions before disappearing behind his own smoke were the primary causes of the *increase* in the separation of the 5BS from the battle cruisers. However, the plain fact remains that, even before the turns, the *initial* separation had already been five miles, which was entirely the result of Beatty's own dispositions.

As the 5BS turned in pursuit of the battle cruisers, *Galatea*'s wireless announced: 'Urgent. Have sighted large amount of smoke as though from a fleet bearing north-north-east.' For the first time, Beatty (and Jellicoe) had confirmation that, at the very least, the 1SG were at sea. Yet Beatty did nothing to dispose his forces in readiness for the coming engagement. With his two weakest ships three miles to the north-north-east, he continued on course south-south-east until 2.52, on south-east until 3.10 and then, at 3.13, turned to north-east. All three turns were ordered by flags only as general signals but they were evidently indistinguishable from *Barham*. Evan-Thomas held on to the south-south-east until 3.05, but he then cut the corners by altering to east-south-east and, at 3.14, to east, thereby reducing the gap by about two miles.[24] However, at 3.21, Beatty broadcast his course and speed by wireless and, at the same nominal time, Evan-Thomas ordered his ships to conform, i.e. north-east at 23 knots. It is regrettable that, at this moment, he appears to have abandoned his independent effort to close the battle cruisers. Nevertheless, none of Beatty's signals give any indication that he wanted the 5BS to concentrate, even when, shortly afterwards, the 1SG were sighted from his battle cruisers, with *Lützow* leading *Derfflinger*, *Seydlitz*, *Moltke* and *von der Tann* on course north-west by north. At 3.30, *Lion* made the general signal by flags: 'Alter course, leading ships together, the rest in succession to east, speed 25 knots.' Clearly, Beatty intended to keep the 5BS on a parallel course. The order was repeated by flags (though without a speed) at 3.32 but the flagship's signallers had again failed to allow for the distance to *Barham*; the 5BS did not turn east until about 3.35, after the signal had been repeated by searchlight, so that the gap increased once more to some eight miles. At this time, the 1SG reversed course, to south-east and then south-south-east, so the range began to fall rapidly.[25]

After the turn east, the 2BCS remained off *Lion*'s port bow, closest to their opponents. At 3.34, Beatty ordered them to 'Prolong the line by taking station astern', but this could be obeyed only by two rapid, 16-point turns to starboard and to port, after which their engines had to be forced at maximum revolutions to make up lost speed.[26] These violent manoeuvres were the very antithesis of 'that steady course which is so important for gunnery',[27] while all Beatty's ships, except for *Princess Royal*, were also handicapped by inaccurate ranges and rates.[28] When, at 3.47, firing between the battle cruisers began at 16,000 yards, the 5BS were still far out of range. As they turned southwards, the engaged British squadrons soon lost gunnery superiority and, at 4.02, *von der Tann* made the hits which resulted in the destruction of the *Indefatigable*. After a lull, Beatty re-engaged but, with *Lion* out of line,[29] *Derfflinger* and *Seydlitz* were able to concentrate on *Queen Mary* until, at 4.26, she was also sunk by devastating magazine explosions.

Only in this second phase of what is called the 'Run to the South' were the 5BS able to give distant, though by no means ineffective, support.[30] In concluding his chapter on the turns to south-south-east from 2.32, Andrew Gordon wrote: 'Having hustled for the 5th BS, and won, VABCF [Vice-Admiral Battle Cruiser Fleet] was about to engage the 1st Scouting Group no better off than if the battleships had stayed in Scapa, and it was substantially his own fault.'[31] During the hour or more that remained before the battle cruisers engaged, Beatty did nothing which could change this verdict. He left the 2BCS in an exposed position, from which they had to struggle into line at the last moment. He threw away the overwhelming advantage over the 1SG which he had been given when the 5BS joined the BCF; indeed, Captain Roskill considered that he did so deliberately, to prevent the battleships upstaging the battle cruisers. Even if he was not guilty of such irresponsibility, Beatty's mishandling of his approach played a large part in his gunnery defeat[32] and the loss of the 2,283 officers and men who died in *Indefatigable* and *Queen Mary*.

Closed up in *Barham*'s A turret, Blackett could only wait for his first sight of the enemy:

> Just before [four] o'clock we loaded and trained on a light cruiser – the first German ship I have seen since the Falkland Islands. At [3].47, we opened fire at about 18,000 yards range. A few minutes earlier, we had seen the flashes of the BC's firing ahead of us. After two salvoes at the light cruiser, both of which failed to hit, we shifted target onto the 2nd German battle cruiser from the left, probably the *Seydlitz*. The visibility was not good but our shooting might have been much better. I saw a number of misses for deflection … We were firing off and on while we could see, and for the first part were not being fired at. After a short time we passed a

> destroyer picking up survivors from an oily patch on the water. I had of course no idea of what it was that had sunk but learned later it must have been the *Queen Mary*. I also saw one of our 'M' class destroyers with her bow out of the water, and very much down by the stern. I did not like it a bit when we began to be fired at, seeing the splashes a few yards short, all their shots falling very close together ... Things did not seem to be going very well then, but I was very cheered to see one beautiful straddle we made, one of our shots bursting on the waterline armour. I saw the flash of it. We then fired four more salvoes rapid and straddled again. After this I saw an explosion aft.

There are some discrepancies between Blackett's account and Captain Craig's report, as well as with the analysis of the firing by John Campbell.[33] Both these sources say that, when the range was 19,000 yards, *Barham* fired initially at the rear German battle cruiser, the *von der Tann*, which received a damaging hit aft from a 15-inch CPC shell at 4.09. At about 4.16, *Barham* shifted target to concentrate with *Valiant* on the second German ship from the left, which was actually the *Moltke*, at 17,000–18,000 yards. *Barham* also changed to AP Lyddite shell, with which, according to Captain Craig, hits could not be seen. This was probably true of the two hits made at 4.16, both of which penetrated the side; however, the first exploded in an outer bunker and started a fire in the ready ammunition of the No. 5 (next to aftermost) 5.9-inch casemate. However, the next two hits, at 4.23 and 4.26, burst on the armour belt, so one of these must have been the hit seen by Blackett. It seems probable that the explosion aft which he described was either the earlier ammunition fire in *Moltke* or perhaps the hit on *von der Tann*, and he misremembered its place in the sequence.

Captain Craig also provides an explanation for the problems with deflection:

> Great difficulty was found in keeping the deflection, due apparently to the enemy constantly zig-zagging, but the difficulty was accentuated by the aloft Director deflection receiver shaking loose, and the electric pointer jamming, this being caused by vibration from our own fire. This made it necessary to shift to the Armoured Director.[34]

Despite *Barham*'s difficulties, the Germans were impressed by the 5BS's 'well-directed fire ... The end ships of the German line were

… soon exposed to a regular hail of 15-inch projectiles, and salvoes of closely spaced shells, fired at extremely short intervals, fell all about them.'[35] Between 4.18 and 4.24, *von der Tann* fired back at *Barham*; this must have been the shooting which Blackett so disliked and it was effective enough to score one hit, though, in striking under water, it did no serious damage.

With his rear ships under heavy fire from the 5BS and threatened with torpedoes from British destroyers engaged between the lines with their German counterparts, at 4.27 Hipper began a succession of turns to port which soon took him out of range. The destroyer spotted by Blackett was probably the *Nomad*, which was hit in the engine room and brought to stop at 4.33.[36] The diary continues:

> We then shifted target. About a quarter to [five] the battle cruisers turned sixteen points and crossed our line of fire. About [5].0pm we also turned and during it got a bad strafing from the German 3rd Division, their crack squadron. As the BC's crossed in front of us I saw that there were only four instead of six, so knew they must have been badly strafed.

While Hipper temporarily withdrew eastwards, Beatty held on south-easterly, with the Second Light Cruiser Squadron scouting ahead, until, at 4.38, *Southampton* signalled by wireless that the enemy battlefleet had been sighted. At 4.40, yet again only by flags, *Lion* made a general signal to 'Alter course 16 points in succession to starboard.' This cannot have been intended for the 5BS, some seven or eight miles astern and once again opening fire on the returning 1SG. By 4.45, they were both heavily engaged; *Seydlitz* took her first 15-inch hit, while a shell striking *Barham* caused the damage discovered by Blackett later on the 31st:[37] 'When I got aft to the gunroom flat, I found the whole place completely wrecked. The gunroom and Eng. Comm's cabin were merged into one and the flat outside riddled with holes.'

The gap between the 5BS and Beatty's battle cruisers was now closing fast. At 4.51, Hipper turned the 1SG about on to a northerly course, while at the same moment *Lion* and *Barham* passed port to port. As Blackett implied, by electing to pass on the 5BS's engaged side, Beatty disrupted their fire at the 1SG (though, in any case, it would soon have been thrown out by Hipper's turn to the north). However, the passage of the surviving British battle cruisers must also have interfered with the fire of the German battleships *Kronprinz* and *Kaiserin*, which had just opened on *Barham*.[38] The *Official Despatches* list a flag signal at 4.48 which repeats the order to alter course 16 points in succession to starboard, but specifically to the 5BS. From a wealth of evidence, Andrew Gordon concludes that this signal was only hoisted at 4.48; that it was still flying when the flagships passed at 4.51; that due to yet another signalling error in *Lion*, it was not hauled down (made executive) until 4.54; that only then did Evan-Thomas lead his ships round to starboard; and that, as a result, the 5BS ended up some 4,000 yards (two sea miles) closer to the High Sea Fleet.[39] This outcome is pretty much in accordance with Captain Craig's report (except for the direction of *Lion*'s turn):

> The *Lion* turned 16 points to Port, the other three Battle Cruisers following her and Vice Admiral Battle Cruiser Fleet ordered 5th Battle Squadron to turn 16 points in succession to starboard. This was done at 4.53 and the squadron hauled in again astern of the Battle Cruisers about two miles.[40]

Gordon also proposes that that the 5BS took up a position on the BCF's starboard, engaged quarter,[41] which does indeed appear to have been the case for the next critical 20 minutes, since *Valiant*'s report states that: 'At 5.13 p.m. … the Fifth Battle Squadron … was altering course slowly to port to get astern of our Battle Cruisers.'[42]

After the turn-abouts by the 1SG and the 5BS, all ships were on the Run to the North. The British battle cruisers fired at the 1SG and, for a time, received fire from both the 1SG and four German battleships. However, Beatty's ships were already drawing out of range and, by 5.10, they had all ceased firing.[43] By contrast, from the moment of their delayed turn, the 5BS were under a heavy fire, as Blackett confirms. He adds additional support to Gordon's conclusion that the Germans did indeed concentrate on the turning-point, even though it is not possible to identify many of the ships concerned.[44] The point of turn itself was fixed, so the change-of-range could be predicted accurately from the known speed and course of each firing ship, while each target ship provided a point-of-aim as it made its turn. However, the deflection was difficult to determine since, in large turns, ships could lose as much as 8 knots of speed;[45] also, any concentration was liable to confuse the spotters. These difficulties probably explain why *Kronprinz* and *Kaiserin*, which were still firing at *Barham*, did not hit her until, according to Captain Craig, 'Shortly after turning'. From Campbell's analysis, this 'bad strafing' began at 4.58, while she had received a further three hits by 5.10.[46]

For most of the Run to the North, ranges were long and visibility difficult and, to a considerable extent, ships had to fire at any target they could see:

> We carried on firing at ranges varying from 24,000 yards down to at the end 8,000. Most of the time we could see nothing but the flashes of their guns. These were very curious. The guns fired in succession beginning with the after gun, so that one saw a succession of flashes, not all at once as with our director or haphazard as in individual. It was horrible seeing the flashes, then waiting for the salvoes to fall ... The terrible part of it was that we could not see them to reply, for they had the modern 'weather gauge' not of wind but of light. We were silhouetted against the bright western sky and they were merged in a great haze.

On the whole, *Barham* and *Valiant* engaged the 1SG while *Warspite* and *Malaya* had to fend off the van of the German battleships, the four *Königs* and three *Kaisers* of the 3rd Division. Historians generally agree with Blackett that the visibility at first favoured the Germans, but this advantage may not have lasted long; *Barham* was not hit again and *Valiant* remained undamaged, but, from 5.05 to 5.30, the 1SG received at least eight 15-inch hits, while ships of the 3rd Division were hit twice at 5.09/10 and four more times subsequently. They did not strike back until 5.20, when *Malaya* received the first of seven hits. Campbell records only two hits on *Warspite* at this time (and, without explanation, attributes them to *Seydlitz*) but, as Gordon proposes, this is probably a considerable underestimate.[47]

Like Blackett, Jellicoe also noticed that the German 'guns do not go off exactly together', while Captain Craig described their salvoes as 'very rapid ripples (almost simultaneous)'.[48] Only the training of German turrets was controlled by director. The layers at each gun were responsible for elevation and they preferred to fire the guns themselves. The ripples from the stern minimised the risk of cordite smoke interfering with guns not yet fired, while their rapidity testifies to the effectiveness of the training of the gunlayers in continuous aim[49] and in firing in quick succession.

The next passage in Blackett's diary seems to refer to the events at 'Windy Corner' at the end of the Run to the North:

> About this time we got our 'five minute hate'. It really lasted much longer and was extraordinarily unpleasant. It is estimated that some five hundred 12-inch bricks were fired at us & the rest of the squadron. How we survived with so few hits I have no idea. Many people say we were saved by one of the armoured cruiser squadrons. They got in front of us and made a very big smoke screen, which was I believe meant to screen themselves, but it effectively screened us and saved us from a far worse strafing. The terrible fate of the ships I did not see – luckily. We do not quite know why Arbuthnot (RA Defense [sic]) got there at all.

As soon as Beatty's light cruisers had sighted the advanced cruiser screen of the Grand Fleet at 5.33, he swung to starboard and renewed the engagement with the 1SG, now yet further damaged by the hits from the 5BS, pushing them to the east. Just before six o'clock, Hipper's light cruisers fought a brief engagement with the Third Battle Cruiser Squadron, which had been advancing ahead of the port column of British battleships (which were then still in their cruising formation). *Wiesbaden* was hit in the engine room and stopped, while Hipper, believing that he was about to encounter a large force of battleships, turned further away. At 6.15, *Iron Duke* made the famous signal 'Equal Speed Charley London', which ordered them to form line astern of the port column.[50]

Meanwhile, the 5BS had been following Beatty but Evan-Thomas decided that, rather than attempting to continue to the head of the line, he should join astern of the battleships:

> 'Barham' led in tur[n]ing about 8 points to port and reducing speed. The leading enemy Battle Squadron (Koenigs) seeing this, opened a terrific fire on the turning point, and 'Barham' was surrounded by a hailstorm of splashes, but no hits of importance were made.[51]

Between the lines, *Defence* (the flagship of Sir Robert Arbuthnot) and *Warrior* had previously hauled to starboard across the heads of the battleship columns, apparently set on the destruction of the already-halted *Wiesbaden.* Then these two obsolete armoured cruisers became the targets for both the 1SG and the leading battleships as the German line loomed out of the mist. *Defence* was soon torn apart by an enormous internal explosion and *Warrior* must soon have shared her fate, except that, as the battleships of the 5BS turned to port, the loss of speed and the disturbed sea state nearly caused *Warspite* to collide with *Valiant*'s stern. In putting her helm hard to starboard, *Warspite*'s steering jammed and she had completed two circles towards the enemy fleet before she was able to regain control and follow her consorts, though not before receiving many hits, including seven on her port side.[52] Blackett was right to be grateful that Arbuthnot's ships initially distracted a good proportion of the German fire. However, *Warspite* soon repaid the 5BS's debt by diverting attention from *Warrior*. Though badly damaged, she was able to stagger out of the battle but, despite *Engadine*'s efforts to tow her home, *Warrior* sank later after all her survivors were taken off.[53] Windy Corner was the last major incident involving the 5BS, but Blackett, still only 18 years old, would soon be deeply affected by the injuries suffered by some of his shipmates. As darkness began to fall:

> We were … allowed to leave our stations to get some supper. In order to get aft it was necessary to go along the mess deck. Many people did not know till then that we had been hit, but one realised it terribly then. There was an extraordinary reek of T.N.T. fumes, which mixed with the smell of disinfectants and blood, was awful. Nearly all the killed, some twenty-four in number, were lying, laid out on the deck, and many were terribly wounded, limbs completely blown off and nearly all burnt.

THE GADGET

After Jutland, *Barham* was sent to Devonport for repairs, during which Blackett enjoyed three weeks' leave. On 8 July, she anchored once more in Scapa Flow and soon returned to her previous routine. Captain Craig could now give some attention to the gadget and, on 7 August, submitted his report to the C.-in-C. concerning 'a rate of change of bearing instrument devised by Lieutenant Edward Bellars[54] and Midshipman Patrick Blackett'. The Admiralty were sufficiently impressed to decide that it should be covered by a secret patent.[55] On 4 October, Blackett noted that 'Bellars received another wonderful document about the hun teaser – the assignment of the invention … which we signed'.

Their invention was an instrument for measuring rate of change of target compass bearing. For long-range gunnery, it was necessary to know this rate (more simply called the bearing rate) in order to determine the change of target bearing during the time of flight of the shell; this was an important component of the deflection, the angle by which the guns were 'aimed off' from the line of sight to the target in order to hit. If both the bearing rate and the rate of change of range were known, an instrument called the Dumaresq could establish the target course and speed and keep both rates, even as the target bearing altered; hence the range and deflection could be kept from salvo to salvo. While Blackett was still at Dartmouth, the Royal Navy had decided to equip its capital ships with Dreyer fire control tables and *Barham* was fitted with the latest model, the Mark IV*; this incorporated an electrical Dumaresq which automatically transferred the range and bearing rates to the table's range and bearing clocks. These tables were provided with separate plotters for recording ranges and bearings against time; the rates could then be measured as the slopes of these two plots.[56]

Because the bearing required was the compass bearing, the plotting pencil for bearings was driven by a differential, which added together the target bearing relative to ship's head and ship's compass course. The relative bearing was received at the table by a stepper-motor receiver wired to a transmitter in the gun control tower. The receiver motor was powerful enough to drive the plotter, but it worked in steps of quarter-degrees, which were too coarse for the small changes in bearing experienced at war-time ranges. The compass course was obtained from a receiver driven by the master Anschütz gyro compass (see Figure 1). However, the receiver itself generated very little torque, so the bearing plot (and other parts of the table) were driven indirectly through what the patent specification calls 'a powerful "relay-system" [but] owing to this necessity of transmitting a fairly high power ... "hunting" takes place which tends to render a plot of little value'.[57]

This 'relay-system' (which today we would call a servo) used an electric motor of sufficient torque to drive the table; the motor then had to be controlled so that its shaft (the servo output) followed the movements of the gyro compass receiver (the servo input). However, a smooth and accurate following action depends on regulating the motor torque according to the difference between the positions of the input and output shafts. This was beyond the capability of the electro-mechanical technology of 1916 (which accounts for the widespread use by contemporary gunnery systems of follow-the-

FIGURE 1
DREYER TABLE MARK IV BEARING PLOT SCHEMATIC

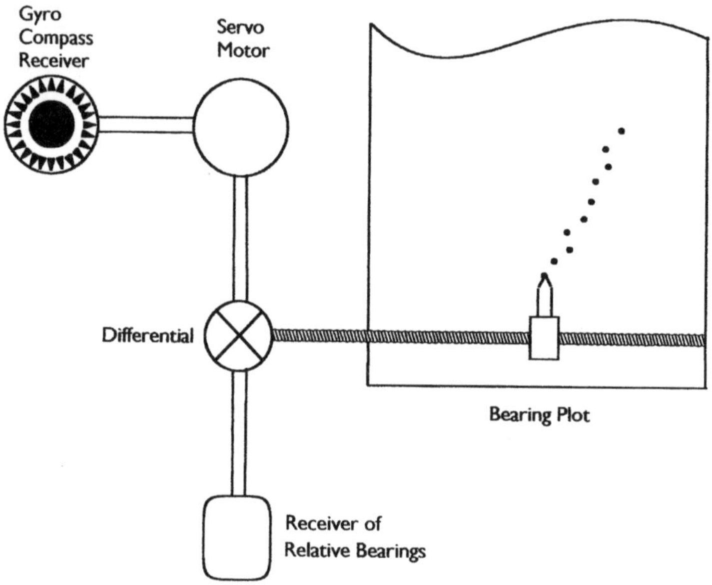

pointer gear, in which the operators were acting as human servo amplifiers). Where, as in the Dreyer bearing plot, automatic operation was preferred, it was necessary to use what may be called a 'bang-bang' electric servo. If the two shafts were exactly aligned, no power was applied to the motor. However, any misalignment, large or small, closed an electric circuit which applied full power to the motor in the sense required to correct the error. Unfortunately, the inertia of the motor and its loads caused the output shaft to overshoot the correct position, producing the characteristic 'hunting' or oscillation. If the input shaft came to rest, the output would eventually settle down; however, if the input continued to move slowly, the output would follow it in a series of small steps.

Blackett and Bellars wisely did not attempt to tackle these fundamental problems, which, in the Royal Navy's fire control tables, were not addressed until the inter-war years.[58] Instead, they proposed a method of measuring the bearing rate directly by observations with a telescope mounted on a modified gyro compass receiver. They arranged for two arms set at right angles to rotate together about the body of the receiver, with the telescope on one arm and an electric lamp on the other. On the compass card itself,

Blackett fixed a narrow slit near the circumference, where it could be illuminated by the lamp. He also made a simple collimator with a lens secured on the card with the slit at its focus. The parallel rays were then directed at a half-silvered mirror mounted at the centre of the card, at 45 degrees to the collimator axis; if the two arms were positioned correctly, parallel rays of light were reflected off the mirror into the telescope (see Figure 2). These light rays established an optical axis which was stabilised in space, even if the ship yawed about its course. The whole receiver was then rotated until the target could be seen in the telescope, after which the images of target and slit were brought into coincidence. If there was no bearing rate and the ship yawed, the two images remained coincident, even as both moved together in the field of view of the telescope.

If the bearing was changing due to the motion of the target relative to own ship, the rate could be measured by rotating the whole receiver. The patent proposed that this rotation should be

FIGURE 2
RATE OF CHANGE OF BEARING INSTRUMENT

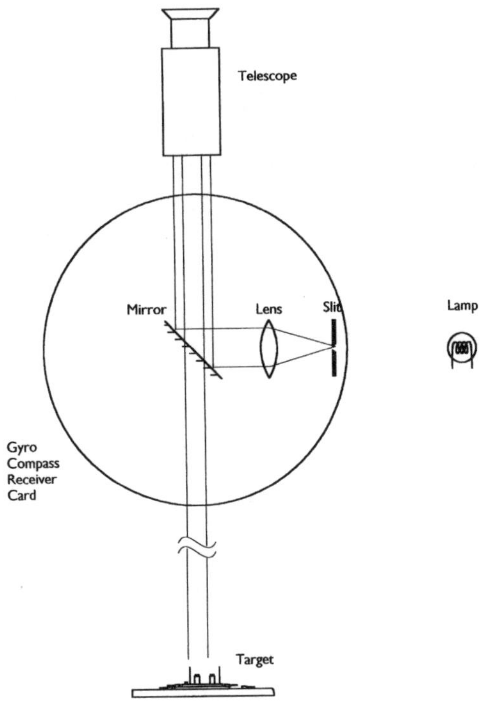

partly controlled by the bearing clock in the Dreyer table. If the table's Dumaresq was correctly set for enemy course and speed, the receiver would turn at the correct rate to keep the slit and the target coincident. However, if the rate was in error, the images would slowly diverge. The rate of a second, local clock (that is, a variable speed drive) could then be adjusted to keep the image of the slit on the target. 'The reading of [this] clock when coincidence is maintained will give the "error in rate of change of bearing".'[59]

On 29 September 1916, Blackett received news of his promotion. On his way south to his new ship (*P17* of the Dover patrol), he called at the offices in Westminster of Elliott Brothers, the company which made the Dreyer tables for the Admiralty:

> After a long wait, Mr Elphinstone[60] came in and I had a talk with him about the Gadget. He was exceedingly nice, and not a bit annoyed at being worried – as I had thought likely. Of course the firm is frightfully busy.

However, after this, no further action seems to have been taken. In his biographical notes, Blackett later wrote: 'The Admiralty ... did not proceed to develop it [our device] – rightly, I think, because it would have taken too long.'[61] Another factor was that, for use with the superior Sperry gyro compass,[62] Elliotts' developed a more sophisticated gyro compass servo which, although it still worked on the 'bang-bang' principle, was probably much less prone to hunting.[63] Even so, there are intriguing links between the gadget and two of Blackett's later inventions.

SERVOS AND BOMBSIGHTS

In 1939, Blackett and F.C. Williams (then an assistant lecturer in the electro-technics department at Manchester) published a paper describing an automatic curve follower for use with the university's differential analyser. Of course, there are similarities between a curve follower and a servo follower and Blackett's wartime experience with the Dreyer table can be discerned in the introduction to the paper:

> The most obvious method would be to use ... a detector device (e.g. a photoelectric cell) ... and to let signals from this detector actuate

> (through relays) a motor driving the y-coordinate lead screw. This method reduces essentially to the process of approximating to a smooth curve by means of a stepped curve [but] this is an unsatisfactory type of motion for driving the disc of an integrator.
>
> A better method is to arrange that the detector shall detect ... the correct value of y ['y-dot', the slope of the curve] then the resulting approximation to the curve will consist of a series of chords.[64]

Blackett and Williams devised a most ingenious photoelectric scanner which registered errors both in slope and in y itself. There were, in fact, no relays but an all-electronic amplifier using vacuum tubes and thyratrons to control the motor which determined the slope. Professor Williams later recalled that, at Blackett's instigation, the curve follower 'was stabilized by adding derivative of error to error, and must have been a very early example of what was to become an accepted technique in wartime automatic tracking'.[65] It would be delightful to be able to claim for Blackett that he was also a founder of control theory. However, the passage quoted earlier shows that the motivating idea for the curve follower was quite different; and the equation describing the feedback loop is not that characteristic of error-rate damping.[66] Furthermore, the paper also states clearly that:

> Usually when alignment is reached inertia of the motor will cause the head to overshoot, and self-oscillation with a natural period of a second or so and a few degrees amplitude ensues. This can be prevented by judicious adjustment ... the motor then cuts out before alignment is reached and inertia carries the head on to the balance position.

This electronic 'backlash' introduced small errors but only in slope and was rapidly corrected; the device could follow a curve smoothly with a mean error of less than one-fortieth of an inch.[67] At this time, the theoretical understanding of stability in complex feedback loops was still in its infancy[68] and this very successful development should be seen as an *ad hoc* solution to a particular problem; even so, it shows that Blackett was once again working close to the limits of current servo technique.

The second link concerns the Mark XIV bombsight and its precursor, the Mark XII. Although the relevant Royal Aircraft Establishment (RAE) files have been destroyed,[69] the Blackett Papers in the Royal Society contain a wealth of material (from official reports and minutes to personal reminiscences) on his bombsight work;[70] what follows is only a brief summary relating to the topics covered in this paper. In September 1939, Blackett began work, at his own initiative, on the design of a bombsight which would enable bombs to be released even while an aircraft was taking evasive action. His design used optical components almost identical to those in the gadget, while both depended on gyroscopes to stabilise the optical axes. Just like the gadget, the bombsight contained a collimator, that is, an illuminated slit (cross-shaped, in fact) at the focus of a lens, which projected parallel light rays on to a glass reflecting plate (see Figure 3). In the sight, the target was observed directly through the plate and the bombs released

FIGURE 3
OPTICAL LAYOUT OF THE MARKS XII AND XIV BOMBSIGHTS

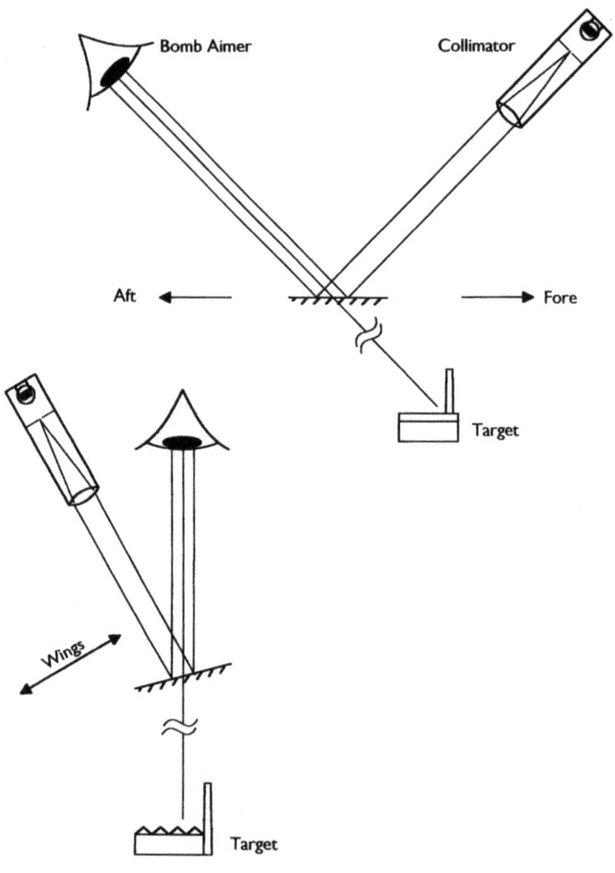

when the target lay under the image of the cross. To maintain aim while rolling, the mirror was gyro-stabilised about the fore-and-aft axis. As in 1916, the gyroscopic reference was based on an existing device; in 1939 this was a standard Sperry artificial horizon. There was, however, one difference. In the gadget, the mirror, lens and slit were all stabilised. In the bombsights, the collimator components rolled with the aircraft. Thus to keep the cross image on the target, the mirror had to rotate by half the angle of roll, which was done with levers giving a two-to-one reduction.

A mechanical computer, which was connected to the bombsight, worked out the correct bombing angle between the collimator and the fore-and-aft axis. In the Mark XII sight, the computer was set for height, airspeed and fore-and-aft level by an additional operator following the instrument pointers. Although tested successfully in September and October 1940, when 20 sights had been made,[71] the device was not generally adopted because of lack of space, particularly in day bombers, for the extra operator. One indication of the advances made in control techniques during the Second World War is that the computer of the Mark XIV sight was set automatically. The development of the necessary servos was begun at RAE by Blackett and Dr H.J.J. Braddick, the latter moving from Birkbeck College in the spring of 1940. Blackett remained in touch after leaving the RAE in September 1940 and the successful trials of the Mark XIV sight took place at the end of June 1941.[72] It is no small irony that Patrick Blackett, who later in the war was thoroughly opposed to the bomber offensive,[73] was one of the principal inventors of the bombsight used by the great majority of aircraft engaged in area bombing.

In his naval diary, Midshipman Patrick Blackett set down a valuable account of life in the Grand Fleet and his own sharp-eyed observations of HMS *Barham*'s part in the Battle of Jutland. The poor results from *Barham*'s bearing plot gave him some valuable insights into the limitations of contemporary servo followers and prompted an early demonstration of his practical skill in optics and instrument-making.[74] In 1938, when he was already deeply involved in defence policy, his collaboration with Williams provided a timely reminder of this early experience with feedback control, a technology which was to prove vital during the coming conflict, not least to the successful development of the Mark XIV bombsight. Finally, it is remarkable how the gyro-stabilisation and optical principles of the bombsight were anticipated by the secret gadget of 1916.

NOTES

1. Entries in P.M.S. Blackett (transcribed by N.M. Blackett), 'Naval Diary 1914–1918'. Historians are greatly indebted to Dr Nicolas Blackett for his transcription of his father's diary.
2. Andrew Gordon, *The Rules of the Game* (London: John Murray, 1996), Chapters 1 and 3.
3. Diary, 18 October 1915.
4. The author is most grateful to Commander Michael Craig Waller, RN, for the opportunity to examine his father's papers, which are an important source for gunnery in the period before the Great War.
5. Unreferenced quotations are from Blackett's diary for the dates in the text.
6. Diary, 9 January 1916.
7. The *Shorter Oxford Dictionary* defines 'cag' as 'to offend, insult' but, in the contemporary slang, it clearly meant a vigorous discussion: Dr N. Blackett's introduction to the diary.
8. Gordon, *Rules of the Game*, p. 51.
9. Correspondence between Beatty and Jellicoe, 21 February to 7 May 1916, in B.McL. Ranft (ed.), *The Beatty Papers*, Vol. I (Aldershot: Scholar Press for the NRS, 1989), pp. 294–308.
10. Gordon, *Rules of the Game*, pp. 48, 54–8.
11. Henceforth, all times are Greenwich Mean Time expressed using the 12-hour clock employed in contemporary reports and descriptions of Jutland.
12. Arthur J. Marder, *From the Dreadnought to Scapa Flow*, Vol. III (Oxford: Oxford University Press, 1978), pp. 37–40, 45–7. This signal did not, however, rule out the possibility that the 1SG were already out.
13. Gordon, *Rules of the Game*, pp. 74–7, 97.
14. This and all subsequent times are *post meridiem.*
15. They were actually the destroyers *B109* and *B110*: V.E. Tarrant, *Jutland: The German Perspective* (London: Arms & Armour, 1997), p. 65.
16. Unless stated otherwise, signals and times, including those for course changes, are from *Battle of Jutland 30th May to 1st June 1916: Official Despatches with Appendices*, Appendix II, Record of Messages Bearing on the Operation, Cmd 1068 (London: HMSO, 1920), pp. 420, 442–55.
17. Commander Michael Craig Waller, RN, 'The Turn to the S.S.E.' (unpublished note, 19 December 1996, copy courtesy of the author). Rear-Admiral Royer Dick warned against trusting the accuracy of times in signal logs; *idem* and Gordon, *Rules of the Game*, p. 603.
18. Stephen Roskill, *Admiral of the Fleet Earl Beatty* (New York: Atheneum, 1981), Chapter 15. Gordon, *Rules of the Game*, Chapter 24.
19. Gordon, *Rules of the Game*, pp. 82, 90–1.
20. Ibid., pp. 545, 557–8, 687.
21. Roskill, *Admiral of the Fleet Earl Beatty*, pp. 326–7. Footnote to Harper's narrative in A. Temple Patterson (ed.), *The Jellicoe Papers*, Vol. II, *1916–1935* (Aldershot: Navy Records Society, 1968), pp. 478–9.
22. Despite the urging of Captain Craig and, perhaps, the flag-commander. Gordon, *Rules of the Game*, p. 82. Marder, *From the Dreadnought to Scapa Flow*, Vol. III, p. 61.
23. Gordon, *Rules of the Game*, p. 92.
24. Marder, *From the Dreadnought to Scapa Flow*, Vol. III, Chart 3. As early as June 1916, Beatty was accusing Evan-Thomas of failing to take the opportunity to close: Ranft (ed.), *Beatty Papers*, Vol. I, p. 368.
25. Tarrant, *Jutland*, p. 78 and Appendix 10.

26. 'With the Battle-Cruiser-Fleet at Jutland', in Papers of Commander G.M. Eady, RN, 86/58/1, Imperial War Museum.
27. Lord Chatfield, *The Navy and Defence* (London: Heinemann, 1942), p. 142.
28. N.J.M. Campbell, *Jutland: An Analysis of the Fighting* (London: Conway Maritime Press, 1986), p. 39. '*Tiger*'s Gunnery Officer', in H.W. Fawcett and G.W.W. Hooper, *The Fighting at Jutland* (London: Macmillan, 1921), p. 424.
29. Chatfield, *Navy and Defence*, p. 143.
30. For the Run to the South, see Campbell, *Jutland*, Chapters 4 and 5.
31. Gordon, *Rules of the Game*, p. 101.
32. For a detailed analysis of tactics, gunnery and fire control during the Run to the South, see John Brooks, 'Fire Control for British Dreadnoughts: Choices of Technology and Supply', University of London: PhD thesis, 2001, Chapter 6.
33. Captain A.W. Craig, 'Report of Action of 31st May, 1916', in 'Battle of Jutland: Reports of Flag and Commanding Officers', ADM 137/302, PRO. Campbell, *Jutland*, pp. 49, 85–90.
34. For the director positions, see John Brooks, 'The Mast and Funnel Question', in John Roberts (ed.), *Warship 1995* (London: Conway Maritime Press, 1995), pp. 53–6.
35. Admiralty, Naval Staff, *The Battle of Jutland (The German Official Account)* from *Der Krieg zur See, 1914–1918, North Sea*, Vol. V by Captain O. Groos, trans. Lt Cdr W.T. Bagot, RN, May 1926, p. 64, Admiralty Library.
36. Campbell, *Jutland*, pp. 50–2. Tarrant, *Jutland*, pp. 91–3.
37. Campbell, *Jutland*, pp. 55, 76–7, 79–80. Blackett's description agrees with Campbell's figure on p. 79 (though this is wrongly timed at 1623).
38. Tarrant, *Jutland*, pp. 101–2, 279.
39. Gordon, *Rules of the Game*, pp. 136–40, 147.
40. Craig, 'Report'.
41. Gordon, *Rules of the Game*, pp. 405–6.
42. H.M.S. *Valiant*, 'Report on Action', 2 June 1916, in ADM 137/302.
43. *Tiger* checked fire at 5.09.45: 'Gunnery Remarks during Action', in ADM 137/1487.
44. Gordon, *Rules of the Game*, pp. 142–6 and Appendix IV.
45. Admiralty, Gunnery Branch, *Manual of Gunnery for His Majesty's Fleet 1915*, Vol. III, p. 173, Admiralty Library.
46. Tarrant, *Jutland*, p. 101. Craig, 'Report'. Campbell, *Jutland*, pp. 126–30, though, for unexplained reasons, he attributes all four to *Derfflinger*, even though *Lützow* and *Seydlitz* were then hitting *Lion* and *Tiger*.
47. Tarrant, *Jutland*, pp. 105–10. Campbell, *Jutland*, pp. 99–100, 104 and Chapter 7. Gordon, *Rules of the Game*, p. 413.
48. C.-in-C.'s confidential despatch, 18 June 1916, in ADM 137/301. Craig, 'Report'.
49. Georg von Hase, *Kiel and Jutland* (London: Skeffington, 1921), pp. 79–81, 83–4. Naval Staff, Intelligence Department, *German Gunnery Information Derived from the Interrogation of Prisoners of War*, October 1918 (C.B. 01481), p. 18, Admiralty Library.
50. Gordon, *Rules of the Game*, pp. 430–40. Tarrant, *Jutland*, pp. 111–17.
51. Craig, 'Report'.
52. Gordon, *Rules of the Game*, pp. 443–8. Tarrant, *Jutland*, pp. 124–30. Campbell, *Jutland*, pp. 173–8.
53. Campbell, *Jutland*, pp. 319, 321–3.
54. In 1942, Captain Bellars was one of two naval officers on the Advisory Committee to Sir Charles Wright, Director of Scientific Research at the Admiralty. The committee was instrumental in bringing Blackett to the

Admiralty to take charge of operational research. Sir Bernard Lovell, *P.M.S. Blackett: A Biographical Memoir* (London: The Royal Society, 1976), pp. 60–1.

55. O. Murray to Captain Craig, 15 September 1916, and provisional patent specification 'Rate of Change of Bearing Instrument', both with the diary transcription.
56. For contrasting assessments of the Dreyer tables and Arthur Pollen's Argo fire control system, see Jon Tetsuro Sumida, *In Defence of Naval Supremacy* (London: Unwin Hyman, 1989), and Brooks, 'Fire Control'.
57. Patent specification. For the bearing plot familiar to Blackett, see Elliott Brothers, London, 'Captain F.C. Dreyer's Fire Control Apparatus Mark IV*', May 1916, *Excellent* Historical Library. Published photographs of the table (e.g. Sumida, Plate 8) are taken from *Handbook of Captain F.C. Dreyer's Fire Control Tables 1918*, C.B. 1456, Admiralty Library; this describes a later type of bearing plot first installed in *Ramillies* in July 1917 but not widely fitted: Admiralty, Technical History Section, *The Technical History and Index, A Serial History of Technical Problems dealt with by Admiralty Departments, 1919*, 'Fire Control in H.M. Ships', TH23, p. 27, Admiralty Library.
58. Air motors, with the air supply regulated by input–output error, were introduced in the fire control tables for *Nelson* and *Rodney*: Admiralty Gunnery Branch, *Handbook for Admiralty Fire Control Table Mark I*, ADM 186/273: Richard Humble, *Fraser of North Cape* (London: Routledge & Kegan Paul, 1983), pp. 81–2.
59. Patent specification.
60. Keith Elphinstone (a director of Elliott Brothers) had been responsible for the detailed design of the Dreyer tables: Brooks, 'Fire Control', Chapter 5.
61. 'Biographical Notes', A.10A, n.d., Blackett Papers, Royal Society Library.
62. The patent specification refers to the 'Anschutz-type of receiver' but, by October 1916, *Barham* had a Sperry gyro compass: A.E. Fanning, *Steady As She Goes* (London: HMSO, 1986), pp. 178–80, 195–6.
63. *Handbook of Dreyer's Tables 1918*, p. 64 and Plate 28.
64. P.M.S. Blackett and F.C. Williams, 'An Automatic Curve Follower for use with the Differential Analyser', *Proceedings of the Cambridge Philosophical Society*, Vol. 35 (Cambridge: Cambridge University Press, 1939), p. 494.
65. Lovell, *P.M.S. Blackett*, p. 48.
66. P.L. Taylor, *Servomechanisms* (London: Longmans, 1960), pp. 83–5.
67. Blackett and Williams, 'An Automatic Curve Follower', pp. 502, 505.
68. Otto Mayr, *The Origins of Feedback Control* (Cambridge, MA: MIT Press, 1970), p. 132.
69. Lovell, *P.M.S. Blackett*, p. 55.
70. Blackett Papers, D.38–58, Royal Society Library, the last containing several versions of Blackett's own reminiscences. See also Lovell, *P.M.S. Blackett*, pp. 53–6.
71. 'Continuously Set Vector Bombsight (Blackett Sight) Trials in Wellington …' with 'Appendix II: Description …', Blackett Papers, D.38, Royal Society Library. The trials were held from 17 September to 11 October 1940.
72. 'Trials of the Mark XIV Bombsight' with 'Appendix II: Brief Description', Blackett Papers, D.40, Royal Society Library.
73. Lovell, *P.M.S. Blackett*, pp. 64–5.
74. Lovell, *P.M.S. Blackett*, pp. 5, 15, 21–2.

6

Blackett at Cambridge

Andrew Brown

While it is commonplace that nothing was ever the same after the First World War, Cambridge University was in many ways unchanged by the conflict. No Zeppelins bombed the city so that the architectural beauty of the colleges was unsullied. Unbroken too was the intellectual lineage of the dons, many of whom had been diverted into tasks related to military needs, but were now free to take up their life's work again. The duration of the war exceeded the usual three years of an undergraduate degree and the lost generation of young men were merely ghosts in the quadrangles and along the Backs. About one in five of those who had joined up straight from public school or who had interrupted their undergraduate degrees were killed in action, with larger numbers blinded, maimed, gassed or psychologically damaged so that they could no longer study. Those who did come up in 1919 were either intact ex-servicemen or younger brothers of the lost generation. The most conspicuous of the former were the 400 in naval uniform scattered among the various colleges; the Admiralty intended them to complete their educations with six months of general studies. They accounted for a quarter of all new undergraduates matriculating in the first six months of 1919, and their arrival was even celebrated by Kipling in one of his less memorable poems, 'The Scholars':

> Oh, show me how a rose can shut and be a bud again! / Nay, watch my Lords of the Admiralty, for they have the work in train. / They have taken the men that were careless lads at Dartmouth in' Fourteen / And entered them at the landward schools as though no war had been. / They have piped the children off all the seas from

the Falklands to the Bight, / And quartered them on the Colleges to learn to read and write!

One of the handful sent to Magdalene College was 21-year-old Lieutenant Patrick Blackett, and for him nothing would be the same again. Surviving a war in which so many friends and relatives had perished brought a purpose and zest to life that transcended the ordinary vitality of youth. On his first night in Magdalene, Blackett was engrossed in a long and voluble discussion with two other new arrivals, Kingsley Martin and Geoffrey Webb. Martin, the son of a Congregationalist minister, had been a conscientious objector and spent two years as a stretcher bearer in France – to him Cambridge offered 'a rare kind of happiness; rather like falling in love without the anxiety'.[1] He read history assiduously as preparation for a career in journalism (he went on to edit the *New Statesman* from 1931 to 1960) but his passion was socialism and the reordering of society. He was described by Beatrice Webb in the early 1920s as 'unkempt and with the appearance of being unwashed ... a fluent and striking conversationalist – intellectually ambitious – with a certain religious fervour for social reconstruction'.[2] His late-night discourses with Blackett were mostly about God, Freud and Marx – very different from subjects that might have been aired in the wardroom, and his influence on Blackett's political outlook is easy to imagine. Geoffrey Webb, a tall, bearded man, had survived a torpedoing while in the Merchant Navy; he habitually wore his blue seaman's jersey and kept all his possessions in a sailor's canvas bag. To complete the nautical image, he kept an outspoken parrot in his room and was once warned by the senior tutor to keep the bird under better control otherwise he would 'consult the Dean whether it is to be regarded as a gramophone or a dog'.[3]

Through Martin, Blackett met some of the most illustrious figures of the day in Fabian and socialist circles: G.B. Shaw, Bertrand Russell, Harold Laski and the Webbs. The Cambridge don who made the greatest initial impression on Blackett was W.H.R. Rivers.[4] He had just returned from Craiglockhart Hospital where his role as a pioneering psychiatrist in the field of war neuroses brought him into close relationship with the poets Siegfried Sassoon and Robert Graves. By 1919 Rivers had attained celebrity status and his study at St John's was, according to another literary figure, Arnold Bennett, 'like a market square. Undergraduates came into it at nearly all hours to discuss the intellectual news of the day.'[5] Blackett had been having serious doubts about continuing in the Navy before the end of the war and it took just three weeks of the heady atmosphere of Cambridge to convince him that he should resign his commission.

Blackett's education at Dartmouth was probably the finest technical and scientific grounding available anywhere in pre-war England, and as a consequence he was superbly equipped for a degree in natural sciences. After little more than a term he gained a second in Part I of the mathematical tripos. He then switched to his chosen subject of physics, using a small notebook kept from the Royal Naval College to record notes on an early lecture by Aston on 'The technique of vacuum apparatus'. Francis Aston had been recruited to the Cavendish by its director J.J. Thomson in 1910 because of his mastery of high vacuum techniques.[6] J.J. Thomson's historic 1897 demonstration that cathode rays consisted of a stream of negatively charged electrons and the determination of their charge per unit mass (*e/m*) depended on using a cathode ray tube containing gas at very low pressure. In the years immediately before the war, Thomson had turned his attention to positively charged particles. Working with Aston, he found that by subjecting these positive anode rays to perpendicular electric and magnetic fields, they could be separated in a parabolic pattern. The deflection of the particles again depended on the ratio of electrical charge to mass, and the parabolas represented different isotopes of the same element. Thus Aston in 1913 had succeeded in separating two isotopes of neon with atomic weights 20 and 22. At the end of the war Aston refined the technique for analysing positive rays and devised the mass-spectrograph, a device of fundamental importance that gave much clearer separation of isotopes and would earn him the 1922 Nobel prize for chemistry.

According to Blackett, he first wandered into the Cavendish Laboratory a few days after arriving at Magdalene. He wanted to see what a scientific laboratory was like. What he found behind the three-storey, grey, stone facade that would grace any Scottish hotel was a concatenation of brick-lined rooms, some of which had been designed with specific subjects – magnetism, optics, acoustics, electricity – in mind. During the war there had been no research and the laboratory workshop had been given over to the manufacture of precision gauges for the armaments industry. Now the Cavendish was bursting at the seams with 50 men like Blackett in naval uniform,

600 undergraduates and a handful of eminent researchers led by the avuncular J.J. Thomson. There were lathes, milling machines, d.c. generators, vacuum pumps, lead batteries, glass-blowing paraphernalia, pendulums with brass and mahogany gleaming. For a young man who loved gadgets from an early age, who was fascinated by new technology and blessed with intellectual curiosity, it was heaven-sent; the only potential problem was posed perhaps by the redoubtable laboratory technicians who watched over the apparatus with a proprietary air.[7]

There was a purpose-built lecture theatre on the first floor and it was here that Blackett was first exposed to another Cavendish luminary, C.T.R. Wilson, whom he would later describe as a 'shy but enduring genius'.[8] In an age when there was no attention paid to teaching technique, Wilson's lectures on light were widely regarded as dreadful, at least in their delivery. He spoke in a quiet Scottish burr and gave his lectures with his back turned towards the audience; as he traversed the blackboard what he wrote lightly in chalk would be removed seconds later by the duster he carried in his left hand! The content of the lectures was completely original and penetrating in its treatment of the subject and Blackett would refer to his hard-won lecture notes for the rest of his career.[9] Twenty-five years earlier, Wilson had invented a piece of apparatus, the cloud chamber, that would bring him lasting fame and would in turn become the chosen instrument for Blackett's scientific virtuosity. As a young post-graduate, Wilson had spent some weeks in an observatory atop Ben Nevis. Above the clouds he had seen the beautiful coloured rings, known as coronas and glories, created by the sun and set out to reproduce them in the laboratory. Almost immediately he found something much more scientifically interesting than the optical phenomena, namely the tracks of charged atoms or ions passing through the chamber that he had made. Wilson patiently perfected his chamber in the years before the war and succeeded with great artistry in making the first photographs of α-, β- and X-ray tracks.

As he walked back to Magdalene from the Cavendish each evening, Blackett would pass a dilapidated-looking house at 1 Free School Lane. On the third floor lived a young philosophy don from Magdalene. His name was Ivor (I.A.) Richards and he was already gaining a reputation as one of the most inspirational teachers and literary critics of his generation.[10] Blackett got to know him through Geoffrey Webb and would frequently climb the pitch-dark, rat-riddled stairs for an audience with him. Richards was typically to be found sitting in his armchair, unshaven, wearing pyjamas and drinking tea. Looking up through his thick spectacles, Richards would be aware of the presence of 'a young Oedipus. Tall, slim, beautifully balanced and always looking better dressed than anyone.' Richards was an eclectic scholar who was deeply imbued with the values of the Cambridge school of humanist philosophers; he had recently written on *Art and Science.* To him, Blackett was alive with 'intelligence, modesty and friendliness', although these qualities tended to be masked by a 'mysterious intense and haunted visage'. Richards was a leading member of a university society, the Heretics, whose guiding principle was to reject 'all appeal to Authority in the discussion of religious questions' and whose debates centred on religion, philosophy and art rather than science. Blackett and Kingsley Martin soon became enthusiastic members and during the early 1920s would have the opportunity to hear and cross swords with Bertrand Russell, Walter de la Mare, Lytton Strachey, Edith Sitwell and Virginia Woolf.[11] Despite the iconoclastic nature of the Heretics, it seemed to Richards that Blackett became 'the leader of his group in many ways'.

Such diversions did not prevent Blackett from taking a first in natural sciences (physics) in Part II. During the long summer of 1921 that followed his graduation, he received a letter from the President of Magdalene inviting him to a college dinner. He was at home in Surrey and was not going to let a strike on the railways prevent him from attending. He cycled to Cambridge and on his arrival learned that he and Kingsley Martin had both been elected to research fellowships. Martin remembered thinking 'that the world was at our feet, an oyster to be opened with the sharp sword of Cambridge intellectualism'. In Blackett's case, such high anticipation would be fully justified by his subsequent research career at the Cavendish. J.J. Thomson had moved on to the mastership of Trinity College the previous year and had been succeeded as director by Sir Ernest Rutherford.[12] Rutherford's expertise was in radioactivity, the forerunner to nuclear physics, and he had built up the world's leading department in Manchester before being lured to Cambridge. While at Manchester he made two fundamental contributions that rivalled his earlier characterisation of α- and β-particles in their lasting significance. First, in 1911, he had been the originator of the now universally familiar planetary model of the atom, with its dense central nucleus. Then at the end of the war he became the first to split the atom – an event which he described to an Admiralty anti-submarine committee as of greater significance than the war itself. By bombarding nitrogen with fast α-particles from a radioactive source, he observed momentary flashes on a distant scintillation screen beyond the expected range of the alphas. He surmised that the scintillations were due to hydrogen atoms or protons and concluded that 'the nitrogen atom is disintegrated under the intense forces developed in a close collision with a swift α-particle, and that the hydrogen atom which is liberated formed a constituent part of the nitrogen nucleus'.

The evidence for this splintering of the nitrogen nucleus was instantaneous and subjective. Rutherford wanted more definite and incontrovertible proof of his conjecture. He believed that this might be obtained using the Wilson cloud chamber which he regarded as 'the most original and wonderful instrument in scientific history'. It consists of a small chamber, filled with air and water vapour, which suddenly expands in volume as a piston is pulled back. The expansion of the gas leads to a drop in temperature and supersaturation with water vapour. Under these conditions the water vapour condenses on any charged particles or ions moving through the chamber and creates a thin track that can be photographed. Even under ideal experimental conditions, only about one α-particle in 100,000 disintegrates a nitrogen nucleus; the challenge was to capture the rare event on film. Rutherford had first given this research project to a young Japanese, Shimizu, who made important improvements to Wilson's original equipment. He moved it towards automation so that expansions could be repeated rapidly and also arranged to take stereoscopic photographs of the tracks through a single lens. Shimizu had to return home unexpectedly, and the project was handed on to Blackett, who found himself 'with a few bits of Shimizu's apparatus in an otherwise empty research room and told to get on with it'. Shimizu had sacrificed some of the sharpness of expansion in Wilson's original design by using a crank to drive the piston, and Blackett restored this feature by installing a simple spring action instead. He also improved the camera arrangement by linking the shutter to the expansion mechanism so that the photograph was taken just as the expansion was completed. The completely automated system could take 1,000 photographs a day giving the tracks of about 20,000 α-particles. He concentrated on analysing the forked tracks formed when an α-particle collides with the nucleus of an atom of gas and showed that these were elastic collisions (like two billiard balls colliding), not the elusive nuclear disintegrations. This work led to the publication of his first scientific papers in 1922 and 1923.[13]

In addition to his own project Blackett, like other young researchers, was expected to lend a hand with the professor's experiments. Rutherford in collaboration with James Chadwick[14] was engaged in a series of scattering experiments to determine which elements other than nitrogen could be disintegrated by α-particle bombardment.[15] Scintillation counting remained the preferred method of detection, and new researchers at the Cavendish had to undergo training in the technique by Chadwick. He tried to instil some reproducibility into the haphazard method by employing pairs of observers, who would each record flashes of light from the screen for a minute at a time. The work was carried out in darkness, often to accompaniment of Rutherford singing *Onward Christian Soldiers*, and Blackett seems to have put in his fair share of hours on this rather tedious watch. While this was duly acknowledged in Rutherford's subsequent papers, no warm personal relationship seems to have developed between the two men. Blackett found Rutherford 'took only a minimal interest in one's work during these years of laborious constructional work: indeed, he was often so impatient for results that the younger research student had often to exert some will-power to resist being unduly hurried'. Rutherford always referred to his research staff as his 'boys' and such paternalism was anathema to a Heretic like Patrick Blackett. Despite the differences in their age and status, there was probably an additional clash of personality between two such born leaders.

Early in 1923, Blackett left Magdalene for King's College, where he had been chosen from an impressive list of candidates for one of two open fellowships. There he came under the sway of John Maynard Keynes, the economist, and told his sister that King's was not a college, more a state of mind. The fellowship brought a little money, but it was insufficient to live on and in May 1923 Blackett applied to the Royal Society for the Moseley research studentship. He explained that he was 'compelled to devote a considerable time to teaching in order to earn a reasonable income … My desire is to devote myself almost exclusively to research for the next few years, but this will not be possible on my Fellowship alone.' With typical fairness, he allowed that there might be another more deserving applicant with no other source of income, but the Royal Society did not agree and awarded him a grant for two years. Blackett's application mentioned his study of 'α-rays through gases, particularly by the Wilson Condensation Method', but gave no hint that he was attempting anything as ambitious as photographing Rutherford's atom smashing.

Another reason for Blackett to be suddenly concerned about his lack of income was that he had fallen in love. The lady was Costanza Bayon, a brilliant language student at Newnham College.[16] It seems likely that they might have met through the Heretics, since she was always more non-conformist and rebellious than he. When their engagement was announced, a disappointed admirer confided to Patrick's sister, 'no doubt he is a very good physicist, but it is his statuesque beauty that I like'. Costanza, familiarly known by her childhood nickname 'Pat', had grown up in Rome and was eager to show her very English man the European way of life. They married in March 1924 and went to Italy for their honeymoon, where Blackett received a letter from Peter Kapitza and other colleagues saying they felt as thought they had 'lost an electron from our innermost ring'.[17] Asking about the probability of his return to the 'normal condition' in England, they supposed 'the return will have to be spontaneous, since the radiation density of happiness will be enough to keep the atom permanently excited, but still an undissociated component of a diatomic molecule'! Prompted no doubt by Pat, Blackett decided that he would like to spend the next academic year with James Franck at the University of Göttingen. Göttingen, with Franck as professor of experimental physics and Max Born in charge of the theoretical side, was becoming recognised as a leading centre for the new, quantum physics.[18] Blackett liked to recall that this request embodied a double heresy as far as Rutherford was concerned – wanting to leave the Cavendish and to study atomic events outside the nucleus – but the professor supported him and wrote to the Royal Society arguing that he should continue to hold the Moseley studentship.

The price for Rutherford's support is plain in that letter: 'I am hopeful that the experiment he is on will have made good progress before he leaves in the Long Vacation.' Rutherford himself left England in July 1924 for a meeting of the British Association in Toronto and would then remain in North America until October. In his absence, Blackett bought himself a new laboratory book and attacked the problem afresh. Work started on 1 August and all the early entries in the book were cryptic and negative. The chamber was plagued by leaks in the vacuum, the spring mechanism needed adjustment and the films taken were blank or of poor quality. On 6 August, Blackett carried out extensive repairs and delicate alterations to the equipment but still recorded 'v. bad. Leak'. A week later he was getting foggy tracks and found that the orientation of the radioactive source greatly influenced the number of tracks. On 15 August he stripped the chamber again and lubricated the piston with gelatine. The following day he was rewarded with 'perfect tracks' and proceeded to photograph 400,000 tracks between then and the end of October. He found six forks in all these tracks which clearly were not elastic collisions but represented the ejection of a proton from a nitrogen nucleus by a fast α-particle. Whereas Rutherford had originally imagined that the α-particle would continue on its way after the collision, Blackett found that there were just two resultant tracks, those of the ejected proton and the recoil atom. This was conveyed to Rutherford in a letter from Chadwick in September: 'Blackett has got two more photographs which are somewhat clearer than the others. They show the track of H particles and the track of the recoil atom, but no track for the alpha.' What Blackett had shown was that, during the collision, the α-particle is itself captured by the nitrogen nucleus forming a new heavier atom that he correctly identified as a previously unknown isotope of oxygen. The discovery was of fundamental importance in the unfolding story of the structure of the nucleus and a triumph for the young physicist, just three years into his research career.

The sabbatical year in Göttingen deepened Blackett's understanding of theory as well as giving him an opportunity to work in the laboratory of another gifted experimenter, James Franck. He returned to Cambridge 'brimful of talk and enthusiasm about de Broglie and wave mechanics etc.'. The Blacketts' home in Bateman Street became a favourite haunt of left-wing and Bohemian academics, and Pat was at least half the attraction. Thanks largely to her spirit, the Blacketts were the 'handsomest, gayest, happiest pair in Cambridge'. By the mid-1920s, Cambridge had largely shaken off the residue of war but had not yet become a vat for fermenting left-wing politics. Blackett's practical support for the General Strike in 1926, when he drove to London to pick up copies of the *British*

Worker, went quite beyond the personal activities of other socialist intellectuals. Although Blackett's primary concern remained his research, he did become an enthusiastic and popular lecturer. Just as he had particularly valued C.T.R. Wilson's lectures on optics, now he taught the subject several Cavendish graduates found his approach revelatory. Blackett also acquired a well-deserved reputation as a virtuoso in the design and execution of experiments. His deep pride in the combined manual and mental skills required to succeed in this field was captured in his classic essay on 'The Craft of Experimental Physics':

> The experimental physicist is a Jack-of-All-Trades, a versatile but amateur craftsman. He must blow glass and turn metal, though he could not earn his living as a glass-blower nor even be classed as a skilled mechanic; he must carpenter, photograph, wire electric circuits and be a master of gadgets of all kinds; he may find invaluable a training as an engineer and can profit always by utilising his gifts as a mathematician … The experimental physicist must be enough of a theorist to know what experiments are worth doing and enough of a craftsman to be able to do them. He is only pre-eminent in being able to do both.[19]

By any measure Blackett was pre-eminent by the late 1920s, his name being well known to physicists throughout the Empire and Europe, although he would not be elected a Fellow of the Royal Society until 1933. In his year at Göttingen, Blackett had met and made friends with many of the leading young scientists on the Continent and was often invited to attend their meetings. In the summer of 1930 he visited Berlin and perhaps because of Pat's Italian background became friendly with another visitor, Bruno Rossi from Florence, who was engaged in cosmic ray research. The two men met again in Rome at an international conference in 1931, where Rossi presented important new data gathered from his ingenious coincidence circuit linking two Geiger counters. A few months after the meeting, Rossi sent one of his research students to the Cavendish to learn the intricacies of the cloud chamber from Blackett, by then the acknowledged master of the technique. Blackett found his new assistant, 'Beppe' Occhialini, full of vitality and passion as an experimenter, and an implacable opponent of the nascent fascism then sweeping Italy. Friendship was irresistible, and inevitably Occhialini taught Blackett about coincidence circuitry and Geiger counters, while he was learning about cloud chambers. According to Blackett, at that time the Geiger counter was a very delicate instrument: 'in order to make it work you had to spit on the wire on some Friday evening in Lent'. By combining the two techniques, Blackett and Occhialini conceived a hybrid system, which no longer relied on rare good fortune to photograph events associated with cosmic rays but captured them almost at will. They placed one Geiger counter above the chamber and one below, linked by a coincidence circuit so that, in order to trigger a photograph, particles would have to pass through both counters and therefore through the expansion chamber. Their first success in seeing cosmic ray tracks was proclaimed by Blackett 'bursting out of the dark room with four dripping photographic plates held high, and shouting for all the Cavendish to hear, "One on each, Beppe, one on each!".'

A Russian, Skobeltzyn, had been the first to photograph the tracks of high-energy cosmic rays: his cloud chamber expanded on a random basis and cosmic ray tracks were visible in only a few per cent of the photographs taken. Following the same laborious procedure, Carl Anderson at the California Institute of Technology was the first to describe the existence of a positron or positive electron in such tracks in September 1932. A month earlier, Blackett and Occhialini had published news of their automated cloud chamber, which could photograph cosmic ray tracks on at least 75 per cent of expansions. They did not mention the many pictures they had obtained where some electron tracks appeared to bend in the applied magnetic field as though they were positively charged, but Blackett had discussed this possibility at some length with the Cambridge theorist, Paul Dirac. In 1928 Dirac had proposed a relativistic theory of the electron, which predicted the existence of an anti-electron, although he was initially reluctant to draw such a startling inference. According to Blackett, no one took Dirac's theory seriously; according to Dirac, Blackett was too cautious in interpreting the abundant evidence that he and Occhialini had assembled. It was characteristic of Blackett the Heretic to maintain a level of scepticism until he was finally convinced. Within a few weeks of Anderson's announcement, Blackett and Occhialini were able to furnish much more convincing photographs that showed positive and negative electrons being born and annihilated, as predicted by the Dirac theory. They also demonstrated that when a cosmic ray particle entered a thin lead plate in their cloud chamber, a 'shower' of subatomic particles was ejected from the opposite side of the plate. Cosmic ray showers would be a fruitful and taxing puzzle for leading theoretical physicists like Heisenberg and Oppenheimer for the next few years.

As a Fabian, Blackett was committed to a non-revolutionary campaign to wear down the capitalist system, but he showed no such patience or dilatory tactics when it came to his career as a scientist. Unlike Chadwick, Rutherford's faithful lieutenant, Blackett did not find subordination a natural or enjoyable state and was anxious to run his own show. When Rutherford tried to force him to increase his teaching load, he emerged from his office 'white faced with rage' and said that 'if physics laboratories have to be run dictatorially ... I would rather be my own dictator'. And so he left to take up the chair at Birkbeck College, London. There was no lasting animosity on either side and in later years Blackett placed Rutherford with Newton and Faraday in terms of the magnitude and duration of his scientific output. In the minds of many of Blackett's contemporaries and students, Blackett was of the same rank.

NOTES

1. K. Martin, *Father Figures* (London: Hutchinson, 1966).
2. Beatrice Webb (1858–1943), wife of Sidney Webb – founder members of the Fabian Society, influential political couple and social historians.
3. Geoffrey Webb (1898–1970), notable raconteur and Slade Professor of Fine Art at Cambridge, 1938–49. No relation to Sidney Webb.
4. W.H.R. Rivers, MD, FRS (1864–1922), physiologist, anthropologist, psychiatrist. Immortalised in Pat Barker's *Ghost Road* trilogy.
5. R. Slobodin, *W.H.R. Rivers* (Stroud: Sutton Publishing, 1997).
6. Sir Joseph John Thomson (1856–1940), Cavendish Professor 1884–1919. His 1897 discovery of the electron earned him the Nobel prize in 1906. Master of Trinity College from 1918 until his death.
7. See J.G. Crowther, *The Cavendish Laboratory, 1874–1974* (London: Macmillan, 1974).
8. Charles Thomson Rees Wilson (1869–1959), the son of a Scottish farmer, awarded the Nobel prize in 1927 for his cloud chamber method; he published his last paper on thunderstorm electricity at the age of 87 years.
9. J. Hendry (ed.), *Cambridge Physics in the Thirties* (Bristol: Adam Hilger, 1984).
10. Ivor Armstrong Richards (1893–1979), English scholar and literary critic. Professor at Cambridge, 1922–29, and then at Harvard, 1939–63. See J.P. Russo, *I.A. Richards: His Life and Work* (Baltimore, MD: Johns Hopkins University Press, 1989).
11. A.J. Ayer (ed.), *The Humanist Outlook* (London: Pemberton, 1968).

12. Ernest Rutherford, born in New Zealand in 1871; his early work on radioactivity earned him the 1908 Nobel prize for chemistry. Cavendish Professor of Physics from 1919 until his death in 1937.
13. A.C.B. Lovell, 'P.M.S. Blackett', *Biographical Memoirs of Fellows of the Royal Society*, 21 (1975), pp. 1–115.
14. James Chadwick (1891–1974) became, in effect, the deputy director of the Cavendish Laboratory under Rutherford. His 1932 discovery of the neutron brought him the Nobel prize in 1935.
15. A.P. Brown, *The Neutron and the Bomb: A Biography of Sir James Chadwick* (Oxford: Oxford University Press, 1997).
16. Prophetically, Kipling's poem 'The Scholars' had gone on to say, 'Lightly dance with them, Newnham maid – but none too lightly believe. / They are hot from the fifty-month blockade, and they carry their hearts on their sleeve.' Earlier, in his diary, Blackett had listed Kipling as 'my favourite'.
17. Peter Leonidovich Kapitza (1894–1984), Russian physicist who came to the Cavendish as a research student in 1921 and was a rival of Blackett's. They worked together for a short time, but their interests diverged – Kapitza becoming pre-eminent in powerful magnetic fields and low temperature physics (Nobel prize, 1978). He was retained by the USSR in 1934, much to Rutherford's distress.
18. James Franck (1882–1964), German physicist who shared the 1925 Nobel prize with Hertz for his investigations of the kinetics of electrons and atoms that confirmed Bohr's atomic theory. In 1933, he publicly resigned from his chair at Göttingen in protest against the Nazis. Max Born (1882–1970), German theoretical physicist who won the 1954 Nobel prize for fundamental contributions to quantum mechanics. He left Göttingen a few weeks after Franck and came to Cambridge. He suggested that since the English insisted on calling theoretical physics 'applied mathematics', the Cavendish should be renamed the Department of Applied Glass Blowing.
19. Reproduced in Crowther, *The Cavendish Laboratory*.

7

Preparations for War

David Zimmerman

Patrick Blackett's work in developing operational research (OR) for Coastal Command and the Admiralty during the Second World War is well known thanks to his own *Studies of War* and Professor C.H. Waddington's, *OR in World War 2: Operational Research Against the U-boat.*[1] We know far less about Blackett's scientific efforts for the Air Ministry prior to 1940, the origins of OR and Blackett's early interest in this type of work. This chapter will examine Blackett's career as a defence scientist from his joining the Tizard Committee in early 1935 until his arrival in August 1940 at Anti-Aircraft Command, Stanmore.

It is generally, but incorrectly, believed that Blackett's first involvement in defence science after leaving the Royal Navy in 1919 occurred when he became one of the original members of the Committee for the Scientific Survey of Air Defence (CSSAD). The CSSAD is better known as the Tizard Committee, after its chairman Sir Henry Tizard. Blackett's role on this committee has never been assessed in any great detail. Blackett passes over his own involvement with the committee in his 1961 lecture to the Royal United Services Institute, 'Tizard and the Science of War', focusing his account almost solely on the efforts of Tizard.

Of all of the members of the Tizard Committee, Blackett's selection was the most unusual. He was younger than the other original members of the committee: Tizard, Professor A.V. Hill and Henry Wimperis, the Director of Scientific Research. While Blackett saw operational service with the Royal Navy in the First World War, the other three had all played an active part in military scientific research during the conflict. Tizard developed techniques for the scientific evaluation of aircraft performance for the Royal Flying Corps. Hill commanded the anti-aircraft section of the military inventions department, which developed equipment and methods of statistically analysing air defence technology. Wimperis headed the Royal Navy Air Service's (later the Air Ministry's) laboratory at the Imperial College of Science where he designed bombsights.[2] Moreover, Tizard and Wimperis continued to be heavily involved in defence science throughout the inter-war years. The same could be said of Professor Frederick Lindemann, whose appointment to the committee in June of 1935 at the insistence of his close friend Winston Churchill, ultimately led to the famous mass resignation of the committee in 1936. Lindemann was a civilian scientist and test pilot at the Royal Aircraft Factory during the First World War. In the 1920s he had served on the first committee which examined scientific means of improving air defence.[3]

All but Blackett were politically conservative. Hill and Lindemann would later run for Parliament as independent conservatives. Blackett was a Fabian socialist and was very much involved in the radical left-wing politics favoured by many young academics during the inter-war years. He had been urged to run as a Labour candidate in the 1922 election. In 1936 Blackett solicited support for a Russian Exhibition, something which more conservative scientists like Rutherford actively disapproved.[4]

Blackett, however, shared several important attributes with all of these men. First and foremost was a deep antipathy to Nazism, which united almost all British scientists whatever their political persuasion. As a result of their close personal and professional connections with German colleagues, scientists were among the first to learn of the oppressive nature of the new regime. In 1924–25, Blackett had spent a formative year in Göttingen studying under James Franck. He found the period 'extremely valuable both by widening my knowledge of physics but also by becoming familiar with the continental way of life'.[5] Hill, Lindemann and Blackett's great mentor, Ernest Rutherford, were among the leaders of a desperate effort to assist German scientists in finding refuge and positions in Britain and elsewhere.[6] Throughout the 1930s, particularly when he was at Manchester, Blackett assisted dozens of refugee scientists to escape from Germany, Italy and Spain.[7] Just before joining the Tizard Committee, Blackett wrote of his deep concern about the extent to which 'science was being used for war preparations, and that many eminent scientists had left Germany, science was being used for anti-working class activities, and scientific fact was being deliberately distorted to accord with Nazi teachings'.[8]

As well, like all members of the Tizard Committee from outside the Air Ministry, Blackett was a member of the Royal Society, having been elected to that august body in 1933. Blackett was already well known as a brilliant experimental and theoretical scientist, and in October 1933 he was appointed to the chair of physics at Birkbeck College. It may also not be a coincidence that all of the original members of the Tizard Committee were based in London.

Like the other scientists, Blackett was already involved in defence research. Well before the formation of the CSSAD, Blackett was overseeing defence-related research through his appointment in early 1934 as a scientific member on the Aeronautical Research Committee (ARC). The ARC co-ordinated and recommended aeronautical research projects, both civilian and military. Its membership came from government, universities and private industry. In 1934 Tizard was the chairman of the ARC, and Wimperis was one of the Air Ministry's representatives.

Before exploring Blackett's role on the Tizard Committee it is necessary to have some understanding as to its nature and operations. Under terms of reference outlined by Wimperis, the Air Ministry formed the committee. Wimperis had several meetings with Tizard, Hill, Lindemann and others in the last few months of 1934, developing the terms of reference before approaching his ministerial superiors. It was agreed that the committee was 'to consider how far recent advances in scientific and technical knowledge can be used to strengthen the present methods of defence against hostile aircraft'.[9] In order to ensure the committee's independence from departmental and external political pressure, it was decided that scientific members would serve voluntarily without pay. It was intended that membership would involve part-time work, attending meetings around once a month, and visiting a number of RAF installations to learn about the current state of the air defences.[10]

In total, the committee met just 50 times between 28 January 1936 and the start of the war. Tizard, the Rector of Imperial College, took on the lion's share of the work between meetings, ably assisted by Wimperis until his retirement, and by A.P. Rowe, the secretary of the committee until his appointment in 1938 to head the Bawdsey radar research establishment. Tizard's biographer has shown that Tizard worked virtually full-time on air defence problems, at first without any clerical support, in order to push through the research programmes initiated by the committee.[11] The most famous and successful of these projects was the development of the radar early warning system.

Tizard was the consummate defence scientist of his era. He was extraordinarily knowledgeable about military technology and generally had a keen sense of what course to steer in developing new weapons systems and techniques. He was a remarkable communicator, able to talk with ease to diverse groups, including politicians, air marshals, generals and admirals, pilots, aircrew, technicians and scientists. Whenever possible, Tizard forged consensus, but he could be as tough as necessary to get his way. While Tizard's falling-out with his friend Lindemann in 1935–36 is famous, normally Tizard forged close personal working relationships with the people he encountered. He was an inspirational leader who had a profound role in shaping Blackett's approaches to defence science. Blackett acknowledged this when he proclaimed that, 'Of the individuals who have influenced me by their personality, I think that Tizard comes next to Rutherford'.[12]

Unlike Tizard, Blackett remained a full-time research scientist until after the war began. The period between 1935 and 1940 was one of his most scientifically productive, as he was heavily involved in his pioneering work on cosmic rays. He wrote, or co-wrote, 49 scientific papers in these four years. His scientific career flourished to such a degree that in 1937 he was given the prestigious position of Langworthy Professor of Physics at Manchester University.

With such an active scientific career, it is not surprising that he did little else for the Tizard Committee than attend meetings and occasionally write a report or visit a few research centres. Blackett, as the most accomplished physicist on the committee, might have been expected to play a significant role in discussions on radar research. However, in 1936, after the reforming of the committee, Lindemann was replaced by Professor E.V. Appleton, Britain's foremost expert on the use of radio reflection in the mapping of the ionosphere. Appleton soon took the lead as overseer for the Tizard Committee, reporting on Robert Watson Watt's research team at Bawdsey.

Blackett, however, did make a significant contribution. He attended almost every one of the meetings and was an active participant in the discussions. Information about the committee's activities is contained in the minutes of the meetings. The minutes are not a transcript of the discussions that took place, but generally record only the decisions reached. Individual contributions are not often identified, yet it is possible to trace Blackett's role and growth as a defence scientist in a somewhat episodic fashion.

Initially, Blackett revealed his inexperience with air defence research. Blackett's first contribution mentioned in the minutes occurred at the meeting of 10 April 1935. The committee held an in-depth interview with Watson Watt over his proposal to use reflected high-frequency radio waves to detect approaching aircraft. During the ensuing discussion Blackett produced a press clipping describing the stopping of cars on the Austrian–German frontier by using electro-magnetic radiation to interfere with the cars' spark plugs. He asked Watson Watt if he thought this was a practical line of research. Watson Watt replied that he 'was dubious of obtaining any effect of this character except by using very high power at a range of few yards'. With this the matter was quickly dropped.[13]

Two other inquiries made in that first year further demonstrate both Blackett's ignorance of flying and his willingness to learn. On 5 November Blackett asked Air Vice-Marshal P.B. Joubert de le Ferte if aircraft in formation could fly for prolonged periods in clouds. Joubert replied that he doubted that a formation could spend more than half an hour in a cloud formation and that it was more probable that occasional cover in clouds would be taken. Later on in the meeting Blackett asked Joubert if it was likely that aircraft would avoid strongly illuminated areas of the sky. The air marshal responded by saying that it was possible that some pilots would shy away, but that others would 'seek these areas on the assumption that they indicated the existence of an important target'.[14]

While Blackett took some time mastering the intricacies of air power, he well understood naval technology. As early as May 1935 he dismissed a proposal to interfere with aircraft by using motor torpedo boats towing kites as being impractical, except in the calmest seas.[15] In October 1937, he suggested that the radar chain be supplemented by a patrol of drifters in the North Sea which would report on low-flying aircraft approaching the coast.[16] This was a good idea, only the subsequent development of the Chain Home Low system of radar in 1938 rendered it moot.

One of Blackett's most important interventions came on 26 July 1937, when he advised that Bawdsey researchers should consult the

Admiralty about range-plotting tables 'in which locations of craft were plotted on a moving time base'.[17] After visiting HMS *Vernon* to view the deviçes, Watson Watt adopted this technology as the basis for range-plotting apparatus at Chain Home radar stations.[18]

In a similar fashion, on at least one occasion, he used his experience as an experimental physicist to suggest a method to measure wind speed and direction by the use of a captive a balloon which would automatically transmit its findings by electrical transmissions. He had used a similar method to obtain data on cosmic rays.[19]

As Blackett learned more and more about air defence he began to take a more active role in the committee. His particular focus appears to have been in efforts made to develop new means of destroying attacking bombers. This included the development of aerial minefields, the placement of explosive devices on balloon barrage cables, a photoelectric trigger to explode bombs in the path of approaching aircraft, infrared guided unmanned flying rams, and unguided anti-aircraft rockets. Starting on 11 November 1936, Blackett made several visits to the Royal Aircraft Establishment (RAE) at Farnborough and other research centres to examine progress in these programmes.[20]

Blackett's involvement with these research programmes is an important reminder that only a part of the Tizard Committee's work involved radar. A large variety of initiatives was undertaken, only a small fraction of which proved to be practicable. Each of these programmes involved a variety of different technologies. For instance, aerial minefields development involved research into new types of cables, the ability of aircraft to cut these cables, new types of fuses for the mines, testing of the effectiveness of small explosives on the aircraft, and the development of helicopters to support the minefield. In the end the minefields proved to be worthless.

Other devices, such as the photoelectric fuse, were the precursors of later successful developments, in this case the proximity fuse. Research into unguided anti-aircraft rockets did lead to an anti-aircraft weapon deployed with a singular lack of success during the Battle of Britain. The research, however, was utilised in the development of unguided air-to-ground rockets used with great effect by fighter-bombers in the last two years of the war.[21]

The Tizard Committee received a number of suggestions from outside inventors and news reports about new air defence devices.

Blackett was involved in investigating at least four of these files brought before the committee. In December 1936 the committee reviewed a proposal by the famous, but then aged, inventor Nikola Tesla to 'bombard aircraft with large numbers of minute particles travelling at very high speed'. Blackett examined the details of the invention and reported back 'that there was nothing of value in them'.[22] In July 1938, Blackett, who was maturing as a defence scientist, dismissed newspaper reports of the use of electro-magnetic and acoustical aircraft detection devices during air attacks on Barcelona, Spain. Blackett told the committee that the source was not 'considered reliable scientifically'.[23]

On 3 January 1939, the committee spent time considering a suggestion for a ram projectile from Messrs Beale and Denman, two consulting physicists. They proposed that they be 'entrusted with an enquiry into a ram which would home in on 'the heated wake behind an aircraft'. Tizard began the discussion by pointing out that the fundamental problem was that no one actually knew if there was a significant heated wake behind an aircraft. Blackett attacked the proposal, believing that some sort of radio scheme would be better for directing the projectile and because he doubted it was possible 'to achieve a suitably controlled projectile'. His personal view

> was that control of the projectile would prove extremely difficult and that, if the aim of the projectile were sufficiently accurate to ensure it meeting the wake behind the aircraft, it would be preferable to equip it merely with a detecting device which would explode it near the target, and rely on the blast or fragmentation effect.

Tizard then put forward the idea that a homing projectile could be in the form of a rocket, and 'that control of it might well be achieved by changing slightly the direction of the stream of gas issuing therefrom'. Instead of following the heated wake, Tizard thought it might prove easier to home in on the turbulence behind an aircraft and 'that it might be possible to devise a simple control which ensured that the projectile remained in the turbulent wake'. After this lengthy discussion, the committee decided that Beale and Denman should not be employed because they had no useful contribution to offer the Air Ministry.

Blackett was more impressed with the dynamite wire barrage proposed by a Dr Goldschmidt in late 1938. The invention was intended to launch explosively a web of wire into the path of an aircraft flying at less than 1,000 feet. Blackett and Hill had a lengthy discussion with the inventor and viewed a working small-scale model of the device. Blackett's 'view was that, if Dr. Goldschmidt could make a large scale apparatus at a reasonable cost and without imposing large demands on the time of the Air Ministry staff, it was advisable to proceed with the development'. Blackett was not gullible, making it clear that he doubted that the dynamite barrage would work in practice. He did believe, however, that there might be some interesting indirect benefits from the programme. Also, he 'pointed out that if knowledge of successful experiments of this nature reached foreign countries, the morale effect would be high'.[24]

This last comment illustrates that Blackett had become a first-rate defence scientist, able to see much more than the simple technical aspects of a device. The very notion of using leaked reports on a new weapon to influence enemy air forces reveals that he looked at every aspect of air defence, including the psychological.

We can also see Blackett's abilities in some of his contributions in discussions on the development of radar. While Tizard and Appleton remained the members principally concerned with radar, Blackett made several noteworthy contributions. He reminded the committee on more than one occasion of the need to remain vigilant about the possibility of the enemy jamming radar transmissions, and he suggested ways in which jamming could be minimised.[25] Aware of recent development in short-wave vacuum tube or valve technology in the United States, in November 1938, Blackett had the committee agree that Appleton should be sent to North America to investigate.[26]

Perhaps Blackett's most interesting contribution occurred in March 1938, during a discussion on means to train radar operators, because it illustrates his ability to combine his combat experience with military scientific development. Bawdsey had unsuccessfully tried to use approaching airliners as targets for interception. These tests had failed because the aircraft operated too low, operated in crowded airspace, and often flew highly divergent courses. Blackett was highly critical of the whole approach, since in operations radar personnel would be focusing their attention on squadrons and not on single aircraft. 'He went on to emphasize the importance in his view of giving practice to the operational personnel in reporting the approach of formations as well as isolated aircraft.' The committee concurred with Blackett and urged that more realistic testing of the radar system be undertaken.[27]

While Blackett enthusiastically contributed to air defence research, there is some evidence that his later moral and intellectual contempt for weapons of mass destruction existed before the war. It appears unlikely that Blackett would have served on a committee dealing with improving offensive weapons. In late 1936, he wrote one of his first papers for the committee on the defensive use of RAF bombers. In the report he made several assumptions: first, that radar, barrages and silhouette schemes in conjunction with fighters made bombers far less effective in attacking the source of enemy air power and enemy military objectives; second, that bombers would still be useful in attacking enemy populations. He wrote to Tizard that 'England, with her dense population close to the coasts and her democratic institutions, is far more vulnerable to [attacks on civil population] than, for instance, Germany, with a less dense and more highly disciplined and protected population'. He argued that the aggressor would always have the advantage. He proposed, therefore, a variety of ways bombers could attack other bombers. 'It would', he wrote, 'avoid the social disadvantage of the present system, that 60% of the new air armaments have no great defensive value, except by the distasteful procedure of resorting to [attacking civilian populations], which may also turn out very ineffective.'[28]

Blackett's interest in developing techniques for bombing the bomber led him into his most extensive involvement in pre-war defence research. On 25 August 1937, Blackett wrote a paper in which he calculated that if a fuse could be developed using optical means or sound to explode in close proximity to an enemy bomber, lethal damage during air-to-air bombing would be achieved 25 per cent of the time, as opposed to a mere 8 per cent using timed fuses. Blackett proposed the immediate development of a new type of detonator which could detect variations in the intensity of light should commence at once.

Research on developing a photoelectric fuse began at the Royal Aircraft Establishment by the beginning of 1938. RAE and Air Defence Experimental Establishment researchers worked in conjunction with ordnance experts at Woolwich. Owing to the inter-service nature of the research, it was supervised by the fuses subcommittee of the Air Defence Research Committee of the Committee of Imperial Defence. Professor A.G.C. Egerton, the co-secretary of the Royal Society, chaired the committee. Blackett was one of the key members of the committee and took the lead in designing a prototype photoelectric (PE) fuse. It was hoped that the fuse would work using a photoelectric cell which would respond to changes in the intensity of light of as little as 1 per cent.

Tests of the PE fuse begin at RAE in the late spring of 1938. A large bomber was flown at 200 m.p.h. 'over at different distances from the "eye" propped up at an angle' for a 2,000-feet drop. By using a movie camera mounted on the aeroplane and which recorded the 'detonations' of the fuse on the film, they developed an accurate means of assessing the performance of the unit.[29] By February 1939, the PE bomb was tested in a series of dropping trials. Two out of five bombs detonated as expected, and it was felt that the causes of the three failures were known and could be rectified. As a result the Tizard Committee recommended that 400 to 500 of the bombs be produced. Metropolitan-Vickers were contracted to build the bombs.[30]

Despite this early promise, however, the photoelectric fuse failed to perform as anticipated. No accounts of the tests have survived, in large measure because most RAE reports were destroyed after the war, but apparently the PE bomb suffered from some fatal flaws. It was soon realised that even if the fuse could be made to function as intended, a new stabilised bombsight would have to be developed in order to allow the attacking aircraft to change course if the target aircraft took defensive action. Existing bombsights required that the bomber fly on a level and straight course and any change of direction or altitude of the target aircraft would make any such attacks futile. It was the lack of a stabilised bombsight that led Tizard to conclude in November 1938 that air-to-air bombing had little future.

Still, testing of the PE fuse continued because it was hoped to incorporate it into other anti-aircraft weapons. Problems, however, continued to plague the programme. Relying on light as a source of activation, no amount of experimentation could make the fuse useful for the night defences. The fuse also proved to be quite delicate, which made it impossible to install into conventional anti-aircraft shells. The PE fuse projects were cancelled in 1940, giving way to a far superior radio proximity fuse.[31]

When war was declared, among academic scientists Blackett was one of the most knowledgeable and experienced about military research. However, unlike many of his less experienced academic colleagues he was not immediately placed full time into a military research programme. For instance, at the outbreak of the war, his contemporary at the Cavendish, John Cockcroft, became the Assistant Director of Research at the Ministry of Supply with special responsibility for radar research.[32] His former student, Bernard Lovell, began work on aircraft interception radar research by October 1939. Instead, on 9 October 1939, Blackett was formally appointed as a principal scientific officer at RAE, but he appears to have worked there no more than two days a week. It remains uncertain why Blackett was not immediately absorbed into the war effort on a full-time basis. It may be that he felt that he required time to suspend his own research and teaching duties at Manchester. It is also possible that when the PE fuse proved not to be practicable, Blackett may have found himself without any clear direction to apply his considerable talents for defence research. This may explain why he began work on designing bombsights at RAE. It is also possible that Blackett hoped that an improved bombsight could be used to make possible attacks by RAF bombers on enemy aircraft.

It is certain that soon after his appointment to RAE, Blackett had a more important role to play in the war effort than designing bombsights. The first suggestion for an alternative wartime position for Blackett was made by Tizard in late October 1939. Tizard recommended that Blackett be placed in charge of a scientific intelligence mission to the United States. For unknown reasons, Blackett was soon dropped from the proposal and, in March 1940, Hill was sent in his place.[33]

The first mention that Blackett would concentrate his attention on operational research seems to stem from the work of the Radio Research Sub-Committee (RRC) of the CSSAD, which was formed in December 1939. This committee took over responsibility for overseeing radar research. Its chairman was Appleton, and members included Blackett, Watson Watt, Rowe and a number of other Air Ministry technical experts. As far as can be ascertained, the Radio Research Sub-Committee existed only until early January 1940, when the CSSAD was disbanded and its responsibilities turned over to a number of new Air Ministry and inter-service committees.[34]

At the second meeting of the RRC, the committee recommended that operational research, which had been removed from the laboratory in September 1939 when Bawdsey researchers were moved to Dundee in Scotland, should recommence forthwith.[35] The

Bawdsey OR group had developed from early radar research, initially focusing its attention on improving the performance of operations rooms. It is from here that the term 'operational research' originates. At first, this work involved improving equipment, such as map counters and plotting boards, used in operations rooms, to distil the vast amount of data being received from radar stations and the Observer Corps into useful information. The research was gradually expanded until, by the summer of 1939, almost all aspects of the air defence system were being placed under scientific scrutiny. When the Bawdsey researchers moved north, Fighter Command Headquarters specifically requested that OR staff be transferred to Stanmore so that they could continue to work closely with RAF personnel to improve the performance of the early warning system.[36] The group was originally named the Air Ministry Research Establishment's Stanmore Research Section. In 1941, the group was placed directly under the Commander-in-Chief, Fighter Command, and renamed the Operational Research Section, Fighter Command.

The pioneering efforts of Bawdsey and Stanmore personnel in developing modern OR is often overlooked. By the start of the war, however, OR was well established in Fighter Command. The head of the Stanmore Research Section, Harold Ladner, and his staff, particularly E.C. Williams and G.A. Roberts, were instrumental in ensuring the radar defence and interception system was operational in time for the Battle of Britain.[37]

The proposal of the Radio Research Sub-Committee to establish another OR group at Dundee came about because the Stanmore group was soon fully involved in improving operational performance of the system and had little time to spare for supporting the research programme on new radar, ancillary equipment and innovative tactical developments. Blackett's interest in pursuing OR research in late 1939 is known from two letters. The first was written on 30 December to Blackett by A.B. Jones, a member of Rowe's staff at Dundee. In the letter, we learn that sometime earlier Blackett had requested that he be allowed to join the radar researchers in Scotland. At the time, however, there was no suitable opening for such an esteemed scientist. However, Jones believed that, as a result of the initiative to form a new OR group, he now needed an individual of 'outstanding ability' to lead it and he offered the position to Blackett. Blackett's first task would be to improve the accuracy of interception, particularly of low-flying German mine-laying aircraft. Jones proposed that this work be coupled with the continued development of aerial minefields, which could be deployed to snag these raiders. Blackett was offered a 'free hand to try any method of interception' he liked and to co-operate with any other research establishment. Jones concluded by telling Blackett, that it was designed to 'be a job after your own heart'.[38]

The second letter was written by Tizard to Rowe on 2 January 1940. Tizard was then the scientific adviser to the Chief of Air Staff, and Rowe was in charge of the Air Ministry Research Establishment (AMRE) at Dundee. The letter spoke of the need to strengthen Ladner's analytical staff and to re-establish OR at AMRE, particularly to work out new means to track the path of low-flying mine-laying aircraft. Tizard wrote: 'I had hoped that Blackett would be able to devote a lot of his time to the work, he is the ideal man for the job.'[39]

Despite this strong support and Blackett's desire to be involved in radar-related OR work, he remained at RAE working on bombsights and other aeronautical equipment until he finally began OR research in August 1940 at Anti-Aircraft Command Headquarters, Stanmore. The reason for this stems from the consequences of the ill-fated move of the Air Ministry Experimental Establishment from Bawdsey to Dundee in September 1939. The objective of the transfer was to move from harm's way Britain's most important research organisation. While the move accomplished the main objective, Dundee was found to be a completely inadequate place to conduct research. There was not enough laboratory space, sensitive equipment was rendered useless by interference from local electrical use, and the area lacked a suitable nearby airbase and radar station. So chaotic was the situation that research virtually ground to a halt and, almost immediately, plans were begun to relocate AMRE to Swanage. Tizard told Rowe that the OR group could not be established until AMRE was up and running in its new premises. Inexplicably, the Swanage move was delayed until mid-spring 1940, by which time Blackett was fully involved with his work at Farnborough and with his participation on a variety of committees. The committees included the RDF (Radar) Applications Committee, and the famous Maud Committee, investigating the military utility of atomic energy.[40]

What Blackett might have felt about the failure to start OR work at AMRE may be surmised from his involvement in the discussions which led to the anonymous publication in July 1940 of the famous Penguin paperback, *Science in War.* The book was based on discussion held at the meeting of a dinner club, 'The Tots and Quots'. The club was organised by the Oxford biologist Solly Zuckerman, and its members included leading liberal and left-wing scientists and social scientists. Of prime concern to the group was the under-utilisation of science in the war effort.

Blackett was a regular member, and was present when Zuckerman invited the Penguin publisher to attend one of the suppers. So impressed was he by the conversation that the publisher suggested that a book based on the discussions he had heard should be put into print within a month. The book was highly critical of the government and urged far greater use be made of scientific resources because 'only scientific method can deal effectively with the new problems which turn up daily, and the issues of the war depend largely on how quickly and how effectively science is used'.[41]

In his account of the creation of *Science in War*, Zuckerman makes only one direct reference to Blackett's role in the discussion. Blackett cautioned his dining companions that scientists could not help in the immediate problems of war production.[42] There is no evidence, however, that Blackett disagreed with the general argument of the book. It is more than likely that he felt himself poorly utilised in the first ten months of the war.

Blackett's decision to leave behind Farnborough and start OR work when another opportunity presented itself should therefore come as no surprise. His arrival at Stanmore put him in direct contact with Ladner's OR group. More research needs to done on the influence of the AMRE's Research Section at Stanmore on Blackett's formative period of OR research. He may possibly have also been instructed by A.V. Hill. Hill had led a similar experimental unit for anti-aircraft defences during the First World War and had introduced Blackett to General Pile, the Commander-in-Chief of Anti-Aircraft Command.

What is certain is that when he arrived at Stanmore, Blackett was already one of Britain's most accomplished defence scientists. He would use his expertise to expand the application of OR outside of Fighter Command. In doing so, he profoundly changed the course of the Second World War and the relationship of science to the conduct of war. He would make the science of OR known to a much wider audience, some of whom would promote the civilian applications of the techniques after the war. Blackett was heavily influenced by his pre-war experiences, and his OR work must be seen as one of the many legacies of the Tizard Committee.

NOTES

1. C.H. Waddington, *OR in World War 2: Operational Research Against the U-boat* (London: Elek, 1973).
2. Guy Hartcup, *The War of Invention: Scientific Development, 1914–18* (London: Brassey's Defence Publishers, 1988), pp. 151–2, 161–2, 164–5, 184, 194–5.
3. From 1925–28 Lindemann was a member of the Anti-Aircraft Research Sub-Committee of the Committee of Imperial Defence. See David Zimmerman, 'Tucker's Acoustical Mirror: Aircraft Detection before Radar', *War and Society*, 15, 1 (May 1997).
4. For more on radical scientists in the 1930s, see Gary Werskey, *The Visible College* (London: Allen Lane, 1978). For Blackett and the Russian Exhibition, see David Wilson, *Rutherford: Simple Genius* (London: Hodder & Stoughton, 1983), p. 489.
5. Blackett as quoted in Sir Bernard Lovell, 'Patrick Maynard Stuart Blackett, Baron Blackett, of Chelsea', *Biographical Memoirs of Fellows of the Royal Society*, 21 (1975), p. 11.
6. Wilson, *Rutherford*, pp. 483–9; The Earl of Birkenhead, *The Professor and the Prime Minister* (Boston, MA: Houghton & Mifflin, 1962), pp. 97–102.
7. Lovell, 'Patrick Maynard Stuart Blackett', p. 76.
8. William McGucken, *Scientist, Society and the State* (Columbus, OH: Ohio State University Press, 1984), pp. 101–2.
9. Secretary, Air Ministry to Hill, 12 December 1934, Sir Henry Tizard Papers (HTT), 58, Imperial War Museum.
10. For the history of the Tizard Committee, see David Zimmerman, *Britain's Shield: Radar and the Defeat of the Luftwaffe* (Stroud: Sutton, 2001).
11. Ronald W. Clark, *Tizard* (London: Methuen, 1965), pp. 116–17.
12. P.M.S. Blackett, 'Tizard and the Science of War', *Studies of War* (New York: Hill & Wang, 1962), p. 118.
13. Committee for the Scientific Survey of Air Defence (CSSAD), Minutes of the 6th meeting, 10 April 1935, PRO AIR 20/181.
14. CSSAD, 13th meeting, 5 November 1935.
15. CSSAD, 7th meeting, 15 May 1935.
16. CSSAD, 35th meeting, 27 October 1937.
17. CSSAD, 32nd meeting, 26 July 1937.
18. CSSAD, 35th meeting, 27 October 1937.
19. CSSAD, 34th meeting, 21 October 1937.
20. CSSAD, 12th, 24th, 36th, 38th, 39th, 41st, 42nd, 44th, 45th and 46th meetings, 10 October 1935 to 9 February 1939; 'Balloon Barrages', Henry Tizard Diary, 14 July 1938, HTT 10; 'Note on a Visit to Woolwich with Professor Blackett', Tizard Diary, 6 March 1939, HTT 11.
21. Guy Hartcup, *The Challenge of War* (Newton Abbot: David & Charles, 1970), pp. 234–7.
22. CSSAD, 27th and 28th meetings, 21 and 24 December 1936.
23. CSSAD, 42nd meeting, 13 July 1938.
24. CSSAD, 45th meeting, 3 January 1939.

25. CSSAD, 38th and 39th meetings, 22 February and 15 March 1938.
26. CSSAD, 44th meeting, 23 November 1938.
27. CSSAD, 39th meeting, 15 March 1938.
28. Blackett to Tizard, 16 December 1936, HTT 32.
29. Ben Lockspeiser, RAE to Blackett, 14 April 1938, Blackett Papers, D13.
30. CSSAD, 46th meeting, 9 February 1939.
31. RAE to Blackett, 4 February 1939, Blackett Papers, D13. 'Time Fuzes for Bombing the Bombers', n.d. but spring 1939, Blackett Papers, D14. 'A Note on the Use of a Stabilised Sight for Use with the PE Bomb', n.d. but spring 1939. RAE Instruction Leaflet No. H277, Blackett Papers, D19. Dowding to Tizard, 15 September 1939, HTT 226.
32. Guy Hartcup and T.E. Allibone, *Cockcroft and the Atom* (Bristol: Adam Hilgar, 1984), pp. 89–90.
33. David Zimmerman, *Top Secret Exchange: The Tizard Mission and the Scientific War* (Montreal and Stroud: McQuill Queen's University Press and Alan Sutton, 1996), p. 51.
34. Minutes of the Radio Research Sub-Committee can be found in PRO AVIA 7/241.
35. Radio Research Sub-Committee of the CSSAD, 2nd meeting, 20 December 1939, PRO AVIA 7/241.
36. Air Commodore K.R. Park, Fighter Command Headquarters to Rowe, Dundee, 16 September 1939, PRO AIR 16/24.
37. For a full account of OR work for Fighter Command up to the summer of 1941, see Zimmerman, *Britain's Shield.* Also see H.M. Barka (ed.), *The War Record of the Operational Research Section, Fighter Command,* unpublished monograph, 31 December 1948, Air Historical Branch; *Complete List of Reports Issued by Research Branch, Fighter Command or its Equivalent from 1940 to October 1947*, PRO AIR 16/1042.
38. A.B. Jones to Blackett, 30 December 1939, PRO AVIA 7/601.
39. Tizard to Rowe, 2 January 1940, HTT 232.
40. For details on Blackett's work at RAE, see Lovell, 'Patrick Maynard Stuart Blackett', pp. 54–6.
41. *Science in War*, as quoted in Werskey, *The Visible College*, p. 263.
42. Solly Zuckerman, *From Apes to Warlords, 1904–46* (London: Hamish Hamilton, 1978), p. 111.

8

Blackett and the Black Arts

Jock Gardner

Two of the more interesting disciplines in the Allied armoury during the Second World War were signals intelligence (SI) and operational research (OR). They displayed some interesting similarities and differences, and both are legitimate fields of study in their own right. However, it would be fair to say that there is no known previous study which has looked at both of these together and considered where, if anywhere, they met at the time. The question posed by the last statement is a very legitimate one and there are good reasons why no meeting of these fields might have occurred: security, the differing culture of the practitioners and some degree of functional mismatch. Such a view was reinforced by the informal opinion held by many researchers that no such junction had taken place. But this was wrong and there was a thriving if somewhat circumscribed relationship between the two communities centred on one of the most important conflicts of the war: the Battle of the Atlantic. Blackett not only had an overall responsibility for this: he produced at least one report under his own signature. The operation of this liaison provides a key insight into the prosecution of that struggle. In investigating this subject, a number of topics of interest emerge: intelligence and OR, the people involved, what they produced and an assessment of the relationship's value.

But before moving on to these, a short digression perhaps ought to be made into asking the question of why the topic of OR is so obscure. Some of the answer for this is fairly obvious: OR practitioners are not usually historians, but neither are most of those involved in the production of intelligence. The compartmentalisation of study also has something to answer for. But another answer must also lie in the rather ugly conjunction of the two words 'historiographical chronology'. Put quite simply, the OR historical literature had largely run out of steam by the mid-1970s.[1] The publication of Winterbotham's *The Ultra Secret* was in 1974, and this opened the floodgates to the stream of signals intelligence literature, and most specifically that concerning Ultra – codebreaking intelligence.[2] By the time that this got into its stride, the history of OR was virtually a dead letter. In fairness, the intelligence official history did not quite neglect OR but nor did it give it much space either.[3] The one reference to the matter of OR and SI is brief but gives the key to the relationship between two parts of the Admiralty: the Operational Intelligence Centre (OIC) of the Naval Intelligence Division (NID) and the OR staff.[4]

A further examination of this liaison will follow but some of the limits to this are set by the survival – or rather lack of it – of much useful primary material. The situation was brought about post-war by a quite proper concern in that period for the security of a vast amount of still highly sensitive material. As a result much of the paperwork held by and originated in the OIC was destroyed with thoroughly good motives. In particular, many working papers were similarly not preserved. Memoirs by those who worked in such places and survived long enough to have their work published in the post-Winterbotham era also make it clear that much of the daily business was done in unminuted meetings and bilateral conversations, either face to face or else by telephone.[5] What have survived are two classes of document: reports issued by the OIC and those by Blackett's own department, latterly known as the Department of Naval Operational Research (DNOR).[6]

INTELLIGENCE AND OPERATIONAL RESEARCH

Intelligence was a pursuit with a considerable pedigree extending back over centuries. Its collection and dissemination can be traced back to at least biblical times. Neither was the breaking of codes and ciphers a new activity.[7] What in the 1940s was relatively new were machine ciphers and radio transmission. The latter made it fairly easy to be aware that an enemy was indulging in communication; the former rendered understanding the words used more difficult. A considerable amount could often be gleaned from a radio transmission without necessarily understanding the plaintext which the cipher concealed. This could take the form of direction finding (thus locating the source of the signal) and traffic analysis, which might yield some clue of deployed strength as well as giving some indication of the type of enemy activity. Full decryption, which started to become available reliably (but sometimes sporadically) from about the middle of 1941, was clearly immensely helpful but was difficult to achieve. During the middle part of the Battle of the Atlantic full decryption of German signals – known as Ultra – might be one of the factors permitting the evasive routeing of convoys away from groups of submarines. A well-developed skill by the middle of 1943 was the use of Ultra intelligence not only to inform current operations but also as an important component of building a very thorough picture of the enemy's order of battle, doctrine and tactical methods.

Operational research, by contrast, was very much a child of the Second World War. Generally acknowledged to have been spurred by the development of radar and the consequent questions concerning the best way to use and organise this powerful sensor, OR advanced rapidly during the war and spread into virtually all fields of warfare and its supporting activities. Its fundamental premise is that scientists can contribute not just to the development of new sensors and weapons but also to the better use of material currently in service. As Blackett himself wrote in 1941: 'The main field of their [scientists in close touch with operations] activity is clearly the analysis of actual operations using as data the material to be found in an operations room.'[8] He went on to note two visceral reactions of military officers to the problems and to suggest palliatives to these: 'In fact, the scientist can encourage numerical thinking on operational matters, and so can help to avoid running the war by gusts of emotion.'[9] His paper goes on to deprecate the attitude that the solution to all current tactical and operational problems lay in the provision of new and markedly better equipment. Although not suggesting that the quest of improvement should be discontinued, he argued instead for the systematic study and thus enhanced performance from existing tactics and material.[10] Thus it can be seen that OR was deeply, largely and normally concerned with the close and numerical study of British activities, not German.

These brief descriptions tend to point to the contrasts between the two disciplines rather than any similarities. The intelligence side may be summed up as being concerned with the enemy, largely non-numerical in its nature and having to form conclusions based on often scanty evidence. OR was related to British activities, highly numerical and working from a much broader and deeper base of knowledge. On such descriptions, there would appear to be little common ground and thus virtually no scope for co-operation.

There are, however, several ways in which to look at organisations and processes. Both intelligence and OR dealt with other entities which used their reports and, in many instances, these were the same bodies. In the context of the Battle of the Atlantic, both intelligence and OR products were used by commands such as the naval Commander-in-Chief, Western Approaches and the Air Force's Coastal Command, as well as the Admiralty itself.[11] Further, both intelligence and OR had as their main stock-in-trade what would now be called information processing. Thus there were similarities as well as differences.

This suggests that there might be some scope for co-operation, but there were two important barriers to such an innovation: one procedural and one of method. The procedural point was that the security surrounding all intelligence method and product was considerable; for Ultra this was especially so. Thus the question has to be asked, how was Blackett or anyone else on the OR staff to learn of Ultra? There are two reasonable possibilities: authorised disclosure or deducing Ultra's existence by other data. On the first, Blackett would have appeared to have received his earliest cognisance of Ultra-based information in April 1943.[12] However, prior deduction cannot be ruled out. On the American side, there is a story of how one OR researcher, Jacinto Steinhardt, deduced from data inconsistencies that some source of information unknown to the researchers must be available and that the operational authorities then admitted appropriate OR staff to the Ultra mysteries.[13] It is possible that a similar event may have occurred on the eastern side of the Atlantic but if this is so, then it has eluded even anecdotal survival. What is clear is that by November 1943 one further member of the British OR staff was not only privy to Ultra information, but had also produced a report drawing largely on such sources.[14]

PLACES AND PEOPLE

Normally, DNOR work was done in their own offices in the Admiralty building in Whitehall. However, the sensitivity of the source material used in drawing up SI reports meant that these could not have been used there. Thus the work was carried out in the Operational Intelligence Centre itself, inside a protected building, the Citadel on the Mall. This was despite the pressures on accommodation there; the work must therefore have been considered of utility and importance.[15] Although the first certain evidence of Blackett's knowledge was in April 1943, the first report known to have been written by an OR researcher later that year was by Leon Solomon, a relatively junior member of the DNOR staff.[16] The only further British documentary evidence that indicates exposure of OR staff to Ultra comes from the signature on a report in August 1944 by E.J. Williams, a researcher of considerable renown who had followed Blackett to take charge of the Coastal Command Operational Research Section (ORS) and was then his assistant director for anti-submarine warfare in DNOR.[17]

There are, however, indications from an American source that Williams's knowledge may go back to an earlier date in 1943. Here the clue comes from a correspondence between Captain H.A. Flanigan, USN, on the staff of United States Naval Forces in Europe in London, and Rear-Admiral F.S. Low, the Chief of Staff of the 10th Fleet at the Navy Department in Washington, DC.[18] The general context was the conduct of convoy operations, a part of which was formed by a discussion of the handling of special intelligence and consequently a comparison of how many people in Washington and London had this knowledge. Flanigan wrote in early June 1943:

> I do not need to tell you of the importance which they attach here to safe-guarding 'Z' [yet another name for Ultra] information. Nevertheless it is known to a reasonably good-sized group, including the 1st Sea Lord, the Vice-Chief of the Naval Staff, … *the two senior scientists in the Admiralty Operational Research, the two senior scientists in Coastal Command Operational Research.*[19]

This might suggest that Williams as a senior member of Blackett's organisation was aware of Ultra rather earlier than the other material would indicate. It also makes it clear that knowledge of Ultra may also have been directly applied to the RAF side of the Battle of the Atlantic as well.[20]

ACHIEVEMENTS AND ANALYSIS

A total of 20 reports were produced between November 1943 and April 1945. Somewhat oddly, there is a marked hiatus after the first report until April 1944. In the intervening period, however, Blackett continued to receive selected SI reports. All but one of the 20 reports were either the sole work of Leon Solomon (the largest number) or else co-signed by E.J. Williams; one report is signed only by Blackett.[21]

There are several ways of grouping the subjects of the reports. Two are adopted here: the general area of warfare that is addressed and the degree to which they deal with enemy activities as opposed to those of Allied forces.

Thus, warfare can be considered in more than one way for these purposes. One is to look at traditional classifications such as anti-submarine warfare (ASW) or mine warfare; another is to consider less used – but probably more useful – classifications. In the latter case, inshore warfare, for example, is a helpful categorisation. However, what this also means is that some of the reports cover more than one class. Thus, the total exceeds the number of reports.

From Table 1 it is clear that ASW is the dominant area, with inshore warfare the second most significant one. However, in three cases, the two warfare fields are both represented in the same report. Anti-shipping is the only other prominent theme, albeit in a relatively minor way. What this suggests is the continuing primacy of the submarine problem even after the withdrawal of German U-boats from the main cross-Atlantic routes in May 1943. Although a judgement made by a historian decades after the event might be that

TABLE 1
OPERATIONAL RESEARCH: SPECIAL INTELLIGENCE REPORTS – ANALYSIS BY WARFARE AREA

Warfare Area	*Number*
Anti-shipping	3
Anti-submarine warfare (ASW)	11
Communications	1
Inshore warfare	8
Mine warfare	1
Shore attack	1

such a continuing stress was wasted effort, this was not so, a point returned to below. The interest in inshore warfare was perhaps more understandable with the majority of the German naval efforts in this late-war period being largely limited to attempts to disrupt the flow of logistics from England to north-west Europe. The subject of anti-shipping operations demonstrates the Allied interest in and interdiction of the remaining, much diminished and much diminishing, German shipping, largely concerned with the supply of raw materials – mostly ore – from Scandinavia. Two comments can be made about the areas with only single appearances. It is perhaps surprising that mine warfare only features once as this was an important aspect of Allied operations at this stage of the war. Perhaps its lack of salience is because of the relatively routine nature of dealing with this problem, it being one which needed much application rather than the combined onslaught of intelligence and operational research. There are perhaps two areas of interest which could be developed further: the continuing emphasis on ASW and the single report on communications.

The clear trend in the SI-based reports stands in clear distinction to the interests shown by the rest of DNOR's output in this period. Paul Sutcliffe has noted that in the 1942–43 period ASW was the staple at over 60 per cent, declining to 35 per cent in 1944 and thence to a mere 10 per cent in 1945.[22] The likely explanation for this divergence is that DNOR generally was concerned with current and recent operations, whereas the SI-issued OR reports were more to do with the developments which the Germans were planning to bring into service in the near future. The former could draw most of its data from Allied observations of operations, but the latter needed information which could only come from intelligence sources and, in particular, signals intelligence. A very specific and important example of this was the one report on communications.

In the first place, this dealt with a German technical innovation of great interest and importance, a system of communication which made a submarine's radio transmissions much less liable to interception at sea. This was done by a system of signal compression or burst transmission, known as 'Squash' to the Allies or *Kurier* to the Germans. The effect of this would be not to allow a direction-finding system fitted in convoy escorts to ascertain the direction from which the signal came, if indeed it was detected at all. The report, using data from the convoy battles of February–April 1943, calculated what would have been the effect of the Germans having had such a device then – and the answers were not at all encouraging.[23] But the importance of this study demonstrated a second significant point – how useful the collaboration between OR and intelligence methods and organisations was. It would have been unlikely, if not impossible, for the talents of the OIC, or even the NID, to have carried out such a study. The later part of the war was typified by several important submarine developments, such as much improved underwater performance, which if they had been fully developed and deployed by the Germans would have had the potential to transfer the initiative in the Battle of the Atlantic back to them. The *Kurier* report was an example of being able to express what the probable effect of a new enemy development might be – in a numerate way. This symbiotic conjunction of two different cerebral disciplines was only possible because of the advanced state of both and a willingness to co-operate.

By contrast, none of these characteristics was evident in Germany, either then or indeed at any time during the war. It is customary to attribute Allied success generally either to outfighting the Germans or to the preponderance of material and economic superiority, but here is a demonstration of yet another area of Allied advantage. It is instructive to look at the German case a little more closely. It is certainly true that they never developed anything remotely like operational research, and the general ambiance of the Third Reich – compartmentalisation, deliberate overlaps and the inbuilt diversion of resources to both wasteful redundancy and significant turf fighting – militated against such a development. But even had this not been the case, there were other barriers. With intelligence product and organisations, there are two linked paradoxes – the juxtaposition of poorer technical prowess at cryptography and the bad exploitation of that product stand starkly against many of the German navy's successes in pure codebreaking up until the middle of 1943. One resolution of this difficulty should lie in the realisation that operational performance is not a matter of comparing two nations' cryptographic quality directly – it has to be related to the targets of such activity. Here it has to be said that the Allied – and in particular the British – record of security of many of their own codes was not good and it was this which allowed the Germans their considerable window on convoy operations, to select an important example.

But there was more to Allied superiority than just this relatively limited point of comparative cryptography. What was also remarkable was the degree of exploitation of the material by the British and then the Americans. Partly as a result of capacity, partly because it was recognised that something could still be learned from German signals which had long passed their very limited period of immediate tactical exploitation, a very detailed picture was built up of German tactics, doctrine and organisation. Whether the Germans suffered principally from a failure of resource or one of imagination cannot be essayed with any degree of rigour, but this ability to project intelligence product at least one level further was undoubtedly a significant Allied advantage.

Such an ability was useful in itself but it was also a critical asset in allowing the operational researcher to turn the talents of that new science to advantage, to lend yet another aspect to understanding the enemy. But the combination of the two skills not only did that; it also allowed a far greater degree of confidence to be enjoyed in the outcome of operations conducted against that enemy. It is also noticeable with the passage of time and the acquisition of practice that OR reports issued under OIC cover moved to dealing rather more with the enemy and somewhat less with Allied operations (see Table 2).

CONCLUSIONS

Collaboration is known to have occurred between British intelligence and operational research staffs in the last third of the Second World War. It may have predated this but there is no known documentary evidence to support such an assertion. Only a small number of OR researchers appear to have been involved: Leon

TABLE 2
OIC REPORTS BY OR RESEARCHERS – ANALYSIS BY SUBJECT

Date Band	*Allied-related*	*Enemy-related*	*Total*
April– September 1943	0	0	0
October 1943–March 1944	1	0	1
April–September 1944	5	4	9
October 1944–May 1945	1	6	7

Solomon, E.J. Williams and Blackett himself. An historical reading of some 20 reports generated by the process suggests that these were at least useful, and probably were of significant value. There is no direct evidence suggesting how they were viewed at the time of writing, nor is there likely to be. Most recipients were fairly senior and almost certainly none survive, and, as far as is known, the only copies now extant of the reports were for the file and were unannotated by customers. Retention of the other copies would not have been encouraged; indeed, their readers would have been prohibited from doing such a thing. The only inference that can be drawn is that the continuity of reporting carries a strong presumption that this was considered to be valuable work. There is only fragmentary anecdotal evidence that any such activity occurred in the USA.[24] In Germany, nothing of the sort took place whatsoever, not least because there was never any effective form of OR.

By their fundamental natures, OR and intelligence inhabit what are normally and indeed properly differentiated spheres of activity; the two key sections of difference are extent of knowledge and concern (usually exclusive) with own or enemy forces. There is, however, room at the margins of both disciplines for useful mutual collaboration. This is what occurred in the last two years of the Second World War and, as far as is known, it is the only example of this taking place in wartime.

NOTES

1. C.H. Waddington, *OR in World War 2: Operational Research Against the U-boat*; (London: Paul Elek Science, 1973) (originally written in 1946). P.M.S. Blackett, 'Operational Research: Recollections of Problems Studied, 1940–1945', in H.G. Thursfield (ed.), *Brassey's Annual: The Armed Forces Year-book, 1953* (London: Clowes, 1953), pp. 88–106. Philip Morse and George Kimball, *Methods of Operations Research* (New York: John Wiley & Sons, 1951).
2. F.W. Winterbotham, *The Ultra Secret* (London: Weidenfeld & Nicolson, 1974).
3. F.H. Hinsley *et al.*, *British Intelligence in the Second World War: Its Influence on Strategy and Operations* (London: HMSO, 1979–1988), 3 volumes in 4. There are a few brief mentions of both OR and Blackett.
4. 'See Appendix 16 [actually 15]. This is an example of the statistical analyses prepared in the OIC, mostly on subjects connected with U-boats, by a civilian scientiest [*sic*] lent to the OIC by the Chief of the Admiralty Operational Research Branch in 1943 (Professor Blackett).' Hinsley, *British Intelligence in the Second World War*, 3:1, p. 286, asterisked footnote.
5. The observations in the last two sentences were largely made from the perspective of the intelligence community. However, Malcolm Llewellyn-

Jones's research, especially his interviews with surviving members of DNOR, has established similar patterns of working.

6. Initially Blackett was appointed to the Admiralty as Chief Adviser Operational Research (CAOR). In June 1944 this changed to DNOR reflecting the growth of his organisation. However, neither expansion nor change of name is marked by the quarterly *Navy List* until April 1945. For simplicity, the organisation will be referred to throughout as DNOR.
7. David Kahn, *Codebreakers: The Story of Secret Writing* (new edition New York: Scribner, 1996).
8. PRO ADM 219/16, 'Scientists at the Operational Level', section 1. It should be noted that Blackett wrote this when he was at Coastal Command. However, the remarks are equally applicable to the naval environment.
9. ADM 219/16, section 2(iii).
10. ADM 219/16, section 6.
11. The Admiralty, unlike the War Office and Air Ministry, was not only an administrative but also an operational headquarters.
12. PRO ADM 223/97, SI 562 of 7 April 1943. Earlier authorised disclosure is possible. Blackett and Rodger Winn, who was the head of the submarine tracking room of the OIC, were both participants in the Assistant Chief of the Naval Staff (U-boats and Trade)'s U-boat Warfare Committee meeting from 31 December 1942. PRO ADM 205/30, p. 32. However, proximity does not allow the inference to be drawn that communication of sensitive intelligence took place. There were several fora where some participants knew of Ultra and others did not. An example is the Anti-U-boat Warfare Committee. See W.J.R. Gardner, 'An Allied Perspective', in Stephen Howarth and Derek Law (eds), *The Battle of the Atlantic 1939–1945: The 50th Anniversary International Naval Conference* (London: Greenhill Books, 1994), p. 525.
13. Keith R. Tidman, *The Operations Evaluation Group: A History of Naval Operations Analysis* (Annapolis, MD: Naval Institute Press, 1984), p. 59. Sadly this account is neither fully documented nor even dated.
14. PRO ADM 223/170, Non-numbered special intelligence (SI) report 'Note on the Mk 24 Mine'. The Mk 24 Mine was a cover name for the first Allied homing torpedo, designed specifically for use against submerged submarines.
15. The point about pressure on Citadel accommodation comes from the research of Dr C.I. Hamilton of Witwatersrand University. Communication, 24 August 1998.
16. As Note 14. Solomon was, at the end of the war, a temporary experimental officer, the lowest level of scientific officer in DNOR. It speaks both for security and perhaps the degree of compartmentalisation of DNOR's work that none of the surviving members interviewed by Llewellyn-Jones have any recollection of him.
17. PRO ADM 223/172, SI Report 1036, 'Note on U Boats fitted with Snort', of 11 August 1944. It is possible that there was a slightly earlier instance of this on 25 July but this is an anomalous document, not carrying any normal indication of OIC provenance. Further, its general subject and style have more in common with the general output of DNOR rather than intelligence OR. PRO ADM 223/261, Unreferenced paper dated 25 July 1944, 'Note on Escort Group Operations in the English Channel, 6th June–10th July 1944'.
18. The 10th Fleet was set up in May 1943 as the USN's principal engine of co-ordination of the Battle of the Atlantic. This was the only known example of operational control of US units being exercised directly from Washington in the same way as the Admiralty did.

19. National Archive and Records Administration (USA), RG 38, 10th Fleet, Box ASM-2, United States Naval Forces in Europe, Flanigan to Low, 3 June 1943 (emphasis added). The correspondence goes on to imply both that the USN's relations with its OR scientists was somewhat bumpy and that they put OR organisations under the relatively low-level control of uniformed officers.
20. This is not pursued directly in this chapter for a number of reasons. RAF Coastal Command was under the operational command of the Admiralty; most of the former's intelligence of this type would have passed through the NID and OIC in any case, and by mid-1943 Blackett had been established in the Admiralty for over a year. However, it is reasonable to assume some degree of communication between DNOR and Coastal Command ORS, not excluding germane specialised matters for those with knowledge of Ultra.
21. This and subsequent analysis of the corpus of the reports is drawn from PRO ADM 223/170, /172, /261, /315, /316 and /317.
22. Paul M. Sutcliffe, 'Operational Research in the Battle of the Atlantic', in Howarth and Law, *The Battle of the Atlantic*, pp. 419–20.
23. PRO ADM 223/261, SI 1254, of 19 March 1945. This indicates two unpalatable effects: greater losses of shipping and reduced sinking of submarines.
24. It is, however, very evident that OR work was done post-war on the efficacy of Ultra. 'A Preliminary Analysis of the Role of Decryption Intelligence in the Operational Phase of the Battle of the Atlantic', US Navy OEG Report No. 66, NARA RG 457 SRH-367, 20 August 1951, and its definitive successor, OEG Report No. 68 of the following year, RG 457 SRH-368.

9

A Clash of Cultures: The Case for Large Convoys

Malcolm Llewellyn-Jones

> One obvious characteristic of operational research … is that it has, or should have, a strictly practical character. Its object is to assist the finding of means to improve the efficiency of war operations in progress or planned for the future … Predictions about the future are of course always subject to much uncertainty, but experience has shown that many more useful quantitative predictions can be made than is often thought possible. This arises to a considerable extent from the relative stability over quite long periods of time of many factors involved in operations. This stability appears rather unexpected in view of the large number of chance events and individual personalities and abilities involved … The more common sense procedure is to abandon the attempt to construct from 'first principles' a complete imaginary operation something like the real one under investigation and to replace it by an attempt to find, both by experimental and by analytical methods, how a real operation would be altered if certain of the variables, e.g. the tactics employed or properties of the weapons used, were varied.
>
> P.M.S. Blackett, May 1943[1]

At an annual salary of £1,200, Professor P.M.S. Blackett was appointed the Admiralty's Chief Adviser on Operational Research (CAOR) in December 1941, having migrated from Coastal Command's Operational Research Section (ORS).[2] Blackett immediately set about gathering a team of eminent scientists in the Admiralty to tackle the task which, as he saw it, was 'the study of *past* operations with the object of extracting the maximum useful lessons to guide planning of *future* operations'. With an apparent perversity he wanted academics who 'knew nothing about the subject beforehand' but who were 'prepared to ask questions that more "instructed" people might not think of asking'. Such people, he thought, would be of the greatest help, for 'too much scientific effort has been expended hitherto in the *production* of new devices and too little in the *proper use* of what we have got'.[3] His abiding concern was the most economical and efficient ways of using existing equipment by improving operational deployments or developing better tactics. The best example of these precepts is perhaps Blackett's most important personal analytical effort – the evolution of the 'case for large convoys'.

Much of the historiography alludes to the shipping crisis that loomed during the winter and spring of 1942–43, caused by the Allies' overly ambitious strategic plans and the escalating shipping casualties after the U-boats returned in strength to the North Atlantic convoy routes, following their 'happy time' off the East Coast of the USA.[4] As the strain came on to the convoy system, it became clear that a remedy had to be found to the heavy losses if the Allied strategic plans were not to be jeopardised. Having analysed the convoy statistics, the narration goes, Blackett concluded that shipping losses would be drastically reduced by the adoption of larger convoys. Then, with some trouble, he 'persuaded the Admiralty to alter the convoy ruling ... [so that] from the spring of 1943 the size gradually increased'.[5] The historiography, then, suggests that the imposition of large convoys, as suggested by Blackett, was a key factor that solved the haemorrhage of shipping losses.

Such a simple explanation will not do, for it paints Blackett's work in primary colours. To begin with, the average convoy size was already growing from the winter of 1942, well before Blackett identified the operational value of large convoys. The swelling numbers of merchant ships, largely from American yards, and the need to increase imports into the UK in preparation for the invasion faced the Admiralty with a crisis but of a different nature. Because more ships had to be convoyed this seemed to imply more convoys, and so more sea and air escorts, and these did not exist.[6] It was the pragmatic solution, or Hobson's choice, as one senior officer put it, that drove the Admiralty into adopting larger convoys, and not Blackett's 'large convoy' analysis. But, crucially, Blackett's analysis did confirm that the course taken was rational and safe.[7] To see how this came about, this chapter will view the issues from the perspective of Blackett's operational research. Underlying all the arguments is the interplay of different professional cultures, between those mainly of the naval and air officers, and those of the operational research scientists, that is, between those whose agenda was to expand force levels and who saw real operational difficulties in large convoys, and those persuaded by the remorseless logic of the data.

Faced with the growing shipping crisis in the autumn of 1942 Churchill formed the War Cabinet Anti-U-boat Warfare Committee on 4 November 1942 'in order to give the same impulse … as had been applied to the "Battle of the Atlantic" [Committee]'.[8] When the new committee met towards the end of the month, with Blackett attending for the first time, A.V. Alexander, First Lord of the Admiralty, outlined the critical shortage of convoy escorts.[9] To meet the Admiralty's needs, even with a greater contribution from American output, British shipbuilding resources would have to be diverted into more escort vessel deliveries at the expense of new merchant ships. But would building additional escorts save more merchant ships from being sunk than would have otherwise been produced? To find out, Churchill's scientific adviser, Lord Cherwell, wondered 'whether it would be possible to obtain more statistical information … on the value of aircraft and escort vessels'.[10] To Blackett, Cherwell's intervention, while making sense, must have caused some irritation. The two had fallen out when both were members of the pre-war Tizard Committee and again in the spring of 1942. At that time Blackett believed that Cherwell's 'de-housing policy' for bombing Germany had been based on overly optimistic calculations. His own figures suggested that with the bomber force at hand the effect on the German war effort would be negligible. He thought that if

> the bombing offensive is to be our decisive war operation, and if it is not likely to be decisively effective till 1944, then there is an overwhelming case for the diversion of the necessary long range bombers to shipping protection immediately.[11]

This, he declared, would then allow the importation of the necessary materials to sustain an effective bomber offensive at a time when

Bomber Command would have better aircraft with improved target location devices. This issue was to rumble on throughout 1942 and into the spring of 1943.

At the turn of the year Alexander, unbowed by heavy shipping losses, declared: 'It is our intention in 1943 to take the offensive against the Axis Powers to the greatest extent possible.' This would need a one-and-a-half-fold increase in the import rate of raw materials, which, together with the build-up of US ground forces in Britain, would impose heavy demands on the convoy programme during the last half of the year. To relieve the strain the Admiralty wanted to boost the level of imports during the first half of the year by shortening the intervals between convoys and reducing losses in the Atlantic by 25 per cent.[12] To do this, the Admiralty pinned its faith on providing air cover in mid-Atlantic with very long-range (VLR) aircraft and augmenting the escort strength by 65 vessels largely with American assistance, a plan that was endorsed by the joint chiefs of staff at the Casablanca Conference a week later.[13]

Meanwhile, Blackett's operational research team had expanded sufficiently to begin the investigation of the value of escorts. Alexander was soon able to present the Anti-U-boat Committee with a memorandum swiftly put together by Blackett from data gathered during 1941.[14] 'The main object of any such analysis', Blackett asserted, 'must be to attempt to estimate in a quantitative way, even if only very roughly, the value of different A/S measures, so as to be able to estimate the probable profit and loss on any proposed plan of operation.' Blackett went on to say that the 'first step must be to study past operations, and to use the lessons learned to attempt to predict the future'. His analysis suggested that a force of 200 long-range (LR) and VLR aircraft, fitted with radar and searchlights for day and night sorties and operating in mid-Atlantic, would save two million tons of shipping in 1943, even allowing for enemy counter-measures. Blackett also estimated that roughly doubling each convoy's escort would halve the losses. If escort carriers were employed, apart from the direct protection they offered, it would be unnecessary to 'seek shore-based air cover', so convoys could sail on more direct, southerly routes, effectively increasing the delivery rate. Overall, each carrier was worth five escorts. Moreover, larger escort groups would sink more U-boats, thereby saving additional ships. Lastly, Blackett observed that slow convoys were considerably more dangerous than fast convoys, which emphasised 'the extreme importance of convoy speed against massed [U-boat] attack'.[15] No record was kept of the committee's deliberations on Blackett's analysis but they asked him, together with Cherwell, 'to submit, as soon as possible, an agreed statistical analysis based on the most recent statistics'.[16]

The research was complex and Blackett's updated report was not available until the Anti-U-boat Committee met again on 10 February 1943.[17] Churchill was just back from the Casablanca Conference and busy preparing for his report to the House of Commons, so Sir Stafford Cripps took the chair. The record of the meeting is sparse and the scope of Blackett's verbal contribution can only be surmised, but he was well prepared with a background note to hand which dwelt on the underpinning operational arguments supporting the detailed statistical paper.[18] This statistical analysis had 'been submitted and discussed in detail with Lord Cherwell during the various stages of its preparation'. This must have been irksome for Blackett because he really disliked Cherwell and, given their earlier disagreements, probably dismissed his scientific judgement. Blackett's paper was intended to recommend 'the best allocation of *existing* resources of escort vessels, aircraft and the faster ships'. The large number of U-boats now in the Atlantic made it impossible to evade their patrol lines, so most convoys would have to 'fight their way through'. However, the surface escorts, unless doubled in strength or with ample air cover, were likely to be overwhelmed by packs of 25 to 30 U-boats and their convoys would lose 15 to 20 ships. Blackett could not see how additional forces could become available in the immediate future except by 'finding new tactics which would lead to a greater economy of escorts'.[19]

With this idea in mind, Blackett and his team had noticed that the losses in convoy did not seem to increase with the size of convoys, though as the escort increased in strength so the number of ships torpedoed for each U-boat in the pack 'decreased markedly'. Blackett calculated that if the escort was increased from six to nine vessels, a 25 per cent reduction in losses could be expected. This could be achieved by joining smaller convoys and thereby combining their escorts. Moreover, larger, and hence fewer, convoys would also benefit from the limited air cover available, which could reduce convoy losses by 64 per cent. The analysis broadly confirmed the marked value of convoy speed and with more data a better estimate of the relative 'safety' of fast and slow convoys was

1. Cody's early aeroplane being inspected by schoolboys. Blackett would cycle to Laffan's plain to watch Cody's flying experiments. (*Source:* Imperial War Museum)

2. A V Roe aeroplane airborne on the first all-British flight, before crash-landing in sewage – an event witnessed by Blackett. (*Source:* Imperial War Museum)

3. The Farman aeroplane in which Blackett cadged a flight as a schoolboy in 1913, and which was flown by F. S. Barnwell. (*Source:* Imperial War Museum)

4. Cadets in their new uniforms waiting to embark on a ferry for the Isle of Wight and the Royal Naval College, Osborne. Blackett is in the centre-right of the picture looking at the camera. (*Source:* From Blackett's own album in the collection at the Royal Naval Museum, courtesy of John Milner, nephew of Blackett)

5. Blackett and fellow 13-year-old classmates at Osborne. (*Source:* Editor's collection)

6. Hawke 1914 – Blackett's term on the steps at Dartmouth. (*Source:* Britannia Royal Naval College, Dartmouth)

7. Mobilisation in 1914 – for a Cadet, packing was merely a question of packing his tea chest. (*Source:* Britannia Royal Naval College, Dartmouth)

8. Blackett's first ship, HMS *Monmouth*, which he joined at Devonport in August 1914, aged 16. (*Source:* Royal Naval Museum, Portsmouth)

9. HMS *Carnarvon*, in which Blackett fought at the Battle of the Falklands, 1914. (*Source:* Royal Naval Museum, Portsmouth)

10. The fast battleship HMS *Barham*, entering Scapa Flow. (*Source:* Royal Naval Museum, Portsmouth)

11. HMS *'P17'*, in which Blackett served as First Lieutenant, mainly on the Dover Patrol. Picture probably taken by Blackett using his own hand-built camera. (*Source:* From Blackett's own album in the collection at the Royal Naval Museum, courtesy of John Milner, nephew of Blackett)

12. HMS *Sturgeon*, at Scapa Flow. Blackett joined her before her transfer to the light forces based at Harwich. (*Source:* From Blackett's own album in the collection at the Royal Naval Museum, courtesy of John Milner, nephew of Blackett)

13. Ship's officers and dog, HMS *Sturgeon*. (*Source:* From Blackett's own album in the collection at the Royal Naval Museum, courtesy of John Milner, nephew of Blackett)

14. Sub-Lieutenant Blackett – cigarette in mouth – teaching HMS *Sturgeon*'s ship's mascot new tricks. (*Source:* Blackett family)

15. Studio portrait of Acting Lieutenant P. M. S. Blackett. (*Source:* Editor's collection)

16. The 1919 intake at Magdalene College, Cambridge. (*Source:* Collection of A. Brown)

17. Rutherford's research group at Cambridge, 1923. (*Source:* Collection of R. Anderson)

18. Patrick Blackett and Costanza Bayon. (*Source:* Collection of A. Brown)

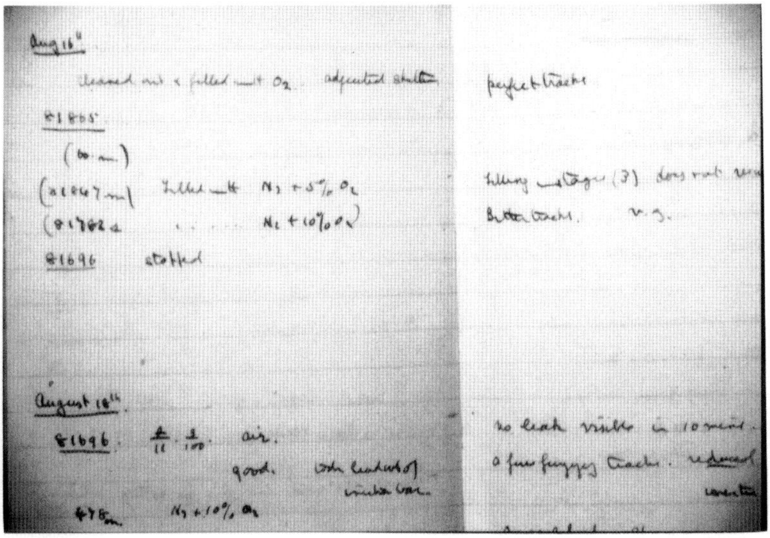

19. 'Perfect Tracks!' Blackett's notebook entry, 16 August 1924. (*Source:* Collection of R. Anderson)

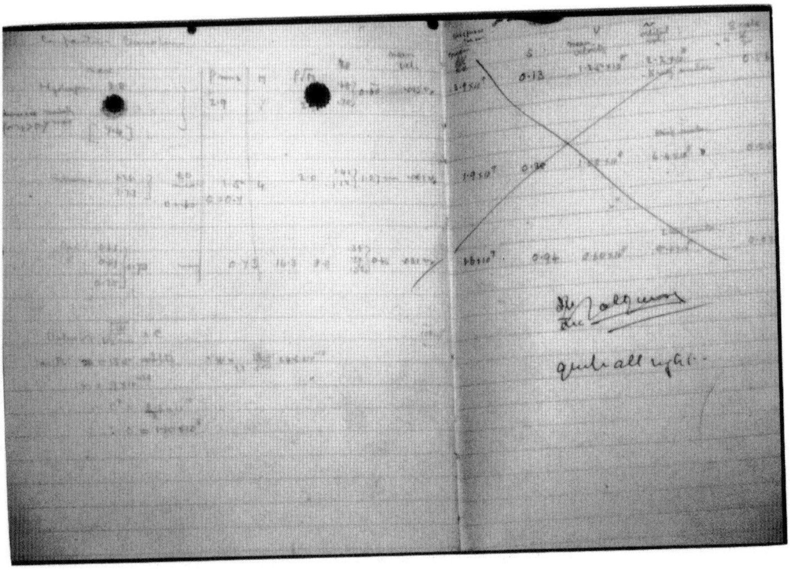

20. On one of his daily inspections, Rutherford has crossed out Blackett's careful observations and written 'all wrong' – later amended to 'quite all right'. (*Source:* Collection of R. Anderson)

21. Blackett dressed for the North Sea in winter. (*Source:* From Blackett's own album in the collection at the Royal Naval Museum, courtesy of John Milner, nephew of Blackett)

22. One of Blackett's lifetime loves was sailing: seen here with Professors A. D. Ritchie and G. P. Thomson about 1929. (*Source:* Blackett family)

23. Blackett with Indira Ghandi, from an album in the possession of the family, inscribed 'Lady Blackett, from the Tata Institute of Fundamental Research, Bombay with warm memories of her great husband, Lord Blackett, who did so much for the Institute, for Indian science and for India'. (*Source:* Blackett family)

24. Jawaharlal Nehru, from the Tata Institute album – with Blackett for once taking a back seat. (*Source:* Blackett family)

25. A rare picture of Patrick Blackett wreathed in smiles (*Source:* Courtesy of Romano Cagnoni)

26. Prime Minister Harold Wilson delivering the Blackett memorial album – which has been edited for the last chapter of this volume. (*Source:* Blackett family; photograph by John P. O'Leary, Department of Aeronautics, Imperial College, London)

calculated. Losses in the faster convoys were some 40 per cent lower than those for slow convoys, because the latter spent 29 per cent longer at sea and the U-boats found it more difficult to concentrate against faster convoys, especially when air cover was present.[20] Blackett's incisive mind had identified the fundamental and easily organised tactical solution – the adoption of larger convoys – though not yet the rational explanation for the observed data. Even so, if evasion was less likely because of growing numbers of U-boats in the Atlantic, then, Blackett thought, larger convoys with heavier escorts offered the opportunity for the escorts to form small striking forces to carry out offensive action against the U-boats and, on occasion, deliberately to seek battle. If one U-boat could be sunk for every two merchant ships then 'a considerable gain would [be] achieved *over a long time*'. Always confident in his own judgements, Blackett doubtless pressed his conviction but his solution fell on deaf ears, at least for the time being.[21]

By selecting favourable data from Blackett's report, the Cabinet Anti-U-boat Committee ascribed a high value to escort vessels, which, Blackett cautioned, was 'a very wide extrapolation from inaccurate data'.[22] With more justification, Admiral Dudley Pound, the First Sea Lord and Chief of the Naval Staff, 'emphasized the urgent need for more V.L.R. aircraft', and the committee noted their great value, yet, in the same breath, also confirmed that only 40 of this type would be made available![23] Overall, Blackett's proposed new tactics with *existing* forces did not sit comfortably with the Naval and Air Staffs. The committee cast about for means to refute Blackett's ideas. They highlighted the U-boats' recent tendency 'to attack convoys from ahead rather than from the flank'. With the wider front of a larger convoy, it might be supposed that the U-boats would find it easier to attack from ahead. The committee felt that this meant that 'the deduction that fewer larger convoys were to be preferred to a greater number of small convoys would no longer be valid'.[24] The committee was persuaded, therefore, before endorsing Blackett's paper, to have it reviewed jointly by Admiral Pound and Air Marshal Sir Charles Portal, the Chief of the Air Staff. The chiefs would also recommend the *size* of air and sea escort forces needed to ensure the reasonable safety of convoys in the light of the changing conditions of the U-boat war. Blackett must have been disappointed. He was sure he was right but while the statistical analysis seemed 'quite reliable' the results were based on a relatively small sample and could be prone to error 'through chance fluctuations'. To make a more convincing case he needed to infer a rational explanation of the results. Blackett and his team therefore embarked on 'an intensive study of all available facts about the U-boat campaign against the convoys' that took several weeks.[25]

Whether or not Blackett's advocacy of large convoys was gaining ground, the situation in the ports was forcing a decision. Since the third quarter of 1942 the net gain of shipping was on the up-turn as new construction deliveries accelerated and, by the end of the year, the number of ships included in ocean convoys was steadily rising, though the number of convoys remained roughly static, no doubt constrained by the perceived shortage of escort groups.[26] On 24 February, Lord Leathers, the Minister of War Transport, reported to the Anti-U-boat Committee that, 'assuming that the number of ships in each convoy should not exceed 60, about 29 ships would have been excluded from a convoy due to leave the United States last evening'. The Admiralty had agreed to this convoy being increased to 80 ships 'with the greatest reluctance', though the United States authorities had also raised objections.[27] The Ministry of War Transport felt there was 'no other means of relieving the present congestion immediately', given the 'difficulty with escorts'.[28] They urged their representatives in the US to represent 'the importance of [larger convoys] to the naval authorities on your side'.[29] This would, in a sense, be embarrassing, because the British had been pressing for additional tonnage but larger convoys would have the effect of reducing the delivery rate (at least in the short term).

The First Sea Lord thought the 'sailing of such large convoys was asking for trouble' and worried that they would prove difficult to handle. But to meet the minimum import requirements, Leathers was convinced that 'we should soon reach a position in which convoys would have to consist of between 70 to 80 ships', even if additional convoys were run.[30] When the committee met in the following week Cherwell chimed in with support for Leathers by pointing out that the consumption of raw materials was outstripping imports. This finally wrung a small concession from the First Sea Lord, who 'undertook to consider the practicability of putting *a few more ships in convoy*', though each should be considered on its merits. Probably under duress, he was forced to waive the previous absolute limitation of 60 ships in convoy.[31] Then, a few days later, the Vice Chief of the Naval Staff, Vice-Admiral Sir Henry Moore, who had been at the Atlantic Convoy Conference in Washington since 1 March, signalled Pound that the choice now lay between:

> (a) … a complete showdown on the whole question of employment of destroyers and escorts in all repeat all war areas
> (b) … [opening] the Atlantic or other convoy cycles sufficiently to enable necessary number of support groups to be provided *and face up to resulting increase in number of ships per convoy …*
> (c) Operating trans-Atlantic convoys with reduced number of groups and accepting a reduced lay over and training period.[32]

The conference had agreed the reorganisation of the Allied convoy responsibilities and next day Moore added that the Americans were likely to go back on the arrangements if the British chose option (a). Pound doubtless knew that the impact on training involved in option (c) would bring vehement resistance from Admiral Horton, Commander-in-Chief, Western Approaches.[33] All of this added to the pressure for Pound to accept a *de facto* increase in convoy size. Losses were escalating in the North Atlantic, and some two-thirds of the losses were ships in convoy. The whole convoy system was under pressure with many escorts out of action from the exceptionally severe weather during the previous few months. The number of U-boats operating in the North Atlantic was still increasing and, as Pound signalled to Moore in Washington on 10 March, 'U-boat Special Intelligence has received a severe setback', which he thought might last two to three months.[34]

That day, with Churchill just recovering from a fever, Cripps again chaired the Cabinet Anti-U-boat Committee to consider comments on Blackett's paper of the previous month in a joint memorandum by Admiral Pound and Air Marshal Portal, the chiefs of the Naval and Air Staffs.[35] To improve protection for trade and troop convoys, the chiefs recognised the advantages of faster convoys and Lord Leathers, too, saw the need to employ the fastest ships in Atlantic convoys but warned that any increase in the convoy speed might lead to more straggling, which had caused serious losses in the past.[36] The chiefs grudgingly accepted, too, 'that on past experience losses have not materially increased with the size of convoys between 20 and 60 ships'. But, they cautioned, while 'this conclusion must be taken seriously into account … conditions now are very different from those from which the majority of the data was collected'.[37] With large numbers of U-boats deployed across the convoy routes all the convoys were likely to be sighted. The First Sea Lord observed that the U-boats were making less use of W/T (wireless telegraphy), so, with less knowledge of their whereabouts, it was more difficult to route convoys evasively. Pound was, of course, alluding to the blackout of Ultra Special Intelligence, reported to him the previous day by Rear-Admiral Edelsten, the Assistant Chief of the Naval Staff (U-Boats and Trade) – ACNS(UT). With the opportunities for evasive routeing thereby seriously eroded, it was expected that several convoys would be attacked simultaneously.[38] Large convoys, having a wide front, were more vulnerable to attacks from ahead, and the difficulties of communications and handling these convoys were greatly increased. 'The Admiralty view', therefore, was 'that convoys *should not be increased above 60 ships and that 40 is better for handling and defence*'. Moreover, the chiefs asserted, to defeat the U-boats the escorts had to be 'strong enough to retain the offensive in the face of heavy and repeated attacks', and to destroy, say, one U-boat for every two merchant ships sunk, a price the enemy could not accept.[39]

At any one time, two-thirds of the convoys were over 600 miles from shore in the mid-Atlantic 'air gap', where only the few VLR aircraft could reach.[40] The most expeditious means of improving convoy safety was by the 'provision of constant air cover' throughout their passage, either by shore- or carrier-based aircraft. There was some scepticism – probably from Portal – as to whether both were needed, so the chiefs decided that, initially, only shore-based aircraft would provide cover.[41] For this task Coastal Command needed 150 VLR and LR aircraft but such numbers could not be generated until October and, in the meantime, the pitifully small force was totally inadequate. Pound had fought Portal – the so-called 'Battle of the Air' – over the allocation of aircraft for Coastal Command throughout 1942 and undoubtedly the First Sea Lord now pushed hard for the earliest increase in VLR aircraft. For Portal this conflicted with his dogged determination to build up the British (and US) heavy bomber force, a policy championed by Churchill. Portal, with one eye over his shoulder at the needs, as he saw them, of the bomber offensive, probably distanced himself from a firm commitment by suggesting the VLR allocations should be monitored and then reviewed later in the year.[42] Pound, too, pressed his parochial interests by claiming, with some justification, that weather conditions might preclude air operations and that convoys would then have to rely on their surface escort. Conventional wisdom in the Naval Staff held that '3 escorts per convoy plus 1 extra for every 10 ships in the convoy' were needed. For most convoys this would mean an escort of six to seven vessels. As Blackett observes, the origins of this formula were obscure. Moreover, it was only intended to apply when air escort was available, so, against the expected scale of attack in mid-ocean where air cover was practically non-existent, the Admiralty abandoned their formula and stipulated that surface escorts must consist of at least 12 vessels. In an attempt to justify this figure, the chiefs noted from Blackett's analysis 'that doubling the escorts halves the losses'.[43] Such reinforcements would require the allocation of American resources in the near term and an accelerated escort-building programme for the future.

Admittedly, at this stage, Blackett had provided little rationale to explain the statistical analysis – an error he later corrected. Yet this does not explain why the chiefs' paper concentrates on the need to build up escort forces, while largely seeking to marginalise Blackett's arguments for large convoys. Both Pound and Portal had achieved rapid promotion and demonstrated professional acumen. Pound was not ignorant of anti-submarine matters. He had, for example, been instrumental in relaxing the safety rules for pre-war submarine exercises in the Mediterranean, which allowed them to demonstrate the effectiveness of night surface attacks.[44] Doubtless, both chiefs were *au fait* with the scientific character of their services, yet, while they may have been comfortable with the 'algebraic' forms of mathematics, they had little education in 'statistical' work. When considering what the operational scientist could offer that the operational staffs could not do themselves, Blackett felt their province lay in exploring just these problems involving the calculation of probabilities, or the theory of errors. In these aspects, he considered the service officers were not generally trained.[45] The executive naval officer, one harsh critic suggested,

> is a man of action and never at a loss. He must make up his mind on every occasion instantaneously and without hesitation … Now just in these characteristics lie his strength and weakness. They make him the finest ship's officer in the world, but they render him unsuitable for work that requires administrative, organizing (if it implies more than 'telling off' parties to work) or reflective capacity,

> and what is more they *prevent him from realizing that there is any kind of work that he cannot do.*[46]

Nevertheless, born from long experience, the two chiefs did possess the prescience needed to determine the force levels necessary to attack Germany in the following year over the beaches in Normandy and in the air, in the Mediterranean theatre, while also taking the offensive against Japan and directly supporting Russia. With a different agenda to that of Blackett and his scientific team, the chiefs were set upon the build-up of their forces for this final confrontation with the Axis powers. In the immediate future Pound, in particular, saw number of escorts as the crucial factor in combating the U-boat menace, and without adequate forces he felt unable to 'accept responsibility for the Atlantic convoy routes'.[47] Blackett, by contrast, was concerned with the most economical way of using existing forces, though he too looked to the future.[48] So Blackett listened to the curious juxtaposition of many of the chiefs' arguments and their rejection of large convoys. His self-confidence, high academic standing, and lack of inhibition through being outside the military and political hierarchies all helped him to command attention. But how much he was able to argue against their case is not clear, though he arrived at the meeting prepared to advocate the immediate adoption of large convoys. Simple calculations showed that, by incorporating all available ships into larger convoys, the delivery rate would be substantially increased. This was true even if the loss rate rose, as the Naval Staff feared, though Blackett thought it a 'quite unduly pessimistic assumption'.[49] If these arguments were offered, the committee ignored them and instead congratulated the chiefs for giving 'a very useful and clear picture of the general problem in the North Atlantic' in their joint memorandum.[50]

Over the preceding week Rear-Admiral Edelsten, ACNS(UT), had proposed the adoption of 120-ship convoys, first suggested by Blackett in early February. The Additional Naval Adviser, Vice-Admiral Usborne, had produced a paper on the advantages of larger convoys and ACNS(UT) had circulated it to elicit views from the Naval Staff.[51] These were mixed. Captain Schofield, Director of the Trade Division, and Captain Eccles, Director of Operations (Home), were unenthusiastic and emphasised the problems of manoeuvring and communications in such large convoys. Captain Clarke, Director of the Anti-Submarine Division, on the other hand, supported the idea, ruefully observing that a '60 ship Convoy is already too big to handle and a bigger one still may not be much worse'.[52] Clarke added a paper dated 9 March 1943 by Dr Whitehead, a member of Blackett's team. In the paper Whitehead summarised the relationship between the number of ships in a convoy and the perimeter to be defended by the escorts. Stated in different terms he had identified the crucial connection between the area occupied by the ships within the convoy and the length of the perimeter to be defended. This was the key that Blackett finally used to account for why the data showed that large convoys were safer.[53] It is intriguing that a similar conclusion had been deduced towards the end of the First World War. When the convoy system was started in 1917 a civilian director of statistics had been appointed. His department concluded that the escort strength requires to be measured not in terms of the number of vessels in convoy, but in terms of the total area comprised within the boundary formed by lines connecting all outer vessels.[54]

This conclusion was subsequently issued in an official publication but Blackett was unaware of this research until much later.[55] Still, Whitehead calculated that increasing the size of convoy from 40 to 78 ships only lengthened the perimeter by one-sixth. The inference was that the same number of, but larger, convoys could be run as at present with the existing escort force and Whitehead noted that 'any additional escorts, over and above the defensive minimum, [could] be used as a local striking force'.[56] At the same time, Usborne's paper on convoys and escorts also referred to the use of a 'V' formation for future convoys, designed to reduce the effects of submarine torpedo attacks – a formation that had also been proposed by Rollo Appleyard of the Admiralty's Convoy Section in 1918.[57] Whether the lineage of Usborne's and Whitehead's ideas owed anything to the earlier work may never be known but, in any case, both papers were among those discussed at a meeting in ACNS(UT)'s office on 15 March.[58] A few days later Edelsten told his U-boat Warfare Committee that the issue of larger convoys 'had been re-examined and a paper would be issued'.[59] A week went by and Edelsten, writing to Horton, thought 'there is always a possibility that we shall have to adopt [120-ship convoys] from Hobson's choice in order to get imports into the country'. By the end of the month Horton agreed 'that in the summer an occasional 80-ship convoy would be acceptable' as long as he had enough notice to ensure that a support group would be available. He also agreed that 120-ship convoys were practical, though this 'merely halves the number of convoys to the detriment of manoeuvrability and administration'.[60] Horton seems to have missed the point that larger convoys were safer.

The specific linkage between the economy of escorts derived from larger convoys and the use of these 'additional' vessels in 'reinforcing' support groups does not appear to have been made by this stage. The need for support groups had already been established in 1942 on tactical grounds. But it was only in February 1943 that Edelsten considered sufficient escort vessels were becoming available to form the groups. Admiral Horton immediately started to plan for the formation of these groups and, from 20 February 1943 at Western Approaches Command, started an imaginary strategic exercise overlaying the actual operational situation, and employing three support groups and three escort carriers with attendant destroyers. The exercise demonstrated that all threatened real convoys at sea during this period could have been reinforced by one of the imaginary support groups.[61] Armed with a report of the exercise, Horton raised the issue at the next War Cabinet Anti-U-boat Committee on 17 March.[62] Pound reported that the Admiralty was already considering the best tactical use of support groups and added that there was one US Navy group already operating, while by the middle of April it was planned to form one Canadian and two British support groups with Home Fleet destroyers, provided the Russian convoys were suspended temporarily. Churchill approved this plan.[63]

Meanwhile, Blackett's fertile brain had been seeking other areas where anti-submarine forces could be employed most economically, such as the comparative value of aircraft used to cover convoys with those used in the Bay offensive. In ACNS(UT)'s opinion Blackett's paper provided 'a most telling argument for the Bay offensive which is hard to refute'.[64] Blackett also noted that VLR aircraft employed on direct convoy protection were about ten times more effective than those on the Bay offensive but, he thought, 'this comparison is misleading', because VLR aircraft represented only a small fraction of the types employed in trade protection. Furthermore, while the enemy could disengage at will from the convoy routes, this was not true for the Bay of Biscay. Blackett believed that the Bay could be made 'almost' impassable to U-boats with a modest force of properly equipped aircraft.[65] Pound, too, pressed for an intensification of the Bay offensive, and a resumption of bombing of the U-boat bases.

ACNS(UT) had previously complained to Pound that the 'bombing of U-boat bases, which might have proved so effective, has now practically ceased when only one-fifth of the target has been bombed. The Bay offensive may prove a decisive factor, but there the build-up is all too slow.' He observed that the bombing of Germany 'may hasten but will never replace the Second Front. A Halifax diverted to Coastal Command will do more towards the security of sea communications than by bombing Germany.'[66]

Air Marshal Harris, Commander-in-Chief, Bomber Command, getting wind of this, waded in with a minute to the Anti-U-boat Cabinet Committee arguing against any diversion of the bomber force to anti-submarine work. His command, Harris avowed, was the 'only effective means open to the United Nations in the immediate future for striking directly at Germany'. To use it against U-boat bases was 'purely defensive ... [and] highly extravagant' and it was more profitable, Harris asserted, to attack 'the sources of [the U-boat's] manufacture'. These ideas, Blackett thought, were 'coloured by the same fundamentally false strategic conception displayed all through these discussions with the Air Staff'. In his opinion, they failed to recognise the bomber offensive as part of the whole Allied strategy and instead tried to paint it as a campaign 'which stands in a different class'. Blackett observed that a 30 per cent reduction in the repair and maintenance facilities in the Biscay ports was all that was needed to have an impact on the Atlantic battle. Harris also exposed his ignorance of maritime tactics when he stated:

> too much emphasis is being given to the possibility of locating U-boats by means of A.S.V. [radar], and too little to the difficulty of attacking them successfully when they are located. Our experience, which is considerable, is that even expert crews find it no easy matter to attack with accuracy even a city by means of H2S [radar]. I am therefore rather sceptical of the prospects of inexperienced crews with A.S.V. Indeed, I feel that the provision of aircraft equipped with this apparatus will mark the beginning rather than the end of the difficulties involved in sinking U-boats.[67]

In Blackett's copy of Harris's paper this paragraph is sidelined in pencil and annotated with 'nonsense!'.[68]

The provision of aircraft for the Atlantic and Bay offensives, and the bombing of Biscay bases were taken together at the War Cabinet

Anti-U-boat Committee on 31 March. Though Alexander made it clear in a note to Churchill that he 'would like to have Professor Blackett in attendance', Blackett was excluded on the pretext that there were now too many attendees. Of course, the bomber lobby, including Harris and Cherwell, were there![69] Cherwell dismissed the modest number of additional aircraft proposed for the Bay offensive as unlikely to be effective. Portal avowed great reluctance to release aircraft from Bomber Command 'on a theoretical calculation' and, Churchill added, it was 'an extremely critical moment for that offensive'.[70] Seeing his moment, Harris poured derision on Pound's wish for the Biscay ports to be bombed and reiterated his clarion call that bombing should be concentrated on Germany. With little support, Pound was forced to accept Portal's suggestion that 'inexperienced' crews should be used against the Biscay ports, as well as the USAAF if targets in Germany were obscured by bad weather. Pound, it seemed, could expect no relief for the hard-pressed escort groups.

The following day, 1 April, Blackett attended ACNS(UT)'s U-boat Warfare Committee. After a general discussion about the imposition of large convoys, the meeting, unable to make a decision, took refuge in the proposal that 'each case must be judged on its merits'. There was no problem with occasional large convoys, Horton said, as long as he could provide the necessary support groups, but he was 'strongly against a succession of large convoys'. Another member of the committee was Admiral Kauffman, United States Navy, chairman of the recently established Allied Anti-Submarine Survey Board charged with making 'a survey of all matters relating to antisubmarine warfare in the Atlantic Ocean'. Kauffman offered the view that 'large convoys were all very well if support groups, good escort groups, and above all air support were present. Otherwise, the risks varied with the size of the convoy.'[71] Given Kauffman's influential position, Blackett must have been exasperated during this exchange. ACNS(UT) was more positive, remarking elsewhere that they had 'been trying in various ways to turn to account the evidence in favour of larger convoys, as disclosed by operational research and past experience' but, he added, the 'practical difficulties of large convoys [were] very real, and [were] not to be lightly dismissed'.[72]

Three weeks later the Director of the Trade Division proposed to open up the convoy cycle to the maximum extent possible, in order to release escorts to form support groups and Blackett summarised a paper his staff was preparing, proposing 70-ship convoys.[73] Three more weeks drifted by until the War Cabinet Anti-U-boat Committee met on 12 May and held a brief discussion on whether the interval between convoys could be opened so as to ease the strain on the escort groups. This would, of course, necessarily mean that convoys would have to be increased in size, unless imports were reduced. However, the committee, including Churchill, remained unwilling to force the issue of larger convoys against the intransigence of the Admiralty. Alexander remarked that the Admiralty 'had previously agreed under pressure to include as many as 60 ships in a convoy and, under very special circumstances, to include as many as 80'. Many of the convoys, however, were still sailing with lower numbers and it 'looked therefore as though some increase ... might be practicable'. It was agreed that the Admiralty, while keeping the question 'under constant review', would prepare a paper in consultation with the Ministry of War Transport.[74]

For some months Blackett had been working on a paper that rounded off 'the case for large convoys'. It was finally ready in late May 1943.[75] The paper contained comparatively little that was new. Most of its elements had appeared in earlier papers or at meetings and, doubtless, it had formed the topic of many informal conversations. But what the paper did was to draw together all the strands of the arguments surrounding the issue of large convoys. He confirmed the crucial finding that 'the average number of ships torpedoed has not varied noticeably with the size of the convoy', even during the period since August 1942 when the tempo of U-boat operations had increased.[76] Simple calculations demonstrated that 'the perimeter, on which the close escort forces move, increases very slowly with the size of the convoy'. This was because the number of ships in a convoy defines the *area* of sea to be protected – but this protection is achieved by patrolling the *perimeter* of the area. Of course, the area increases in proportion to the *product* of the length and breadth, while the perimeter increases in proportion to the *sum* of the length and breadth. So, as the dimensions increase the area expands at a much faster rate than does the boundary.[77] In fact, as Dr Whitehead had shown in early March, the perimeter of a 78-ship convoy was only one-sixth longer than that for a 40-ship convoy. This fundamental geometric comparison explained why a U-boat was just as likely to be detected attacking a 40-ship convoy with six escorts as it was when attacking a 78-ship convoy with seven escorts. Yet, once a U-boat penetrated the screen, it was presented with a surfeit of targets but could only sink the same number of ships, irrespective of the convoy's size, because of the U-boats' limited reloading capability.[78]

Blackett reasoned that if the convoy size was increased one-and-a-half-fold, the number of convoys would be reduced by a third.[79] With the economy of escorts from larger convoys, the vessels that would have been used in close escort could be formed into support groups to reinforce threatened convoys. With reinforced escorts, convoy losses would be reduced by at least two-thirds. When the two factors were compounded Blackett estimated that by '*increasing the average size of convoy by 50%, and thus decreasing the number of convoys, we can hope to reduce the losses to about one half*'.[80] Moreover, with fewer convoys at sea the close escort groups would have longer lay-over periods in port where they could carry out continuation training.[81] Also, with fewer convoys, a higher proportion of support groups could be maintained, so '*that the chance of an attacked convoy getting a support group [would] be approximately trebled*'. Furthermore, 'the offensive actions of the increased numbers of support groups would lead to the sinking or damaging of many more [U-boats]'. Blackett, having conferred with Coastal Command ORS, pointed out that fewer convoys would also allow an increase of 40 per cent in the air cover given to each convoy.[82] Presumably, the effectiveness of these arrangements would rely on the Admiralty's ability to direct the support groups and aircraft to threatened convoys, which Blackett undoubtedly understood. He was already involved in improvements to the H/F D/F organisation and its co-ordination with the Admiralty's Operational Intelligence Centre, and, at least from April 1943, he had knowledge of special intelligence.[83]

Yet if these tactical changes were to be adopted, Blackett realised they had to cope with the changing situation in the Atlantic. So, he reasoned, the reinforced escorts for individual threatened convoys would provide a counter to the trend of the U-boat packs attacking in larger mass. Support groups would also be able to provide an outer screen, especially across the convoy's extended front, and the more concentrated effort of VLR aircraft would enhance protection. Above all, the adoption of large convoys could be 'achieved immediately, without waiting for any special equipment, the only cost being a very small immediate loss of trade'. Blackett had discussed this problem informally with Ministry of War Transport officials. An increase of 50 per cent in the average convoy size would reduce the frequency of convoy arrivals and some ships would be delayed waiting to join the larger convoys. But it was estimated that the reduction in deliveries owing to delays would be compensated threefold by the lower loss rate on passage, which would also lead to an accumulating gain in tonnage over the long term. Nor was the proposal anticipated to cause 'undue congestion at the ports – unless two or three large convoys arrive simultaneously' and this could be avoided. And with better protection the need for evasive routeing would be reduced, so convoy passage times would be shortened, thereby improving the delivery rate further. As naval dogma was that a 60-ship convoy represented the practical handling limit, Blackett examined the convoy reports up to January 1943 and found that, though commodores disliked large convoys, they did not report any great difficulties with convoys up to 83 ships.[84]

With this paper Blackett completed his formal work on large convoys, but, as with any big organisation, the real dynamic exchange of ideas in the Admiralty occurred in a welter of informal discussions that engaged much of Blackett's time. He 'had the bearing rather of a military man' – he had served at sea in the Royal Navy during the First World War – and this 'remained a powerful influence throughout his life'. Blackett 'was tall, handsome, with an air of authority about him, courteous and quiet spoken' and at 'any level of society … never felt any inferiority'. Moreover, 'it is fair to say there was rarely a middle way with him'.[85] This, combined with his obvious social conscience and left-of-centre politics, may have irritated less intellectually gifted sailors and airmen. Some may have seen Blackett's report as too theoretical.[86] Of course, the record of what happened in these face-to-face meetings has evaporated with the passing of the players and the passage of time. Often things were committed to paper only after they had ceased to be operationally significant or to tie up loose ends.[87]

What Pound and Portal thought of Blackett's idea is hard to judge and, in a way, is of little consequence, for they had different plans. The chiefs' focus was on the build-up of forces for the final defeat of the Axis powers and Pound's *de facto* acceptance of larger convoys was as much because of the burgeoning mercantile fleet as any conscious policy. Operational commanders, like Horton, were opposed to the routine introduction of large convoys 'until considerable reinforcements of escort vessels [were] available'.[88] However, other senior officers in the Admiralty accepted Blackett's ideas. A month before Blackett's paper was issued Admiral Edelsten, for example, had neatly summarised the Naval Staff's attitude: 'We must undoubtedly exploit the large convoy to the limit of what is practicable, but we must do this by the gradual process of eliminating, step by step, the present limitations.'[89] This did not amount to an unambiguous change in Admiralty policy. Even in the middle of May the Deputy Director of the Trade Division could still talk about a *trial* with two forthcoming convoys being combined into a single large 80-ship convoy.[90] Early in the following month, Leathers once more exposed the real catalyst for change. At the Cabinet Anti-U-boat Committee Leathers said it 'was probable that we might frequently find in the next few months that about 100 ships would be available to sail in a convoy'. Pound repeated that 'the Admiralty were fully alive to the importance of including as many ships as possible in each convoy and that this would be done, provided that escorts adequate to the size of the convoys could be made available'.[91]

By the summer of 1943, whether by conscious policy or serendipity, all the ingredients of Blackett's proposals, including larger convoys, were in place. From May onwards shipping in the North Atlantic deliberately 'followed a standard path along the Great Circle Route', thereby reducing passage time and increasing delivery rate, just as Blackett had foreseen five months previously.[92] A month later the southern routes were similarly fixed, so that Atlantic convoy tracks were effectively following 'tram lines'. With the opening of the cycle, 80-ship convoys became commonplace and, as Blackett had concluded, the whole system proved more economical in its need for close escorts.[93] When the German U-boats returned to the convoy routes it was the tactical expertise of the close escorts, support groups, escort carriers and VLR aircraft operating around large convoys, supported by better use of intelligence and technology, that soon smashed their renewed assault. Between 10 April and 1 December 1943 the enemy lost 63 U-boats while only managing to sink 45 ships from mid-ocean convoys. The enemy's new weapons, like the Gnat anti-escort torpedo, were of no avail and the U-boats deserted the mid-ocean convoy routes and abandoned pack tactics. But the enemy's defeat was not just because of the Allied personnel and material advantages: 'fundamentally, the Allies made better use of their resources'.[94] Blackett would have delighted in this conclusion and was undoubtedly right when he observed: 'the policy of running large convoys with the resulting economy in escort vessels played an important part in facilitating the transfer of numbers of anti-submarine escort vessels from the Atlantic to support the invasion of Normandy in June 1944'.[95]

Large convoys of 100 or more ships were regularly running by the middle of 1944, reaching a peak with the Canadian-escorted 167-ship convoy HX 300 that August. Thereafter, although the total number of ships convoyed escalated, the average convoy size fell, probably because the large frigate-building programme was delivering escorts in abundance and more individual convoys could be run.[96]

So, in the end, how far did Blackett influence the Admiralty to adopt larger convoys? As he candidly, if ruefully, testifies, 'many other factors were changing in the Atlantic battle at the same time … [and since] the battle was virtually won by the summer of 1943 the advantage of changing to large convoys could not be directly tested'. Indeed, the whole issue was overshadowed when catastrophic U-boat losses precipitated their withdrawal from the North Atlantic convoy routes on 24 May 1943.[97] Blackett was, however, somewhat unfair in suggesting that it was 'most unfortunate that we did not appreciate the advantage of large convoys much earlier'. As he rightly recognised, the problem was 'one of considerable scientific difficulty'.[98] A First World War analyst had astutely observed:

> At all times of danger or crisis, the natural tendency is to seek defence in a simple device ready to hand. It is important to observe, however, that simplicity is needed in the final manipulation, and not necessarily in the design or construction … [so if the] result of the struggle with complexity is simple and adequate, the task is successfully accomplished. Thus in devising improved means for the defence of convoys, however complicated it may be in the planning, it will be justified if it helps towards a simple and effective plan.[99]

Blackett would have echoed this view. He was also distracted from the spring to the winter of 1942 by the prolonged internecine dispute between the Naval and Air Staffs over bombing policy and the allocation of sufficient VLR aircraft for the Atlantic battle, at a time, Blackett later thought, when his staff could have been looking at convoy organisation. It was not until the autumn that Blackett had started to explore the relative value of building escorts or merchant ships, spurred by the discussions in the War Cabinet's Anti-U-boat Committee. The analysis had revealed the relative safety of larger convoys but it took until the summer of 1943 before the full impact of this result was understood and explained. But, in trying to formulate his ideas, Blackett was faced with naval prejudice against large convoys, based on worries over tactical ship handling and an overriding desire, at least at senior level, for more powerful escort forces, particularly for future operations.

Ultimately, Blackett's research did not lead directly to the imposition of larger convoys. It was the burgeoning volume of shipping that drove, by *force majeure*, the swelling convoy sizes. But it was Blackett's strong and logically argued work that persuaded commanders gradually to accept that large convoys really did work. There is a parallel with the value of special intelligence, in the sense that Blackett's 'case for large convoys', together with all the underpinning analysis, made a huge contribution to that vital ingredient for military success, *confidence* – confidence that the war was being fought to its best advantage, given the resources available.

NOTES

1. P.M.S. Blackett, 'A Note on Certain Aspects of the Methodology of Operational Research', May 1943, Royal Society, Blackett Papers (RSBP), D86, pp. 1–2.
2. J.P. Walsh, Admiralty, to CAOR, 16 March 1942, RSBP, A16. In 1944 Blackett's title was changed to Director of Naval Operational Research (DNOR), though this title appears in references for all reports produced by his team from 1942 onwards.
3. 'Operational Analysis: Its Relation to Intelligence and Plans', talk given to Combined Intelligence Sub-Committee, Washington, 13 December 1943, RSBP, D90. Professor Sir William McCrea, letter to the author, 7 April 1998. Sir William was a member of Blackett's team from 1943 onwards. Similar sentiments come from Professor Cruickshank, another erstwhile, albeit brief, member of DNOR. Professor D.W.J. Cruickshank, letter to the author, 27 June 1998. Samuel Eliot Morison, *History of United States Naval Operations in World War II*, Vol. I: *The Battle of the Atlantic 1939–1943* (Boston, MA: Little, Brown, 1988), p. 221 (emphasis added).
4. For a detailed exposition of this problem, see Kevin Smith, *Conflict over Convoys: Anglo-American Logistics Diplomacy in the Second World War* (Cambridge: Cambridge University Press, 1996). Smith's main arguments are distilled in Dr Roger Sarty's review in *Northern Mariner*, 8, 2 (April 1998), pp. 123–5. Eric J. Grove (ed.), *The Defeat of the Enemy Attack on Shipping, 1939–1945: A Study of Policy and Operations*, Vol. 1B (Plans and Tables), rev. edn (Aldershot: Ashgate

for the Navy Records Society, 1997), Plans 16(4) and 16(5); this was originally issued as the classified Staff History in 1957 in two volumes, and authored by David Waters and Frederick Barley of the Admiralty's Naval Historical Section. See also W.J.R. Gardner, 'Prelude to Victory: The Battle of the Atlantic, 1942–1943', *Mariner's Mirror*, 79, 3 (August 1993), pp. 305–17, for a detailed operational account.

5. Bernard Lovell, *P.M.S. Blackett: A Biographical Memoir* (London: The Royal Society, 1976), pp. 66–7.
6. See, for example: 'Correspondence and Brief for Lord Hankey's Motion in Secret Session of House of Lords: "To Call Attention to the Present Position of the U-boat Campaign" and to Move for Papers', February 1943, PRO ADM 1/14878; and message from Ministry of War Transport, London to British Merchant Shipping Mission, Washington, via Sparks, New York, Limit Bilge 2670, 24 February 1943, PRO MT 59/30.
7. Paul M. Sutcliffe, 'Operational Research in the Battle of the Atlantic', in Stephen Howarth and Derek Law (eds), *The Battle of the Atlantic 1939–1945: The 50th Anniversary International Naval Conference* (London: Greenhill Books, 1994), pp. 425–6; John Terraine, *Business in Great Waters: The U-boat Wars 1916–1945* (London: Leo Cooper, 1989), p. 554; and Donald Macintyre, *The Battle of the Atlantic* (London: Pan Books, 1969), pp. 155–7. For a later view, see Michael Gannon, *Black May* (London: Aurum Press, 1998), pp. 110–13. For the growth in shipping output, see Grove, *Defeat of the Enemy Attack on Shipping*, Vol. 1B, Plan 35.
8. AU(42), 1st meeting, 4 November 1942, PRO CAB 86/2. The earlier Battle of the Atlantic Committee had last met on 20 May 1942. See 'War Cabinet. Battle of the Atlantic Committee. Conclusions of a meeting on 20 May 1942', BA(42), 2nd meeting, 21 May 1942, CAB 86/1. For an outline of this committee's work see Max Schoenfeld, 'Winston Churchill as War Manager: The Battle of the Atlantic Committee, 1941', *Military Affairs* (July 1988), pp. 122–7.
9. AU(42)12, A.V. Alexander, 'Provision of Escort Vessels: Memorandum by the First Lord of the Admiralty', 23 November 1942, CAB 86/3, pp. 58–9. AU(42), 4th meeting, 25 November 1942, CAB 86/2.
10. AU(42), 7th meeting, 16 December 1942, CAB 86/2. Lord Cherwell was appointed Paymaster-General on 20 December 1942 but remained, in effect, Churchill's confidant on scientific matters.
11. P.M.S. Blackett, 'Notes on the Effects of Bombing', 15 August 1941, RSBP, D59; CAOR, 'Effect of Bombing Policy', CAOR [spring 1942], RSBP, D65; and Lord Zuckerman, *Six Men Out of the Ordinary* (London: Peter Owen, 1992), p. 23; CAOR to D. of P., 10 November 1942, RSBP, D70. Also: 'Effect of Bombing Policy: Report by CAOR' [spring 1942], RSBP, D65; P.M.S Blackett, *Studies of War: Nuclear and Conventional* (London: Oliver & Boyd, 1962), pp. 223–7.
12. AU(43)1, 'A/S Warfare in Relation to Future Strategy', Memorandum by First Lord of the Admiralty, 5 January 1943, CAB 86/3, pp. 147–8, 150.
13. AU(43)29, 'Security of Sea Communications', Note by the Secretary, E.G. Clifford, 30 January 1943, CAB 86/3. The Admiralty later revised the escort deficit to 58 vessels. See AU(43)7, 'A/S Warfare in Relation to Future Strategy – Revised Proposals in Accordance with AU(43) 1st meeting, Item 12', Memorandum by the First Lord of the Admiralty, 11 January 1943, CAB 86/3, pp. 164–5.
14. AU(43), 2nd meeting, 13 January 1943, CAB 86/2. Blackett's team working on convoys included Professor E.J. Williams (Blackett's deputy), L. Solomon, K.V.

Thimann, Dr H.R. Hulme and J.H.C. Whitehead. See DNOR 21/43, L. Solomon and K.V. Thimann, 'Statistical Analysis of Effect of Surface Escort of Convoys', 29 January 1943, RSBP, D80, and ADM 219/37; and J.G. Crowther and R. Widdington, *Science at War* (London: HMSO, 1947), p. 102. This last pamphlet was later withdrawn from sale. My thanks to Rear-Admiral J.H. Adams for a copy.

15. AU(43)8, P.M.S. Blackett, 'The Value of Escort Vessels and Aircraft in Anti-Submarine Warfare', 11 January 1943, CAB 86/3, pp. 168–70.
16. AU(43), 2nd meeting. AU(43), 3rd meeting, 20 January 1943, CAB 86/2.
17. AU(43), 6th meeting, 10 February 1943, CAB 86/2.
18. P.M.S. Blackett, CAOR, 'The A/S War. What is to be done?', 5 February 1943, RSBP, D79. Points raised in this paper appear in subsequent comments offered by the chiefs of the Naval and Air Staffs. This paper was seen by Admiral Usborne. See also 'Convoys and Escorts. Remarks by ANA to ACNS(UT)', n.d., Naval Historical Branch, Box 'Trade Protection', File 'Size of Convoys'. ANA's memo was issued no later than 9 March 1943.
19. AU(43)40, P.M.S. Blackett, 'Progress of Analysis of the Value of Escort Vessels and Aircraft in the Anti-U-boat Campaign', 5 February 1943, CAB 86/3, Covering page (emphasis added) and p. 241 (also in RSBP, D79); Sir Bernard Lovell, letters to the author, 19 August and 4 September 1998; ACNS(H) to First Sea Lord, 20 December 1942, Churchill College Archive Centre, Roskill Papers, 5/13, and 'The A/S War', 5 February 1943, RSBP, D79, *passim.*
20. AU(43)40, 'Progress of Analysis', 5 February 1943, CAB 86/3, pp. 241–3; DNOR 21/43, L. Solomon and K.V. Thimann, 'Statistical Analysis of Effect of Surface Escort of Convoys', 29 January 1943, RSBP, D80, and ADM 219/37, pp. 4–5. Marc Milner, *North Atlantic Run: The Royal Canadian Navy and the Battle for the Convoys* (Annapolis, MD: Naval Institute Press, 1985, reprinted, 1986), p. 190.
21. 'The A/S War', 5 February 1943, RSBP, D79, p. 5 (italicised words added in pencil in the original). The view of Blackett's character is from Sir Andrew Huxley, 'Science and Politics: The Blackett Memorial Lecture', *Interdisciplinary Science Reviews*, 10, 1 (1985), pp. 15–21. Sir Andrew, a member of Blackett's team, kindly gave the author a copy of his article.
22. AU(43)40, 'Progress of Analysis', 5 February 1943, CAB 86/3, p. 242.
23. Air Vice-Marshal Slessor, Commander-in-Chief, Coastal Command, was present; see Commander-in-Chief, Coastal Command, 'Policy for the Employment of V/L/R Aircraft in the North Atlantic in the Present and Near Future', Note by Commander-in-Chief, Coastal Command, 14 February 1943, CAB 86/3.
24. AU(43), 6th meeting, 10 February 1943, CAB 86/2, pp. 103–4. It seems very likely that Pound offered this comment.
25. P.M.S. Blackett, *Studies of War*, pp.231–2. Admiral Horton and Commander Winn (Admiralty Operational Intelligence Centre) confirmed U-boats were deliberately approaching convoys from ahead at periscope depth to avoid radar detection by the escorts. 'Minutes of the Eighth Meeting of the U-boat Warfare Committee', 18 February 1943, ADM 205/30, p. 48 reverse. Blackett regularly attended these weekly meetings, chaired by Rear-Admiral J.H. Edelsten, ACNS(UT).
26. Grove, *Defeat of the Enemy Attack on Shipping*, Vol. 1B, Plans 15 and 35.
27. Morison relates a similar incident. He claims that in March Churchill had persuaded Hopkins to lobby Roosevelt on 'the R.N. concept of optimum size of transatlantic convoys'. As a result a 'double' convoy was sailed, though Admiral

King objected. See Morison, *History of United States Naval Operations in World War II*, Vol. X: *The Atlantic Battle Won May 1943–May 1945* (Boston, MA: Little, Brown, 1990), p. 22, n. 14. Could Churchill have actually supported Blackett's view on larger convoys and tried to outflank the Admiralty?

28. Message from D. Gibbs, Combined Shipping Adjustment Board, London, to Combined Shipping Adjustment Board, Washington, SABLO 181, 23 February 1943; Message from Leathers, Ministry of War Transport, London, to Salter, British Merchant Shipping Mission, Washington, via Sparks, New York, Limit Bilge 2670, 24 February 1943, MT 59/30.
29. Message from D. Gibbs, Combined Shipping Adjustment Board, London, to Combined Shipping Adjustment Board, Washington, SABLO 181, 23 February 1943, MT 59/30.
30. AU(43), 8th meeting, 24 February 1943, CAB 86/2, p. 115.
31. AU(43), 9th meeting, 3 March 1943, CAB 86/2, pp. 124–5 (emphasis added).
32. 'Personal and private for 1st S.L. from V.C.N.S.', B.A.D. Washington to Admiralty, 8 March 1943, Churchill College Archive Centre, Roskill Papers, 5/14 (emphasis added). Stephen Roskill, *The War at Sea 1939–1945*, Vol. II: *The Period of Balance* (London: HMSO, 1956), p. 358; and Marc Milner, *The U-boat Hunters: The Royal Canadian Navy and the Offensive against Germany's Submarines* (Annapolis, MD: Naval Institute Press, 1994), pp. 25–6.
33. 'Personal and private for 1st S.L. [from] V.C.N.S.', 9 March 1943, Churchill College Archive Centre, Roskill Papers, 5/14. Admiral Horton had despatched a strongly worded paper to the Admiralty on the topic of escort group training on 5 December 1942. See W.S. Chalmers, *Max Horton and the Western Approaches* (London: Hodder & Stoughton, 1954), pp. 162–3.
34. Pound is referring to Ultra information. Grove, *Defeat of the Enemy Attack on Shipping*, Vol. 1A, pp. 91–2, gives the percentage loss as 67 per cent or 68 per cent. Jürgen Rohwer, *The Critical Convoy Battles of March 1943: The Battle for HX.229/SC.122* (London: Ian Allan, 1977), p. 187. F.H. Hinsley, *et al.*, *British Intelligence in the Second World War: Its Influence on Strategy and Operations*, Vol. II (London: HMSO, 1981), pp. 562, 750. In the event Bletchley Park was able to penetrate the new Enigma setting after only nine days.
35. AU(43), 10th meeting, 10 March 1943, CAB 86/2, p. 130. AU(43)68, 'Security of North Atlantic Convoys', Memorandum by the Chief of the Naval Staff and the Chief of the Air Staff, 8 March 1943, CAB 86/3, pp. 311–15.
36. AU(43)53, Lord Leathers, 'Losses of Merchant Ships. Notes by the Minister of War Transport', 20 February 1943, CAB 86/3, p. 279.
37. AU(43)68, 'Security of North Atlantic Convoys', 8 March 1943, CAB 86/3, p. 314.
38. AU(43), 10th meeting, p. 131; Patrick Beesley, *Very Special Intelligence: The Story of the Admiralty's Operational Intelligence Centre 1939–1945* (London: Hamish Hamilton, 1977), pp. 176–7; Hinsley, *British Intelligence*, Vol. II, p. 570. W/T, or wireless telegraphy (i.e. radio), was extensively used by U-boats at this stage of the campaign to co-ordinate their search for, and approach to, convoys. The Allies were able to fix the location of many of these high-frequency radio transmissions by direction finding, known as H/F D/F, or huff-duff, both from shore stations and in many of the escorts.
39. AU(43)68, 'Security of North Atlantic Convoys', pp. 311, 314 (emphasis added). A convoy of 60 ships was some six miles in breadth and two miles in depth. Peter Gretton, *Crisis Convoy: The Story of HX231* (London: Peter Davies, 1974), pp. 5, 10.
40. Depicted in Grove, *Defeat of the Enemy Attack on Shipping*, Vol. 1B, Plan 16(5).

41. AU(43), 10th meeting, pp. 130–1. AU(43)68, 'Security of North Atlantic Convoys', pp. 312–13. The provision of an air base in the Azores was an important adjunct to this policy and was being discussed by the Joint Planning Staff and the Foreign Office.
42. AU(43)68, 'Security of North Atlantic Convoys', p. 315; Robin Brodhurst, 'Admiral Sir Dudley Pound (1939–1943)', in Malcolm H. Murfett (ed.), *The First Sea Lords: From Fisher to Mountbatten* (London: Praeger, 1995), pp. 193–4; Denis Richards, *Portal of Hungerford* (London: Heinemann, 1977), pp. 259, 311.
43. AU(43)68, 'Security of North Atlantic Convoys', p. 313; AU(43)7, 'Revised Proposals', CAB 86/3 (emphasis supplied); Blackett, *Studies of War*, pp. 230–1.
44. Arthur J. Marder, *From the Dardanelles to Oran: Studies in the Royal Navy in War and Peace, 1915–1940* (London: Oxford University Press, 1974), p. 46, n. 23. Brodhurst, 'Admiral Sir Dudley Pound', p. 185. Alex Danchev, 'Waltzing with Winston: Civil–Military Relations in the Second World War', in Paul Smith (ed.), *Government and the Armed Forces in Britain, 1856–1990* (London: Hambledon Press, 1996), p. 214.
45. P.M.S. Blackett, DNOR Report No. 17/42, 'Scientists at the Operational Level', 31 October 1941, ADM 219/16. Professor Sir William McCrea suggests as much. Conversation with the author, 18 June 1998. David Waters, the Naval Staff historian, makes a similar observation about the lack of suitably qualified staff officers. D.W. Waters, 'The Use and Operational Importance of Statistics relating to Shipping Defence', 16 August 1957, Naval Historical Branch, DWW77A.
46. These comments, apparently from Alistair Denniston, were directed to the use of executive officers in the intelligence field, but the point is the same here and would apply to air force officers. Patrick Beesley, *Very Special Intelligence: The Story of the Admiralty's Operational Intelligence Centre 1939–1945* (London: Hamish Hamilton, 1977), p. 6.
47. AU(43), 10th meeting, p. 131. AU(43)68, 'Security of North Atlantic Convoys', p. 315.
48. Apart from evidence from his operational research papers, it was also a characteristic part of his general outlook. Sir Bernard Lovell, letter to the author, 19 August 1998.
49. CAOR, 'The Case for an Immediate, even if Temporary, Increase in the Size of Convoys', 5 March 1943, RSBP, D79.
50. AU(43), 10th meeting, p. 131. There were advantages to being a civilian, Professor D.K. Hill remembers, while another of Blackett's team recalls the informality of DNOR's relationship with the Naval Staff. Sir Andrew Huxley remembers Blackett saying something like: 'The great advantage of being a civilian was that you could answer back to senior officers.' Professor D.K. Hill, letter to the author, 16 August 1998; interview with Professor Sir William McCrea, 17 April 1998; and interview with Professor Sir Andrew Huxley, 3 August 1998. Professor Zimmerman draws the same conclusion: see David Zimmerman, *The Great Naval Battle of Ottawa* (London: University of Toronto Press, 1989), p. 152.
51. U.T.1/43, 'Size of Convoys', Proposal by ANA to ACNS (UT), 6 March 1943, Naval Historical Branch, File 'Size of Convoys'. (The papers in this file all appear to be typed transcripts of originals.) Admiral Usborne was the Additional Naval Adviser (ANA) to ACNS(UT). Information supplied by Ninian Stewart, 9 September 1998. Usborne based his argument on Blackett's 'The A/S War', RSBP, D79.
52. C.P. Clarke to ACNS(UT), 9 March 1943; B.B. Schofield, DTD, to ACNS(UT),

8 March 1943; and J.A.S. Eccles to ACNS(UT), 19 March 1943 all in Naval Historical Branch File 'Size of Convoys'.

53. Dr Whitehead, CAOR (A/SW), 'Size of Convoy and Escort. Perimeter to be defended', 9 March 1943, Naval Historical Branch File 'Size of Convoys'.
54. D.W. Waters, 'Notes on the Convoy System of Naval Warfare, Thirteenth to Twentieth Centuries', Part 2, 'First World War, 1914–1918', March 1960, p. 995, para. 51, Historical Section, Admiralty Library. Also Arthur J. Marder, *From the Dreadnought to Scapa Flow: The Royal Navy in the Fisher Era, 1904–1919*, Vol. V: *Victory and Aftermath (Jan. 1918–June 1919)* (London: Oxford University Press, 1970), pp. 99–100, n. 33.
55. Dr Nicolas Blackett remembers his father talking about evidence from the First World War favouring the use of large convoys. E-mail to the author, 16 September 1998. It is likely that this conversation took place in the post-war period. D. W. Waters, 'The Science of the Admiralty', *Naval Review*, 51, Part I (October 1963), p. 400.
56. 'Size of Convoy and Escort. Perimeter to be defended'.
57. Rollo Appleyard, Naval Staff, Convoy Section, 'The Elements of Convoy-Defence in Submarine Warfare', 3 April 1918, Admiralty Library, P880, p. 28.
58. It is interesting to note that the Naval Staff historians, David Waters and Frederick Barley, independently derived the 'law' of large convoys in their post-war analysis. Grove, *The Defeat of the Enemy Attack on Shipping*, Vol. 1A, pp. xix, 37.
59. 'Minutes of the Twelfth Meeting of the U-boat Warfare Committee', 18 March 1943, ADM 205/30. The document has not been located, unless Edelsten was referring to Blackett's subsequent paper, 'The Case for Large Convoys', produced in May 1943 (ADM 219/19). Blackett's paper certainly contains many of the items discussed at ACNS(UT)'s meeting, particularly the concept of convoy size and the length of the screen perimeter – see text.
60. 'Minutes of the Thirteenth Meeting of the U-boat Warfare Committee', 25 March 1943, ADM 205/30. Admiral Horton to Rear-Admiral Edelsten, 'Remarks on ANA's Paper on "Convoys and Escorts"', 30 March 1943, Naval Historical Branch File 'Size of Convoys'.
61. UT37, 'Admiralty Review of Anti-U-boat Warfare Committee', 20 August 1943, ADM 205/30, p. 23; AU(43), 12th meeting, 24 March 1943, CAB 86/2, p. 139; Chalmers, *Max Horton*, p. 158; 'Inside Story of Events Leading to the Defeat of the U-boat Campaign in 1943. Winston Churchill's Decisive Directive', Captain H.N. Lake, DSO, DSC, RN Retd., Miscellaneous Papers of Captain Lake, WWII, 7, pp. 4–5, Churchill College Archives Centre. For an uncritical use of Lake's papers see Geoffrey Penn, 'Convoy versus U-boat in World War II', *Naval Review*, 85, 4 (October 1997), pp. 361–3.
62. And not on 24 March, as Lake remembers. Captain H.N. Lake, Miscellaneous Papers, 7, p. 5. Lake's paper was, from internal evidence, written somewhere between 1965 and 1971. He admits that his memory for detail was fallible.
63. AU(43), 11th meeting, 17 March 1943, CAB 86/2, p. 139. AU(43)90, 'Battle of the Atlantic', Memorandum by the First Sea Lord, 22 March 1943, CAB 86/3. Winston S. Churchill, *The Second World War*, Vol. V: *Closing the Ring* (London: Reprint Society, 1954), p. 208. The issue was taken at the War Cabinet Anti-U-boat Committee meeting on 31 March, of which more later.
64. P.M.S. Blackett, CAOR, 'Note on Relation Between the Use of Aircraft to Give Cover to Convoys and in the Bay', 22 March 1943, ADM 205/30, p. 213. Edelsten's comments were handwritten on 23 March 1943.
65. 'Note on Relation Between the Use of Aircraft to Give Cover to Convoys and in the Bay', 22 March 1943, pp. 214 and reverse.

66. AU(43)90, 'Battle of the Atlantic', 22 March 1943, CAB 86/3, pp. 392–5; 'Review of U-boat Situation', ACNS(UT), 16 March 1943, ADM 205/30, p. 212.
67. AU(43)96, Air Marshal A.T. Harris, 'The Battle of the Atlantic: Memorandum by the Air Officer Commanding-in-Chief, Bomber Command', 29 March 1943, RSBP, D71, pp. 1–3.
68. CAOR, 'Bombing of U-boat Bases', [30 March 1943], RSBP, D76.
69. AU(43)100, Note by the Secretary of the War Cabinet, E.E. Bridges, 29 March 1943, CAB 86/3; 'Committee', 1942–45, PRO Premier 3/414/1, p. 128. The 'other' Admiralty attendee was Edelsten.
70. AU(43), 13th meeting, 31 March 1943, CAB 86/2, pp. 153–7.
71. 'Minutes of the Fourteenth Meeting of the U-boat Warfare Committee', 1 April 1943, ADM 205/30, p. 57; Morison, *United States Naval Operations*, Vol. X, p. 16. The joint British–US board had been set up on 8 March 1943.
72. 'Mammoth Convoys. Summary by ACNS(UT)', 16 April 1943, Naval Historical Branch File 'Size of Convoys'.
73. 'Minutes of the Seventeenth Meeting of the U-boat Warfare Committee', 22 April 1943, ADM 205/30, p. 61 reverse. The minutes do not make clear what paper Blackett used, though it is likely to be a draft of 'The Case for Large Convoys', which was finalised in May.
74. AU(43), 18th meeting, 12 May 1943, CAB 86/2, pp. 185–6.
75. DNOR Report No. 2/43, CAOR, 'The Case for Large Convoys', [May 1943], ADM 219/19. The numbering of the report as 2/43 suggests that the paper was in preparation from early 1943 and Blackett indicates as much in *Studies of War*, pp. 228–34 *passim.* The exact dating of the report remains problematic. At the Anti-U-boat Committee meeting on 12 May the Admiralty were asked to prepare a paper but it was not needed until the Minister of War Transport returned from Washington, where he had been at the 'Trident' Conference with Churchill. The conference did not finish until 25 May – ironically just as the U-boats withdrew from the Atlantic. AU(43), 18th meeting, p. 186. Winston S. Churchill, *The Second World War*, Vol. IV: *The Hinge of Fate* (London: Reprint Society, 1954), pp. 630–53. Blackettt's paper does not seem to have been formally submitted to the War Cabinet for review, CAB 86/2 *passim.* In his 'Notes for Lecture on Science and the U-boat War', DNOR, May 1943, RSBP, D87, p. 17, Blackett, referring to 'The Case for Large Convoys', says that such analysis 'can lead to conclusions on which action *can be* taken immediately'. This contrasts with earlier examples of operational research on which, he says, action *was* taken. The conclusion is that 'The Case for Large Convoys' was probably ready towards the end of May but was never formally reviewed by the Cabinet Committee.
76. The relevant percentage loss rates were:

January 1941 and April 1943:	
Large Convoys, average of 53 ships	1.7%
Small Convoys, average of 33 ships	2.6%
August 1942 to April 1943:	
Large Convoys, average of 53 ships	2.9%
Small Convoys, average of 33 ships	4.0%

These figures *included* stragglers from the convoys. Both the Admiralty and the Ministry of War Transport were concerned that larger convoys would lead to more straggling and therefore greater loss. Blackett's results showed this not to be the case. 'The Case for Large Convoys', p. 1 and Appendix I.

77. 'The Case for Large Convoys', p. 1. Blackett's figures were drawn from Dr Whitehead's calculations made in early March and were based on practical convoy shapes. For a simplified geometric treatment see D.W. Waters, 'The Mathematics of Convoy', *Navy International* (May 1978), pp. 22–6, 78.
78. 'The Case for Large Convoys', p. 1; Crowther and Widdington, *Science at War*, p. 101.
79. Since only a small part of the widely spaced U-boat pack could be homed on to an individual convoy and that the process could take up to 30 hours. See AU(43)84, Air Officer Commanding-in-Chief, Coastal Command, 'The Value of the Bay of Biscay Patrols', 22 March 1943, CAB 86/3, p. 370.The difficulties of U-boats homing to convoys was confirmed in a DAUD paper written in 1944. See 'A/S Warfare 1944', Commander H.J. Fawcett, RN Papers, 2/4/5, pp. 9–10, Churchill College Archives Centre. DNOR also noted in early 1944 that in the past their navigational and homing capability had been poor, so that many of the boats in a pack spent up to 70–90 per cent of their time searching for the convoy sighted by one of their number! See Report No. 12/44, L. Solomon, 'Note on U-boats with High Submerged Speeds', 18 February 1944, ADM 219/98, p. 1.
80. 'The Case for Large Convoys', p. 1 (emphasis added).
81. This argument was doubtless aimed particularly at Admiral Horton, C.-in-C., Western Approaches, who was repeatedly on record emphasising the need for continuation training for his escort groups. See: AU(43), 16th meeting, 21 April 1943, CAB 86/2, p. 175; 'Minutes of the Seventeenth Meeting of the U-boat Warfare Committee', 22 April 1943, ADM 205/30; AU(43), 18th meeting, p. 186; Chalmers, *Max Horton*, pp. 163–4 and *passim.*
82. 'The Case for Large Convoys', p. 1 (emphasis supplied). The close co-operation between DNOR and Coastal Command ORS is confirmed in C.H. Waddington, *OR in World War 2: Operational Research Against the U boat* (London: Elek Science, 1973), p. 222. The book was originally written in September 1946 but remained unpublished until 1973.
83. Meeting, 25 January 1943, ADM 205/30; see also Chapter 8 above. H/F D/F, or high-frequency direction finding, was used to locate enemy ships or U-boats at sea. It was colloquially known as 'huff-duff'.
84. 'The Case for Large Convoys', pp. 1–4. Horton would have disagreed, especially for convoys in bad weather and particularly fog. See Horton to Edelsten, 'Remarks on ANA's Paper on "Convoys and Escorts"'.
85. Professor D.K. Hill, letter to the author, 16 August 1998. Sir Bernard Lovell, letter to the author, 19 August 1998.
86. An American captain in London, writing to the Chief of Staff, 10th Fleet in Washington, commented that the 'Operational Research people ... work up a good many things which have some value and considerable interest, but their conclusions are not always correct because they don't know the practical and material difficulties which stand in your way, and sometimes these conclusions are phrased in such a positive way that they may seem irritating'. Captain H.A. Flanigan to Rear-Admiral F.S. Low, 3 June 1943, NARA RG38, 10th Fleet Box ASM-42, United States Forces in Europe. (I am indebted to W.J.R. Gardner for a copy of this letter.) A year later the Director of the Anti-U-boat Division accused an OR report of being 'too theoretical'. See Report No. 66/44, E.J. Williams, DNOR, 'A/S Operations against Snort U-boats working inshore', 29 August 1944, ADM 219/148.
87. Interview with Professor Sir William McCrea, 17 April 1998.
88. Horton to Edelsten, 'Remarks on ANA's Paper on "Convoys and Escorts"'.

89. 'Mammoth Convoys'.
90. 'Minutes of the Nineteenth Meeting of the U-boat Warfare Committee', 13 May 1943, ADM 205/30.
91. AU(43), 20th meeting, 9 June 1943, CAB 86/2, pp. 195–6.
92. AU(43)8, 'The Value of Escort Vessels and Aircraft in Anti-Submarine Warfare', 11 January 1943, CAB 86/3, p. 170.
93. Milner, *The U-boat Hunters*, pp. 39–40; 'The Case for Large Convoys', *passim.*
94. David Syrett, *The Defeat of the German U-boats: The Battle of the Atlantic* (Columbia, SC: University of South Carolina Press, 1994), pp. 261–4.
95. P.M.S. Blackett, *Studies of War*, p. 233. Certainly the case was made, and adopted, for maximising the escorts for the D-Day convoys at the expense of Atlantic convoys. See 'Overinsuring versus Underinsuring Overlord from the U-boat and W-boat Threat', 30 March 1944, Commander H.J. Fawcett, RN Papers, 2/8, Churchill College Archives Centre.
96. Captain C.D. Howard Johnston, Director Anti-U-boat Division to ACNS(UT)', 2 June 1944, Naval Historical Branch File 'Size of Convoys'. Milner, *The U-boat Hunters*, pp. 139–40. The conclusion is drawn from Grove, *Defeat of the Enemy Attack on Shipping*, Vol. 1B, Plans 9 and 35. Sir Edward Bridges to Prime Minister, 25 January 1945, PRO Premier 3/414/1.
97. AU(43), 19th meeting, 26 May 1943, CAB 86/2, p. 188.
98. P.M.S. Blackett, *Studies of War*, p. 233.
99. Appleyard, 'Convoy-Defence in Submarine Warfare'.

10

The Case against Area Bombing

Paul Crook

On 11 February 1960 Patrick Blackett gave the Sir Henry Tizard memorial lecture to the newly founded Institute for Strategic Studies (a body Blackett hoped might shed some much-needed scientific light upon crucial human matters such as the nuclear threat). This lecture was to become a foundation document that helped shape our present thinking about the mass bombing of civilian populations in war. Britain's decision in 1942 massively to bomb German cities, largely in order to erode civilian morale, followed heated debate waged among the armed forces, scientists and politicians. The famed skirmish between Churchill's scientific adviser Lord Cherwell ('the Prof') and the brilliant Sir Henry Tizard, key scientist at the Air Ministry, has become the stuff of legend. After the war controversy continued to rage over the operational success and ethics of 'area bombing', the largely indiscriminate blanket bombing of cities, the end product of the Royal Air Force's almost hypnotic attraction to the concept of strategic bombing. Blackett was a traditionalist appalled at the concept of total war. He disbelieved in both the ethics and operational effectiveness of area bombing. He had been a major player in the events of 1942. Now, in the 1960s, he and another radical scientist, C.P. Snow, wartime boffin and novelist, helped form the historiography of the Tizard–Cherwell feud. Blackett and Snow, and sympathisers like J.D. Bernal, had been on the losing Tizard side in 1942. By dramatising this dispute within the very precincts of policy-making (Snow's 'corridors of power'), Blackett and Snow snatched victory from the jaws of their wartime defeat. Tizard, their hero, was rehabilitated, while the conservative 'outsider' Cherwell was found guilty of poor judgement or worse. This chapter will deal with this process of myth making and add a brief reality check from what we now know of events.[1]

First some context. The pure doctrine of strategic bombing developed in the inter-war period, and envisaged the smashing of a foe's war capability and will. The targets would be large cities and industrial heartlands. But the doctrine never achieved complete hegemony in the military thinking of the major powers. Germany and the United States were countries where army influence was strong. There was scepticism that wars could be won by air offensives alone. The enemy would still need to be defeated on the ground. There were doubts about the operational feasibility of strategic bombing. British military thought contained much ambivalence. Britain was close to Germany and vulnerable to a bombing blitz. However, strategic bombing offered the glittering prospect of winning victory without entanglement in a Continental ground war. This was consistent with traditional British diplomacy, and struck a chord in a national psyche still scarred by horrific memories of the trench warfare of 1914–18. The mass bombing doctrine was embraced by Sir Hugh Trenchard, Chief of Air Staff between the wars, and by his young followers Charles Portal (Chief of Air Staff during the Second World War) and Arthur 'Bomber' Harris, later Chief of Bomber Command. The doctrine proved highly resistant to ethical or operational criticisms, essentially because it empowered the RAF. As Blackett, a Navy man, put it, the Allied bombing offensive 'was a product of the rise of the air forces of the world and of their determination to evolve a strategic role for air power that would make them independent of the two older services, the army and the navy'.[2]

The result was (according to critics like Blackett) a weakening of co-operation between the RAF and the other services, an obsession with bombers rather than fighters, and poor progress in solving the navigational and bomb-aiming technicalities involved in 'precision' bombing. As a designer of the Mark XIV bombsight at the war's start, Blackett was vitally interested in such weaknesses in Bomber Command. They resulted in heavy casualties being inflicted by German anti-aircraft and fighter defences during daylight raids made on key oil installations and submarine bases in the first phase of the war. Bomber Command still relied upon outmoded medium-range bombers (such as Blenheims), and was fatally slow to realise the need for long-range bombers carrying heavy loads and heavy-calibre machine-guns for defence. The appearance of fast new fighters, radar, better searchlights and ack-ack rudely shook the idea of the invincibility of the bomber. The extremist faith in strategic bombing as a single war-winning factor waned, but it was by no means dead within the Air Force.

Bombing Germany became a political necessity, after Dunkirk and the blitz, with Churchill in command. It was designed to shore up home morale and international support. As the defects of 'precision' bombing at night emerged, the RAF edged inexorably towards area bombing. Portal (who became Chief of Air Staff in October 1940) advocated in July 1940 a plan of hitting key industrial targets, but with the consolation that errant bombs would not be wasted. Scientific analysis of results was notably primitive. The Butt report of August 1941 concluded from photographic evidence that night bombing was seriously inaccurate, largely owing to navigational defects. Only one-third of attacking aircraft got within five miles of their targets. This shock hastened both the scientisation of Bomber Command and the adoption of area bombing, the rapier abandoned for the bludgeon. By late 1941 the Air Staff was demanding 4,000 front-line heavy bombers, never economically feasible, and had plans to raze over 40 populous German towns. Churchill was sceptical of exaggerated claims for bombing, but nevertheless supported a massive bomber build-up. A bombing directive of 14 February 1942 made clear that the primary objective of operations should be to destroy the morale of the enemy civil population, especially industrial workers. Eight days later 'Bomber' Harris became Chief of Bomber Command. He thus inherited – and went on enthusiastically to implement – the strategy of a massive air offensive against the German heartland.

After the failure of the German blitzkrieg in Russia, and the entry of Japan and the United States into the war, the Allies reaffirmed a policy of wearing down the German war effort by bombing. However, critical differences of opinion continued to surface in Britain over strategic priorities and the effectiveness of bombing. The issue was freely canvassed in the country and in Parliament in early 1942. Within official circles, critics such as Admiral of the Fleet Sir Dudley Pound pressed for greater concentration of air power on the crucial sea war in the Atlantic. The future of Bomber Command and area bombing seemed in the balance when Cherwell made his crucial intervention. We will return to the details later, but, briefly, Cherwell minuted Churchill on 30 March 1942. He calculated – on the basis of damage inflicted by German raids on Birmingham and

Hull – that 10,000 heavy bombers blitzing main cities could destroy the homes of one-third of the German population by mid-1943. This would break the German war will. Cherwell's minute found favour with the Air Staff, but was seriously questioned by Tizard. At heart, Tizard wanted air power to complement a broader armed strategy. In the ensuing wrangle, Cherwell triumphed over Tizard, and area bombing was given a higher priority than its operational critics – Blackett to the forefront – wanted.

This was the setting for Blackett's 1960 lecture. It laid down the basic framework of radical science writing on the Tizard–Cherwell dispute. As noted elsewhere in this volume, Blackett had been a political radical in the 1930s. Although a moderate Fabian socialist, he was closely associated with Marxist scientists like John Desmond Bernal, J.B.S. Haldane, J.G. Crowther and Hyman Levy in what has been called 'the Visible College' of the scientific left.[3] Blackett had discovered the positron while working at the Cavendish Laboratory, in the radical anti-war ethos of Cambridge. His lifetime friendship with Tizard also dated from this period. In 1934 Blackett served under Tizard, chairman of the Aeronautical Research Committee. He saw himself as a disciple of Tizard:

> I have never failed to find stimulus, entertainment and enlightenment from his company. Though sometimes a little irritable, he was essentially warm-hearted and very wise. Of the individuals who have influenced me by their personality, I think Tizard comes next to Rutherford.[4]

Like his mentor J.B.S. Haldane, Tizard wanted to make official circles conscious of the national significance of science. Blackett particularly valued Tizard's initiative, through the Biggin Hill experiment, in starting the process of getting fully fledged operational research sections attached to all major commands of the three services, something which gave Britain a vital edge over the Third Reich in the war. Blackett recalled that Tizard had the capacity, not only to inspire younger men in the services and university, but also for setting the cat among the official pigeons and for pricking complacency. These things won him some enemies among the upper hierarchy. Blackett was Tizard's appointee to the Air Defence Committee, which did vital work in developing radar before the war. Professor F.A. Lindemann (later Lord Cherwell),

Churchill's man on the committee, had little faith in early-warning radar systems, and proved to be a disruptive presence. Blackett was a key player in having Lindemann ousted from the committee in 1936. Thus began the chronic feud between Tizard and Lindemann.

Blackett recounted that feud in his 1960 lecture. Lindemann regained the upper hand on the outbreak of war when he became Churchill's personal scientific adviser. Tizard, the civil servant mandarin within the Air Council, soon found himself marginalised in what Blackett described as the 'taut, executive, war-time machine' (p. 649). This was despite Tizard's brilliant success at the Air Ministry in 1939–40, when he masterminded an exchange of scientific secrets between Britain and the United States, something that was to aid immeasurably the war effort. Tizard became dissatisfied with his role, first at the Ministry of Aircraft Production and then at the Air Council:

> On the one hand he was too senior to do his own devilling among the files at the lower levels of the machine ... and on the other hand, he had too much self-respect to acquire influence by becoming a courtier. Tizard evidently felt that he was not wanted in Whitehall and so he accepted the presidency of Magdalen College, Oxford. (p. 649)

This ousting of the ablest British scientist to apply himself to the problems of war was, in Blackett's opinion and that of many others, a disastrous turn of fortune for the British war effort. It was clear that Tizard's defeat on area bombing had helped to precipitate his departure.

Blackett's recollection of the bomber controversy has Churchill early in 1942 'extremely anxious that everything possible should be done by Bomber Command to help the hard-pressed Soviet armies in Stalingrad' (p. 650). Cherwell's proposal was for a bombing offensive aimed primarily against German working-class housing, an easier target than spread-out middle-class housing or difficult-to-hit factories or military establishments:

> So far as my memory goes, the paper claimed that it should be possible within the stated period [until autumn 1943] to destroy 50 per cent of all houses in all towns of more than 50,000 population in Germany, if Britain concentrated all her efforts on the production of bombers and used them for this purpose. Tizard studied this paper in detail and concluded that the estimate of the number of houses likely to be destroyed in the next eighteen months was five

> times too high. At that time I was director of Operational Research at the Admiralty, and I was asked to comment on the Cabinet paper. I came independently essentially to the same conclusion as Tizard – I think I estimated the error as six-fold. The main mistake made in the Cabinet paper was to assume that all bombers which would be delivered from the factories in the next eighteen months would in the same period have dropped all their bombs on Germany. The year or more from the completion of a bomber to the completion of its average operational life of twenty sorties had not been fully allowed for.

Blackett pointed out that the US Strategic Bombing Survey after the war

> showed that the number of houses actually destroyed in the assigned period was only one-tenth of the estimate in the Cabinet paper: this agreed rather closely with Tizard's and my estimates, allowing for reduced numbers of bombers actually supplied to Bomber Command. (p. 650)

There were some interesting inaccuracies in Blackett's recollections. Most importantly, Cherwell's minute to Churchill did not in fact single out working-class housing. Also it estimated that 'the great majority' of inhabitants of Germany's 58 towns of over 100,000, or 'about one-third of the German population', would be turned out of house and home.[5] Again, Blackett was notably modest, or diplomatic, about his role in affairs. As we shall see, he was closely involved in the row over area bombing in 1942. As the Admiralty's operational expert on bombing, Blackett used his scientific clout to make the Navy's case against area bombing, and he supplied Tizard with ammunition to use against Cherwell's de-housing plan. One may be permitted to doubt that they arrived at their conclusions entirely 'independently'. Blackett recalled that Tizard and he went unheeded:

> By this time a certain allergy to arithmetic was spreading in Whitehall ... The story goes that at that time in the Air Ministry it was said of anyone who added two and two together to make four, 'He is not to be trusted; he has been talking to Tizard and Blackett'.

Disagreeable tales circulated that those making such calculations were defeatists. The Air Ministry agreed with Cherwell 'and the policy of dehousing the German working-class population, with the object of lowering its morale and will to fight, became a major part of the British war effort' (p. 650). Blackett endorsed a rare post-war comment by Tizard on the affair:

> Experience has shown that a nation, with toughness, stamina and a will to live and work, can stand far more punishment in the form of bombardment of cities and homes than most people thought possible before the trial. No one thinks now that it would have been possible to defeat Germany by bombing alone. The actual effort in man-power and resources that was expended in bombing Germany was greater than the value in man-power of the damage caused. (quoted p. 650)

Blackett made a link between the wartime controversy on bombing policy and the bitter disputes that were then being engendered by atomic weapons. Each case left a trail of personal antagonisms. However, Blackett's sober narrative of events in 1942 stirred few waves when it appeared in March 1960 in *Nature.*

If Blackett had given the essential facts of the Tizard–Cherwell feud, it took C.P. (later Lord) Snow to raise it to high drama. He did so in his Godkin lectures for 1960, soon published as *Science and Government* (1961). Snow and Blackett had been involved in Cambridge radical science in the 1930s. Snow, who worked on solid-state photochemistry at the Cavendish, edited the popular scientific magazine *Discovery*, dedicated to socially responsible science. He and Blackett were critics of Establishment science (which Snow later described as 'an agreement, largely unspoken and very largely unconscious, to preserve substantially the present web of power-relations'[6]). As Mary Jo Nye has indicated in her Chapter 14, Snow and Blackett often met in Whitehall corridors of power during and after the war (Snow was wartime chief of scientific personnel for the Ministry of Labour), and both worked for the anti-nuclear cause. Snow used these experiences as the basis for his cycle of novels *Strangers and Brothers*, and in *Corridors of Power* (1964) he used Blackett as the model for the physicist Francis Getliffe. He had already (1959) popularised the schism between 'the two cultures' of the humanities and science–industry.

Snow was concerned to caution against the perils of secret government in an age when a handful of men, including scientists, made life-and-death decisions for humanity: witness the area bombing offensive and the decision to make an atomic bomb. The

Tizard–Lindemann story enabled Snow to indict the excesses of committee politics, hierarchical politics and court politics. Lindemann was the grey eminence to Churchill, a 'solitary overlord', a source of bad judgements and bad choices. Snow's lecture vividly depicted the polar tensions between two brilliant, but temperamentally different scientists: Tizard, 'English of the English', a trained techno-bureaucrat, a radical full of traditional loyalties (all qualities shared by Snow, and Blackett); and Lindemann, rich and 'quite un-English', full of repressions and venom.[7] Snow's vignette incorporated some subtly racial codes, and it was to become the basis for Lindemann's later 'demonisation'.[8]

Snow made the bombing row the high point of his drama. He closely followed Blackett's account of events (complete with inaccuracies), spiced with his own recollections:

> At the time I heard some talk of the famous cabinet paper. I have to say this about my own attitude and that of the people I knew best. We had never had the conventional English faith in strategic bombing, partly on military and partly on human grounds … The strategy had not been thought out. It was just an unrationalised article of faith … I think it fair to say that Lindemann had always believed in this faith with characteristic intensity. (pp. 47, 49)

In Snow's opinion Tizard's critique of Lindemann's calculations was impregnable, enough to demolish the whole bombing strategy. Lindemann's bombing estimates were out by a factor of ten. Yet in the hysterical atmosphere that prevailed, the more informed view was squashed: 'I do not think that, in secret politics, I have ever seen a minority view so unpopular.' There was 'the faint but just perceptible smell of a witch hunt … Strategic bombing, according to the Lindemann policy, was put into action with every effort the country could make' (pp. 50–1). Snow considered the whole thing a colossal misjudgement operationally. Not only that. He made clear his own feeling that a strategy of razing half the houses in Germany was simply inhuman, and would be judged as such by future people living in a more benevolent age.

A lively debate ensued, with a number of Cherwell's wartime colleagues springing to his defence and attacking Snow's impartiality. They included Professor R.V. Jones, who had been Chief of Scientific Intelligence, and Lord Birkenhead, Cherwell's biographer. Both attempted to narrow the differences between Tizard and Cherwell. They tended to depict the dispute as essentially about means rather than principles.[9]

Blackett for his part gave a glowing review of Snow's book for *Scientific American*, declaring that 'I can vouch for the fundamental truth of Snow's account of what went on. Moreover, I think that his description of the conflicts and his penetrating insight into the characters of the two men is brilliantly carried out.'[10] Blackett gave some interesting personal insights. We know of his youthful enthusiasm for the Air Force and his invention of the Mark XIV bombsight. Yet his concept of war remained in key senses part of a much older tradition. He said regretfully of the bombing offensive:

> So far as I know, it was the first time that a modern nation had deliberately planned a major military campaign against the enemy's civilian population rather than against his armed forces. During my youth in the Navy in World War I such an operation would have been inconceivable. (p. 192)

Blackett added some details about his own involvement. In March 1942 (he said) Churchill had asked the Air Staff how they thought they could best help the beleaguered Russians by stepping up the bombing offensive against Germany. The Air Staff report was sent to the Admiralty, who sent it on to Blackett for comment, as Director of Operational Research:

> Since the Air Staff estimates in this paper of what the bombing campaign had hitherto accomplished seemed to me to be based on very flimsy evidence, I set about checking the claims by the simple method of noting what the German blitz on England had accomplished and calculating from this what our much weaker attack should have done to Germany. The result was startling. It seemed probable that the German casualties from our bombs could not have been much more than the loss of trained air crews. Further, I estimated that the reduction of industrial production was less than 1 per cent. So on these two counts the direct effect of the British bombing offensive of 1940 to 1942 seemed nearly a dead loss.

Blackett took these calculations to Lindemann:

> In effect he accepted my calculations and realized that neither by the casualties inflicted nor by the interruption of production was

> our bombing offensive likely to bring much relief to the Russians. So he switched the objective to the destruction of German housing. (pp. 192–3)

The story then followed the familiar lines of his Tizard lecture. Blackett added that from his talks with Lindemann at the time 'I became aware of that trait of character which Snow so well emphasizes': this was his almost fanatical belief in some particular operation or gadget to the almost total exclusion of wider considerations:

> Bombing to him then seemed the one and only useful operation of the war. He said to me (unfortunately I have no record of this conversation, but he probably said the same to others) that he considered any diversion of aircraft production and supply to the antisubmarine campaign, to army co-operation or even to fighter defence – in fact, to anything but bombing – as being a disastrous mistake. Lindemann even suggested that the building up of strong land forces for the projected invasion of France was wrong. Never have I encountered such fanatical belief in the efficacy of bombing. (p. 193)

Blackett believed that the high priority given to saturation bombing made it very difficult to get adequate air support for the vital Battle of the Atlantic. Again he emphasised the report of the US Strategic Bombing Survey after the war, which showed without doubt that area bombing was an expensive failure:

> About 500,000 German men, women and children were killed, but in the whole bombing offensive 160,000 US and British airmen, the best young men of both countries, were lost. German war production went on rising steadily until it reached its peak in August 1944. At this time the Allies were already in Paris and the Russian armies were well into Poland. German civilian morale did not crack. Perhaps it is not surprising that the [US report] seems to have had a rather small circulation; it is to be found in few libraries and does not appear to have been directly available, even to some historians of the war. (p. 194)

Snow used Blackett's piece in *Scientific American* in a 'Postscript' written to justify his own reading of events.[11]

In 1961 there appeared the official history of the strategic air offensive, written by Sir Charles Webster and Noble Frankland. This included detailed documentary evidence on the Tizard–Cherwell affair. The official history had the great virtue of seeing the dispute not as a piece of stage drama, but as the outcome of complex historical, strategic and administrative forces. The history made it clear that Cherwell's memo had not initiated area bombing (see above). It was embraced in an atmosphere of inter-service rivalry and scepticism about the effectiveness of Bomber Command and mass bombing. Churchill himself wavered between offence and defence, between belief in a pugnacious bombing strategy that would destroy German morale and caution that this might drain support from other priorities (such as protection of the Fleet and Fighter Command). Webster and Frankland nevertheless judged that the bombing force remained 'the only weapon with which Britain could strike directly at Germany, and remind Russia of an ally in the West'.[12]

Webster and Frankland analysed closely Cherwell's celebrated minute of 30 March 1942. Churchill always asked for simple calculations, so Cherwell gave him simple calculations. Bombers produced over the ensuing 15 months would on average drop about 40 tons of bombs during a lifetime of 14 operational sorties. Cherwell calculated from a study of raids on Birmingham and Hull that one ton of bombs dropped on a built-up area demolished about 20–30 dwellings and dehoused 100–200 people. Hence 40 tons of British bombs would make 4,000–8,000 Germans homeless. Given a forecast output of 10,000 heavy bombers by mid-1943, if even half the total load of this force dropped on 58 German towns housing over 100,000 people, the great majority of their inhabitants (about one-third of the German population) would be turned out of house and home:

> Investigation seems to show that having one's house demolished is most damaging to morale. People seem to mind it more than having their friends or even relatives killed. At Hull signs of strain were evident, though only one-tenth of the houses were demolished. On the above figures we should be able to do ten times as much harm to each of the 58 principal German towns. There seems little doubt that this would break the spirit of the people. (quoted p. 332)

The Air Minister and the Chief of Air Staff accepted the Cherwell minute as strengthening their policy demands for more bomber production, even though, as the official historians dryly remarked, 'these policy decisions could not be justified by the probability calculations themselves because the calculations seemed probable only to those who, in any case, believed in the policy' (pp. 332–3).

Webster and Frankland printed a key memo of 20 April from Tizard to Air Minister Sir Archibald Sinclair and Cherwell, which questioned Cherwell's estimates on almost every front. Tizard computed from Ministry of Aircraft production figures that Bomber Command would receive only 7,000, not 10,000, aircraft by June 1943. He disputed that aircraft would complete an average 14 sorties, or be able to hit targets designated with the tonnage estimated. Night navigation was difficult under heavy opposition, and new radar aids would not be ready until April 1943. Even with Bomber Command expending all its resources on area bombing (neither wise nor possible), no more than 50,000 tons of bombs could be dropped (compared with Cherwell's 200,000–400,000). Spread over 58 towns this would be only three to four times as devastating as German bombing in Hull and Birmingham. Such a result 'would certainly be most damaging but would not be decisive unless in the intervening period Germany were either defeated in the field by Russia' or prevented from any further advance.[13] Tizard conceded in an accompanying letter to Sinclair:

> I should like to make it clear that I don't disagree fundamentally with the bombing policy, but I do think that it is only likely to be decisive if carried out on the scale envisaged by the Air Staff, which, if I remember rightly, contemplated a front line strength of 4,000 aircraft and a rate of reinforcement of 1,000 heavy bombers a month. We cannot achieve this this year, or even until next year, so if we try to carry out the policy with a much smaller force it will not be decisive, and we may lose the war in other ways ... I am very keen about the greater and better use of the Air Force against enemy ships of war.[14]

Cherwell was dismissive of Tizard's critique (although scarcely denying many of his own fallacies). He replied that he was only using rough estimates, and that, even if Tizard's projections proved to be realistic, the effects would still be 'catastrophic'.[15] The official history judged both sets of calculations to be 'extremely approximate'; there were many imponderables; and the dispute was best seen as 'really no more than an illustrative reflection, in somewhat more scientific terms, of the issues which divided the counsels of the Air and Naval Staffs'. Cherwell won the day, despite his flawed forecasts, because he had Churchill's ear, and because his plan seemed to fulfil Churchill's demand that 'there must be a design and theme for bringing the war to a victorious end in a reasonable period' (pp. 335–6).

Rather like scripture, the official history could be read in many ways. Both sides appealed to it. In his *Postscript* (1962), Snow printed large slabs of the official history's version of the Tizard–Lindemann exchange as self-evident vindication of his own reading of events.[16] However, strikingly at odds with his posture of candour, Snow failed signally to reproduce the key letter from Tizard to Sinclair (20 April 1942) which made it clear that he did not disagree fundamentally with the bombing policy. Snow's evasiveness on this letter has generally escaped attention.

Ronald Clark's biography of Tizard in 1965 used new materials, and presented Tizard as less preoccupied with war morality than with strategic priorities. Tizard was pictured as the detached, in some ways politically naïve, scientist seeking the most cost-effective war plan. However, beneath the mask, Tizard was horrified that highly trained bomber crews were being expended on targets that were, objectively speaking, not worth the cost. Blackett supplied Tizard with the statistics on exactly this point of loss of crews (yet strangely the issue was hardly raised during the confrontation with Cherwell). It appeared from Clark's account (and evidence from other sources now available) that Blackett and Bernal played a seminal role in causing Tizard to question area bombing. Blackett's continuing view was that blanket bombing of cities was not a decisive war weapon and that long-range bombers were better deployed on shipping protection.[17] Clark showed that in December 1941 Bernal, scientific adviser at the Ministry of Home Security, talked with Tizard about his department's ongoing survey of the raids on Hull and Birmingham. Tizard also discussed the survey with Solly Zuckerman, its co-author, who was working with Bernal at Home Security on the physics of bomb blasts. A few weeks later Tizard advised the Vice-Chief of Air Staff: 'The war is not going to be won by night bombing.'[18]

Blackett had also been keeping Tizard informed about his detailed statistical study of enemy bombing deaths, carried out for the Navy. Blackett later explained how at Operational Research in early 1942 he had calculated likely civilian casualties in Germany. To do so it was necessary to use data about German attacks on Britain in 1940–41 as a basis. These showed that, roughly, loss of industrial production, damage to buildings and civilian casualties were about proportional to the weight of explosives dropped. Instead of estimating casualties from first principles, Blackett used the quicker, and generally more reliable, method of employing known results of one bombing offensive where casualties were known to predict the effect of another offensive where the casualties were not known:

> In the ten months from August 1940, to June 1941, the total weight of bombs dropped on the United Kingdom by the enemy was about 50,000 tons, that is, at the average rate of 5,000 tons per month. The number of persons killed was 40,000, or an average of 4,000 per month, giving 0.8 killed per ton of bombs. Static detonation trials showed that the British G.P. bombs then in use were about half as effective as the German light-cased bombs of the same weight. Hence, these bombs should produce only 0.4 killed per ton, when dropped under the same conditions. Our bombers had further to go to their targets, the enemy towns are less easy to find, and are smaller, and no radio aids were then available. One must therefore assume that the fraction of bombs falling in built-up areas in Germany was not more than half of the fraction of German bombs falling on built-up areas in Great Britain. Hence, we should expect about 0.2 killed per ton of bombs dropped. During 1941 an average of about 2,000 tons of bombs were dropped on Germany per month. The expected number of killed is therefore 2,000 × 0.2 = 400 per month.[19]

Tizard wrote in his diary of 17 February 1942:

> Blackett came to see me with his note about civilian deaths in Germany. He makes out a good case for these not being much higher than our own losses of trained crews of bombers. Bernal left his summary of the results of German bombing of England. Taken as a whole the effect on production and morale has been surprisingly small.[20]

The next day Tizard provocatively urged upon the Minister of Aircraft Production ‘that a calm dispassionate review of the facts will reveal that the present policy of bombing Germany is wrong; that we must put our maximum effort first into destroying the enemy’s sea communications and preserving our own'. The only advantage he saw in bombing Germany was that it forced the enemy to lock up a good deal of effort in home defence:

> The heavy scale will only be justified and economic at the concluding scale of the war when (or if) we are fortunate enough to have defeated the enemy at sea and to have command of it. Until this time is ripe, everything is to be lost by concentrating on this bombing offensive.[21]

It is clear that by this time Blackett was regarded as a fly in the ointment by the Air Staff. Tizard had sent a memo of 20 February to Air Chief Marshal Freeman, lamenting the alarming losses suffered by Bomber Command (728 planes in 34 weeks), probably as many casualties in trained crew as the number of Germans killed. Freeman retorted, 'my first reaction is that you have been seeing too much of Professor Blackett'.[22] In April Cherwell's controversial dehousing minute was circulated for comment within Whitehall. Blackett submitted on 16 April a detailed criticism of this paper, objecting that Cherwell's estimate of what could be achieved was at least 600 per cent too high.[23] Tizard used this in his attempt to rebut Cherwell. However, Tizard was inclined to retreat at vital moments. In a conciliatory letter to Cherwell of 20 April (apparently accompanying his key memo of the same date), Tizard conceded that 'you certainly have more access to the right information than I have', and stated, 'I don't really disagree with you fundamentally, but only as a matter of timing'. Clark described this letter as curious, 'a tribute to Tizard's political innocence as well as his integrity'.[24]

Finally, a brief word about the Hull–Birmingham bombing survey.[25] Solly Zuckerman suggested the survey to Cherwell during conversation in Christ Church common room in August 1941, when the 'Prof' was much concerned about hostile reaction to the bombing offensive.[26] With Cherwell's backing the inquiry was conducted by the Ministry of Home Security's team at Princes Risborough laboratory, headed by Bernal and Zuckerman. As Bernal later recalled, it was one of the most elaborate studies ever undertaken of large cities under bombing. They had two teams of about 40 workers each, which investigated everything in great detail down to 'the number of pints drunk and aspirins bought in the chemists'.[27] The report was not completed until 8 April 1942, a week after Cherwell's celebrated minute. However, Zuckerman recalled that he kept feeding the 'Prof' with information as it emerged, and we have seen that Tizard was similarly kept abreast by Bernal and Zuckerman. In his autobiography in 1978, Zuckerman printed, apparently for the first time, the secret report's conclusions (astonishingly the full report is restricted until the year 2020, so has been denied to historians). 'In neither town', the report concluded,

> was there any evidence of panic resulting either from a series of raids or from a single raid ... There is no evidence of breakdown of morale for the intensities of the raids experienced by Hull or Birmingham (Maximum intensity of bombing 40 tons per square mile).[28]

Cherwell in his minute spoke of 'signs of strain' at Hull and predicted that ten times this degree of bombing in Germany would break the spirit of the people. As Zuckerman perceptively noted in his autobiography, although the report was the basis of Cherwell's vital minute, it had never been reproduced in the writings over the controversy:

> What I find curious is that no-one who has ever written about the exchanges between Cherwell, Tizard and Blackett, not even Webster and Frankland, has noted that although the Prof used the results of our study to claim that bomber raids of the intensity that Hull and Birmingham had experienced were 'most damaging to morale', this was the very reverse of what we had stated.[29]

It seems then that radical science polemic failed signally to exploit compelling evidence that would have exposed Cherwell to charges of duplicity over his use of the Birmingham–Hull bombing survey. This evidence was passed on by Bernal and Zuckerman to Tizard at a vital stage in the area bombing debate of 1942, but Tizard lacked killer instinct and failed to use it. Later, in 1961, a number of factors inhibited Bernal from opening up a full-scale assault on Cherwell, which would certainly have utilised the Hull–Birmingham report. These factors included Zuckerman's good-mannered reluctance to attack Cherwell, his growing political estrangement from Bernal (who was too doctrinaire in the post-war period for Zuckerman's liking), and the historical happenstance that Bernal had not kept full documentation of events in 1942.

In 1961, on his return from a visit to the Soviet Union, Bernal wrote a long letter to Snow, praising Snow's lecture and explaining his own involvement in events. (The two knew each other well, and Snow had used Bernal as the model for the brilliant, womanising crystallographer Constantine in his first novel, *The Search*, in 1934.) Bernal detailed the history of the bombing survey and its aftermath:

> Cherwell very naturally did not like this report but he found his way to twisting it to his purpose by saying that as the result showed that the degree of bombing produced by the Germans had had a negligible effect on production, this proved that a much heavier bombing was bound to have enormous effect if used on German cities! This breathtaking logic was absolutely characteristic of the man.

Bernal also remarked that both he and Blackett felt that Cherwell's worst fault 'was his deliberate and I think dishonest neglect of what we came to call the operational factor': the ratio between what happens in the field and what is deduced from trials carried out under the best possible conditions.[30] Bernal drafted a letter to the *Times*, a more restrained version of his letter to Snow.[31] Bernal apparently suggested that he and Zuckerman sign the letter. Zuckerman pointed to flaws and gaps in Bernal's account (he was much more exact than Bernal in keeping records) and felt that Bernal was being unfair to Cherwell.[32] He later recalled:

> My own view was that it was inappropriate for us to participate in a public argument about two men whom we had both known, particularly as the draft letter was heavily slanted against the Prof. Having been reminded of the record, Bernal then agreed that no letter should be sent.[33]

Thus the damaging evidence about Cherwell's misuse of the Hull–Birmingham survey did not surface in 1961. Zuckerman commented to Bernal at the time:

> I'm amused at the partial truths that are emerging about the 1942 change in bombing policy. My files are complete – and I have a fear that both Charles Snow and Patrick Blackett are jumping much further than the facts at their disposal justify.[34]

Historiographically, we may conclude, it was Blackett who set the basic scenario of the Tizard–Cherwell feud, which was then mythologised by Snow. Blackett, as an operations pioneer, wrote about the dispute in essentially operational terms, although he had an underlying moral objection to the ruthlessness of modern total war. As he read it, in the aftermath of the blitz, when the debate was fuelled by motives of *realpolitik* and vengeance, the sober scientific judgement of Tizard lost out to Cherwell's obsessed policy of razing Germany. Blackett and most radical scientists firmly believed that area bombing had been exposed as a tragic and expensive failure. Blackett noted cynically that the US Strategic Bombing Survey had documented this, but had been virtually suppressed in post-war Britain. Beneath his cool appraisals, Blackett felt a deep indignation mixed with a sense of guilt that he had not done more:

> If the Allied air effort had been used more intelligently, if more aircraft had been supplied for the Battle of the Atlantic and to support the land fighting in Africa and later in France, if the bombing of Germany had been carried out with the attrition of the enemy defences in mind rather than the razing of cities to the ground, I believe the war could have been won half a year or even a year earlier. The only major campaign in modern history in which the traditional military doctrine of waging war against the enemy's armed forces was abandoned for a planned attack on its civilian life was a disastrous flop. I confess to a haunting sense of failure, and I am sure that Tizard felt the same way. If we had only been more persuasive and had forced people to believe our simple arithmetic, if we had fought officialdom more cleverly and lobbied ministers more vigorously, might we not have changed this decision?[35]

It is merely hypothetical whether more pugnacious politicking by the Tizard camp would have won the day, or whether their alternative operational strategies would have shortened the war. What can be said is that the key historiographical debate of 1961 was supercharged by emotions emanating from 1942, as it was also conditioned by the growing impact of the nuclear debate. The case against area bombing became for Blackett, and others, the case against nuclear strategy.

NOTES

1. This chapter is a shortened and revised version of my article 'Science and War: Radical Scientists and the Tizard–Cherwell Area Bombing Debate in Britain',

War & Society, 12 (1994), pp. 69–101. I am grateful to the editors of this journal for permitting me to use this material.

2. P.M.S. Blackett, 'C.P. Snow's Account of the Role of Two Scientists in Government', *Scientific American*, 204 (1961), p. 192. The context presented here is based upon standard authorities, including the official history: Sir Charles Webster and Noble Frankland, *The Strategic Air Offensive Against Germany*, Vol. 1: *Preparation* (London: HMSO, 1961); also Max Hastings, *Bomber Command* (London: Pan, 1979) and R.J. Overy, *The Air War 1939–1945* (London: Europa, 1980).
3. Gary Werskey, *The Visible College: A Collective Biography of British Scientists and Socialists of the 1930s* (London: Allen Lane, 1978; repr. London: Free Association Books, 1988), p. 216 and *passim*. Blackett was involved in the Association of Scientific Workers (closely linked with the Cambridge Scientists' Anti-War Group). The Association was dominated by Marxists (such as Bernal and Levy) after W.A. Wooster became General Secretary in 1935 (p. 235).
4. P.M.S. Blackett, 'Tizard and the Science of War', *Nature*, 185 (5 March 1960), p. 652 (Tizard Memorial Lecture). Subsequent page numbers in the text refer to this source.
5. Cherwell to Churchill, 30 March 1942. The whole text is printed in Webster and Frankland, *Strategic Air Offensive*, pp. 331–2. The minute was circulated by the Prime Minister to the Defence Committee on 9 April and was thus not strictly (as Blackett described it) a Cabinet paper emanating from Cherwell's Paymaster-General's office in April. More on all this in the text.
6. C.P. Snow, 'The Irregular Right', *Nation*, 182 (24 March 1956), p. 238.
7. C.P. Snow, *Science and Government* (London: Oxford University Press, 1961), pp. 6, 11, 67.
8. For example, Norman Longmate in 1983 contrasted Tizard, 'the good-natured, rational, balanced, extrovert Englishman', with the German-descended Cherwell, the intense, unscrupulous foreigner, 'a monstrous snob … his chief pleasure lay in ruthlessly pursuing vendettas … The curious fascination which this repellent, inhibited, un-clubbable, un-English figure exerted upon Churchill has often been remarked upon': *The Bombers: The RAF Offensive against Germany* (London: Hutchinson, 1983), p. 130 and generally Chapter 3. Cherwell's friends vigorously denied such characterisations.
9. For a fuller account of the reception to Snow, see Crook, 'Science and War', pp. 76–81.
10. Blackett, 'C.P. Snow's Account' (1961), p. 191.
11. C.P. Snow, *A Postscript to Science and Government* (Cambridge, MA: Harvard University Press, 1962).
12. Webster and Frankland, *Strategic Air Offensive*, p. 187, and generally pp. 331–6.
13. Memo from Tizard to Sir Archibald Sinclair and Lord Cherwell, 20 April 1942, quoted in Webster and Frankland, *Strategic Air Offensive*, pp. 333–4.
14. Letter from Tizard to Sinclair, 20 April 1942, quoted in Webster and Frankland, *Strategic Air Offensive*, pp. 334–5 (not to be confused with the memo of the same date to Sinclair and Cherwell).
15. Cherwell to Tizard, 22 April 1942, quoted in Webster and Frankland, *Strategic Air Offensive*, p. 334.
16. Snow, *Postscript*, pp. 24–7. Snow declared: 'The facts are so eloquent that, if I had had the Lindemann and Tizard papers before me, I should just have printed them without comment' (p. 24).
17. For example, P.M.S. Blackett, CAOR, to D. of P., 10 November 1942, Blackett Papers (Royal Society), D70, cited in Malcolm Llewellyn-Jones's Chapter 9 (note 11) of this volume.
18. Tizard to Sir Wilfred Freeman, 24 December 1941, cited in Ronald W. Clark, *Tizard* (London: Methuen, 1965), p. 308. Also Solly Zuckerman, *From Apes to*

Warlords: The Autobiography (1904–1946) of Solly Zuckerman (London: Hamilton, 1978), p. 145. Blackett discussed briefly his role in these events in his 'Recollections of Problems Studied, 1940–45', *Brassey's Annual* (1953), repr., Blackett, *Studies of War: Nuclear and Conventional* (Edinburgh and London: Oliver & Boyd, 1962), pp. 223–5.

19. P.M.S. Blackett, 'Operational Research', *Advancement of Science*, 5 (1948), pp. 37–8 (Appendix C, Document II, 'Examples from Bombing Offensive'). The article is reprinted in Blackett, *Studies of War*, pp. 169–98 (Appendix C, pp. 195–7).
20. Tizard diary entry, 17 February 1942, cited in Clark, *Tizard*, p. 309.
21. Tizard to Minister of Aircraft Production, 18 February 1942, cited in Clark, *Tizard,* p. 309. Shortly afterwards, Tizard admitted to the minister that he had been 'perhaps too provocative' and that 'the difference of opinion is not so much one of object but one of timing' (ibid., p. 309).
22. Cited Clark, *Tizard*, p. 310.
23. Ibid., p. 311.
24. Tizard to Cherwell, 20 April 1942, cited in Clark, *Tizard*, p. 312 (same page for Clark's comment).
25. Crook, 'Science and War', pp. 81–9. The interested reader is referred to this article for full documentation and debate about what follows.
26. Zuckerman, *Apes to Warlords*, p. 140 and pp. 139–48 for the bombing survey and report. Zuckerman and Cherwell were fellows of Christ Church, Cambridge, and Zuckerman respected Cherwell. Zuckerman, a pioneer endocrinologist, was a moderate leftist during the 1930s. He, Blackett and Bernal were members of the 'Tots and Quots', a 'liberal-left' London dining club which Zuckerman had founded in 1930 (pp. 89–90, 109ff.).
27. J.D. Bernal to C.P. Snow, 11 April 1961, Add. 8287/87/J217, Bernal Papers, Cambridge University Library.
28. 'Quantitative Study of Total Effects of Air Raids (Hull and Birmingham Survey)', Ministry of Home Security and Experiments Department, 2770, 8 April 1942, published as an appendix in Zuckerman, *Apes to Warlords* (quotes pp. 143, 405).
29. Zuckerman, *Apes to Warlords*, pp. 145–6.
30. Bernal to Snow, 11 April 1961, Add. 8287/87/J217, Bernal Papers, Cambridge University Library.
31. Bernal to *Times* (draft), 27 April 1961, Add. 8287/87/J217, Bernal Papers, Cambridge University Library.
32. Zuckerman to Bernal, 30 April 1961, 1 May 1961, Add. 8287/88/J267, Bernal Papers, Cambridge University Library.
33. Zuckerman, *Apes to Warlords*, p. 147. Zuckerman criticised Snow's account, which 'seems to be based on no more than hearsay (he was certainly not involved in the argument), and his pictures of Cherwell and Tizard, with both of whom I worked closely, seem hardly real to me. I cannot see the Prof as some kind of Second World War Dr. Strangelove' (p. 145).
34. Zuckerman to Bernal, 17 April 1961, Add. 8287/88/J267, Bernal Papers, Cambridge University Library. Bernal's response is not recorded, but we may guess it from an article he wrote on the dispute for the communist *Daily Worker*, 29 April 1961, p. 2. In it he made a savage attack upon Cherwell, 'a single ultra-reactionary' controlling scientific policy, and area bombing, always 'the doctrine of those who hate and despise the common people', and now (1961) it 'survives in an infinitely more horrible and militarily futile form in the era of the atom bomb'. Bernal condemned the bombing strategy as a monstrous diversion of effort, badly needed elsewhere, and dictated by an objective 'of fighting the third world war against the Soviet Union before the second against Germany was well won'. However, bafflingly, Bernal did not mention even here Cherwell's 'twisting' of the Hull–Birmingham report. It seemed almost to have become taboo.
35. Blackett, 'C.P. Snow's Account', p. 194.

11

The Father of Operational Research

Richard Ormerod

A major event in the calendar of the UK Operational Research Society is the annual Blackett Lecture given by a leading public figure. The text of the lecture is subsequently published in the *Journal of the Operational Research Society*. Blackett's role in setting up the society and initiating the journal (originally called the *Operational Research Quarterly*) is thus remembered and he is celebrated as the founding father of operational research (OR). Blackett's activities in seeding new OR groups in Britain's war machine during the Second World War have been amply recorded.[1] In the only paper in the first issue of the first volume of the *Operational Research Quarterly*, Blackett himself says: 'The main outlines of the growth of operational research in the armed services during the second world war have been described in numerous articles and books and are certainly sufficiently well known not to need repetition here.' He goes on to suggest that others knew more than he did about 'the actual practical results attained since the war by application of these methods to the great task of increasing the efficiency of our social system and the well-being of our population'. He concludes: 'Leaving aside, therefore, both its history and its present achievements, I wish to touch on some points relating to its methodology and its organisation.'[2] In this chapter, taking the lead from Blackett himself, I will pass over his wartime achievements and concentrate on the evolution and development of the profession and discipline that arose out of his efforts and those of other pioneers of the time. Like Blackett, I will touch on some points relating to OR's methodology and organisation. Unlike Blackett, I will also comment on some of the practical results.

In his paper Blackett poses three questions about operational research. Is it new? If so, in what way? Is it scientific? He addresses the last question first, concluding that the answer must be yes because most definitions of OR include some such phrase as 'the application of the scientific method'. Reflecting on what is meant by 'scientific method', he continues as follows:

> A broad but eminently reasonable view is that scientific method consists of a systematic method of learning by experience (Jeffreys). In more detail, scientific method may be defined as that combination of observation, experiment and reasoning (both deductive and inductive) which scientists are in the habit of using in their investigations (Yates).[3]

In answer to his first two questions Blackett points out that other statistical, economical and social scientific analysis applies the scientific method to the complex data of human society. Despite this, in his view the difference is that the other subjects were aimed at political action to influence policy whereas OR's appreciable degree of novelty lies

> in the level at which work is done, in the comparative freedom of the investigators to seek out their own problems, and in the direct relation of the work to the possibilities of executive action. Dr. Kittel's well-known definition of operational research as 'a scientific method for providing executives with a quantitative basis for decisions,' expressed this clearly, or, as another writer has put it, operational research is social science done in collaboration with and on behalf of executives.[4]

For the next 20 to 30 years Blackett's view that OR is a scientific activity conducted for executives in relative freedom would be typical of the views held by most in the UK OR fraternity. However, later, these views became the subject of debate and controversy.

Blackett's choice of subject for the first paper in the new journal is not surprising: the question of what it is that defines a discipline or profession is crucial at its birth. Immediately after the war the government set up the Committee on Industrial Productivity (CIP), which produced a draft report, *The Principles and Practices of Operational Research.* This strongly advocated the application of OR in a wide set of peacetime settings.[5] However, a subsequent covering note to a shortened redraft produced by the Treasury's Economic Information Unit included the comment:

> the more we read the literature which has been circulated about it, the closer we come to the conclusion that operational research is merely a term covering a whole range of sensible activity (already known, studied and applied under other names), arbitrarily, and to no purpose, differentiated from other sensible activity.[6]

These issues are seldom satisfactorily resolved at birth and the question of definition remains important later in the life of the profession or discipline as debates continue about the domain of activities, the relationship with neighbouring disciplines and the rules for membership. Much is, of course, simply determined by what those people who choose to operate under the banner of OR do in practice. It also depends on how the actual and potential clients of the services perceive the tasks that can best be given to those who operate under the banner of OR. The military successes of OR led in the UK to enthusiasm for the application of OR to civil problems after the war. Initial efforts to establish OR in the government sphere were faltering[7] but the groups established in the newly nationalised coal industry[8] and the steel industry[9] flourished. Early studies included the use of statistical techniques, queuing theory, inventory models and simulation (initially by hand, later on the computer). Of course, many of the problems could be satisfactorily resolved without sophisticated techniques at all, the solution being apparent once the situation had been appraised and the data gathered. Simulation stands out as the technique that proved most valuable in diverse industrial situations. However, most commentators agreed that it was not the techniques that defined OR but its conduct by scientists who applied the scientific method.

During the formative years much excitement was generated by two developments. First, efficient algorithms were developed in the US for the solution of linear programmes. As computer power grew it also became possible to tackle integer, quadratic and goal programming. Collectively these mathematical programming techniques could be used to tackle a wide variety of problems including resource allocation, transportation and production scheduling. The international oil companies in particular, who at that time managed their operations as planned activities from wellhead to petrol pump, used the new techniques extensively. Second, the development of critical path analysis and its use on the US Polaris construction project led to its obligatory application for large, governmental construction projects on both sides of the Atlantic.

OR was at its height in the 1960s with industrial OR groups flourishing, interest in the commercial and service sectors growing, take-up in the UK civil departments of government progressing gradually, and attempts to apply the techniques to governmental planning and budgeting being energetically pursued. Various surveys track the take-up of OR,[10] which, despite difficulties of comparison,[11] demonstrated the very widespread utilisation of OR in the UK. OR had thus been established as an activity of practical value.

Mercer identified 766 OR groups (defined by the existence of members of the OR Society), 87 per cent of which contained three or fewer people. By then some professional trappings had been established in the form of a society with an annual conference and a journal. Blackett was one of the four founding members of the Operational Research Club in 1948, which was later renamed the Operational Research Society. This was the first OR society in the world. The Operations Research Society of America followed in 1952. As noted above, Blackett was the first author to publish a paper in the *Operational Research Quarterly*, which was the first OR journal in the world to be published. The first issue was 15 pages long and Blackett's paper was less than four pages of what we today call A5 paper. I particularly like the first sentence of the Editorial Notes: 'To justify burdening the scientific world with yet another journal, two conditions must be rigorously fulfilled: undoubted utility and the utmost brevity.' Academic life today would be very different if these standards had been upheld. The first issues could be obtained for three shillings a copy or through an annual subscription of ten shillings (post-free). By the 1960s both the society and the journal had become established and respected world-wide. Despite this, the society did not introduce a mechanism to restrict entry or maintain professional standards: young OR workers could not obtain a professional qualification in OR. The society remained essentially an open club of people who wanted to be associated together. Whether or not this was the right strategy to adopt, it had a profound effect on the nature of the society, its activities and its membership.

In the 1960s OR started to be established in university engineering, economics and business administration departments. Later it would become established in mathematics and management departments and business schools. The first dedicated chair in OR was established at Lancaster University in 1964. OR was thus becoming established as an academic discipline as well as a professional activity. However, university training was not a prerequisite for membership of the OR Society nor for practising OR.

In the 1960s OR held out the hope that a scientific approach would bring a more professional, rigorous approach to planning and other managerial problems. Many companies were at this time adopting divisionalised structures to gain better control of increasingly complex national and international operations. OR was part of the technocratic infrastructure used to apply rationality and control. During the 1970s there was evidence that the management agenda was moving on and confidence that OR was the answer to management problems was starting to wane. For instance, a declining number of articles in the *Harvard Business Review* featured OR. This was, in part, a natural consequence of the absorption of the new ideas by management, in part because OR was being challenged by other management disciplines such as marketing, strategy and organisational behaviour, and, in the UK at least, in part because management itself was starting to become more professional, requiring less support. It may also have been the case that OR approaches were better fitted to resource allocation and control than to the more entrepreneurial approach demanded by the rapidly developing consumers markets. Externally, the scientific approach to management, within which OR was positioned, came under attack. Internally, concern started to be expressed about the direction OR was taking.

There were a number of dimensions to this concern. At a time when the nature and scope of science itself was being hotly debated, OR's status as a scientific discipline that aided management decision-making was questioned. OR's emphasis on quantitative analysis was said to be ill suited to many managerial problems where qualitative aspects were important. There was a danger of concentrating on that which could be measured rather than on that which was important;

of giving weight to objective, numerical data rather than subjective, qualitative factors; of concentrating on the parts rather than the whole. This unease was ironically given impetus by the great success of the mathematical programming and other optimising techniques. These techniques worked on delimited areas of interest, required reliable information and usually assumed a single objective such as profit maximisation. The computer-derived 'optimum' with its unchallengeable logic offended those who felt that, in the process of formulating the problem in such a way that the computer could perform its trick, many of the important dimensions were left out or marginalised.

The success of the optimising techniques, which organisations did find useful, and which were eminently teachable, led to a greater emphasis being placed on them. This emphasis was fed by the new Master's courses in management science and OR at universities. These courses were increasingly becoming the main source of recruitment for industrial, commercial and governmental OR groups. As the greater knowledge of, and reliance on, OR techniques moved into practice, concern mounted that the craft of investigation and advice was giving way to the instrumental provision of a technical service. A social as well as a functional point was at issue here.

In the UK, OR had become established in a peculiarly British way which reflects the use of graduates in the civil service. Oxford and Cambridge had over the years geared themselves to supply the upper echelons of the British Establishment in general, and the civil service in particular. As Elliot Krause, an American sociologist, relates:

> Civil servants are recruited for general work, on the assumption that brilliant amateurs, with first-class degrees from Oxford and Cambridge, can learn any task: such generalists are preferred to those with scientific and technical backgrounds, whose expertise might be limited by their specialities. This principle of amateurism – that superior men of general ability are preferable to technicians – and the belief that all those with science and social science backgrounds *are* technicians – still prevails; since the 1970's there have been many more appointments for midlevel science and technical graduates, but not in the administrative class.[12]

There is, of course, plenty of evidence that in times of stress, such as wartime, the 'brilliant amateurs' were clever enough to recognise the value of science and technology as the stories of, for instance, R.V. Jones, Zuckerman and Blackett himself attest. The struggle to be heard was, however, formidable.

OR groups in nationalised industries provided a career route for Oxford and Cambridge mathematics and science graduates who, despite their technical background, established themselves as general providers of advice to senior executives, much as their classics, humanities and history colleagues in the civil service provided advice to ministers. OR workers were able to see themselves as an elite, despite, as Krause puts it, 'the overwhelming cultural bias of the British upper class, and thus of British institutions generally, against technical expertise, the very possession of which signifies social unacceptability'.[13] Any emphasis on technique thus threatened to reduce the status to which OR workers aspired and reduce their standing with their client, the senior executives.

Closely linked to the concern about the dominance of techniques was the worry that OR was becoming increasingly concerned with low-level operational and planning issues rather than those with strategic and policy implications. Although it was expressed as a functional concern that best use was not being made of OR's potential, the underlying issue was the lack of influence on and access to the corridors of power. Paradoxically, another stream of criticism was that OR had become the unquestioning servant of powerful interests in large organisations and was failing to provide similar support for the weak who had no access to expensive resources.

In retrospect, a further criticism of OR is that it failed to initiate, or at least strongly associate itself with, some of the important managerial developments that it might have been expected to champion. Notions of quality are now embedded in most companies, but OR largely ignored the quality movement. Perhaps ideas such as 'quality is free' sat uneasily with OR's micro-economic notion of trade-off of substitutes. Nor did OR's acknowledged expertise in the area of inventory management lead it to run with concepts such as Kanban, just-in-time and SMED (single minute exchange of dies) set-up reduction programmes. Something was amiss. One explanation is that the intellectual calibre of the peacetime activists did not match those in the war, though this is unlikely as OR personnel during the war were not uniformly of high quality nor always put to good use.[14] There are also plenty of examples of excellent intellects being attracted to OR after the war. My preferred explanation is that OR workers, embedded in internal OR groups, were inward-looking, the concern being organisational survival rather than the entrepreneurial activity of developing concepts for general application, across companies and industries. This highlights a weakness in the term ‘operational research’, a term which may lead one to expect the research to give generally applicable results. However, the research referred to is detailed, grounded research, carried out to solve a local problem in a particular context. OR was not so much concerned with scientifically building a body of generally applicable knowledge as with the engineering of change suited to local circumstances. Particular, local solutions were therefore sought, and if they satisfied the sponsoring managers that was success enough. Perhaps organisational constraints and assumptions were too easily accepted. OR practice was also inward- looking in the sense that it was slow to draw on other disciplines. There are some honourable exceptions to this in the use of social science by the pioneers of soft OR (see below) but the point stands. For instance, ideas in economics have been mainly taken up and made practical by strategists, and those in psychology and sociology by organisational behaviourists. Perhaps there has simply been too much intellectually demanding material for the limited population of mainly mathematicians, scientists and engineers to grasp and make practical (for this reason, if for no other, OR activists should value the social scientists, economists and those from other disciplines in their midst). Whatever the explanation, the failure of OR to grasp and champion some of the most successful ideas on its own patch is disappointing.

There were some positive results emanating from all the talk of crisis and the agonising about what OR is or ought to be in the UK. Some initiatives were set away on OR in underdeveloped countries and OR in communities. In addition, a number of approaches that were rooted in social as opposed to natural science were identified as representing a new school of thought now usually referred to as ‘soft OR’. The soft OR methods are designed to help groups of people work together on unstructured, ‘messy’ problems where the scope, dimensions and objectives of the issue need to be determined. This was a useful response to telling criticism. However, it had two effects.

First, OR is now less securely located within science. This may not in practice matter as science has become a less secure place to be intellectually located. Moreover, if the purpose of a science is to build a generally applicable body of knowledge, I am also not convinced that OR ever was a science. Rather it is a professional activity that undertook research into particular, local situations to seek locally applicable understanding and improvements. Second, a wider gap has been opened up with the US. The US has not gone down this particular avenue.

Just as the forward momentum of OR was beginning to falter, it was given a new lease of life by the introduction of the personal computer (PC). PCs proved a cheap, flexible and portable tool on which to test algorithms, build models and interact with the client. They reduced the OR groups' dependence on IT support and they provided an opportunity to help client departments make use of their new purchases. More importantly, OR workers suddenly became much more productive. Despite all the concerns, OR activity levels in the UK continued unabated throughout the 1970s and well into the 1980s.

The UK OR Society recently failed to get a sufficient number of its members to vote in favour of obtaining professional status for its members. In any case, it is difficult to see the society as ever being more than a weak professional grouping. In fact, those professional groupings that have traditionally been relatively strong in the UK (for instance, the medical profession) are today increasingly dominated by state and capital, as has long been the case for teachers (who mainly work in state institutions) and engineers (who mainly work in companies owned by shareholders). The only professional groupings substantially to advance their power and interests in recent years have been the accountants and management consultants. It is of more than a little interest that while internal OR groups within industrial and commercial firms have declined over the past ten years, OR groups within management consultancy firms have been rapidly increasing.[15] The rapidly growing management consultancies, operating on a fee-for-service basis, remain free of state and capital domination (in other words, the consultancies are generally owned and run by the consultants themselves, who share the profits). Although the Institute of Management Consultants (IMC) is still establishing its position, it already offers the Certified Management Consultant qualification for individuals and a Certified

Practice scheme for firms. It seems possible that in time most OR practitioners will gravitate towards this and other professional bodies that offer professional status. The OR Society seems destined to become a club of individuals who enjoy the association with the subject's history, the academic discipline and other OR-orientated practitioners. It is possible to imagine that the OR Society could in time be absorbed, becoming a chapter within the IMC. However, this development seems likely to be successfully resisted by those who would see this outcome as surrender to a more overtly capital-serving body, the diminution of its role as an academic society, and a loss of something worthwhile in both historical and human terms. The continued independence is likely to be reinforced by the continuation of the much larger US profession and other OR societies around the world.

The activities of OR practitioners today can be grouped under three headings: (i) developing and deploying algorithms embedded in information systems, (ii) helping clients in organisational settings address issues and seek improvements, and (iii) contributing to the debate about the purpose and direction of public institutions and policies. I refer to these three areas of activities as smart bits, helpful ways and things that matter:[16]

- *Smart bits.* With information technology enabling the capture, production and manipulation of data in ever-increasing quantities, the need for algorithms and logical routines has never been greater. OR algorithms are used to forecast demand, order stock, schedule production, control maintenance, allocate resources, maximise revenue, design networks and assess risks in organisations ranging from supermarkets to banks and from manufacturing to telecommunications.
- *Helpful ways.* In many instances OR consultants are less concerned with providing technical expertise on appropriate algorithms than simply helping to address the problem as presented by the client by whatever means are appropriate. This could involve a debate about means and ends, organised as a series of structured workshops bringing together various stakeholders. It may involve an assessment of the feasibility, costs and benefits, and risks of a research programme, or a major investment, or a change in policy. It could involve the specification and design of a decision support or planning system

for a senior executive, or an air traffic controller or a post office teller.

- *Things that matter.* Every so often an OR approach will contribute to a public issue. This may be in the form of an Audit Commission report on some aspect of the NHS, an analysis of AIDS-related policies, a report on the effect of the electricity pool, or an evaluation of the relative performance of schools. Very often academics are best placed to contribute to such issues.

I would classify most of the frequently quoted Second World War examples as helpful ways: there were no sophisticated algorithms and no computer systems to embed them in. I suspect that the challenge of the investigations lay in the craft skills of observation, conceptualisation and data gathering, and the organisational skills of gaining access to the problem and earning the confidence of the decision-makers. I imagine that the mathematics of the solution was well within the capabilities of the scientists employed. It could be argued that the subjects addressed were things that matter, and, in a sense, that was certainly the case. However, in the first instance, I would classify most of the activity as helpful ways since the investigators were generally working to find technical solutions to defined problems rather than working on the implications at the policy level. In other words, they were engaged with means rather than ends. These generalisations are based on a weak and distant understanding of wartime OR and I am applying distinctions which I believe are relevant today, but may not have been then.

On reading accounts of wartime exploits I am struck by the close linkage between technology and operational capability on the one hand and military strategy on the other. This can, of course, be true of civil enterprises as well. Thus, less intrusive surgery reduces the requirement for hospital beds, leading to the need to review the balance of investments in equipment, staff and hospital facilities. OR may be involved in exploring the deployment of the new technology and its consequences or it may sometimes be providing the new technology itself. An example of the latter, which originated in the airline industry, is referred to as yield management. Airlines have developed decision-making aids with embedded algorithms to enable them to determine at any point of time before take-off whether to sell a seat to a customer on a particular tariff. The capability provided has enabled airlines to grow the market for low-cost seats for the general public and as a consequence provide a frequent service for business customers prepared to pay higher prices. In effect, the business traveller cross-subsidises the intrepid traveller in order to gain the convenience of a readily available, frequent service. All parties gain from the arrangement. The OR in the decision support system ensures that, as each request for a seat purchase is dealt with, the right balance is struck between filling the plane up with the low-tariff customers who are prepared to book early, and maintaining some seats for late-booking, high-tariff business travellers. Without the ability to work out the consequences of accepting a booking or not in real-time, the airlines could not ensure that they fill their seats, maximise their revenues and provide an attractive service to different sets of customers. Yield management is now being applied to hotel bookings, car hire and an ever-wider set of circumstances.

Today there are 28 countries in the European Federation of OR Societies (EURO) and 45 in the International Federation (IFORS). Membership of the UK Society is stable. Nevertheless, in 1988 the American sociologist Abbott cited OR as a profession in regression, a state of decline which he says the evidence shows is irreversible.[17] The reality is a little more complex and a little less dramatic. The model of OR as an activity conducted by internal OR groups with a good deal of choice as to which issue to tackle, essentially Blackett's model, is on the way out. A new model of highly specific investigations and developments conducted by external specialist firms and management consultancies is alive and flourishing. In time, the supply side will sort itself out with the specialist companies dominating the provision of the smart bits, external consultancies dominating the provision of helpful ways, and academics dominating the contribution of OR to things that matter. This is not an unequivocally happy outcome. There was, and still is, great merit in the sort of grounded, detailed investigation that is the hallmark of good traditional OR. It has been argued that the Japanese were successful in developing lean production because they were atheoretical, lacked sociological awareness and based their thinking on a very detailed knowledge of how things work. Thus the technically efficient, goal-oriented, socially aware OR consultants of tomorrow may get things done and satisfy their clients but they may miss the potential implications or the valuable insight as they rush to the next challenge. Only time will tell. I am confident, however, that the more relaxed, reflective times are behind us and the pressures that have resulted in the decline of internal OR groups will continue. I should hasten to add that I have seen no evidence of a decline in military and governmental OR.

Blackett's child is alive and well. In some sense it has reached and passed its maturity. This should be no surprise 50 years on. The OR profession was for a time the centre of managerial attention. It had its golden era. It is now a small professional grouping that has found its niche. Few people realise that OR lies behind many everyday events, providing the algorithms for airline reservation systems, checking the creditworthiness of loan applicants and calculating the replenishment quantities required by supermarkets. Despite its important role in today's society, OR lacks pomposity, it includes many, diverse interests and has demonstrated a certain capacity for survival. We would all wish as much for our own children.

NOTES

1. See, for instance, J.F. McCloskey, 'The Beginnings of Operational Research 1934–1941', *Operations Research*, 35 (1987), pp. 143–52; J.F. McCloskey, 'British Operational Research in World War II', *Operations Research*, 35 (1987), pp. 453–70; M. Kirby and R. Capey, 'The Origins and Diffusion of Operational Research in the UK', *Journal of the Operational Research Society*, 49 (1998), pp. 307–26; and the references contained in the above articles.
2. P.M.S. Blackett, 'Operational Research', *Operational Research Quarterly*, 1 (1950), pp. 3–6.
3. Ibid.
4. Ibid.
5. See Kirby and Capey, 'Origins and Diffusion of Operational Research'.
6. Quoted in Kirby and Capey, 'Origins and Diffusion of Operational Research'.
7. See J. Rosenhead, 'Operational Research at the Crossroads: Cecil Gordan and the Development of Post-War OR', *Journal of the Operational Research Society*, 40 (1989), pp. 3–28.
8. See R.C. Tomlinson, *OR Comes of Age* (London: Tavistock, 1971).
9. See R.H. Colcutt, *The First Twenty Years of Operational Research* (Old Woking: Unwin, 1965); H.G. Jones, 'Early OR in the Steel Company of Wales', *Journal of the Operational Research Society*, 43 (1992), pp. 563–7.
10. C.F. Goodeve and G.R. Ridley, 'A Survey of OR in Great Britain', *Operational Research Quarterly*, 4 (1953), pp. 21–4; B.H.P. Rivett and R.L. Ackoff, *A Manager's Guide to Operational Research* (Chichester: Wiley, 1963); A. Mercer, 'The Membership of the Operational Research Society', *Operational Research Quarterly*, 19 (1968), pp. 371–6.
11. See Kirby and Capey, 'Origins and Diffusion of Operational Research'.
12. E.A. Krause, *Death of the Guilds: Professions, States, and the Advance of Capitalism, 1930 to the Present* (New Haven, CT: Yale University Press, 1996).
13. Krause, *Death of the Guilds.*

14. See N. Lawrie, unpublished paper (1996), presented at the History of OR stream of the 1996 UK Annual OR Conference, which quotes from Zuckerman's biography.
15. See R.J. Ormerod, 'Beyond Internal OR Groups', *Journal of the Operational Research Society*, 49 (1998), pp. 420–9.
16. See R.J. Ormerod, 'The Role of OR in Shaping the Future: Smart Bits, Helpful Ways and Things That Matter', *Journal of the Operational Research Society*, 48 (1997), pp. 1045–56.
17. See A. Abbott, *The System of Professions: An Essay on the Division of Expert Labour* (Chicago, IL: University of Chicago Press, 1988).

12

Blackett and Nuclear Strategy

Philip Towle

In 1948 P.M.S. Blackett made his first, most extensive and most radical contribution to the debate on nuclear strategy with the publication of *Military and Political Consequences of Atomic Energy*.[1] It came at a time when there was very little published work in the field and it established his reputation as a sceptic about the wisdom of Western nuclear policy. He was to alter his attitudes from time to time, to the efficacy of deterrence and to the potential for tactical nuclear weapons, but his position as a critic was set. As he put it himself in 1948, with a combination of bitterness and defiance:

> I found I have singularly failed to write a recipe for action which would be likely at the present moment to commend itself to the political taste of my fellow countrymen. But for this the state of the world, not I, must take the blame.

His sympathetic obituarist in *The Times* claimed that, in the context of the ever-worsening Cold War, Blackett's book 'seemed to many to be inhumanly cold, perverse, and probably communist'. One reviewer described it as 'the fullest explanation and justification of the Soviet attitude to atomic energy which has been published in this country' and another advised readers to disregard his 'odd tendency to view in a rosy light any Soviet attitudes, and to be critical of the natural degree of caution showed by the United States'.[2]

Blackett was a disappointed man in 1948. He was regarded as too left wing to be a welcome adviser to the Labour government elected in 1945 with a mandate to transform the British economy and society. He was appointed to the Advisory Committee on Atomic

Energy but found himself increasingly at odds with the views of other members and even more so with the ideas about nuclear deterrence being spread by Jacob Viner, Bernard Brodie and other American strategic writers. It was, as his obituarist wrote, 'the only obscure period in his adult life'.[3]

All Blackett's writing on nuclear strategy was profoundly influenced by his assessment of the effects of the bomber offensive against Germany and of the motives for the two atomic bomb attacks on Japan. Blackett believed that the bomber offensive had neither been the decisive factor in bringing about the Allies' victory, nor even cost-effective. Until 1943 the weight of bombs dropped was less than the weight dropped by the Germans on Britain in 1940. After this date, even though Britain had devoted about 40 per cent of its war effort to the bomber offensive and some 47,000 airmen were sacrificed by Bomber Command, the German economy continued to thrive, and in 1944 it produced more aircraft than Britain for the first time during the war years. Even in the Pacific war, where Japanese houses were far more vulnerable, the conventional bomber offensive on its own had not brought Tokyo to its knees. That required the defeat of its forces on land and sea, and the interdiction of its communications and trade routes.[4]

Blackett believed that such defeats had brought Japan to the point of surrender before the atomic bombs fell on Hiroshima and Nagasaki. Japan was ready to lay down its arms, but Washington wanted a quick victory, to pre-empt Soviet forces participating in a major way in the defeat of Japan and to demonstrate the power of its new weapon. The first bomb was dropped on 6 August, the Soviet Union declared war on Japan two days later, its armed forces began to overrun Manchuria on 9 August, the day on which the second bomb was dropped on Nagasaki, and Tokyo surrendered on 14 August. Blackett, therefore, concluded:

> Let us sum up the three possible explanations of the decision to drop the bomb and its timing. The first, that it was a clever and highly successful move in the field of power politics, is almost certainly correct; the second, that the timing was coincidental, convicts the American government of a hardly credible tactlessness [towards the Soviet Union]; and the third, the Roman holiday theory [to justify the cost of the Manhattan project], convicts them of an equally incredible irresponsibility.

In Blackett's view, the nuclear attacks were the beginning of the Cold War not the end of the Second World War, but the scientists and others involved on the US side could not admit, even to themselves, that the bombing of Hiroshima and Nagasaki was unnecessary to achieve Japan's surrender and to avoid the loss of thousands of Allied lives.[5]

Blackett drew a number of conclusions from this analysis. One was that the civilian nuclear strategists, Bernard Brodie, Jacob Viner and others, were exaggerating the potential effectiveness of nuclear weapons against the Soviet Union and thus of deterrence. To achieve the same damage to Russian targets as the Allies had achieved in the Second World War, when they dropped millions of tons of conventional bombs but failed to make the Axis surrender, the United States would need 400 nuclear weapons. It would be very difficult to drop these on Soviet targets from aircraft because fighters would be very much quicker and more manoeuvrable than bombers for many years to come. Eventually, rockets developed from the German V2s would carry nuclear warheads, but not for the next ten years, and it would be 25 years before they had inter-continental ranges. Submarines powered by hydrogen peroxide might launch nuclear missiles near to enemy coasts but it seemed unlikely that this would be an effective way of waging war.[6]

Despite the inability of nuclear weapons to defeat the Soviet Union, Washington was much more likely to use them than Moscow. This was partly because the United States had made so much greater use of strategic bombing in the Second World War, partly because of the exaggeration of their effects and partly because of the US fear of incurring casualties. General Marshall claimed that the US had suffered 'staggering' casualties in the Second World War although, in fact, they were only three times the road deaths suffered during that time. Nevertheless, to avoid casualties and fighting a continental war, Washington might resort to nuclear weapons. This would not be decisive and the threat to use such weapons would not be sufficient to deter Soviet actions. 'Enough has been said', Blackett concluded,

> to show convincingly the obvious truth – though a truth somewhat obscured by a wave of very inaccurate and superficial reasoning based on the destructive power of the atomic bomb – that a war between America and Russia would be of world-wide extent and would be a war of all arms, and certainly of very long duration. The

> first World War lasted four years; the second, in spite of the technical advances or perhaps because of them, lasted nearly six years.[7]

It is clear from this very brief summary of his published views why Blackett's analysis was so unpopular in 1948. In the years immediately after the Second World War people in Britain and the USA were only too conscious of the effort which had gone into the bomber offensive. They were very reluctant to accept that it might not have been 'cost-effective' and that resources might have been better re-deployed to close support aircraft, maritime patrol aircraft and ship-borne fighters. One can contrast Blackett's views with those expressed by Lord Tedder in the Lees Knowles lectures in Cambridge the previous year; Tedder did not claim that the bomber offensives had won the war on their own, rather that they had worn down German and Japanese strength and forced them on to the defensive. 'Step by step and from losing the battle of Britain, the Germans had been forced back more and more on the defensive. More and more was their effort diverted to passive defence.' Tedder's conclusion was 'that the outstanding and vital lesson of this last war is that air power is the dominant factor in this modern world'.[8] The argument over the efficacy of the bomber offensive continues down to the present but it has now become a historical battle rather than an emotional and political one. In 1948 this was not the case. Today most historians would agree with Tedder that the bombers had forced the Japanese and Germans on to the defensive and 'wasted' their resources, making victory in the ground and naval battles much easier. On the other hand, as Blackett pointed out, they failed in their primary purpose of breaking the will of the German and Japanese nations.[9]

The argument that Washington dropped the nuclear weapons on Japan to pre-empt Soviet expansion and impress Soviet leaders was, and remains, controversial. Certainly the Japanese were looking for a way to end the war, but they were justifiably anxious about how the Allies would treat the Emperor and consequently they were not, yet, prepared to accept unconditional surrender, despite their losses on land and sea. Senior members of the government also had great difficulties in communicating sensibly and openly among themselves, let alone with their publics and with the armed forces, and this prevented systematic analysis of the desperate situation in which they found themselves.[10] Blackett argued that the Allies could have allowed the conventional war to continue, but the deaths of prisoners in Japanese hands and of combat troops would also have continued, even if a landing in Japan had proved unnecessary. Thousands would have died if the orders to kill all the POWs had been carried out. Blackett was simply wrong to claim that 'no appreciable loss of American lives would have resulted from' delay. As it was, the growing losses in the struggles on the Pacific islands, and the fact that so much money and effort had been expended on nuclear weapons and that the Manhattan project had acquired a momentum of its own, all played a part in the decision to drop the bombs. So too did what the British embassy in Washington called 'the exterminationist anti-Japanese feeling of the man in the street'. Certainly, if fear of the Soviet Union was a major factor, it was not the only motive.[11]

Blackett's attitude to the bomber offensive and to the attacks on Hiroshima and Nagasaki could be considered 'cold and anti-Western', particularly in the intensifying Cold War. His analysis was picked up the next year by the radical MP Konni Zilliacus in his widely read denunciation of the West, *I Choose Peace*:

> The explosion of the atomic bomb at Hiroshima and Nagasaki blew to pieces the rickety structure of friendship between the Western Allies and the Soviet Union ... The real reason for this unparalleled act of barbarity, says Professor Blackett, and pretty well proves his case, was to deprive the Soviet Union of a share in the victory big enough to give her an important influence on the peace settlement. The two bombs that struck down a couple of hundred thousand civilians, old and young, men, women and children, in strange and hideous ways, many dying in long-drawn-out agony, were intended not so much to end the anti-Japanese war as to begin anti-Soviet and anti-Communist intervention in the Far East.

Zilliacus was expelled from the Labour Party.[12]

Blackett's dismissal of US losses in the Second World War and his belief that the US would be 'trigger happy' with nuclear weapons were deeply wounding. The British government was at this time trying to bind the US ever more deeply to European defence because it was unable to finance the British occupation zone in Germany, to balance Soviet power and to halt the spread of communist influence in Greece and Turkey. Yet Blackett was warning that the Soviets would have acquired nuclear weapons in the next five years and this would make Britain vulnerable to a Soviet response against a US attack. In such circumstances, Blackett advised neutrality unless

> America, in peace time, installed many tens of divisions in Europe, so as to be on the spot if war did break out. But this policy raises such exceedingly difficult political problems both in Europe and America that it is rather unlikely to be followed.[13]

Fortunately his prognosis was to prove too pessimistic. The outbreak of the Korean War in 1950 convinced Washington that ground forces would have to be kept in Europe to deter Soviet expansion for as long as the threat remained. They were to remain there for more than half a century.

One way out of the dilemmas presented by the nuclear threats, which Blackett sketched so clearly, was outlined in the Baruch plan presented by Washington to the United Nations in 1946. This would have allowed for the abolition of nuclear weapons and the control by the UN itself of all major civil nuclear facilities. Blackett was, quite rightly, deeply sceptical of the feasibility of such a proposal and it had, indeed, been rejected immediately by the Soviet Union. Blackett believed that any arms control agreement negotiated between the two sides would have to involve conventional as well as nuclear weapons. He wisely argued that the UN would not be allowed ownership or control of nuclear plants or of armed forces, at least for many years, despite the negotiations being carried on at that time. But, above all, he believed the plan failed because,

> in its attempt to secure nearly complete security for America, it was inevitably driven to propose a course of action which would have put the Soviet Union in a situation where she would have been subservient to a group of nations dominated by America.[14]

As a distinguished nuclear physicist, Blackett contended that British and American commentators underestimated the importance of civilian nuclear power for countries which lacked their coal or oil resources. Thus, he rejected the views of those who argued against all nuclear research on the grounds that it would be too dangerous and would encourage states to develop nuclear weapons:

> The development of atomic power is likely to prove extremely important for the progress of the relatively under-industrialised countries ... The unique mobility of nuclear fuel renders it ideal for the purpose of providing cheap power in regions remote from other energy sources.[15]

His enthusiasm for nuclear power was criticised at the time by a reviewer in the *Royal Engineer's Journal* for making 'a mistake very common among scientists, namely of underestimating the engineering difficulties in applying scientific discoveries'.[16] Despite such scepticism, Blackett's enthusiasm continued long after other British scientists, like Kathleen Lonsdale, were warning of the difficulties of disposing of nuclear waste, the catastrophic effects of an explosion in a power station and the encouragement which civil nuclear power gave to the spread of atomic weapons.[17]

Blackett's book was unpopular and his views were widely rejected. Sir Norman Angell's lavishly praised appeal in *The Steep Places* for the development of the Commonwealth into a confederation of democracies and for unity between the United States and the British Commonwealth to balance Soviet power, or Dame Barbara Ward's support for a federation of Western states in *Policy for the West* were much more palatable. Ward, the deputy editor of *The Economist*, was far more critical than Blackett of the Soviet leaders for their 'deadly mixture of arrogance and suspicion', but believed that it was possible for 'the West to mobilise sufficient military strength to deter the Russians from thinking they can manage a local aggression too speedily for effective counter-action to be possible'.[18]

As a former naval officer with extensive experience of maritime affairs, Blackett was willing to tackle technical military issues and to challenge the emerging consensus on deterrence. Ward, Angell and most other civilian writers focused on political issues in the 1940s. The review of Blackett's book by H.C. Wimperis in *International Affairs* concentrated entirely on his criticism of the Baruch plan and ignored his strategic ideas.[19] When they were discussed, Blackett's attacks on both the bomber offensive and the use of nuclear weapons against Japan were considered by many to be extreme. The fact that they were carefully and forcefully argued only added to the distrust they evoked.

Later critics, like Lawrence Freedman, have argued that Blackett's analysis was quickly outdated because the military balance was changing so rapidly.[20] Blackett was right to predict that the Soviets would soon acquire nuclear weapons, although the arms race proceeded faster than he expected. Intercontinental ballistic missiles (ICBMs) and ballistic missile firing submarines appeared long before his 25-year period had expired. Blackett was probably correct in 1948 to believe that nuclear weapons would not have brought an East–West war to an end quickly, and that deterrence was less effective than many suggested. But time was not on his side. The development of the hydrogen bomb was to make a prolonged nuclear war an impossibility, as he quickly realised himself. Finally, as many were prone to do at that time, Blackett exaggerated the benefits of civil nuclear energy, particularly for underdeveloped states. Even today, half a century later, such benefits are, at best, controversial and, many would argue, grossly inflated. Yet some of his other insights have enduring relevance. In the midst of the US and, indeed, international debate on missile defences and the danger from rogue states, it is salutary to recall Blackett's dismissal of the fear expressed by US Secretary for War, Henry Stimson,

> that an unsuspecting United States itself might be defeated in a few days by a very much smaller nation [with nuclear weapons]. The obvious result has been to stimulate a hysterical search for 100 per cent security. Since there can be no such complete security for America, except through world hegemony imposed by America, Mr Stimson's view, which is very widely accepted, justified a drive towards world hegemony by America in one form or another … Perfect security from any of the dangers besetting humanity is clearly not attainable.[21]

Blackett's next distinctive foray into the nuclear field occurred in 1956, when he was invited to Trinity College, Cambridge, to follow Lord Tedder and others and to give the Lees Knowles lectures, which were later published as *Atomic Weapons and East–West Relations.* It is not unfair to say that these were less interesting, because less radical, than his previous work. Above all he was now less sure of his targets. By and large Blackett had accepted the principle of deterrence and Brodie's claim that nuclear weapons had changed the world. As he put it, 'all-out total war has been made very unlikely by the great superiority on both sides of atomic offensive power over defensive possibilities'.[22] On the other hand, Blackett still believed that the West was relying too much on nuclear weapons to balance Soviet forces. It was unwilling to spend funds on civil defence or on its conventional armed forces and hence it was pushed towards an unrealistic strategy of massive retaliation. 'One thing is certain,' he wrote, of British doctrine on the possible use of nuclear weapons, 'the amount spent on atomic weapons, their carriers and on the active and passive defence measures to meet an enemy atomic attack' was grossly inadequate to make the doctrine effective.[23]

This was, in fact, one of his continual refrains; the West could not afford to cut conventional forces, nor were nuclear weapons a cheap option because of the expenditure they would require on civil defence, if they were to have any credibility. Blackett was hardly the only writer to argue thus in the 1950s. But governments could only spend on defence what their publics were willing to concede and their economies could stand. Britain had 841,000 men under arms in 1951 and 700,000 still mobilised six years later. Britain spent 4,707 million dollars on defence in 1953. Defence expenditure per head was 7.6 times as great in 1952 as it had been in 1890 at the height of its Empire.[24] According to Ward's figures, Britain spent 7.4 per cent of its national income on defence in 1949/50, against 5.9 per cent spent by the US, 5 per cent spent by France and 2.5 per cent spent by Norway.[25] Balancing economic against military demands is always a difficult exercise but, in retrospect, a historian might well feel that governments were better judges of this question than commentators like Blackett. By peacetime standards they were spending very heavily indeed on defence; no wonder they balked at doing more. As the 1956 Defence White Paper wisely put it, 'the continued economic strength of the free world is an essential element in our ability to resist Soviet aggression and the burden of defence cannot be allowed to rise to a level which would endanger our economic future'.[26]

Blackett, by contrast, was critical of the West's reliance on science and technology in the form of nuclear weapons instead of the conventional forces governments believed they could not afford. He pointed out that the West had 17 million men under arms at the end of the war, against 12 million Soviet forces. It was much richer; why could it not have invested enough in conventional forces to keep up with Soviet forces? In any case, Blackett had an exaggerated view of the efficacy of Soviet science and scientific education, and he thus believed it was unwise to rely on scientific advantage. He was also critical of the notions that it was necessary to keep ahead in the nuclear arms race. 'It was a dangerous will-o-the-wisp which might well have enticed the West into waging a preventive war.' It was to be another decade before US Defence Secretary Robert McNamara finally accepted Blackett's judgement that the West could accept Soviet equality in the numbers of nuclear weapons and thus that effective arms control talks could begin.[27]

Blackett ridiculed Winston Churchill's 1948 claim that 'nothing stands between Europe today and complete subjection to communist tyranny but the atomic bomb in American possession'.[28] He pointed out that, if atomic weapons had not been invented, the West would have acted differently. 'Anyone who believes Churchill's rhetoric about atomic bombs having saved Western civilisation must take a much poorer view than I do of the good sense, the high ability, the keen courage and the massive material power of the West.' The Soviet Union had suffered appallingly in the Second World War and would thus not have attacked in 1948 anyway. Realistically, as most would agree today, its primary objective was to recover, though it was also determined to ring itself with satellite states as a buffer against attack.

All these ideas were interesting and many were prescient but the lectures really came alive when Blackett turned to the victimisation of the American nuclear scientist, J. Robert Oppenheimer, and his dismissal from office in 1954. Blackett clearly felt great sympathy for his fellow physicist and friend. He talked of Oppenheimer's 'personal vulnerability due to his left wing past' and must have been only too well aware of the parallels between their careers.[29] Suspicions of Oppenheimer grew when his General Advisory Committee opposed a crash development programme for hydrogen bombs, even though it was in favour of developing tactical nuclear weapons to strengthen the West's European defences. Furthermore, the suspicion remained after Oppenheimer pronounced himself in favour of developing hydrogen bombs in 1951, when Edward Teller came up with a much more efficient way of building them. Despite his belated support, Oppenheimer had done enough to raise fears about his political reliability when the Cold War was at its height and Senator Joseph McCarthy was proceeding with his anti-communist witch-hunt.

Blackett believed that Oppenheimer's initial doubts stemmed from his experience with the use of atomic bombs in 1945. Blackett quoted the moment in the Congressional hearings on Oppenheimer's loyalty, when he was asked at what point he began to doubt the wisdom of producing hydrogen bombs. The scientist replied: 'I think it was when I realised that this country would tend to use any weapon they had.' Thus, Blackett felt Oppenheimer agreed with him that atomic bombs need not have been dropped on Japan to force its surrender in 1945. They were aimed against the Soviet Union.[30]

In the 1956 lectures Blackett reverted to a number of other issues he had raised in 1948. He lashed the Baruch plan again as 'the illegitimate offspring of the idealism of conscience-stricken scientists and the conservative realism of hard bitten statesmen'. Far from abolition of nuclear weapons through the plan leading to peace, if it had been accepted, Russia would have contravened it in some way and this might well have been made an excuse for war. However, Blackett's final conclusion about arms control was both optimistic and right: 'we have to learn to live with bombs ... and every year we live with them without using them is one step towards the possibility of a real agreement on how first to control them and how then to abolish them'.[31]

Blackett's last substantial book on nuclear weapons was a collection of essays entitled *Studies of War* and published in 1962. All through this period he had been a close and critical observer of the defence debate and of the evolution of strategic thought, participating in a study group on the subject at the Royal Institute of International Affairs. In his lecture at Chatham House in April 1958 he quoted Eliza Doolittle's threat, 'Say one more word and I'll scream.'[32] He enjoyed taking issue with many of the new generation of defence intellectuals. Thus he dismissed Henry Kissinger's claim in *Nuclear Weapons and Foreign Policy*, published in 1957, that the West should rely on tactical nuclear weapons to make up for its inferior conventional deficiencies. Blackett suspected that tactical weapons would actually disadvantage the West, because they could be used by an aggressor to attack key strategic points such as ports, headquarters and communications. Blackett also examined the alternative suggested by the writer Stephen King-Hall, another former naval officer, that it would be better to accept a Soviet occupation of western Europe if it could not be defended conventionally, and that opposition should be confined to passive resistance for which governments should make massive pre-attack preparations.[33] Blackett pointed out that this was to take far too pessimistic a view of the West's ability to defend itself conventionally. One might add that it was also to take too optimistic a view of the efficacy of passive resistance to occupation by a totalitarian power, even if King-Hall believed such resistance might have to last for decades.

Given his general ideas on nuclear weapons, Blackett was particularly horrified by the Defence White Papers masterminded by Duncan Sandys. These increased British reliance on deterrence and reduced the efficacy of its conventional defences by abolishing conscription, the very opposite course to that advocated by Sir Basil Liddell Hart, Blackett and other critics. 'Britain was left without an operational defence policy ... on which realistic military planning and training could be based.' From Blackett's point of view, 'the criticism of the 1957 and 1958 White Papers [was] overwhelming'. He went on, 'in my view the card house of our defence policy erected on a policy of bluff and politics has collapsed and will never be resurrected in its old form'.[34] That was hardly to prove the case, though it was true that NATO fumbled in the 1960s towards the strategy of flexible response which relied less wholeheartedly on nuclear retaliation than Sandys suggested was the optimum policy. It is difficult now to recapture the incredulity and fury with which Sandys's White Papers were received. A quarter of a century later, in the middle of the House of Lords' debate on the Falklands War, Lord Wigg blamed them for the task force's lack of air cover. The 1957 White Paper was 'the most disastrous document that has ever been introduced by a British government. It was a dishonest document.'[35] In contrast to the Sandys' approach, Blackett advocated a combination of unilateral British nuclear disarmament and joint efforts towards arms control. He believed that

> Britain should content herself with (a) inducing as many as possible medium and low rank nations to join the Great Power Safety Catch Club (b) obtaining a reasonable promise from both great powers that no atomic weapons will be given to any other powers, free of their own safety catch; this assured, Britain should follow the Labour Party proposals to cease production of her own A and H bombs, dismantle her stocks and submit her atomic installations to international inspection, as would all members of the club.

With the exception of his espousal of British unilateralism, this was in fact precisely what was to happen over the next decade, when

Blackett was working in Labour's Ministry of Technology. The Nuclear Non-Proliferation Treaty was negotiated as the basis of a non-nuclear club of nations and included a commitment by the nuclear weapon states that they would not give nuclear weapons to other countries.[36]

Blackett's last book on nuclear strategy was given a very different reception from his first, which the *Royal Engineers Journal* believed had provided material for Gromyko's speeches at the UN.[37] It was warmly, almost reverentially reviewed in the *Royal United Services Institute Journal* for February 1963 by Cyril Falls, the former Chichele Professor in the History of War at Oxford University. Falls argued that Blackett's 'early university training, together with his abilities and his experience, made it inevitable that he should be called upon for aid in dealing with the deadly menace of the atomic bomb'.[38] He went on to commend Blackett's essays to the journal's readers 'in all confidence'. His views were indeed now much closer to the conventional wisdom.

Blackett brought a combative, sceptical mind to the problems of nuclear strategy with which governments, military officers and academics wrestled in the Cold War decades. He was by no means always right, either in his political or his technical judgements, but his books on nuclear weapons have survived better than much contemporary writing and are still worth reading half a century later. His ideas are 'not accepted as platitudinous' as his obituarist argued and they combined military and political analysis in a way which was very rare in Britain in the early years of the Cold War. He was wrong on the utility of atomic energy as a source of cheap power for the Third World, about the practicality of missile-carrying submarines and about the timing of the development of ICBMs. His judgements about the Soviet Union were also sometimes mistaken. Soviet science was nothing like as effective as he suggested and their figures for the numbers of scientists being trained were simply bogus. Comments by Ward, Angell and others about Soviet society were far closer to the truth than Blackett's sparse observations. He was wrong about the prospects of the US stationing forces in western Europe to deter a Soviet attack and exaggerated the funds which Western governments could devote to defence over the decades of the Cold War. However, his views on nuclear proliferation and on accepting Soviet nuclear parity with the West were belatedly espoused by Western governments in the 1960s. Blackett was dogmatic, but he was willing to change his ideas on deterrence and other basic issues. Governments ignored his opinions and moved towards greater reliance on nuclear weapons in the late 1950s to keep the cost of defence under control, but Blackett ensured that the opposite strategy was thoroughly ventilated.

His writings on nuclear weapons must often have pleased the Soviets, if they bothered to read them. He sympathised with the way their brilliant Manchurian offensive had been eclipsed by Hiroshima and Nagasaki in August 1945, justified their rejection of the 'specious' Baruch plan, praised their technological achievements, suggested that they were less likely to use nuclear weapons than the Americans and that they would not attack the West, at least until they had recovered from the horrendous damage caused by the Nazis. By contrast, he dismissed US fears of attack as a neurotic misinterpretation of the lessons of the Japanese attack on Pearl Harbor, played down the sacrifices they had made in the Second World War, insisted that they had used nuclear weapons unnecessarily against Japan in 1945, argued that Britain would be safer as a neutral in the Cold War in 1948, ridiculed most of the writings by US nuclear strategists and deplored the West's reliance on superior technology to balance Soviet power.

It was not, therefore, surprising that his views on nuclear weapons were, as his obituarist argued, considered 'cold, perverse and probably communist' in the darkest period of the Cold War. They represented the ideas of a tough-minded and radical physicist, who was determined to look at the strategic arguments from both points of view, and who both relished and resented being in a minority at odds with the government and with the conventional wisdom.

NOTES

1. P.M.S. Blackett, *Military and Political Consequences of Atomic Energy* (London: Turnstile Press, 1948).
2. Blackett, *Military and Political Consequences*, p. VIII. Obituaries from *The Times*, 1971–1975, Newspaper Archive Development, Reading, 1978, pp. 49–50. Reviews of *Military and Political Consequences of Atomic Energy* by KHT in *Royal Engineers Journal* (September 1949), p. 195, and by H.E. Wimperis in *International Affairs*, 25, 2 (1949), p. 199.
3. *The Times* Obituaries. On US nuclear strategy, see Philip Bobbitt, Lawrence Freedman and Gregory Treverton, *US Nuclear Strategy: A Reader* (Basingstoke: Macmillan, 1989).
4. Blackett, *Military and Political Consequences*, Chapters 2 and 3.

5. Blackett, *Military and Political Consequences*, p. 126. For the opposite criticism, often made, that Roosevelt was too apolitical and too trusting of the Soviets, see J.F.C. Fuller, *The Conduct of War 1789–1961* (London: Eyre & Spottiswoode, 1962), pp. 297 ff.
6. Blackett, *Military and Political Consequences*, especially pp. 48 ff.
7. Blackett, *Military and Political Consequences*, p. 4 and Chapter 6. Marshall is quoted on p. 71. For a later assessment of the US military effort in the Second World War, see William L. O'Neill, *A Democracy at War* (New York: Free Press, 1993).
8. Lord Tedder, *Air Power in War* (London: Hodder & Stoughton, 1948), pp. 44, 123.
9. See, for example, R.J. Overy, *The Air War 1939–1945* (London: Europa, 1980); John Terraine, *A Time for Courage: The Royal Air Force in the Second World War* (New York: Macmillan, 1985); Robin Neillands, *The Bomber War: Arthur Harris and the Allied Bombing Offensive 1939–1945* (London: John Murray, 2001).
10. Henry L. Stimson, *On Active Service in Peace and War* (New York: Harper, 1948), Chapter 23. Robert J.C. Butow, *Japan's Decision to Surrender* (Stanford, CA: Stanford University Press, 1954); Leon V. Sigal, *Fighting to a Finish: The Politics of War Termination in the United States and Japan, 1945* (Ithaca, NY: Cornell University Press, 1991).
11. On hatred of Japan, see John Dower, *War Without Mercy* (London: Faber & Faber, 1986) and H.G. Nicholas (ed.), *Washington Despatches 1941–1945* (London: Weidenfeld & Nicolson, 1981), p. 299. For anger over the prisoners of war, see *The Memoirs of Cordell Hull*, Vol. 2 (London: Hodder & Stoughton, 1948), p. 1598. For the conditions of the POWs, see John Fletcher-Cooke, *The Emperor's Guest, 1942–1945* (London: Leo Cooper, 1972); Thomas Pounder, *Death Camps of the River Kwai* (Cornwall: United Writers, 1977); Aidan MacArthy, *A Doctor's War* (London: Robson, 1979).
12. K. Zilliacus, *I Choose Peace* (Harmondsworth: Penguin, 1949), pp. 97, 236.
13. Blackett, *Military and Political Consequences*, p. 77. For a devastating dismissal of the advantages for Britain of neutralism, see Norman Angell, *The Steep Places* (London: Hamish Hamilton, 1947), p. 105.
14. Blackett, *Military and Political Consequences*, p. 108, *passim.*
15. Blackett, *Military and Political Consequences*, Chapter 8.
16. KHT, review in *Royal Engineers Journal.*
17. Kathleen Lonsdale, *Is Peace Possible?* (Harmondsworth: Penguin, 1957), pp. 18–19.
18. Angell, *The Steep Places*; Barbara Ward, *Policy for the West* (Harmondsworth: Penguin, 1951), pp. 11, 25.
19. Wimperis, review in *International Affairs.* Solly Zuckerman also refers to Blackett's book in his autobiography, *Monkeys, Men and Missiles* (London: Collins, 1988), pp. 182ff., and laments that, when Blackett asked him for comments before publication, he concentrated only on Blackett's views on bombing and was 'less interested in Patrick's strategic vision and political arguments'. Blackett's views were clearly too wide-ranging even for someone of Zuckerman's breadth.
20. Lawrence Freedman, *The Evolution of Nuclear Strategy* (London: Macmillan, 1981), p. 63.
21. Blackett, *Military and Political Consequences*, Chapter 10.
22. P.M.S. Blackett, *Atomic Weapons and East–West Relations* (Cambridge: Cambridge University Press, 1956), pp. 2, 34.
23. Ibid., p. 31.

24. ISS, *Military Balance 1972–1973* (London: International Institute for Strategic Studies, 1972), p. 74. Alan T. Peacock and Jack Wiseman, *The Growth of Public Expenditure in the United Kingdom* (London: Allen & Unwin, 1968), p. 56.
25. Ward, *Policy for the West*, p. 81. The great virtue of this book was that it integrated economics and defence in a way that Blackett, Strachey, Angell and others were unable to do.
26. Statement on Defence 1956, Cmd 9691, para. 9.
27. Blackett, *Atomic Weapons*, pp. 63 ff.
28. Ibid., pp. 67 ff., p. 95 ff.
29. Ibid., pp. 72 ff.
30. Ibid., p. 78.
31. Ibid., pp. 92 ff.
32. P.M.S. Blackett, 'Nuclear Weapons and Defence: Comments on Kissinger, Kennan and King-Hall', lecture given in April 1958 and published in *International Affairs* (October 1958).
33. Stephen King-Hall, *Defence in the Nuclear Age* (London: Gollancz, 1958), Chapter 13. P.M.S. Blackett, *Studies of War* (London: Oliver & Boyd, 1962), p. 70.
34. Blackett, *Studies of War*, pp. 86–7. For Liddell Hart's views at this time see his *Deterrent or Defence* (London: Stevens, 1960). For other troubled intellectuals' views, see John Strachey, *On the Prevention of War* (London: Macmillan, 1962) and George Kennan, *The Nuclear Delusion* (London: Hamish Hamilton, 1984), pp. 3–10. For a more optimistic view, see Evan Luard, *Peace and Opinion* (London: Oxford University Press, 1962).
35. Parliamentary Debates, House of Lords, 14 April 1982, columns 323–6.
36. Blackett, *Studies of War*.
37. See Note 3. For the Soviet view at this stage, see Documents on Disarmament 1945–1959, Vol. I (Washington, DC: Department of State, 1960).
38. Cyril Falls, 'Studies in Operational Research', *RUSI Journal* (February 1963), pp. 62 ff.

13

Blackett in India: Thinking Strategically about New Conflicts

Robert Anderson

Invited to lunch at the Nehru home in January 1947, Patrick Blackett was seated beside the acting Prime Minister. Jawaharlal Nehru knew of Blackett's experience in war and military affairs, and asked him how long it would take 'to Indianise the military', meaning both its command structure and its weapons production and supply. He was not yet the Prime Minister and India was not yet an independent nation. Blackett's reply was a challenging one, obliging Nehru to explore two different kinds of strategy and thus two different military set-ups. For the 'realistic' strategy Blackett preferred, he told Nehru that Indianisation could be completed in 18 months: this would prepare India for conflict with other similar powers in the region. For the 'unrealistic' strategy, in which India would prepare for conflict with major world powers, Blackett predicted it would take many, many years to 'Indianise'. Nehru liked his approach, and wrote to him soon afterwards to ask Blackett to advise him on military and scientific affairs. From this invitation much followed. One wonders if Nehru's memory cast back to 1924, when his father, Motilal Nehru, with Mohammed Ali Jinnah, was a member of the first committee to try to accelerate the process to 'Indianise' the military (the Skeen Committee). The question the Prime-Minister-to-be posed to Blackett, like other questions in India, had a long history.

In describing some of Blackett's activities in India and relationships with Indian leaders and their problems, my purpose is to convey – mostly in his own words – the problems he perceived and the solutions he advocated. Through this we get an understanding of the changing context in which he worked, and the evolution of his thought and practice as a consultant and intervenor.

Twenty years after he first set foot in that country, Patrick Blackett was thinking about his influence on military and scientific developments in India. In a free-ranging interview with B.R. Nanda in 1967 he selected his influence as military consultant as probably more important than his other role as scientific intervenor.[1] This is in marked contrast to Indian perceptions of him, which focused mainly on his influence on large scientific research organisations. There is truth in both views, as I will show. (By 'intervenor' I mean a role more penetrating and involved than 'consultant'. This was the role in which Blackett intervened and accepted some responsibility in the development of specific institutions of the scientific community.)

But Blackett rightly points to his relationship with Prime Minister Jawaharlal Nehru as crucial to his influence in both spheres. Nehru identified with and trusted Blackett because both had been to Cambridge, held favourable attitudes to 'political' socialism and were cautious about the same kinds of people, including 'the Americans'. In turn, Blackett acknowledges Nehru to be unusually receptive to his ideas and approaches, more receptive than his own British Prime Ministers of the period to 1964 (such as Attlee or Churchill). What Blackett does not say is that Nehru acted on his ideas not just because of Nehru's personal receptivity, but also because Blackett's ideas were acceptable to a handful of other influential people in India, such as scientists Homi Bhabha and Sir Shanti Bhatnagar, and also to D.S. Kothari and senior military officers like General J.N. Chaudhuri. Few of these people would have been untouched by Blackett's multitude of interests and torrent of energy, and would therefore have paid attention to his presence. But, more importantly, Blackett articulated ideas they had, supported them in their efforts and made connections at the highest level to people outside India for them. And, finally, his influence coincided with and extended the work of his old Cambridge colleague A.V. Hill, who had been deeply involved in India since 1943 and continued to play a role among Indian scientists similar to Blackett's. To this nexus of trusting and increasingly familiar relationships should be added the force of a number of material factors and ideas, making what Blackett said and did even more influential in elite Indian political and scientific circles.

The most powerful person in science in India just before independence, Sir Shanti Bhatnagar, was also in a position to invite foreign experts to visit and work in India. At the 1946 Empire

Scientific Conference in London, P.C. Mahalanobis and Bhatnagar proposed a scheme called 'Short Visits of Scientists from Abroad' and Mahalanobis followed up with a final list (based on lists drawn up by people like Meghnad Saha) which included Robert Oppenheimer, Norbert Wiener and Niels Bohr, as well as familiar British names like Patrick Blackett, J.B.S. Haldane, Sir Henry Dale, Sir Henry Tizard and Joseph Needham. Nehru agreed to sign the invitations to give these visits prominence.[2] It is probable that Blackett met some Indian scientists in London at the month-long Empire Scientific Conference in 1946, including Homi Bhabha. Eventually most of the individuals on this list visited India and got involved – some more, some less – in the development of their own fields and research institutions.

When Blackett received an invitation late in 1946, signed by Nehru, he accepted. The Council of Scientific and Industrial Research (CSIR), of which Bhatnagar was the Director, paid for Blackett's first trip to India. He was asked to address the Indian Science Congress (of which Nehru was president) and also the Association of Scientific Workers of India. Blackett had been a committed member of this association in Britain since the 1930s, and the objectives of the Indian association were identical: to increase the applications of scientific rationalism in politics and planning, and to improve the working conditions of scientists. His old Cambridge colleague and head of the association in Britain, the physicist J.D. Bernal, was influential in getting the Indian association recognised, but the impetus for its development came from India.[3] Nehru himself was favourable to the association. The British association experienced a great political shift from 1947–48 onwards, with British communists like Bernal leaving it, and thousands of laboratory technicians joining it as a kind of trade union from the early 1950s. In India it retained its original intellectual, planning and agitational character for at least the next 30 years. During his 1947 visit Blackett received an honorary degree from the University of Delhi, an event requiring months of planning and Blackett's foreknowledge. Evidently, he decided in the autumn of 1946 to go to India. It appears that while travelling in India to the meetings of the Indian Science Congress in early January 1947, Blackett and Nehru found themselves on the same plane, and managed to talk.[4] Shortly afterwards, Blackett went for lunch at Nehru's home in Delhi. Much of Blackett's engagement in India resulted from these conversations with Nehru.

This British expert became sought after precisely as the sun was setting on the British Empire, as physics was taking a strategic turn, and as military development was becoming a national and commercial complex in which university-based scientists gradually played a less central role, particularly in contrast to Blackett's experience in Britain over the previous ten years (that is from about 1938 to 1948). In 1947–50, when his reputation was deepening in India, the full consequence of the end of the Second World War was evident. The British presence in India had to end, but it ended so slowly that Britain's reputation in India worsened after the war. The Indian adjustment to the new world power, the United States, was complicated by the sudden emergence in 1947 of Pakistan. The British adjustment to the US was also difficult and uncertain, and there was tension before the formation of NATO (North Atlantic Treaty Organisation) and CENTO (Central Treaty Organisation) in 1949. The United States was a major power in Asia too, with bases in Japan, Taiwan and the Philippines. British and French colonies in Asia (like Vietnam) seemed vulnerable. When the first Soviet atomic bomb was exploded in 1949 (years before the Allies had predicted it), military bases in northern Pakistan acquired a new significance to Britain and the United States. When the victory of the Communist forces in China was complete in 1949, large diverse populations and a great arc of land from the Baltic to the Pacific lay to the north of India, all 'marching to a different drummer'. The Anglo-American approach to India would have been complicated enough after 1947 without Pakistan, a Soviet atomic bomb and a communist China. But, with these factors, it was very complicated indeed. A year later, in 1950, these very complications led to a war in Korea, during which US military planners thought they would use an atomic bomb. India was a secondary consideration to the great powers as the Cold War evolved, but occasionally became a sharp and pressing consideration, and was usually an irritant. And, as a stage on which to demonstrate another kind of economic and political development, both from the rivalrous view of the great powers and from the view of the Indian government that Blackett served, India became a most prominent example. India also had a huge reserve of British pounds at this time, and its currency was intimately linked with sterling.

It is difficult to give a measure of Blackett's influence in India. Blackett's papers in the Royal Society seem incomplete, and we do not have a thorough record of all of his activities in India. Most of his communication with Nehru and Bhabha is still unavailable. We cannot easily calibrate his experience in India with his other activities and relationships in the rest of his large life. In the 1967 interview he remarked: 'I had no official status in defence matters except as an advisor to Nehru.' Since his defence reports were marked 'Secret', and his consultations were not widely known, it is understandable that his public reputation was largely in the field of scientific research institution building. However, he sensed that his greater influence lay in the military. In tracing his relationships with key Indian figures and institutions, I often learned more about India than I did about Blackett. It is his appraisal of others, usually very decisive, that reveals most about him. It is clear India had a great influence on Blackett.

Blackett's father's brother was a missionary in India, his mother was the daughter of Sir Charles Maynard, an officer in the Indian Army around 1857, and his mother's uncle was a tea-planter in Assam. Perhaps because of these associations, or in spite of them, Blackett stated he had not wanted to go to India before it achieved independence. We shall see that he was horrified by the 'Colonel Blimp culture' among some of the British in India. Though he was proud to be there during the great change to independence in 1947, he was soon to discover both how old lines of dependence were maintained and how new lines of interdependence were established. He was thus an early harbinger in the mid-1960s of the whole discourse on the proper role of science and technology in newly independent developing countries.

THE PROFESSOR AND THE PRIME MINISTER

> He was a superb leader. But he did not know how to get things done very well.[5]

Few Prime Ministers anywhere at that time had the appreciation of and responsibility for science and scientists that Nehru did. He was the direct minister with portfolio – with powerful secretaries (like deputy ministers elsewhere), one for atomic energy, the other for industrial research and natural resources. Nehru was also intimately involved in two subjects – defence and economic planning. He was also Minister for External Affairs. He kept these five files close to him, and met directly with the scientists responsible for them. The indirect evidence is that Nehru discussed many issues within his responsibilities with Blackett, judging from comments in letters written by Bhabha, Bhatnagar, Mahalanobis, Saha and others. Scientists and officers soon learned that one way to Nehru, and simultaneously to Bhabha or Bhatnagar, was through Blackett's ear. From 1948 onward, Blackett usually stayed in the Prime Minister's Residence, often for weeks at a time. In 1948 his wife Costanza stayed with him. He received his correspondence and phone calls there. If Blackett got inspired about your project or problem, his energy knew no bounds. Blackett, of all people, believed in the possible. This must have appealed to Nehru. Moreover, Nehru's beliefs that the state should lead in the economy, and that the government could do almost anything if it tried were largely Blackett's own beliefs. This awesome role and responsibility forecast by Nehru was something Blackett seems to have thought this large group of scientists could actually meet. These beliefs were to have long-term consequences in India.

During the years when Nehru was formulating the movement of non-aligned nations, he tried his ideas out on Blackett, who was very receptive to them and probably contributed to them through discussion and debate. (We do not have documentary evidence for this yet.) Blackett spoke most approvingly of this part of India's foreign policy, and showed how India could not possibly win an arms race, not even with nuclear weapons. He said in 1967:

> I think you [India] would have split up if you had to fall into the western orbit in the first five years of independence. I think it was [Nehru's] great contribution of showing that non-alignment is a thing that is feasible ... I did not think it was feasible at the time.[6]

Blackett went on to say about Nehru that

> he had a bit too much intellectualism to solve the problem. He spent, from one point of view, too much time talking ... He liked intellectual company. (And he did not get it except in Homi Bhabha and people like that.) He had extreme informality and charm; his physical presence was extremely attractive; he was very engaging, with a shy sort of smile. He was sort of light-hearted. I liked this about him. But he spent too much time, I think, on science anyway.

> Considering the amount he had to do, running a country of that size, the amount of time he did spend with us was indeed surprising. On the whole, he liked me and others more as companions than as consultants.

Although we know the closeness of the relationship between Nehru and Blackett, we do not know its frustrations, or what value Nehru privately placed on Blackett's advice. Blackett was candid about Nehru in 1967, saying:

> He was a superb leader. But he did not know how to get things done very well. He believed in science in a rather naïve way. We all did at the time. He was not more naïve than other people. It was enormously valuable that he should put science first in making Indians scientifically minded. But science is only part of the game and the real effect of science comes from producing wealth ... Now India is finding out that the problem of turning science into wealth ... is very much more difficult than just doing science. It is not his fault that he did not fully understand this.

Blackett's deepest critique was about implementation and action:

> Nehru did an enormous amount to get non-scientists to understand what was scientific. But his regime did not do nearly as well in implementation. What he lacked were hard-headed industrial-minded Ministers who could push on the agricultural programme, the industrial programme.[7]

PATRICK BLACKETT AND INDIAN SCIENTISTS

> We were all scientifically naïve. We thought science was the solution to everything. I do not think I was very conscious of it explicitly earlier in this period.[8]

Nehru did, of course, have two scientists as hard-headed secretaries of his portfolios. They were not elected but had, as secretaries to the government, direct access to him, often more than any elected minister. They had unelected 'deputy minister' status, but were as powerful as ministers, in my opinion, building systems and institutions, developing regulations, and writing international agreements. One was Homi Bhabha, the physicist whom Blackett first met at Cambridge in the 1930s, in charge of the atomic energy programme and the laboratories (including his own in Bombay) which were funded through it. Bhabha was an extraordinary man with his finger on the strategic pulse. At the time of his death in 1966 Blackett called him 'my best personal friend'. Blackett went to parties at Bhabha's house, had his portrait sketched by Bhabha, had Bhabha to stay at his own house (for example, in 1946 in Manchester, before Blackett first went to India). The other powerful secretary was Sir Shanti Bhatnagar, a chemist trained at Lahore and the University of London, who was the head of the Council of Scientific and Industrial Research and who also reported directly to Nehru. With Sir Shanti, Blackett also formed an on-going personal relationship, until Bhatnagar's early death in 1955. They had frequent meetings in London as well as Delhi.

In addition, Blackett was friendly with Prasanta Mahalanobis, a physicist trained at Cambridge, who became a renowned statistician and built the influential Indian Statistical Institute in Calcutta. Mahalanobis too had quasi-ministerial status, saw Nehru regularly and shaped Nehru's entire approach to economic planning, which we know was one of Blackett's continuing passions. Mahalanobis (and, perhaps more ambiguously, Nehru) was committed to a centrally planned state-driven economy. This definitely appealed to Blackett, along with Mahalanobis's commitment to, and reputation in, statistics. At not quite so senior a level, Blackett's advice shaped the career of Daulat Singh Kothari, another Cambridge-trained physicist who became the Scientific Adviser to the Minister of Defence in 1948 and headed the Defence Science Organisation when it was established in June 1949. This organisation in Delhi was modelled on the one Blackett had prescribed in 1946 for the United Kingdom. Kothari eventually held the most important positions in the politics of education and universities in India, including being chairman of the University Grants Commission. Together these men controlled larger budgets for construction and employment than anyone else in the scientific community.

From the late 1940s, the scientists Blackett knew were travelling regularly: Bhatnagar to Norway to negotiate a heavy water deal,

Bhabha to Ottawa to negotiate a reactor, Kothari to Moscow to purchase troop transport aircraft, Mahalanobis to Washington to look at the new large computers. As they passed through London they all kept in touch with Blackett. Blackett visited their institutes, gave lectures there, examined their doctoral students, helped select candidates for appointments, appraised new research programmes and then promoted them if he liked them. These same scientists were also friends with A.V. Hill, whose influence upon science and the military in India began in 1943, four years before Blackett's own relationship with that country. The Blackett friendship in some senses was an extension of the Hill friendship. It provided the basis for professional advocacy and intervention within the scientific community. Hill knew Bhatnagar very well, and advised Bhabha on the establishment of his own institute. As personal friends of Blackett's, these men (Bhatnagar, Kothari) also asked him to watch over their children and other relatives when they studied or worked in London, which he did.

The relationship between Bhabha and Blackett was different from the others. They had already known each other well at Cambridge, where Bhabha (11 years younger than Blackett) studied under Paul Dirac. At a weekend conference in Manchester in 1937 Bhabha established himself in Blackett's eyes as an independent-minded physicist. In the company of Heisenberg, Bhabha (aged 28) challenged Blackett (aged 39) who insisted that the quantum theory of radiation must fail at higher energies because there could be no particles heavier than electrons in the penetrating component of cosmic rays at sea level. Bhabha persisted patiently in saying that there was a penetrating component heavier than the electron. According to an observer, Blackett stubbornly resisted this idea at the conference, but a few months later conceded that an energetic electron could produce a cascade shower, according to the Bhabha–Heitler theory, and the penetrating component of cosmic rays must consist of a new type of particle with mass intermediate between the electron and the proton.[9] Bhabha travelled extensively in Europe, was not dependent on a laboratory and could discuss his work with all the influential physicists of the day. His international scientific reputation was thus already well established before the war. When the war actually began he was on holiday in India, and so had to stay there. He wrote more openly to Blackett than he did to many others. For example, in 1941, Bhabha wrote to him from India: 'the attitude of the Government is as die-hard as ever. The mis-rule would astonish you.'[10] A reluctant experimenter in physics, Bhabha preferred a more theoretical mathematical physics, but he liked the practical gleam in Blackett's eye, and was delighted when Blackett got the Nobel prize in 1948 for work with the cloud chamber in the early 1930s in Cambridge. Bhabha made a commitment to cosmic ray studies in India from 1939 onwards. He asked Blackett to lend him the big magnet that Blackett had built at Cambridge and Manchester for cosmic ray research in Bangalore in 1941, but apparently it was never sent. When Bhabha built the Tata Institute of Fundamental Research (TIFR) in Bombay, Blackett was in on every step. Each time Blackett went to India, often at someone else's expense, Bhabha would command part of Blackett's schedule and arrange meetings for him, including introductions to the captains of industry with whom he was very well connected through the Tata family and other Bombay Parsee networks.

Blackett could not have had more a powerful and effective set of intermediaries in India, nor a more secure base from which to criticise and challenge Establishment thinking. That some of his friends constituted part of the Establishment and wanted similar changes within it, only enhanced his influence.

BLACKETT AS MILITARY CONSULTANT

> On the whole I think my views about the Indian armed forces expressed in 1948 have not proved too incorrect.[11]

Patrick Blackett was proud of his involvement in military affairs in India, and appears to have gained considerable insight from the experience. A window opened for Blackett upon a new world of poor countries which were trying, like India, to build a scientific and technological community that applied its skills to socio-economic problems, as well as building up a modern military infrastructure. Although this task for poor countries is not something to which he appears to have given much previous thought, he threw himself into it in the 1950s. At the same time, however, he soon realised with regret that much of the effort of poor countries was drained away in the importation of costly weapons systems. Thus he argued that India should define very carefully what armed conflicts it would face, and should choose its weapons for those conflicts with equal care. He correctly realised that the military forces would be used in conflicts inside India, particularly after the 1948 experience in Hyderabad and Kashmir. And he saw the conflict in India between defence and science, and the need to address the imperative of the era, which was then, as now, to reduce poverty. The conflict between the interests rooted in industrial and economic development with interests in scientific and defence policy was unresolved throughout Blackett's period. They were all competing for the same scarce resources. Nevertheless, he seems to have become more conscious of this conflict as he got older, although as a consultant he did not have to face it personally.

His advice ranged from the most concrete, like arguing for specific new positions and arranging for specific appointments, to a general concern for the development of a weapon like the tank or an organisation like the Defence Science Organisation. Then there was his wider commitment to cultivating certain ways of thinking, ways we would now call 'systemic', to do with how systems operate and how they can be understood dynamically in the field. This wider commitment was explained in terms of strengthening Indian strategies for economic development, industry and defence. At the core of these strategies glowed Blackett's own holy grail, the pursuit of science in its purest, most difficult and most exciting form, what his friend Homi Bhabha and others now called 'fundamental research'. He later reflected that he had not been conscious of the over-simplification in his approach to science and development, and began to re-think what he (and evidently his closest allies in India) believed about science in the 1940s and 1950s. During this entire early period as military consultant, Blackett was actively promoting his own scientific projects in India. In 1948 he was already in transition away from the subject for which he won the Nobel prize that year (cosmic rays) to the question of the reversal of the earth's magnetism. He lectured on 'the origins of cosmic rays' and 'reversely magnetised rocks', and proposed projects on white dwarf stars. He supervised the collection of lava and rocks in India in the 1950s and 1960s for his project on geomagnetism. He presented – for his friends and for casual observers – a unique combination of the theoretical and the practical. His 1948 combination of winning the Nobel prize, launching a book about a critique of cold war logic and being put on the US government's *non grata* list won hearts and minds in India.

His rare ability to combine the practical and theoretical as a scientist was also fully realised in Blackett's work as military consultant. It was physiologist A.V. Hill who involved Blackett in military research committees, starting with radar in 1936, and Hill and Blackett communicated frequently about new weapons and strategic questions prior to Hill's departure for India in 1943. Hill preceded Blackett as a military consultant in Delhi, where he spoke to senior military staff in India in 1943 about the value of science and scientists, gave a lecture on operational research and reported on his appraisal of the situation to the Viceroy. Hill himself had established a special group of physicists and mathematicians in the First World War with a responsibility to develop the ability to defend London against Zeppelin attacks. This group was called 'Hill's Brigands' during that war. When Lord Mountbatten needed scientific advisers in 1943 in Supreme Allied Command, Hill was instrumental in getting physicist J.D. Bernal and physiologist Solly Zuckerman to work for him, and Bernal spent the last weeks of 1944 in Calcutta, on the Arakan coast of Burma and at the HQ in Kandy, Ceylon.

Blackett, who moved effortlessly during the war between the naval and air force 'camps' in the British military, already had long experience of inter-service competition when he served on defence committees. Despite being classified as a naval expert, he developed the 'Blackett bombsight' (Mark XIV) that was standard equipment on Allied bomber aircraft, and specialised in bomber/bombing strategy and studies. He persuaded the Navy to form a group of physicists, astronomers, chemists, mathematicians, biologists and physiologists (six of whom were or would become Fellows of the Royal Society, two of those winning the Nobel prize) and this group became known as 'Blackett's Circus'. By November 1943 he had access to Ultra secret code material.[12] He knew Paul Rosbaud, the German physicist who supplied Churchill with a crucial assessment of the lack of progress of Werner Heisenberg and his team on an atomic bomb. He debriefed the captured German nuclear physics team at Farm Hall, just outside Cambridge, in September 1945, being the person asked for by both Heisenberg and Eric Welsh, the intelligence controller of Paul Rosbaud, the nuclear spy. 'It was a measure of confidence between the three men that Blackett was brought to Farm Hall.' It is probable that Rosbaud read the final draft of Blackett's 1948 book.[13] He sat on the key committees (or talked regularly with people like Sir John Cockcroft, Sir Henry

Tizard, Sir Rudolph Peierls and Sir James Chadwick who sat on committees) that bridged the public and secret uses of nuclear fission.

In addition, Blackett knew everybody interested in other future weapons. The contacts he had made at Cambridge, before leaving in 1933, gave him access almost everywhere. Moreover, throughout this period he understood all the engineering required to apply fission to both weapons and power generation. In 1946 he received the US Medal of Honor for his work on the Mark XIV bombsight. Yet, in 1948 he suffered a sudden drop in reputation in official American circles, reflecting the rise of 'anti-communism' and Senator Joseph McCarthy. President Truman issued the 'Loyalty Order' for federal employees in March 1947, and eventually suspicion reached physicist Robert Oppenheimer. Between 1947 and 1951 Attlee, the British prime minister, chaired the Cabinet Committee on Subversion. It applied the concept of 'negative vetting' which established a list of people who might constitute a risk to security. The discovery of the physicist-spies Fuchs and Pontecorvo by UK and US intelligence agencies was under way. Blackett's isolation in Britain was partly because of his book criticising the development of nuclear weapons for war, partly because of his friendship with British members of the Communist Party (like Bernal), and partly because of his relationship with Soviet scientists like Kapitza (whom he had nevertheless not done much personally to save from Stalin before the war). American advice probably played a role in his isolation; the bigger context for the treatment of this distinguished scientist was the British (Labour) government's effort to secure US loans to stave off their balance-of-payments crisis, and a mutual military security agreement (including nuclear weapons) with the Americans. Blackett was a disposable symbol in this shift, as moves like this were expected to appease some of the numerous Anglophobes in the US government. But observers of the British scene at the time remarked on the severity of the turn against him in defence and policy circles. Curiously, however, in 1949 he travelled again to the US for extensive talks with scientists and strategic analysts in the context of the publication of the American edition of his book on nuclear weapons. With so little evidence available, and so little open debate about nuclear weapons, Nehru would probably have read and discussed Blackett's book with him shortly after its publication in 1948, though we do not yet have evidence of their discussions about it.

It is his uncommon range of abilities and experience that made Blackett valuable to India, particularly his skill in the comparative analysis of military systems. Despite the chaotic changes going on around them, his friends in India correctly evaluated his value to their objectives. In the period between 1945 and independence, Britain was preoccupied with many issues in India but scientific development was not really among them. As the end drew near, Blackett briefed the Viceroy and British Commander-in-Chief Field-Marshal Auchinleck in Delhi, and Prime Minister Attlee, Sir Stafford Cripps and Lord Mountbatten (poised to be appointed to be the last Viceroy) in London about his intensive meetings in India with Nehru and members of the Atomic Energy Committee and Board of Atomic Research (Bhabha, Bhatnagar, Meghnad Saha) in early 1947. The subject of all these meetings was 'the atomic energy set-up in India', and he was also soliciting their commitment to assist his friend Homi Bhabha, whom Nehru had already identified as his own champion of atomic energy and nuclear research.[14]

In 1945 and 1946 Blackett was on the subcommittee on future weapons for the chiefs of staff of the British armed forces. He chaired the Harwell atomic power committee from May 1946, and was a member of the powerful Advisory Committee on Atomic Energy between August 1945 and April 1949, including after its renaming as the 'Nuclear Physics Committee' in January 1948, when Chadwick became chair and Blackett was vice-chair. Blackett was instrumental in having Tizard appointed to this committee, asking Stafford Cripps to include Tizard to strengthen an independent point of view in the committee (Tizard had supported Blackett in the 1942 strategic bombing controversy with Lindemann and others). Both Blackett and Tizard took the position that the UK should not develop atom bombs, should leave that project to the Americans, and should obtain some protective nuclear guarantee from them. This was not the position approved by Cabinet, and Blackett was identified again as a nonconformist. The British decision to develop nuclear weapons was taken in January 1947. Blackett had to leave the committee and return all of its documents in 1948. But Blackett was not just a physicist who understood nuclear strategy, he was also a naval officer with practical experience in war. In this he had something in common with the new Viceroy of India, Lord Mountbatten, with whom he would gradually become friendly. They had both been at Cambridge in 1919, but Blackett's meeting with Mountbatten on returning from his first trip to India in 1947 was not a great success. 'I wish I had been able to see Mountbatten alone,' he said,

> he was obviously much more sensible than [General] Ismay but still disappointed me a bit. He seemed very keen on finding all the arguments on why India should remain in the Commonwealth. It may be that this will in the end happen, but to over-stress our desire for it to do so would seem to me a mistake.[15]

Blackett had been convinced, in January and February, by people in Delhi who said Britain should leave India within three months, not six or nine. This relationship between Mountbatten, Blackett, Nehru and India was to be important; if Mountbatten had not generally respected Blackett's work, he could have undermined his effectiveness in India. From the friendly letters they exchanged in 1971–72 ('Dear Dickie', 'Dear Pat'), it appears that Mountbatten maintained throughout a respect for Blackett's activities in India, and Blackett would have known a great deal about Mountbatten's activities.

In 1967 Blackett reminisced, with characteristic confidence, about the experience of going to India to try to influence the defence establishment, and why he was selected:

> Nehru spoke to all the scientists, but I was the only scientist there with professional military experience; five years at sea in the first war, and four years amidst the application of scientific methods to modern warfare. So it was not very accidental that Nehru chose me to advise him.[16]

Five years later he said, with continuing satisfaction: 'On the whole I think that my views about the Indian armed forces expressed in 1948 have not proved too incorrect.'[17] Blackett's memory in 1967 was consistent with his first report in 1948. After the Indian conflict with China in 1962 and Pakistan in 1965, Blackett said that his effort from the beginning had been to prevent the unnecessary and costly introduction of weapons and strategies which would not have practical value, and to focus attention on the military risks which India did face. The most pervasive problem he faced was, Blackett said, that

> Indian officials and advisors were thinking purely from a Whitehall angle. There was an appalling psychological dependence on every word that Whitehall speaks. I understand in the beginning, in 1948, there was very little time and experience to think for yourself. But a great many of your problems are due to imitative adoption of

> Whitehall habits. Actually a lot of that thinking should not be exported anywhere. Some of it is not even good here.[18]

Blackett met the chiefs of the armed forces every time he went to India, and the Minister of Defence and the Minister's scientific adviser. He gave a talk to the chiefs of staff in the War Room each time, toured armaments and aircraft factories, appraised candidates for strategic analysis positions, and interpreted strategic implications of the Cold War into the Indian context. He got into the details of building tanks and developing rockets in India. He said, with great satisfaction in the 1967 interview, 'I like to think that … I saved India a lot of money by discouraging her from buying too much big and expensive Western equipment'. He distinguished between the Indian and British military risks to which new weapons were to be the solution. For example, in 1948 he advised the British forces to follow a rapid programme to develop supersonic fighter-planes, whereas for India he took a more cautious approach, and did not support integrated production of jet-fighters under licence in India until seven years later when he proposed a lighter, more versatile, transonic fighter based on an Anglo-Dutch model designed by people whose reputation he knew very well. Underlying Blackett's 1948 report is 'the understanding that it is the intention to make India as nearly as possible a self-supporting defence entity as may be at the earliest possible date' according to Abraham, who notes the remarkable similarities to the objectives of A.V. Hill's work during the war. 'Yet this understanding was neither invented by Blackett nor did it come from Hill. Blackett took the quotation on self-reliance verbatim from the "Report on Defence Science" (1946) written by Dr O.H. Wandsborough-Jones, a British defence scientist advising the colonial Indian government.'[19] One wonders whether the ideal of self-reliance was so immediately attractive to Blackett because he was sympathetic to the 1930s-style Fabian socialism which stressed self-reliance, and also because the experience during most of the Second World War required it of Britain, particularly before the entry of the United States in the war.

But, more importantly for him, he forced chiefs of forces and defence ministers to define what kind of wars they expected to fight, who the probable enemies were and what the risks were. He gave shrewd appraisals of his first adversaries, the admiral with whom he disagreed over the Navy's future, the air marshal and the chief of staff of the Army. These British officers commanded the Indian forces, and the transition to Indians in command was not quick. The first Indian officer, Vice-Admiral Katari, became the Chief of Naval Staff only in April 1958. In the case of the Navy, Blackett was intimately aware of Admiralty thinking and planning, and was known to everyone as a naval expert (despite his immense knowledge of aircraft). So the naval drama is, though smaller in scale, perhaps richer in nuance. Admiral Parry 'was a very nice man', said Blackett in 1967, 'but he tried to sell India, or make her buy, four fleet aircraft carriers which would have required 16 new destroyers to protect the carriers'. (These were light carriers of about 16,000 tons, then in great surplus, and being sold cheaply to friendly navies to raise money. Blackett might also have known that it was the Royal Navy's policy not to sell a carrier to India that year, because it felt that the Indian Navy was not ready to maintain one. His advice, and the Royal Navy's position, coincided, but for different reasons. This kind of carrier was eventually approved for purchase by India in 1957, and this British ship, which had commenced construction in 1943 (but was not completed during the war), was actually commissioned at sea in 1961 and renamed INS *Vikrant.*) The Blackett report on the Indian Navy is the only subject on which there was Cabinet disagreement in India. In order to prove that India could not afford the consequences of Admiral Parry's plan, Blackett had to strengthen his argument by obtaining, from friends in Whitehall, secret estimates of costs of ships currently under construction by the Royal Navy in 1948. The military situation in India was quite volatile. Blackett had also probably heard about the mutiny in the Indian Navy in the previous year. Vice-Admiral Parry returned fire a few days after seeing Blackett's report: 'I personally think you are being unrealistic in your fundamental assumptions – particularly that India should only prepare for a local war against an imaginary opponent of comparable overall strength to herself.'[20] Parry had planned an expansion in which India would experience a world war with current weapons of all types, building its Navy to protect India's sea links in all directions.

The British Admiralty rejoined first with instructions that India should simply defend the coastline and harbours of India, instructions that gradually enlarged to be that India's Navy should complement the strength and force structure of the total Commonwealth navies in case of a global war. These instructions came from no less a figure than the First Sea Lord, who was, by 1951, Lord Mountbatten. Because the Commander of the Indian Navy was, right through to 1956, a British-appointed and British-paid admiral, Mountbatten exercised great influence over the Indian Navy's development, and obtained from its chief all the intelligence the British needed about its strengths and weaknesses. The story of India's purchase of a second cruiser from Britain provides an extraordinary tour through the public and private lives of the players. A second cruiser was negotiated in 1949–50, but put on hold owing to the Korean War. Parry wrote plaintively to Mountbatten in 1951 that 'if the question [of the cruiser] has to be shelved very much longer we shall have to make some rather drastic decisions'.[21] The shelving of the cruiser continued, so, during one of Nehru's London visits in 1951 when he dined with the Mountbattens, the cruiser was discussed. Mountbatten urged him to write to Prime Minister Attlee to ask for the cruiser, which Nehru did.[22] Gradually the Admiralty came to the view that the second cruiser should be sold to India, but the Indian government was coming to the view that they should not accept it. 'During this period the roles of the major players got reversed.'[23] Three years later, the (British) Commander-in-Chief of the Indian Navy, Vice-Admiral Pizey, wrote to Mountbatten to describe the decisive role that Edwina Mountbatten played in convincing Nehru to override the objections and delays of finance and defence ministry officials about the cruiser. Pizey stated: 'it was mainly due to [her] "whisper" in the right direction that we managed to speed up the government's acceptance of the second cruiser ... The speed at which things happened over a certain weekend was really quite remarkable.'[24] Although Blackett's name is unmentioned, this story is relevant because it shows the tangled web of affection and loyalty within which Blackett worked, the interdependence of British and Indian buyers and sellers of major military equipment, the interplay of commercial and strategic calculations, the role of the Mountbattens, and the continuing direction coming from Britain.

The Air Force Chief Air Marshal Elmhirst, Blackett stated in his 1967 interview about his first report in 1948, 'tried to make India buy long-range bombers', which would ruin India while being useless in local wars. Worse, he said, long-range bombers would have been dangerous to India, inducing massive and uncontrollable retaliation. For the Chief of the Army Blackett had more respect.

General Bucher was less intellectual but wiser than the others. He was born and brought up in India, and understood what it was about; he knew the terrain. He immediately spotted that the arms salesmen were trying to sell us things like these tanks without telling us they were too big to cross our bridges.[25]

It cannot have escaped Nehru's attention that it was very useful to have an expert like Blackett with a network in Whitehall to appraise the plans of India's (British) defence chiefs with their own networks in Whitehall.

Blackett also discovered at first hand the post-war 'Colonel Blimp culture' in India, which enraged him, and reported to Sir Stafford Cripps that he had just met General H.L. Ismay in 1947 with Lord Mountbatten in London. Ismay (who was also born in India, and would become Secretary of State for the Commonwealth in 1951) 'produced more "Blimpisms"', said Blackett, 'than I have heard from anyone for ages. He did not seem to me to have a clue as to the real situation in India. He just doesn't know the facts.'[26] Blackett had experienced this culture at closer range a few weeks before, when he joined an expedition which had been planned for bird watching but which (in anticipation of Blackett's being unable to join in) was changed to bird shooting. Blackett's love of birds was well known, and his first lecture at Cambridge was partly about bird watching. In the end, Blackett (not sympathetic to shooting birds) joined the expedition. 'I was invited by a British General, who was a friend of mine … We drove out some 20 miles from New Delhi', he said:

> and then looked for partridges by drawing a rope across the top of a small sugar field. The villagers soon came along, all with their Gandhi caps, to protest against the party shooting in their fields, without even asking permission – adding that the last shooting party had shot a peacock, which of course are sacred birds. This is what was translated to us. The leader of the shooting party told the villagers that they were not harming the crops and they had no intention to shoot peacocks. The villagers looked surly but did not protest any further. Later in the afternoon the shooting party was driving slowly along an irrigation dyke when a peacock was seen on the dyke about a hundred yards ahead of the cars. The leader of the shooting party stopped the car, jumped out and raised his gun. But before he had fired an Indian woman walked up the bank of the

> dyke between the car and the peacock. The leader lowered his gun and said 'what a bore, now we won't have peacock at the Club tomorrow'. Two years later at a cocktail party in New Delhi I was introduced to a man whom I recognised as the leader of the (to me) memorable shooting party. He is a British diplomat. This [incident on the dyke] was January 1947, at a time of acute civil disturbance and with the end of the British Raj only a few months ahead. One would have thought that all Britishers would have been on their best behaviour. Was the shooting party typical of the heyday of the British Raj?[27]

Presumably Blackett knew the answer to this rhetorical question, and this helped explain why he did not wish to go to India before its independence.

In his 1948 report to the Minister of Defence Blackett listed those weapons which should not be on India's list for development, as follows: atomic weapons, chemical warfare, supersonic jets, high-performance jets and guided missiles. All of these were unsuitable, he said. At the same time Blackett grasped from the beginning what not all Indians or British realised – that, despite 200 years of a deeply intertwined military development, British forces were not likely to play any further role in conflicts involving India, and that foreign troops with these weapons were not likely to be based in India. Blackett soon saw Indian troops deployed inside India, in Hyderabad and Kashmir. Nehru wrote a remarkably long letter to Blackett to thank him for his work, to praise the Indian military success in Hyderabad, and to say that the war risk over Kashmir had subsided: 'I think definitely that there is hardly any chance of war between India and Pakistan. Of course the Kashmir issue remains and it is a difficult one.'[28]

Blackett says he gradually elaborated a theory of marginal war, preparing India for war with a country the size and force of Pakistan, and not with Russia or a Western power. He did not mention China. 'The Pakistan war [of 1965] was an exact example,' he said in 1967, 'countries of similar makeup fought each other to a stand-still, more or less.' He tried constantly to redirect the Indian attraction to grandiose military projects. By 1949 he had gained the public glow of winning a Nobel prize, something he did not have on his first two visits in 1947 and early 1948. He had also been told, in 1948, he was *persona non grata* in the US, and was later detained by American officials when his Canadian plane refuelled briefly in Florida in 1950. This may have added to his stature in India where there was a camaraderie among and respect for those who spent time in the prisons of a well-known 'big power'. It is a measure of the deepening of the Cold War that Blackett was awarded the Medal of Honor by the US in 1946 and quietly declared *persona non grata* by the US in 1948. The change in the international climate was equally dramatic: Churchill's 1947 'Iron Curtain' speech in America provided a figure of speech to conjure the new state of affairs. The US sought to install and secure a monopoly of knowledge surrounding atomic energy and weapons. On the Western Front in 1948, the Berlin Blockade posed again the risk of a war in Europe between the Allies and the Soviets. In 1949 the Chinese communist revolution was successful, and the USSR tested their first atomic bomb in August. Because of these changes, because India had become a member of the UN, because CENTO was being planned, and because India's views on the Korean War were receiving wide publicity, India was now being taken a little more seriously. A new and alternative model of development was evidently needed, by India as well as others. Over the next five years Nehru articulated his policies of non-alignment, trying to build enduring relationships with south-east Asia and China, and trying to limit the extent to which India became dependent on the Americans.

The atmosphere surrounding Blackett's work for Nehru in 1948–50 was turbulent. Indian scientists like Bhabha, Bhatnagar and Kothari were thrown into work that had immediate strategic implications. They worked in a more conflictual world, particularly after partition and the military operations directed by the Indian Army in 1948. No longer did foreigners direct these activities, but Indians. Less than a year after independence, a young Hindu zealot assassinated Mahatma Gandhi in his garden in Delhi, creating a martyr and settling a leadership question; the people around Nehru would now be fully in charge (with Patel's death in 1950 it would be Nehru alone who guided the Congress Party). Gandhi's rootedness, like many of his followers, became a progressively more nostalgic force; Nehru's cosmopolitan, patrician and elitist leadership was without serious challenge, even from the Hindu extremists who privately approved of partition and Gandhi's death. The partition and Gandhi's assassination were a chilling and dramatic closing and opening of possibilities. These were the possibilities and constraints that Blackett had to address.

Concerned about the costs of licensed defence production, and about capturing more benefits in India from Indian innovations, Blackett asked Shanti Bhatnagar in 1948 to provide him with a list of all patents held by Indians which might be applicable to defence production. In 1950 Bhatnagar sent him all 'the various projects which have been patented, exploited, or under consideration for exploitation'.[29] In another era this information would have been considered top secret. He then began to examine production facilities. His tours of armaments factories were an observational displeasure. He recalled a factory set up north of Bombay by the Swiss arms manufacturer Oerlikon:

> absolutely four million pounds went down the drain. India did not want new prototype weapons like Oerlikon did, Indians wanted to manufacture existing weapons. The factory had some refugee-Germans trying to invent recoil-less guns, under the charge of a charming ICS man who had been to Oxford and who did not know anything about machine tools in the first place.

In 1967 he went on:

> You ran your Bangalore electronics factory down. It is running all right now. But it took ages to get it going, because the people in charge had no knowledge of it. One of the Defence Minister's followers was a poet. He was so embarrassed. He did not know one machine tool from another.

Elsewhere Blackett said that he should not be misunderstood: 'I am deriding my civil servants just as much. They thought they could run anything, being at Oxford.'[30]

As part of 'Indianisation', Blackett immediately advised Nehru to establish a new research function within the Ministry of Defence. Until this time most research had been carried out in Britain. There were a few Technical Development Establishments under the Indian Army with the purpose of providing inspection and quality control in ordnance factories. Although the officer corps were well trained and educated, scientists and engineers were not involved. A few weeks after giving his first major report to Nehru on defence in 1948, Blackett wrote to the Minister of Defence, 'I am delighted with your choice of Dr. Kothari to be scientific adviser to the Defence

Ministry. I am in complete agreement with his views on these matters.'[31] Daulat Singh Kothari, whom he helped to become the Scientific Adviser to the Minister of Defence and who thus headed the new Defence Science Organisation (later the Defence Research and Development Organisation), had first met Blackett in the Cavendish Laboratories in Cambridge in the early 1930s. Trained by Saha at Allahabad, Kothari was a theoretical astrophysicist who had seen how Rutherford's experimental laboratory was organised, and how stars in it like Blackett functioned. This new Defence Science Organisation in Delhi was modelled on the one Blackett had just prescribed for the United Kingdom. Since it was first housed in the new National Physical Laboratory (of the CSIR), and borrowed scientists and equipment from it, there was around 1950 a deep integration of personnel in defence research and industrial research. The close relationship between Bhabha, Bhatnagar, Kothari and Blackett – and all of them with Nehru – reinforced the structural advances of such integration. Kothari now joined the group of science developers who had institutes to build and positions to fill; within months of starting, Kothari received a letter from his revered teacher, Meghnad Saha, enquiring about a job in defence research for one of Saha's sons.[32] By 1951 Blackett was channelling all Indian requests for employment (on defence matters) directly to Kothari. In 1953, for example, Bhabha heard of Blackett's visit to Delhi and telephoned Kothari from Bombay to ensure adequate time was set aside from his defence work for a visit to TIFR in Bombay. Kothari then informed Meghnad Saha and P.C. Mahalanobis in Calcutta of the Blackett visit to TIFR, and they immediately wrote to Blackett to have their institutes put on the itinerary. Curiously, Blackett does not seem to have developed a relationship with K.S. Krishnan, the physicist who was Director of the National Physical Laboratory and also member of the Atomic Energy Commission.

Blackett decided to intervene in training. Having overseen the creation of a Defence Science Organisation, in 1950 he urged the creation of functional groups such as the Weapons Assessment Team and the Operational Research Group. By 1951 he was clearing the way for Indian defence scientists to spend a year at Cambridge and in the UK Operational Research Group. He also acted as intermediary for the appointment of the first Director of the Indian Institute of Armament Studies, a Briton who was previously at the

RAF College. At that time Blackett and Kothari discussed a naval research laboratory for Bombay. Although Blackett wanted a focus on real problems, he also said from the beginning (to the Minister of Defence), 'It is most important to realise ... that a research and development establishment must often keep a considerable number of its personnel employed on work which promises no immediate or tangible results.'[33]

Blackett played this catalyst and promotional role for operational research in Sweden too, beginning with the very high access granted him when he received the Nobel prize in 1948, and continuing through the 1950s.[34]

In the years following independence there were immediate pressures on Indian leaders to face the new (and uncertain) position of the country in a hardening Cold War environment. Blackett understood this environment as well as anyone else, although his interpretations of it were unconventional. After the 1948 Berlin Blockade was broken, attention turned in August 1949 to the Soviet atomic bomb tests and the success of the Chinese Communist Party in taking full control of China. The Americans, confused by events, realised with chagrin that their efforts in China had been futile, and were chastened to admit that even their most rigorous controls on information had not stopped the Soviets from developing their own atomic bomb. French and Dutch military forces had been fighting unsuccessfully in Vietnam and Indonesia to preserve their colonial territories, and the march of North Korean and Chinese troops into Seoul in 1950 decisively opened Allied eyes to the risk to their interests in Asia. Particularly because of its policy of non-alignment India began to be taken slightly more seriously by the Americans. The Indian Ambassador in Washington had prepared the ground for Nehru, and the US Ambassador to India wrote a formal request to the President for five years of economic assistance. Nehru did not like the conditions that the US put on these loans, and did not pursue the request vigorously during his 1949 visit (in part because he found his relations with President Truman and Secretary of State Acheson so difficult). The Indian Ambassador and then Nehru himself discussed possible loans for wheat and steel with the Americans in 1949. President Truman's response was that India should apply to the World Bank for these loans. Following this US rejection, Nehru then suggested to Krishna Menon (High Commissioner in London) that they should 'align with the US somewhat and build up our economic and military strength'.[35] Despite its inconsistency with the non-alignment policy, the signal had been sent, and grain from Canada and the US eventually began arriving in 1950–51, after prolonged official negotiation.[36]

As a confidant of Homi Bhabha, Shanti Bhatnagar and Nehru, Blackett understood what the Indians were doing in atomic research from the beginning, and he thus sometimes avoided explaining this publicly. Since 1944 the security of India's thorium and beryl had been a quiet but steady theme in Anglo-American politics. In 1951 the story emerged in Washington that President Truman had made an explicit connection between a new 'Grain for India' plan and the fact that India held three-quarters of the world's monazite/thorium. As it was known in London which person understood the implications of this connection, the editor of the *Daily Telegraph* telephoned and wrote to Blackett asking for an interview. Blackett's disingenuous reply was: 'I have nothing to tell you which would be of use to you nor do I have any comment on the report.'[37] By now Blackett had become quite familiar with India's rocks and minerals because of his new interest in geomagnetism, so he would have known. There are differing views of how forthcoming Blackett was about enquiries like this. Some, including those who met him, say he was ready to explain situations or his work in an informal manner to people who were not well known to him, others (basing their opinion on reading his papers) that he typically refused interviews and requests for informal help.

By this time, although Bhabha was regularly meeting his official counterpart and old Cambridge friend Sir John Cockcroft, Director of the Atomic Energy Commission, he could always get another view from Blackett, whom he met at least twice a year, and usually more. Blackett helped Bhabha indirectly too. For example, he met the scientific attaché to the Indian High Commission in London in 1951 who Bhabha said was 'studying the organisation of institutions where nuclear and atomic research is in progress'. Although the UK Atomic Energy Authority treated this survey very cautiously, Blackett knew it was being done for Bhabha and Bhatnagar, and he gave his views on the proper organisation of an atomic research and development system, drawing on his intimate knowledge of the organisational set-up in Britain.[38]

Committed to atomic energy, and tactically (if not morally) opposed to atomic bombs, Blackett never lost sight of the importance of conventional weapons. To Nehru in 1951 he wrote, gently promoting Kothari's influence, 'I have heard from Kothari that he is carrying on energetically the investigations we started on tank and anti-tank gun performance.'[39] At the same time, however, Blackett was talking to people in London about new weapons like rockets, as he did with H.A. Sargeaunt, Deputy Scientific Adviser for the Army Council in the War Office, Whitehall. 'Kothari's group', reported Sargeaunt from Delhi,

> is certainly making great strides, and I think there is no doubt that when you next come you will be impressed. My feeling is that they must now think in terms of specific Indian problems rather than copying the problems of other nations.[40]

This was the very goal which Blackett was striving to achieve – he perceived a predisposition to adopting the solutions developed elsewhere to problems which were not theirs. Nevertheless, Blackett was supportive of new initiatives like rockets, which did not have to be British: 'when I was there at Christmas the Minister was particularly keen on a French rocket weapon which sounded very good'.[41] Notwithstanding his proximity to the Indian High Commission in London and his meetings with Krishna Menon, Nehru's adviser on foreign and military policy, there is an absence of correspondence between Blackett and Menon in the Blackett Papers. This suggests that they met frequently enough (or read accounts in newspapers) to know each other's views, but that they did not develop a close relationship. In one sense Menon might have seen Blackett as competition for Nehru's attention, and a person not wholly committed to the kind of socialism Menon wanted.

According to Blackett, one personal military planning triumph occurred in 1955. It was an application of the principle which his friend Homi Bhabha was following in atomic energy, namely to decide on the appropriate technology, to import a prototype and get training in production, and to set about producing the technology in India. Blackett realised that since he was engaged not only in weapons evaluation but also in the merger of defence policy with industrial policy and macro-economic policy, these economic, social and military objectives would be in conflict. He understood that planning had to take into account such conflict. Blackett was just learning about the socio-economic and political complexities of

India. After the use of Indian forces inside India in Hyderabad and Kashmir, Blackett had to think strategically about kinds of conflict he had not seen before. It is important to remember the strategic context of the time. In 1954 and 1955 friendship treaties had been concluded and visits exchanged between both China and the USSR and India. In 1955 the Soviets 'expressed a willingness to sell advanced military aircraft' to enhance their offer to build a steel mill in India.[42] (But one notes that the first MiG fighters only actually arrived in India in 1963, after India's conflict with China.) And Nehru was at the height of his non-aligned strategy, chairing the Bandung Conference on non-alignment just before the Gnat fighter deal was initiated between India and Britain. It was also in 1954 that India increased the size of its dollar reserves and proposed cutting the rupee free from sterling in order to follow an independent exchange rate policy. Fearing 'a break in a uniform sterling front and damage to the international role of sterling' (and critical of the increase in dollar reserves), the Bank of England and the Chancellor of the Exchequer pleaded with India not to present its proposal to the Commonwealth summit meeting. There was, at the same time, speculation on the pound and thus a sharp fall in the value of Indian sterling reserves, which were still very healthy, at £542 million pounds.[43] These reserves were still held, at the time, in the Bank of England. So, for political and economic reasons, Britain should have been very pleased with Patrick Blackett's influence as a military consultant in the Gnat contract.

The triumph Blackett alluded to concerns jet-fighters. The Indian Air Force already had a Vampire fighter, constructed from airframes built in Bangalore and imported British engines. Like others, Blackett proposed an aeronautical research and development establishment from the beginning, 'if India is to build an air industry'.[44] But in 1955 Blackett's proposal was radical and risky: to start building a fighter much lighter than the Vampire and to build both the airframe and the engine. The choice, argued Blackett, should be the Gnat, a transonic aircraft with a ceiling of 50,000 feet and thrust of 4,800 lb compared to Vampire's 3,300 lb. It was easier and cheaper to manufacture than alternatives, thus giving (said Blackett) two Gnats for every conventional fighter, and more quickly. The catch was that it had not been combat-tested. Blackett later said that, although the Gnat was still not fully operational, its designer came to Delhi and made a very convincing argument which eventually convinced most present including myself. In fact I became a very strong advocate for going into mass production before waiting for the full tests of the Gnat had been carried out: this meant gambling on the outstanding ability of Petter as designer and Folland as Chief Engineer.[45]

The discussions about the jet-fighter 'often became vehement', said Blackett. 'I think that the majority of service pilots were against the Gnat but there was strong enough support from some of the technical staff at the Ministry to win the case eventually.' (The Scientific Adviser's Report described the Gnat as 'severely utilitarian', which might have been unattractive to pilots who wanted something fancy.) India was stepping into a zone of high uncertainty, Blackett said;

> one has also to recognise the fact that during these days of terrific rate of development in fighter-aircraft, it is very difficult to forecast what current types would actually (if ever) find their use in war. Many types would never see war. They would, however, have served the purpose of leading to more effective successors, eventually leading to the nth successor which sees battle.[46]

Here Blackett the planner triumphed, arguing that the Hindustan Aeronautics Limited programme 'should consist of items which are a requirement for the Services (or better still for the Services as well as civil aviation), and which are within its technical reach and resources'. Blackett later took pride in the report that led to the Gnat instead of heavier and more sophisticated aircraft. The Gnat performed very well in both wars with Pakistan in 1965 and 1971, but, he noted wryly, 'it never became an important aircraft in the Royal Air Force'.[47] The Gnat did, however, become the main jet training aircraft for the Royal Air Force for many years.

Not all his advice was accepted, however, following the success of the Gnat deal. Kurt Tank, a leading designer of the Focke-Wulf team during the Second World War, was brought to Bangalore. Blackett recalled:

> another occasion when I think a wrong decision was made. This was the plan to bring to Bangalore Dr Tank, who was famous in the last war for his brilliant German fighter designs. The plan was that

> Tank should design a quite new supersonic fighter which would be designed, manufactured and tested in India. I was strongly against this as I thought it too big a step from a simple trainer designed and built at Bangalore to a supersonic fighter. My views were not accepted. This project was a very big one. A few such aircraft were made but I did not hear of their use in either of the two Pakistan–India wars.[48]

Here Blackett's views are controversial; some observers say the fighter, called the HF 24, that Kurt Tank developed played a significant role in the 1971 war between India and Pakistan; others point out that the 1969 Report of the Committee on Aeronautics (chaired by C. Subramaniam) criticised the HF 24 and that the aircraft never received full approval.

After revelations of the unprepared and ill-equipped state of military forces during the 1962 conflict with China, and the subsequent resignation of Krishna Menon as Minister of Defence, there was a complete review of Indian armed forces. Blackett's knowledge of the past was now useful again and, in the context of a letter on the progress of cosmic ray studies, Bhabha wrote by hand in the margin, 'I hope you will agree to take on the job of reviewing our Defence Research organisation, if asked to do so later'.[49] In 1967 Blackett said that his military consulting declined as time went on, but there was still an admiral of the Navy included in a dinner party given for him at the High Commissioner's Residence in Delhi in 1965 (plus the Cabinet Secretary, arguably the most influential person around the Prime Minister), and he was asked to read a confidential report on precision optical manufacturing (with military applications) in 1966. By this time, of course, he was President of the Royal Society and thus very busy. But he kept up his study of Indian scientific and military institutions, and continuously used his influence to improve conditions for doing research. He formed a long friendship with General J.N. Chaudhuri whose command of Indian forces at Hyderabad in 1948 Blackett had admired (there is a letter in Blackett's papers showing this, written much later). I recall being asked by General Chaudhuri at McGill University in 1970 whether I had spoken with Patrick Blackett about science and scientists in India and, if not, he advised that I should do so quickly: 'he knows the facts', said Chaudhuri.

A study of Patrick Blackett's work for the military in India up to 1964 reveals some things that were not widely known. Although

Blackett's presence in India for military work was always public knowledge, it is the other work he did with scientists that took on greater importance. Although his seminal 1948 report to the Minister of Defence remains secret in India to this day, his military persona was not clandestine. However, it was as a physicist who had won the Nobel prize that Blackett circulated among scientists and intellectuals and who naturally acquired a reputation for the development of science. On the basis of evidence available so far, I do not think that Blackett's work as scientific intervenor was a camouflage for Blackett as military adviser. Nor do we yet have any evidence about Blackett's possible role in providing intelligence and influence for Britain. For example, in a recent study of the use of British scientists by British intelligence agencies in this period, Paul Maddrell found no trace of Blackett in the files.[50] An explanation, Maddrell suggested, is that intelligence agencies were preoccupied with science and secrecy in Europe and the USSR, contributing to their indifference about what could be learned via India or via Blackett. They may have presumed that nothing of importance could be learned via India. Another explanation is that because he was not trusted by the governments in power he was an unreliable source, too 'pro-Soviet', and perhaps unlikely to be useful. Again, in a review of evidence related to the uses of air bases in India and Pakistan for UK strategic offensive bombing plans against the USSR, Aldrich and Coleman found no trace of Blackett's name.[51] This last absence is 'counter-intuitive', in that Blackett was an acknowledged bombing expert at the very time when Britain was trying (in 1946–49) to secure access to airbases (not just in Peshawar) from which to reach industrial targets deep in the Soviet Union. Despite his personal antipathy to the idea of offensive bombing of the USSR, it is nevertheless conceivable that such agencies could have found informal ways to learn what Blackett knew, which would have been considerable.

Few foreigners, if any, have played a role in independent India such as that played by Patrick Blackett between 1947 and 1972. As a military consultant he initiated a debate about the effective role of scientific research in military development, and promoted the conditions and careers of scientists attached to defence research, particularly up to about 1964. This was a period of dramatic change in India, with an emphasis on comparatively low-cost military development (particularly when compared with later periods). The same period also marked the steady decline in India's foreign exchange reserves, and Blackett understood how this decline would influence major strategic programmes, determine the level of imports, influence relations with rich countries and establish the volume of subsidies sought by the Indian government. An argument for 'self-reliance' became more and more necessary, although paradoxically was increasingly difficult to put into practice as reserves dwindled. He argued for (and against) new weapons, learned how these developments or purchases were financed, and helped in some instances to make appointments and close deals. He reinforced an attitude of 'self-reliance' already in circulation in the 1940s – articulated by Indian scientists long before any real prospect of independence for India – and which traded on the momentum of Gandhi's and Congress's idea of a self-reliant industry, made-at-home goods and independent-minded politics. While Gandhi would not have imagined this idea applied to military development, Nehru and his political allies/advisers learned that it would be a policy of necessity, simply because there could be few alternatives. At the same time, Blackett's independent views on nuclear weapons and 'the arms race' were a stimulant to discussions with Nehru, Homi Bhabha and other scientists. He was a regular guest of the chiefs of staff, discussing both disarmament and armaments. In this sense there was an official acceptance of his presence and advice. During this period India learned how to optimise the potential of great-power rivalry, and to use this rivalry to obtain favourable terms for commercial and military contracts and agreements. But, most importantly, Blackett helped Indian leaders to rethink military development and concentrate on relevant conflicts of a local and regional nature.

BLACKETT AND THE COUNCIL FOR SCIENTIFIC AND INDUSTRIAL RESEARCH

> What has gone wrong, I think, in some government research stations is that the principle of scientific freedom has sometimes been misapplied to mission-oriented R and D, where it is largely inapplicable.[52]

It is not as a military consultant, however, but as an intervenor in scientific affairs and adviser to the research system that Blackett was and is best known in India. He came to understand its political economy, specifically the political limits of the influence of the scientific community and the way in which very scarce economic resources were (or were not) mobilised within it. Blackett and Bhatnagar (and Nehru) often discussed the development of the vast government research organisation, the CSIR, but after the visit of the winter of 1955–56 Blackett is curiously absent from India for seven years (according to his own records). The 1956 Gnat fighter deal seems to end the first phase of this involvement, which began in 1947. Until his sudden death in January 1955 Bhatnagar was in regular communication with Blackett, and they sometimes toured CSIR laboratories together. Blackettt's deeper involvement with the CSIR seemed to occur after 1963–64, during which period his work as a military consultant gradually decreased. He appears to have liked Bhatnagar and approved of the general direction of the CSIR's evolution as the state's applied research system, even if he saw research that was not being or could not be applied. In the eight years that Blackett knew him (1947–55), he helped Bhatnagar a great deal. Bhatnagar valued Blackett's influence with Nehru, and supplied Blackett with the list of patents he needed for a study of defence production. Bhatnagar worked hard to find good appointees for his laboratories, and was always looking outside India for candidates. There is no clue in the papers whether Blackett advised for or against the appointment of non-Indians, but he certainly assisted Bhatnagar, Kothari and Bhabha to identify candidates abroad. In 1951, Blackett interviewed a Canadian metallurgist working in London who wanted to 'get a job in India and settle there permanently'. Bhatnagar said the new National Metallurgical Laboratory was already 'in the charge of a brilliant young Frenchman', and he welcomed the arrival of this Canadian, W.K.A. Congreve, from London, with Blackett's favourable opinion based on a metallurgist colleague's expert recommendation.[53] A.V. Hill played a similar role at this time, looking internationally for good candidates for Bhatnagar, but Hill already had a much longer and deeper involvement in the development of the CSIR, starting in 1943.[54]

At the same time as he investigated patents, Blackett was inspired by a research project on solar power at the National Physical Laboratory (NPL) in Delhi, and went to considerable lengths to obtain French reports for the Indians in 1951. It is curious Bhatnagar could not obtain these directly, because an agreement (involving

Bhatanagar) was signed that year between France and India on scientific co-operation, including rare earths and nuclear power.[55] The NPL solar-powered cooker project did not deliver on its promise, but Blackett's papers do not reveal evidence of the extent of Bhatnagar's embarrassment or Nehru's displeasure with its failure. Blackett's involvement in the NPL was to become much deeper in a few years. A series of problems arose within the CSIR with respect to leadership of the National Physical Laboratory after the death of K.S. Krishnan in 1961, and Blackett was appointed by the Minister of Scientific Research and Cultural Affairs (Humayun Kabir) to conduct what the newspapers called a 'Full Enquiry at NPL'. Moreover, one of these news stories said that 'the Director's post ... was offered to Professor Blackett last year, but he declined it'.[56] There is no trace of this offer in the Blackett Papers at the Royal Society, but the idea may have been presented in person, and is consistent with the esteem in which Blackett was held.

Publicity about his NPL Enquiry prompted his old friend from London, biologist J.B.S. Haldane, to invite Blackett to visit for a discussion about CSIR. Writing from Orissa, and with seven years' experience of living and working in India, Haldane drew Blackett's attention to what he must learn before he formed an opinion about the CSIR, and provided Blackett with the following advice:

> I don't envy you your job. Considerable efforts will be made at the top to prevent you from finding out the truth, and when you do get through to unofficial sources you will hear some outrageous lies from people who cannot imagine an uncorrupt reason for doing anything. I advise you to get hold of the contract offered to junior scientific workers (such as myself) agreeing to go anywhere at a month's notice.[57]

Blackett worked fast at the NPL, and submitted a report in a month. He recommended reorganisation of the whole laboratory, moving some or most of those who worked largely in basic research to a new Centre for Advanced Physics at the University of Delhi, moving those in rain and cloud physics out to the Meteorological Department, moving potential manufacturing units in radio, glass and ceramics out to join their industries, and defining the work of remaining divisions more clearly while enhancing communication among them. Blackett found a culture of administrative rigidity in the

NPL where most people fought to define and protect the boundaries of their work. In effect, what he said was that the NPL lacked purpose. He had earlier criticised the fact that the CSIR had pressured Sir K.S. Krishnan to leave basic research in a university, offering double his professor's salary, to ask him to try to build a research tradition applied to industrial problems. Blackett had seen this same phenomenon at Britain's National Physical Laboratory at Teddington. Both Blackett and A.V. Hill criticised this practice in India. D.S. Kothari also criticised Bhatnagar for taking scientists away from the universities, but his own Defence Science Organisation did the same thing, when it could. Bhatnanagar and Kothari argued that there was no other source of competent people. The CSIR set up a committee to review Blackett's report, tour the laboratories, and recommend how the Executive Council of NPL should respond to it. In April 1963 this committee reported to the Executive Council that 'The Committee finds itself in general agreement with the spirit of the Blackett report.' Its own assessment for its implementation was that

> there should be enough flexibility so that when an individual project is taken up which requires that scientists from different disciplines be brought together, then it should be possible to do this without difficulty. This aspect has been sorely neglected hitherto.

There was an exception to their approval, however, in that 'the Committee was not at all in favour of one possibility indicated by Professor Blackett, that of completely amalgamating the proposed Centre for Advanced Physics with the Delhi University'. The report suggested instead an institute like the Saha Institute in Calcutta that was autonomous from but very close to the university, with university participation in its governing body. The members of this committee included M.G.K. Menon of TIFR (author of the report), R.C. Majumdar of Delhi University, A.K. Saha and B.D. Nag Chaudhuri of Calcutta's Saha Institute of Nuclear Physics – the latter three had been students of Meghnad Saha – plus J.C. Kapur, W.M. Vaidyaya and L.C. Verman.[58] The Menon Committee proposed changes that did not always satisfy Blackett, and on his copy, beside the issue of the Centre for Advanced Physics, he noted: 'All this does not agree with my recommendations.' Much may be learned from a study of this era and these individuals in the NPL. Blackett was well aware of the complicated historic relations between universities and government laboratories; the debate was already loud about how universities were being deprived of good researchers and so could not demonstrate how good research was also a form of training. On the other hand there was equally loud criticism that universities were inhospitable to good researchers, and this criticism was based on an assumption that government laboratories actually were the source of most good research in India. For a historical explanation of this contested relationship, see the recent essay by Raina and Jain.[59]

The saga of the NPL reached Blackett again in late December 1964, when the Director-General of the CSIR, Husain Zaheer, wrote to him:

> I am afraid matters have not improved very much during the past year. The Director, whom we appointed last October, had eventually to be removed from service. [It is unclear whether he meant P.K. Kichlu.] The main defect was that he could not get on well with his younger colleagues. Now we are on the lookout for appointing a Director.

It was the Director who would have to implement the changes.[60] Blackett had just been in India, and discussed with Zaheer his opinion that the Chinese were far advanced in electronic instruments. (This was not the first time this warning to India had been sounded by a British physicist: newspapers throughout India had carried the statement of Blackett's friend J.D. Bernal in December 1954 that 'China has made more rapid progress in science than India'. Speaking in Madras, Bernal said this in the context of his support for the 'Five Nehru–Chou Principles', and his condemnation of the arms race. Nehru, who had, like Bernal, just returned from China, was keen to meet Bernal in Delhi to hear his views, according to Bernal's papers.)

The 1962 military conflict with China caused a rapid and agonised re-appraisal of India's development and military requirements. Homi Bhabha was appointed chairman of an Electronics Committee in 1963, charged to plan the mobilisation of Indian resources for increased research, development and production in electronics. Zaheer accepted Blackett's warning about the Chinese and electronics, and quickly outlined the steps two CSIR labs were taking – one in electronic engineering in Palani and the other in scientific instruments at Chandigarh – but Zaheer did not admit (in his 1964 letter) that the underdevelopment of electronics was retarding India. The real issue was not simply electronic instruments for researchers, or electronic engineering for production and military systems, but was also consumer electronics and, more fundamentally, the supply and delivery of electricity itself. Homi Bhabha had just negotiated contracts in 1963 with Canada and the US for nuclear reactors that were intended to solve this problem once and for all. Or so many people thought.

Blackett was, at this stage, newly appointed adviser to the Minister of Science in the new Labour government. His relationship with the CSIR certainly continued, though soon Blackett became President of the Royal Society and was even busier. But he did not lose interest. For example, he received a copy of the confidential report written by C.G. Wynne of Imperial College for the Director-General of the CSIR about optical designing.[61] At the same time, Wynne also wrote Blackett a long personal account of his visits to National Aeronautics Ltd, the Glass and Ceramics Institute, and commercial firms, lamenting the amount of money wasted in assistance to India and the frustration of talent in research centres like the Glass and Ceramics Institute in Calcutta. Wynne reported that everyone in India recognised the strategic necessity of a developing a high-precision optical glass industry, and that everyone thought India was proceeding too slowly towards that goal, but everyone blamed someone else. This conformed with the views of a wide range of Indian and foreign opinion on many matters of strategic necessity, and this negative opinion reached the Scientific Advisory Committee to the Cabinet in 1966–67, thus initiating a wide review of success and failure in the scientific and industrial community.

In a way Wynne's 1966 report gave Blackett his subject for the Nehru Memorial Lecture a year later. This lecture was attended by Prime Minister Indira Gandhi and reviewed in all newspapers. He called for thinking about 'the innovation chain' from research to production, albeit in a somewhat linear way of thinking about innovation. He wanted industry in India involved in the process of innovation from its inception at the laboratory stage. He criticised the 'sanctity' of basic research. Blackett's Nehru Lecture was gleefully received in some government and industry quarters, because it shook things up a bit. Some researchers, whose lives depended on the 'sanctity' of basic research, felt he had attacked them, and some researchers felt betrayed because Blackett's lecture seemed to undermine them, even in the laboratories founded by Homi Bhabha and so often visited by Blackett himself. This was a widespread reaction after the lecture among scientists in India, in both Bombay and Calcutta. Blackett probably never heard this reaction to his lecture, and would not have understood that researchers 'in the ranks' thought the support for basic research was fragile. He was now communicating at a level very far removed from researchers 'in the ranks' and it appeared that he thought that support for basic research was sufficiently strong. A few days later he wrote to Atma Ram, Director-General of the CSIR: 'it has been quite clear in recent months that our ways of thinking are very similar ... I do realise the difficulty you will have in guiding Indian policy in a new direction.'[62] Up to this date Blackett had not attacked so publicly what he viewed as the irrelevance of much research in India, including basic research. This was an extraordinary period in India, because there was uncertainty around the 1967 election and the rupee had just been devalued. The brief thrill of the 1965 war with Pakistan had been forgotten, replaced with worry about a severe drought and famine in Bihar and eastern Uttar Pradesh, confrontations with the American President, and the death of Shastri early in 1966. Foreign exchange reserves had fallen to their lowest level since independence. The secretly planned devaluation of the rupee in June 1966 from Rs 4.76 to Rs 7.50 to the US dollar (Rs 13.33 to Rs 21 to the UK pound) caused massive curtailment of importation of industrial and scientific supplies and equipment (among other essential items). It also brought even stronger pressures for self-reliance and import substitution. Blackett's Nehru Lecture eight months after the devaluation, with its call for more realistic thinking about innovation, played on the historical sensitivity among elites that was caused by these other events. Blackett also now admitted the importance of market forces in innovation, something he seldom discussed in India. He was fresh from the experience as adviser to the new Ministry of Science and Technology in the UK, a ministry created by Prime Minister Harold Wilson in 1964, partly at Blackett's suggestion. He had a hand in drafting Wilson's speech on 'the white heat of technology', had a new appreciation of a resurgent British industry and understood the mutual frustrations experienced in the relations between industry and government laboratories.

Blackett's influence extended right into the laboratories at this time. For example, to Atma Ram, he criticised 'the otherwise excellent man Varma, talking lightly about starting to design an electron microscope at NPL. It seems that all you and I have been saying has not been taken in at all.'[63] His influence also reached Delhi University, where Blackett had been involved in planning a transfer of a small accelerator from the Cavendish Laboratories at Cambridge to Delhi; at first Blackett thought it would be a good machine for training purposes, but he examined the project carefully when he visited India, only to realise

> that the machine was asked for not by physicists at all but by engineers who wanted some way of playing around with high voltages. I do not think they should be allowed to do this, as the techniques have almost no relevance in any other branch of engineering. The fact that they should want to do this shows, I think, the underlying drive towards prestige subjects, which is quite a danger in India as well as here.[64]

Was this remark about disdain for engineers, about preference for training as opposed to 'playing around' or about conquering the impulse for prestige? Although it is difficult to say, I think it is about Blackett trying to help Atma Ram fight entrepreneurial 'chaos' and bring order and control in 'his' laboratories, as much as it was about avoiding unnecessary importation or engineers doing research which others had already done elsewhere.

Right through this busy period, Blackett kept up with correspondence and visits until his final visit in 1971, aged 73. The last visit was a nine weeks' tour through the heat of India in March–May 1971. While there, in March, he observed the re-election of his old friend Indira Gandhi as prime minister. Apart from Pakistan's brutal crackdown in Dhaka on leading political and intellectual figures, and the movement of refugees to India, the conflict with Pakistan over Bangladesh had not really yet developed. Prior to Blackett's journey, Atma Ram's intention to resign as Director-General of the CSIR had been signalled to Blackett, and the opportunity arose to appoint someone younger. With a distinct reduction of his military contacts, Blackett toured all his familiar scientific sites like TIFR and the National Physical Laboratory, plus new ones like the Space Research Centre and Bharat Heavy Electronics, and a dozen CSIR institutes. He met the most powerful man in Indian science, Vikram Sarabhai, and also M.G.K. Menon, Y. Nayudamma (who soon succeeded Atma

Ram at the CSIR) and Pitambar Pant of the Planning Commission. He toured the Trombay atomic research centre (renamed after Bhabha) with astronomer S. Chandrasekhar from the University of Chicago, someone he had known since the early 1930s. Although the CSIR paid the expenses of Blackett and his wife Costanza on this last journey, he was also invited to advise the Indian Statistical Institute (by P.C. Mahalanobis) and the University Grants Commission (by D.S. Kothari). His conversations with Indira Gandhi showed Blackett that, although she retained her father's respect for science and scientists, she had also preferred to press forward in the debate which gradually linked 'science' more strongly to 'technology'. Indira Gandhi was determined to see more practical results from the state's massive investment in industries relying on science and technology. This was the request she evidently made to Blackett to help her, as is shown below. Whereas her father had aligned science with 'education' and 'culture', Indira Gandhi joined in the move in the 1960s to link 'science' to 'technology'. She was also prepared to redesign institutions to achieve this and, like her father, took a direct interest in key appointments. For example, during 1971, she agreed that the administration of the atomic energy and space programmes should be divided, and she engaged in the selection of people to lead both of these agencies.

Various laboratory directors wrote to him in 1971, while in India and afterwards, to ask him to persuade Atma Ram to promote their objectives, improve liaison with CSIR headquarters in Delhi and provide more freedom for their scientists to innovate. Basically, they were lobbying him, about which Blackett wrote to Atma Ram later. Not opposed to their pleas, Blackett nevertheless said the central problem facing some CSIR laboratories was that they had

> shown a tendency toward rather basic research without always having any very definite practical goal. Some of the work seems to me to be more suitable for university departments than for government research stations, which were undoubtedly set up with the general goal of producing practical results of use to industry and agriculture. This tendency towards purity is by no means only to be found in India [he then mentioned the same tendency in the UK]. I think there are two main reasons for this drift to purity. One is that it is often much easier to do good basic research than good applied research of interest to industry. The second reason is the

> widespread misapplication (in my view) of the principle of the importance of the 'freedom of science' ... In the field of basic curiosity-driven research, it is fully established that able research workers should be given the greatest possible freedom to plan and execute their own research ... What has gone wrong, I think, in some government research stations is that the principle of scientific freedom has sometimes been applied to mission-oriented R and D, where it is largely inapplicable, instead of only to curiosity R and D where it does apply.[65]

In particular, he said that some laboratories

> do not always seem to understand the importance of directing work towards a market requirement and close collaboration with industry, and so are surprised when their work is wasted. Then there are some individuals in certain stations who don't seem to be trying very hard to do anything useful but think it is more important to advance basic research.

His recommendations again pointed to strengthening the powers of the governing body of the CSIR over the strategic direction of its laboratories (leaving the tactics 'firmly in the hands of the Directors'). He said India should study how Harwell atomic research centre and industry co-operated, and how government funds were available to industry scientists (not just to government scientists) for this co-operation. He praised the Central Leather Research Institute (directed by Nayudamma) for appointing four economists to its staff, thus providing it with an understanding of its markets and clients superior to other CSIR laboratories. He did not exempt industry from criticism, saying 'the backwardness of much of Indian industry itself' was partly to blame. But Blackett pointed to a CSIR study of ten years' experience with £10 million expenditure on 23 industrial pilot plants, which concluded that the plants 'brought in little financial return'. Without acknowledging Ram's impending retirement in his report, Blackett complimented Atma Ram's speeches and articles as 'particularly eloquent'. Back in London, however, he politely discouraged an Indian initiative to nominate Ram as a Fellow of the Royal Society.

This last tour occurred in the middle of a Review Commission of the CSIR conducted by retired Justice Sarkar, to which Blackett himself made a presentation, and Blackett asked the High Commissioner in London in September 1971 for an early copy of the Sarkar Commission's report. This is further evidence that at the age of 73 he was passionately interested in India and enjoyed his influence in its scientific community. He felt the scientific community had reached a certain maturity and should be able to tackle the practical problems that confronted India, namely poverty and population. Blackett discussed this with Prime Minister Gandhi, whom he had now known for 24 years (since she was 30 years old). Before leaving India in 1971, he wrote to Atma Ram to propose a new advisory group for the Prime Minister, to advise her

> about the areas in which efforts should be most concentrated – in a way, a 'task laying down body'. In order that R & D would have a relation to economic growth, this body should have an economist on it, and to ensure implementation of the assignments should include a high official ... This work should not be hampered on the plea of freedom for scientists. It must be appreciated that scientists are not free to do whatever they wish, certainly not in the field of applied science ... In order that this evaluation of present activities and assignment of future tasks is done unhampered and expeditiously, no lobbying should be allowed and the issues should not be bogged down in those superficial discussions and to and fro arguments which can always be produced. The stakes are high, time is short, and there is no room for irrelevant arguments. Now when conditions have been created in the country, thanks to the thinking generated recently, this is the opportunity to give concrete shape to the R & D related to economic growth. Even in allocation of resources, at the most 10–20% may be earmarked for basic research, the rest should be devoted to applied work bearing on economic growth.[66]

This was the voice of Blackett from the late 1930s ('the stakes are high, the time is short'), drawing on his war-time experience advising the War Office and the Cabinet – in which, nevertheless, there were often 'to and fro arguments', few of which were really 'irrelevant' even when he disagreed with them. Blackett's role in the strategic bombing controversy of the Second World War is a perfect example, and he knew that scientists did not always win these contests anyway.

Blackett was not alone in his criticism of the scientific community. Writing from New York, Mahalanobis warned Blackett that he did not like what he what was going on in India: 'Indian science is in a state of confusion ... The immediate future does not look too bright ... because we still remain a structured hierarchical system.'[67] Blackett, however, remained an optimist about India, ready to try new things. As an example, while President of the Royal Society, he promoted the idea of a new school of genetics on the campus of the Indian Statistical Institute in Calcutta during 1969–70, before Mahalanobis died. This institute was where Blackett's friend J.B.S. Haldane had first gone to work when he left Britain to live in India in 1956. The genetics school was not built.

PATRICK BLACKETT AND VIKRAM SARABHAI

Quite far from the politics of the CSIR, Blackett had formed a friendship with Vikram Sarabhai, the Cambridge-trained physicist who was appointed Bhabha's successor as Secretary to the Department of Atomic Energy in 1966. Sarabhai studied at Cambridge as a teenager, and then returned after the war to complete his doctorate in 1947. Because the war had changed the composition of the physics department at Cambridge so greatly, there was no one present to examine Sarabhai's thesis in cosmic ray physics. So Blackett was asked to be the examiner, and Sarabhai (aged 28) was sent to Manchester for the examination. Evidently they got on well, because Sarabhai became known in the Blackett household as 'my father's student'. They soon met again in India in 1948, and Blackett went to Ahmedabad in 1958 to dine at the Sarabhai house and see the Physical Research Laboratory that Sarabhai was building. Perhaps Blackett recognised that Vikram Sarabhai, who was then 39, would be an important force in science in India. He may have heard that Sarabhai had been discussed for a possible role in the CSIR after Bhatnagar's sudden death in 1955. After the dinner, Sarabhai wrote to Blackett to discuss their mutual interest in the explanation of the anomalies in the divergence of the actual terrestrial magnetic fields from an ideal single dipole field. Geomagnetism was by then Blackett's passion. Sarabhai was beginning to direct his gaze to India's role in space. A further dinner in London was proposed, with more conversation about how to finance scientific research because

Sarabhai was in the middle of establishing an industry-funded textile research laboratory at the time.[68] Blackett saw Sarabhai when he was in India or in London, and prepared a moving obituary for him at the international cosmic ray conference in Jaipur. Unfortunately, there are no other letters between the two men in the Royal Society archives.

PATRICK BLACKETT AND HOMI BHABHA

Along with their love for physics, Blackett and Bhabha shared a love of mountains. When these pleasures were combined, the joy was great. They both visited the cosmic ray laboratory up in the Alps. Blackett wrote to Bhabha in 1951:

> we have nearly 60 photographs of V tracks from the Pic du Midi and it looks as if there are at least three separate neutral masses, two being greater than protonic mass! Herr Gott certainly has made the world very complicated.[69]

Long forgotten was the disagreement over the mass of the penetrating component of cosmic rays at sea level. In February 1955 Dag Hammerskjold announced that Bhabha would be the president of the first conference on the peaceful uses of atomic energy in Geneva that year. W. Bennett-Lewis of Atomic Energy Canada Ltd was on the planning committee for the conference, and the discussion of Indo-Canadian co-operation, which began in Colombo Plan circles, blossomed between them there. Considerable pressure had been brought to bear, from Nehru through Krishna Menon (then in New York), to ensure that someone (Bhabha?) from a 'neutral' country would chair the conference. More decisively, the British government also championed Bhabha's candidacy for the chair. Bertrand Russell appears to have championed this objective too. It was now that Nehru cabled Bhabha in Geneva giving him full freedom to negotiate the terms of collaboration with Canada on the Canada–India Reactor. He had already negotiated the installation of a British research reactor in the previous year.

By the end of 1955 the US and USSR had exploded both fission and larger fusion (thermonuclear) bombs, and the UK had exploded fission bombs. Bhabha and Blackett had formed the opinion that these were unlikely ever to be used in war. Evidently they also agreed in the view that the original Hiroshima and Nagasaki bombs had been unnecessary. Perhaps Bhabha had grown to accept Blackett's 1946 view that these bombs were not simply aimed at Japan but were also the first act in a cold diplomatic war with Russia, to limit the USSR's expansion in Asia. (It should be remembered that even for people with their kind of connections (for example, both knew Robert Oppenheimer well) the Manhattan Project evidence was still secret, and thus their interpretation of that situation would have been based on an understanding that some of the facts were concealed from them.) Therefore, when an authoritative American source revealed something, it was considered valuable. Bhabha wrote to Blackett quoting at length and with approval the views of Admiral William Leahy, the Chief of Staff who served under both Presidents Roosevelt and Truman, that the atomic bomb was not tactically necessary. Although this is clearer to us than it was to them, we should not miss the point – meaning that Bhabha was well informed and did not believe some of the mythology surrounding the use of the bomb in the ending of the war.[70] Moreover, at the time Bhabha was participating in a year-long review of recently declassified evidence on the use and effects of nuclear explosions, soon published by the government of India, with a foreword by Nehru.[71] Perkovich says that Bhabha told Blackett in 1958 that he hoped to develop nuclear weapons, and this is certainly consistent with what Bhabha told other people around that time.[72]

Because Bhabha had confided in him a great deal, Blackett kept abreast of current strategic thinking in Delhi, and in atomic energy/nuclear weapons circles elsewhere. I think this larger view was made possible, despite their differences, by a number of similarities – common background in physics at Cambridge and a sense of belonging to an international community of scientists. Blackett's passionate interest in the role of science and technology in developing countries matched Bhabha's. Blackett's intellectual grasp of strategy easily matched Nehru's and Bhabha's, because he probably knew things they did not, even in the late 1950s and early 1960s when he is said to have been out of the British policy loop. According to Nye, Blackett realised in the early 1950s that he had underestimated the lethal effects of radioactive fallout, and had not anticipated the rapid development of missiles able to deliver small hydrogen bombs. 'However, Blackett continued to argue during the

1950s and 1960s that conventional and nuclear disarmament should be negotiated in parallel.'[73]

I do not know what Blackett would have thought if he knew that his friend Homi Bhabha was the person who (had he lived long enough) would have been in charge of the project to test India's first nuclear bomb in 1974. It is interesting to note that Blackett tried to bring Bhabha into the Pugwash Conference in 1961. Bhabha replied, rather disingenuously, that it would take him too long to study the issues for that particular meeting, and instead recommended Vikram Sarabhai. By this time, Bhabha was, I think, more caught in an official net than he realised and felt constrained to speak even among fellow scientists about nuclear policy. India was taking a strong stand for disarmament in the Test Ban Treaty negotiations in 1961, and when Bhabha spoke, even informally, it reflected on national policy. Nevertheless, Bhabha arranged and attended a lecture by Blackett in Delhi in early 1962 on 'Military Policy and Disarmament', and he and Blackett did attend the Pugwash meetings in 1963. One year later, after Nehru's death, the first Chinese atomic bomb was exploded in October 1964. Bhabha complained that there was no protection for countries capable of making atomic bombs but which had refrained from doing so. He said that a climate favourable to such countries must be created immediately. Bhabha probably got the new prime minister's agreement to a project that prepared India for an underground nuclear explosion, in late 1964. A few months later Bhabha announced that India could make a nuclear bomb in 18 months:

> 'We are still 18 months away from exploding either a bomb or a device for peaceful purposes, and we are doing nothing to reduce that period.' Eighteen months was the figure Dr. Bhabha cited a year ago and he said the situation had not changed since then.[74]

These news reports refer to a statement Bhabha made ('eighteen months ago') in October 1964, after the Chinese bomb test.

What Blackett might not have understood or accepted at the time was that nuclear weapons were becoming to be seen in India as a great symbol of national prestige, a symbol made by scientists and engineers around which political parties and non-political groups would gradually join together people of otherwise differing views. Of course, there were other motivations, such as the influence of the

Chinese bomb and two wars with Pakistan, but this symbolic one was more important. It is not clear what position Blackett took with regard to Bhabha's preparations in 1964–65, but it is highly unlikely that they failed to discuss it. The question of nuclear weapons for national prestige had faced Blackett before, in Britain, and he argued against prestige there too. It is not clear that Bhabha ever took such a position against nuclear weapons. Many people assert that he always favoured them, though the evidence here is ambiguous too, at least until about 1956.

It is, finally, at Bhabha's unfortunate death in an air crash in the Swiss Alps in 1966 – at which there was little opportunity for Blackett to mourn – that friends of Bhabha were drawn closer together. Blackett spoke on the radio in London most feelingly about Bhabha; this may have been re-broadcast in India, and was certainly widely quoted in Indian papers, because Bhabha was considered a national hero. Letters came to Blackett, thanking him for his speech, and recognising that Blackett himself had lost a special friend; letters came from men and women who had liked Bhabha greatly – like the new Prime Minister Indira Gandhi. Blackett was identified, in these letters as 'a true friend of India', and on an emotional level. It is curious that the biographical appraisal of Bhabha written for the Royal Society records is not by Blackett but by Sir William Penney, the scientist behind the UK's nuclear weapons programme, a man who went rarely to India, but who had known Bhabha since the 1930s.[75]

Blackett knew he had been tough on India and had openly shown his frustration with its conditions. At the same time, he had created a circle of affection through his friendships there, and had found talented and effective people who were doing the kind of things he believed in. His wife Lady Costanza Blackett said that in the later years of his life he cared more passionately about his work in India than he did about most other things.[76] It is for historians of Indian military and scientific development to judge what Blackett achieved in India, and what consequences his work had. We know little of how Blackett was appraised outside the charmed circle in which he normally moved, and new historical research is necessary to understand how this new type of defence consultant and scientific intervenor was viewed by others. If Britain made use of Blackett as a source of intelligence after 1947, we do not yet know how. Did they think more carefully about India and south Asia as a result of listening to Blackett? On the evidence, I think Blackett's influence in British policy towards India was limited. Did India get unseen benefits through Blackett and his connections? Did Blackett's interventions promote or inhibit Indian self-reliance? The evidence here shows that, whatever Blackett achieved in India, he did so only through co-operation with a number of powerful people and through the prestige he brought from British (and international) science and politics. His world reputation as a consultant, a term he himself used, says a great deal about the continuity and interconnection of the Indian and British scientific, military and political elites at the time. It also says much about Indian awareness of British political culture and how to use its resources. This awareness extended widely, including, among others, the London School of Economics, the Royal Society and Cambridge University.

The evidence suggests that there is sometimes an interesting, creative and useful role for outsiders as intermediaries. In another 50 years, if we were to look back then on Blackett's role in this formative period, I think we should find that his objectives in India are enduring: that is, to improve the working conditions of people doing research, to distinguish carefully between the objectives of scientific institutions, to cut away the bureaucratic brambles which grow up around the practice of research and spend money wisely, to think carefully about the things which can be developed locally instead of being imported and to balance the state's insatiable desire for technical prestige with enhancing ordinary people's abilities to provide a better life for themselves. I do not know what role the military will have in India in 50 years time, but Blackett advocated a realistic appraisal of the relations between the state and the military, and limitations on the military's growth and influence. That surely would not change in a democratic country like India.

Not long after Bhabha's death, when Blackett received his Order of Merit in 1967, he received a letter from senior civil servant A.J. Kidwai whose words capture the perspective in which Patrick Blackett was viewed by a certain generation as part of the lineage of people considered as friends of India. 'To no other people outside this country', says Kidwai, 'have you given the same sense of belonging. And no one after Harold Laski has had the same impact on Indian minds as you.'[77] This statement is more important to consider now, when a younger generation of well-educated Indians do not even know who either Patrick Blackett of the Royal Society or

Harold Laski of the London School of Economics actually were, or even the significance of their relationships with India.

VISITS BY PATRICK BLACKETT TO INDIA

1947	1963
1948	1964
1950	1965
1953	1966
1954	1967
1955	1971

(according to his note in the Blackett Papers, Royal Society)

Institutions visited (usually many times):

- Universities (Delhi, Bombay, Calcutta, Madras, etc.)
- Tata Institute of Fundamental Research, Bombay
- Saha Institute of Nuclear Physics, Calcutta
- Indian Institute of Science, Bangalore
- Indian Statistical Institute, Calcutta
- Physical Research Laboratory, Ahmedabad
- All laboratories of the Council of Scientific and Industrial Research, e.g. Glass and Ceramics, Metallurgy, Roads
- National Physical Laboratory, National Chemical Laboratory
- National Aeronautical Laboratory, National Metallurgical Laboratory
- All defence laboratories and all defence production sites.

NOTES

1. P.M.S. Blackett, interview (in London), with B.R. Nanda of The Nehru Library, Delhi, 27 July 1967.
2. P.C. Mahalanobis to S.S. Bhatnagar, 28 August 1946, NISTADS Archive, Delhi.
3. On the history of the association in Britain, but without mention of its Indian counterpart, see Gary Werskey, *The Visible College: A Collective Biography of British Scientists and Socialists of the 1930s* (London: Free Association Books, 1988), 2nd edn.

4. Itty Abraham, personal communication, 9 February 1999.
5. Blackett, 1967 interview.
6. Blackett, 1967 interview, Royal Society Archives, p. 4.
7. Blackett, 1967 interview, Royal Society Archives, pp. 4–5.
8. Blackett, 1967 interview.
9. Bernard Lovell, 'Bristol and Manchester – the years 1931–1939', in R. Williamson (ed.), *The Making of Physicists* (Bristol: Adam Hilger, 1987), pp. 158–9. About Bhabha's relationship with Heisenberg, see David Cassidy, *Uncertainty: The Life and Science of Werner Heisenberg* (New York: W.H. Freeman, 1992).
10. H.J. Bhabha to P.M.S. Blackett, 1941 (day/month missing), Royal Society Archives.
11. P.M.S. Blackett to B.R. Nanda, 8 February 1972, Royal Society Archives.
12. A number of references to Blackett's role during the war, including his extraordinary network of influential contacts, can be found in Guy Hartcup, *The Effect of Science on the Second World War* (London: Macmillan, 2000).
13. Arnold Kramish, personal communication, 19 February and 20 April 1999.
14. P.M.S. Blackett to S. Cripps, 17 February 1947 and 11 March 1947, Blackett Papers, Royal Society Archives. Cripps had a special interest in India, having taken two British diplomatic missions there, and was just about to become – in the middle of the 1947 crisis – the chief government supervisor of the British economy, including its vast nationalisation programme. For these reasons Cripps appears to have been an informal 'Secretary of State for India'. See Chris Bryant, *Stafford Cripps* (London: Hodder & Stoughton, 1997). I am indebted also to Peter Clarke's lecture on Cripps's negotiations in India at Simon Fraser University, Vancouver, September 1999.
15. Blackett to Cripps, 11 March 1947.
16. Blackett, 1967 interview, p. 4.
17. Blackett to Nanda, 8 February 1972.
18. Blackett, 1967 interview, p. 7.
19. Itty Abraham, *The Making of the Indian Atomic Bomb: Science, Secrecy, and the Postcolonial State* (London: Zed Books, 1998), p. 56.
20. Vice-Admiral Parry to P.M.S. Blackett, 7 September 1948, Royal Society Archives.
21. Vice-Admiral Parry to Lord Mountbatten, 2 January 1951, cited in Jaswant Singh, *Defending India* (London: Macmillan, 1999), p. 122.
22. J. Nehru to C. Attlee, 28 January 1951, quoted J. Singh, *Defending India*, p. 123.
23. Singh, *Defending India*, p. 123.
24. Vice-Admiral Pizey to Lord Mountbatten, 23 March 1954, cited J. Singh, *Defending India* p.124.
25. Blackett, 1967 interview, p. 7.
26. Blackett to Cripps, 11 March 1947.
27. Personal communication, Nicolas Blackett, 5 October 1998, including a copy of a letter typed shortly after the event.
28. J. Nehru to P.M.S. Blackett, 26 September 1948, Royal Society Archives.
29. S.S. Bhatnagar to P.M.S. Blackett, 29 December 1950, Royal Society Archives.
30. Blackett, 1967 interview, p. 8.
31. P.M.S. Blackett to Baldev Singh, Minister of Defence, Delhi, 30 September 1948, Royal Society Archives.
32. M.N. Saha to D.S. Kothari, 21 July 1948, Saha Institute Archives, Calcutta.

33. P.M.S. Blackett, Report to the Minister of Defence, 10 September 1948, Royal Society Archives.
34. 'Blackett stayed in Stockholm for ten days, and he gave several lectures and had many informal discussions with leading Swedish scientists from universities and from the recently founded National Defence Institute. He also met high-ranking military officers. Blackett's wartime experience and his personal charisma created a strong interest in OR and was one impetus for establishing OR in Sweden' (p. 385). 'Furthermore, Blackett arranged for a British OR specialist, CEG Bailey, to come to Stockholm in February 1951 to give three lectures on operations research to an audience of officers, academics, and civil servants' (the National Defence Institute became 'the spider in the military web') (p. 386). Arne Kaijser and Joar Tiberg, 'From Operational Research to Future Studies: The Establishment, Diffusion, and Transformation of the Systems Approach in Sweden, 1945–1980', in Agatha Hughes (ed.), *Systems, Experts and Computers* (Cambridge, MA: MIT Press, 2000).
35. Cited Robert McMahon, *Cold War on the Periphery: The United States, India, and Pakistan* (New York: Columbia University Press, 1994), p. 49.
36. Ibid., p. 69.
37. P.M.S. Blackett to L. Bertin, 24 February 1951, Royal Society Archives.
38. High Commission for India to P.M.S. Blackett, 18 August 1951, Royal Society Archives.
39. P.M.S. Blackett to J. Nehru, 31 January 1951, Royal Society Archives.
40. H.A. Sargeaunt to P.M.S. Blackett, 9 May 1951, Royal Society Archives.
41. P.M.S. Blackett to H.A. Sargeaunt, 29 May 1951, Royal Society Archives.
42. McMahon, *Cold War on the Periphery*, pp. 219–20.
43. G. Balachandran, *The Reserve Bank of India 1951–1957* (Delhi: Oxford University Press, 1998), p. 617.
44. P.M.S. Blackett, 'Scientific Organisation for the Defence Services', 8 September 1948, Royal Society Archives.
45. 'A Note Prepared by the Scientific Adviser on the Visit of Professor P.M.S. Blackett – 27 December 1954 to 15 January 1955', 15 January 1955, and Patrick Blackett, *aide-mémoire* (typed, n.d. – probably 1972), Royal Society Archives.
46. 'A Note prepared by the Scientific Adviser'.
47. Blackett, *aide-mémoire.*
48. Ibid., p. 40.
49. H.J. Bhabha to P.M.S. Blackett, 3 August 1963.
50. Paul Maddrell, 'Britain's Exploitation of Occupied Germany for Scientific and Technical Intelligence on the Soviet Union', unpublished Ph.D. dissertation, University of Cambridge, 1999. See also Paul Maddrell, 'British–American Scientific Intelligence Collaboration during the Occupation of Germany', *Intelligence and National Security*, 15, 2 (Summer 2000).
51. Richard Aldrich and Michael Coleman, 'Britain and the Strategic Air Offensive Against the Soviet Union: The Question of South Asian Air Bases, 1945–1949', *Journal of the Historical Association* (October 1989), pp. 400–28.
52. P.M.S. Blackett, Report to the Leverhulme Trust, 12 May 1971, Royal Society Archives.
53. S.S. Bhatnagar to P.M.S. Blackett, 22 April 1951; P.M.S. Blackett to S.S. Bhatnagar, 27 April 1951, Royal Society Archives.

54. The relationship between Hill and Bhatnagar is one of the subjects of my forthcoming book, *Nucleus and Nation.*
55. On the history of the solar power research at the NPL, see Shiv Visvanathan, *Organizing for Science: The Making of an Industrial Research Laboratory* (Delhi: Oxford University Press, 1984).
56. *Statesman* (Calcutta), 24 January 1963.
57. J.B.S. Haldane to P.M.S. Blackett, 25 January 1963, Royal Society Archives. On the relationships between Blackett, Bernal and Haldane, see Werskey, *The Visible College.*
58. M.G.K. Menon *et al.*, Report to the Executive Council, National Physical Laboratory, 9 April 1963, Royal Society Archives. The best assessment of Blackett's report in the overall context of the National Physical Laboratory remains the excellent Shiv Visvanathan, *Organizing for Science.* It is curious that despite so much frank public discussion about the CSIR there is so little serious academic analysis of the socio-economic and intellectual history of its major institutions.
59. Druv Raina and Ashok Jain, 'Big Science and the University in India', in John Krige and Dominique Pestre (eds), *Science in the Twentieth Century* (London: Harwood Academic Publishers, 1997).
60. H. Zaheer to P.M.S. Blackett, 9 December 1964, Royal Society Archives.
61. C.G. Wynne, Report on Optical Designing, for CSIR, June 1966, Royal Society Archives.
62. P.M.S. Blackett to Atma Ram, 4 December 1967, Royal Society Archives.
63. Ibid.
64. P.M.S. Blackett to A.J. Kidwai, 29 November 1967, Royal Society Archives.
65. P.M.S. Blackett, Report to the Leverhulme Trust, 12 May 1971, Royal Society Archives.
66. P.M.S. Blackett, 'Personal Notes – Atma Ram', n.d., probably April–May 1971, Royal Society Archives.
67. P.C. Mahalanobis to P.M.S. Blackett, 29 June 1971, Royal Society Archives.
68. V. Sarabhai to P.M.S. Blackett, 14 February 1958, Royal Society Archives.
69. P.M.S. Blackett to H.J. Bhabha, 13 February 1951, Royal Society Archives.
70. H.J. Bhabha to P.M.S. Blackett, 21 April 1955, Royal Society Archives. For the entire discussion of the consequences of using the bomb see Gar Alperovitz, *The Decision to Use the Atomic Bomb and the Architecture of an American Myth* (London: Harper Collins, 1995).
71. Government of India, *Nuclear Explosions and Their Effects* (Delhi: Publications Division, 1956).
72. George Perkovich, *India's Nuclear Bomb: The Impact on Global Proliferation* (Berkeley, CA: University of California Press, 1999), p. 35. Bhabha's efforts to build an Indian capacity for the bomb is a subject of my forthcoming book.
73. Mary Jo Nye, 'A Physicist in the Corridors of Power: P.M.S. Blackett's Opposition to Atomic Weapons Following the War', presented to Conference on Patrick Blackett, Imperial College London, April 1998.
74. Anthony Lukas, 'India Rules Out Secret Atom Test', *New York Times*, 29 November 1965. See also Patrick Keatley, 'The Brown Bomb', *Guardian* (London) 11 March 1965.
75. As president, Blackett would have chaired the meeting at which the assignment to write Bhabha's obituary (which had to be written by a Fellow

of the Royal Society) was made. But Blackett himself appears not to have written anything about Bhabha. Even in his 1967 interview with B.R. Nanda, a year after the crash, Blackett talked very little about Bhabha because the interview was expressly about Nehru.

76. Personal communication, Sir Bernard Lovell, 24 April 1998.
77. A.J. Kidwai to P.M.S. Blackett, 21 November 1967, Royal Society Archives.

14

A Physicist in the Corridors of Power

Mary Jo Nye

O! curs'd device! base implement of death!
Fram'd in the black Tartarean realms beneath!
By Beelzebub's malicious art design'd
To ruin all the race of human kind …
That ne'er again a knight by thee may dare,
Or dastard cowards, by thy help in war
With vantage base, assault a nobler foe,
Here lie for ever in th'abyss below!

Orlando Furioso, Ludovico Ariosto
IX, 83–84, translation, John Hooke[1]

In his novel *Corridors of Power* (1964), one of C.P. Snow's main characters is the physicist 'Francis Getliffe', who, as Snow described him:

> had thought more effectively about military-scientific strategy than anyone had … he had not long before screwed himself up to write a pamphlet. In it he had said that there was no military rationale behind the nuclear policy. This analysis got him into trouble, mostly in America, but also in England. In some Right-thinking circles, it had seemed not only preposterous, but also heretical, and something like wicked.[2]

The Getliffe character is largely modelled on the physicist P.M.S. Blackett (1897–1974), Nobel laureate in physics in 1948.[3] Lord Snow knew Blackett well. During the late 1920s and early 1930s their paths frequently crossed in Cambridge where Blackett was working in

Ernest Rutherford's Cavendish Laboratory and Snow was engaged in molecular spectroscopy while a Fellow at Christ's College.[4] In the war years and afterwards, they met in government ministries in London, and in the 1950s they were part of the dinner group of scientists and politicians who were convened to advise Hugh Gaitskell and Harold Wilson on science policy for the Labour Party. Thus, Snow knew precisely Blackett's position on nuclear policy, as well as the outrage it provoked in the US and the UK.[5]

Historians have analysed the attitudes of American scientists towards the first military use of the atomic bomb in the war against Japan, as well as the efforts of American scientists from 1945 to 1947 to ensure civilian control over an atomic energy commission and to set up international control of atomic energy research and development. It has been noted, however, that few American scientists spoke out publicly against the expansion of the American nuclear arsenal immediately after the war. Indeed opposition became legally risky after President Truman issued the 'Loyalty Order' for federal employees in March 1947, an order soon copied by State legislatures.[6]

Historians have noted, too, that there was very little opposition among British scientists to the development of an atomic arsenal in the UK. Exceptions were Kathleen Lonsdale and Lionel Penrose, both Quakers, Nevill Mott and left-wing scientists including J.D. Bernal, E.H.S. Burhop, C.F. Powell and Blackett, all officers of the allegedly communist-infiltrated Association of Scientific Workers.[7] Among these, Blackett was the most outspoken and the most vilified of British scientists who opposed American and British nuclear policies from the mid-1940s to around 1960. One of the few comparable cases is that of the chemist Linus Pauling in the United States who campaigned publicly against nuclear weapons and against war.[8]

Blackett was neither communist nor pacifist, and he had no argument with war. Why did Blackett the real physicist, like Getliffe the fictional physicist, take an outspoken and unpopular political position on matters of nuclear policy immediately following the Second World War? How unusual was it for a scientist to speak out on issues of broad military strategy and international relations, and how precisely were his views received? Did Blackett's opinions have any effect in the long run? The experiences of Blackett in his public campaign against atomic weapons illustrate the risks to a physicist of writing about a subject other than physics, as well as the circumstances that might compel one to do so.

BLACKETT'S EARLY SCIENTIFIC CAREER

P.M.S. Blackett was the consummate insider and outsider in British science and politics. A Londoner by birth, he was the only son and the second of three children of Arthur Stuart Blackett, a stockbroker, and Caroline Frances, daughter of an army officer. Blackett entered Osborne Royal Naval College in 1910, and he was studying at Dartmouth Royal Naval College when the Great War began in August 1914. He saw action in the Battle of Falkland Islands in 1914 and the Battle of Jutland in 1916. His Navy experiences were formative of his later personal style and military views.[9]

In January 1919 the Admiralty sent Blackett and other officers to Cambridge to study. He resigned from the Navy three weeks later and embarked upon the mathematics and natural sciences tripos in physics, joining Ernest Rutherford's Cavendish Laboratory in 1921 and becoming a Fellow of King's College. He spent the academic year 1924–25 with James Franck in Göttingen, following his marriage to Costanza Bernadina Bayon.[10]

At the Cavendish, Blackett became one of the pre-eminent experimental physicists of his generation, using the cloud chamber to study the expulsion of protons from atomic nuclei hit by fast alpha-particles. In 1924, from some 23,000 photographs showing 415,000 tracks of ionised particles, he identified eight tracks that showed the path of a proton ejected from a recoiling nitrogen nucleus and the capture of an alpha-particle by a nitrogen nucleus, creating an isotope of oxygen. Blackett's soon-classic paper, published in the *Proceedings of the Royal Society* in 1925, included photographs that have been widely reprinted ever since.[11]

While improving methods of detection of charged particles, Blackett became interested in cosmic rays. His new focus led to a stunning paper with G.P.S. Occhialini who came from Rome to work with Blackett at the Cavendish. In late 1932 they made photographs showing the track of a positive electron in a shower of cosmic rays. The experimental success was seated in a clever design using Geiger counters to trigger expansion of gas in the Wilson chamber. Since they tied the experiment into their friend Paul Dirac's prediction of an anti-matter for the electron (a kind of energy hole),[12] it was they, rather than Carl Anderson at Pasadena, who first offered the idea of pair production as the proper explanation of the experimental effect that constituted the discovery of the positron.[13]

In 1933 Blackett moved to Birkbeck College to head his own laboratory,[14] setting up equipment for detection of cosmic rays 100 feet below ground at an unused platform in Holborn tube station.[15] With the return to London, Blackett, who had been pro-Labour for a decade,[16] began speaking on the BBC in 1934 in a series of programmes on science and society organised by the left-wing scientists Julian Huxley, Hyman Levy and Desmond Bernal.[17] While arguing for the moral values and material advantages of scientific rationalism, Blackett nonetheless denied that there could be scientific consensus in matters of politics, a view that was only to be reinforced by events of the next couple of decades.[18]

Attracted by the resources of a large university supported by local industrial interests, Blackett accepted a position at Manchester in 1937 as Langworthy Professor of Physics. In August 1939 news of the Soviet–German non-aggression pact stunned Blackett, who had been an outspoken sympathiser for the Soviet experiment in socialism.[19] It was clear that the war that had been feared was inevitable. Blackett had already been enlisted, in 1935, by Henry T. Tizard, then Rector at Imperial College, to advise the Air Ministry on priorities for national defence. The Tizard Committee argued that highest priority in spending should be given to the development of radar, against the objections of Oxford physics professor Frederick A. Lindemann, who was to become Winston Churchill's scientific adviser in 1939. The matter of radar was the first of Blackett's confrontations with Lindemann.[20]

OPERATIONAL RESEARCH AND ATOMIC WEAPONS, 1940–48

In the spring of 1940 Blackett became a member of the committee with the intentionally meaningless acronym MAUD to advise the British government on the feasibility of Britain's developing a fission bomb. Blackett found himself the lone member of the MAUD committee recommending against an independent British effort and urging joint collaboration with the United States in North America, advice that ultimately prevailed.[21]

At the outbreak of the war, Blackett joined the instrument section of the Royal Aircraft Establishment where he worked on the design of the Mark XIV bombsight, which eliminated the need for a level bombing run at the time of bomb release. In August 1940 Blackett became scientific adviser to the Anti-Aircraft Command (AAC), organising an operational research group to advise the AAC on co-ordinating the use of radar sets, guns and mechanical calculators in the air defence of London. He joined Coastal Command in March 1941 and worked at the Admiralty from January 1942 to the summer of 1945, heading a group whose accomplishments included dramatic improvements in techniques for using airborne radar to find German submarines. Blackett's experiences in operational research were decisive for the post-war views that he developed on strategic weapons.

Invited by Prime Minister Clement Attlee to join a new Advisory Committee on Atomic Energy in August 1945, Blackett's views quickly diverged from majority opinion.[22] He not only opposed British development of atomic weapons, but argued in favour of a neutralist foreign policy for the United Kingdom. Failing to sway members of the atomic energy committee, including his former Cavendish colleague James Chadwick, Blackett circulated his opinions publicly, first in a pamphlet published by the Fabian Society, *The Atom and the Charter* (1946), and then in the widely read book *Military and Political Consequences of Atomic Energy* (1948), which appeared in the United States under the dramatic title *Fear, War and the Bomb* (1949).[23] Just before his book appeared, in May 1948, the Labour government announced in Parliament that the official decision to produce atomic weapons had been made secretly in January 1947 in a committee that included Prime Minister Attlee and Foreign Secretary Ernest Bevin.[24]

From the war's end, and despite growing concern in London and Washington about Soviet domestic and foreign policy, Blackett began arguing the need to maintain contact and co-operation with the Soviet Union.[25] He criticised the plan presented by Bernard Baruch to the United Nations Atomic Energy Commission in June 1946, which recommended an international authority for control and inspection of all atomic materials. The Baruch proposal included the recommendation of explicit penalties for violation of atomic-weapons controls, penalties that would be exempt from veto in the Security Council, where the Soviet Union was a permanent member.[26] Blackett opposed the veto exemption as impractical.

From 1946 on, while head of the physics department at Manchester, Blackett began putting together materials that appeared in his 1948 book.[27] In a letter to his Manchester friend and colleague

Michael Polanyi, Blackett wrote: 'You speak as if it is always a duty to publish the "truth." If I had published the truth of what I have known of parts of our war effort, I would certainly be locked up. Should I have done so?'[28] Now, in 1948, Blackett made public his views about the military strategy that had been carried out by British and American air forces in the past war and his misgivings about present policies.

The matter of strategic nuclear weapons was not the first instance in which Blackett took a minority position against an implacable majority. While at the Admiralty, Blackett incensed some members of the government and the Air Ministry by arguing against Lindemann's recommendation in April 1942 for saturation bombing of civilian housing in German cities. At the time, Lindemann estimated that 50 per cent of all houses in German towns of more than 50,000 population could be destroyed by autumn 1943 and that the effects on German morale and infrastructure would be devastating.[29] In contrast, Tizard, Blackett and Bernal were among those dissenters who argued the inefficacy of Lindemann's strategy, based on recent information about Japanese bombing in China and German bombing of Birmingham.[30] Blackett fought hard, with considerable success by mid-1943, for the diversion of anti-civilian air effort to the bombing of German submarines using improved methods of airborne radar.

The wartime civilian bombing strategy, Blackett wrote publicly in 1948, had been arrived at because of earlier failures of the RAF to pinpoint and hit specific industrial and military targets. Thus civilian bombing constituted 'a technically debased form of the original conception'.[31] Worse than British use of this strategy during the past war, he wrote, was the new development in American public opinion of accepting the tactics of mass destruction as a normal operation of war, a view that Blackett condemned as ethically immoral and militarily ineffective. A visit to the United States following the American mid-term elections in 1946 also convinced Blackett of a conservative turn in American politics and a willingness to talk about preventive war.[32] Polanyi expressed similar misgivings to Blackett after a return from the United States, despite Polanyi's long-time distrust of the Soviet Union.[33]

As he examined available US military reports on the bombing of Germany and Japan, Blackett became convinced that air war had not, and could not, win a war independently of ground troops. He extended the argument to atomic weapons, warning that it was a mistake for Americans so to overestimate the decisive effects of aerial bombardment and so to fear the power of nuclear weapons that they sought absolute security from atomic weapons by the unworkable provisions of the Baruch plan.[34]

The US McMahon Act of August 1946, which created the Atomic Energy Commission and forbade any sharing of atomic information with another foreign power, including Canada and Great Britain, was a grave mistake, in Blackett's view. It reneged upon the successes of international co-operation during the past war, and it ignored the legitimate desire of the Soviet Union for the development of new sources of power from atomic energy. If the McMahon Act was to be the American position, the UK should not seek to develop atomic bombs at all, and the UK should remain politically neutral in the growing confrontation between the United States and the Soviet Union.[35]

Most controversially of all, in 1948 Blackett expressed extreme worry that the US had not been open to meaningful accommodations with the Soviet Union for some time. By way of making this point, he voiced an argument now familiar, but then novel, that the United States had used atomic weapons in Japan in early August 1945 'not so much as the last military act of the Second World War, as the first act of the cold diplomatic war with Russia'. The Americans, Blackett charged, made a political decision to force Japanese surrender before the mid-August date agreed upon by the Soviets and Americans for the Soviet Army's invasion of Manchuria. The United States wanted to keep the Soviet Union out of Asia.[36]

Blackett's book appeared in Britain in autumn 1948 at the very time that it was announced that he was the recipient of the 1948 Nobel prize in physics. The Nobel award brought his book even more publicity than it might have had, especially outside Britain. Facing pages in the *Manchester Guardian* carried columns entitled 'Nobel Prizes: Professor Blackett and Mr T.S. Eliot' and 'The Atomic Problem: Professor Blackett's Book'.[37]

There was widespread criticism from both friends and foes that Blackett was too harsh on the Americans.[38] Frederick Osborn, who became Deputy US Representative to the United Nations Atomic Energy Commission in May 1949, debated with Blackett on the BBC in December 1948. He wrote to Blackett that he would not discuss the matter of US motives in using atomic bombs in Japan and that he was certain that Blackett was wrong, especially regarding Secretary of War Henry Stimson and General George Marshall.[39]

Blackett's charge of the inefficacy of aerial bombing during the Second World War also was much disputed.[40] Blackett was accused, too, of giving too much credence and too much encouragement to the Russian position in the UN and of ignoring the fact that Andrei Gromyko had rejected any form of international ownership or supervision of atomic materials.[41] The *New York Times* science correspondent, Waldemar Kaempffert, thought that Blackett was performing a useful service in toning down doomsday predictions, but that he had gone too far in denying the dangers of atomic weapons.[42]

By the early 1950s Blackett realised that he had misjudged the persistent lethal effects of radioactive fallout. He also underestimated the rapidity with which missile-delivery systems would be developed and equipped with relatively small 'super' or hydrogen bombs. However, Blackett continued to argue during the 1950s and early 1960s that conventional and nuclear disarmament should be negotiated in parallel.[43] Nor did he doubt his expertise in this discussion. To the comments of one reviewer that 'Science and politics do not readily mix together – at least not in one person'[44] and of another that 'because a man is a success in physics it does not follow that he is well qualified to elucidate political issues',[45] Blackett's rejoinder was obvious: 'Why I should stick to Physics any more than you or Friedwald I cannot quite conceive. Anyway I have spent eleven years of my life in warfare. That gives me a title to talk about it.'[46]

A four-part series of reactions to Blackett's book appeared in the *Bulletin of Atomic Scientists* in early 1949, with comments by sociologist Edward Shils, then teaching at the London School of Economics and the University of Chicago, the physicist Philip Morrison, Senator Brien McMahon and the Russian journalist M. Marinin.[47] The Russian's remarks put Blackett in a bad light by extolling his book's virtues and characterising Baruch as 'an old-time wily speculator from Wall Street'.[48] McMahon called Blackett an apologist for the Kremlin, while Shils characterised Blackett as a 'master of artful and intelligent distortion'.[49]

Morrison had a different point of view. He deplored the *ad hominem* attacks on Blackett, supported Blackett's principal military conclusions that a major war would not be a 'three-week aerial expedition', and recommended that disarmament discussions should include both conventional and atomic weapons. While not accepting

Blackett's characterisation of the Hiroshima bomb as the first act of the Cold War, Morrison offered some personal testimony:

> I can testify … that a date near August 10 was a mysterious final date which we, who had the daily technical job of readying the bomb, had to meet at whatever cost in risk or money or good development policy. That is hard to explain except by Blackett's thesis.[50]

However, the attitude of most American physicists, particularly those who worked on the Manhattan Project, is better represented by Columbia University physicist I.I. Rabi, who wrote a scathing attack on Blackett and on Blackett's arguments for an April 1949 issue of *Atlantic Monthly.* Rabi castigated Blackett for writing 'like the amateur he is' on international affairs and for manifesting 'the hopeless confusion of the average Englishman' about American attitudes and politics.[51] Worse, Rabi wrote, Blackett had abused his responsibility as a scientist by writing so disastrously for a lay audience in a field outside his special field of competence. And further, Blackett had not worked on the atomic bomb during the war, his recent professional interests had not been primarily in nuclear physics, and the contents of his book often 'show that his thinking in this is that of an outsider'. In Rabi's opinion, Blackett's uninformed knowledge of atomic weapons resulted in the failure to see that the atomic bomb 'has made obsolete' the methods of conventional warfare.[52] A year later the United States was in a shooting war in Korea.

POLITICISATION OF A SCIENTIFIC MAN: DEBATES TO THE 1960s

For Blackett, his role in these debates on atomic policy gained him a reputation broadly as a communist fellow traveller. In the United States this meant that the FBI kept files on him, making use of an informant's false claim in 1951 that Blackett had admitted affiliation with the Communist Party of Great Britain 'on the occasion of the founding of the World Federation of Scientific Workers in Paris, France, in the Summer of 1946'.[53] Blackett and his wife were detained and questioned about his political views in Tampa, Florida in 1951 when their Canadian plane made a refuelling stop *en route* from Mexico City to Toronto.[54] As late as 1960 Blackett had to be given a special visa at the American Embassy in London to enable him to enter the United States.[55]

Blackett's socialist views and his friendships with British communists and with Russian scientists were well known. Among German scientists detained at Farm Hall from July 1945 to January 1946 was Werner Heisenberg, who speculated in his first days at Farm Hall on the reasons that British scientists had not been brought immediately to see the German scientists:

> It may be that the British Government are frightened of the communist professors, Dirac and so on. They say 'If we tell Dirac or Blackett where they are, they will report it immediately to their Russian friends [such as] Kapitza.'[56]

As Jeremy Bernstein notes, this is a bizarre statement in almost every way. Dirac and Blackett were not communists, and Kapitza was dismissed in 1946 from his physics institute for refusing to work on nuclear weapons development.

Blackett was despatched from his summer cottage in Wales in late August 1945 to interview the German scientists. Informed that General Leslie Groves wanted the Germans to be treated as prisoners of war or to be settled into British universities, Blackett argued for their return to Germany. To the argument that the German scientists might be hijacked by the Russians, some British physicists jested that this might be good for the UK and the United States since German backwardness in atomic weaponry would retard the advance of any Russian nuclear programme.[57]

Reflecting later on the increasing amounts of time that he had begun spending in the late 1940s in writing essays for public affairs journals like the *New Statesman*, *Encounter*, *Endeavour* and *International Affairs*, Blackett noted that he began seriously to study politics, international affairs and strategies of war following the rise of Hitler in Germany and the coming of the Spanish Civil War. In joining the Tizard Committee in 1935, Blackett realised that his early naval service had given him an understanding of the attitudes of service men.[58] Among his naval experiences he vividly remembered the Battle of Jutland, in particular gazing through a periscope at a patch of oily water in which a dozen survivors, from a crew of 1,200 men, were clinging to pieces of wreckage from the battle cruiser *Queen Mary*, one of two British battle cruisers blown up by the German Navy. Jutland taught him, he repeated on several occasions, the danger of assuming superiority over the enemy in military technique and the folly of failing to design defence measures against the offensive weapons in which one claims superiority.[59]

Further, Blackett recalled in 1961, he had felt increasing alarm during the war at hearing BBC broadcasts treat the bombing of German civilians as a viable and normal strategy of war. Blackett perceived a steady brutalisation of military and civilian attitudes about the practice of war. In his view, the senseless destruction of refugee-swollen Dresden in February 1945 paved the way for the August bombing of Hiroshima and Nagasaki. Foreboding about a future in which military policy countenances annihilation led Blackett to devote large amounts of time to opposing atomic policies despite his desire to immerse himself in scientific research.[60]

In this opposition, there is considerable continuity in Blackett's attitude toward the matter of strategic conventional and nuclear bombing. In the 1940s in governmental memoranda he emphasised the importance of land forces in military campaigns and the need for the Air Force to protect ground troops and supply lines, both on land and sea. In these memoranda, Blackett voiced the opinion that the Air Force was seeking to establish itself as the strategic offensive force, leaving the Navy with the defensive role of guarding communications and the Army with the role of occupying the enemy's country after defeat from the air.[61]

By the 1950s Blackett was arguing that the only sensible military policy in Europe was to develop a strength in land forces that more nearly matched Soviet land forces in Europe, instead of relying on airborne nuclear weapons. It is hard not to think of Blackett as a Navy officer as he decried what he called the 'Jupiter complex of the airmen' threatening mankind with atomic thunderbolts.[62]

Blackett became increasingly concerned, too, about the advocacy of tactical nuclear weapons by Gordon Dean, chairman of the United States Atomic Energy Commission from 1950 to 1953, and then by Henry Kissinger, professor of politics at Harvard University, in 1957.[63] As Blackett saw it, Kissinger's rules of engagement were a prescription for limited nuclear war contained in Europe.[64] Kissinger's argument that American soldiers could be trained more successfully than Soviet soldiers in the use of nuclear tactical weapons was dismissed by Blackett as 'poppycock – and very dangerous'.[65]

Most repugnant to Blackett were the applications of game theory to 'scenarios' of nuclear war, as worked out by scholars associated with the RAND Corporation, the Hudson Institute, Princeton University, and other university and government-associated 'think tanks' and operations research groups. In March 1961 Blackett delivered a speech to military officers in the Royal United Services Institution. He argued that operational research (OR) groups had been able to make substantial contributions during the Second World War not only because they were in close contact with executive officers who were running the war, but because the OR group members believed their conclusions to be accurate and felt morally responsible for them. Operational research cannot substitute for traditional military judgement and wisdom, he argued, but rather provides a useful supplement.[66]

In contrast, recent conclusions of civilian military analysts associated with the RAND Corporation, Blackett said, 'seem to me wrong and dangerous'. Since no large-scale nuclear war had ever occurred, there was no body of operational data on real events on which to base a common-sense analysis such as was available to wartime operational research groups. Worse, the new writings in operational research embodied a 'nauseating inhumanity' which, Blackett wrote, expressed a 'strain of deep social pessimism combined sometimes strangely with an almost neurotic contemplation of destruction'.[67]

Albert Wohlstetter's 'The Delicate Balance of Terror' had appeared in *Foreign Affairs* in January 1959. Wohlstetter argued that it is sane and rational for a country to initiate a first and 'surprise' nuclear strike.[68] Blackett rejected these kinds of arguments as well as the conclusions of Princeton University's Oskar Morgenstern and RAND's Herman Kahn in calculating nuclear risks. Morgenstern's *The Question of National Defense* (1959) followed the RAND Corporation's classified *Report on a Study of Non-Military Defense* (1958) edited by Kahn.

The RAND study, like Kahn's 1960 book *Thermonuclear War*, assumed two levels of nuclear attack and figures for civilian casualties which Kahn deemed 'plausible'. The conclusion was that the United States could survive nuclear war if measures of 'non-military', that is, 'civilian', defence were taken immediately in preparation for war.[69] In 1962 Kahn augmented his earlier studies with the book *Thinking about the Unthinkable*, discussing both limited nuclear war and all-out nuclear war, and laying out what he called 'scenarios' and 'games' that might be played out.[70] RAND Corporation studies argued the need for a civil defence programme that was estimated to cost hundreds of billions of dollars.[71]

Dismissing American fears of a 'missile gap' with the Soviet Union, Blackett argued, as he had done since the 1940s, for parallel reductions in conventional and nuclear weapons, noting that the growing power of China was an additional reason for urgency in this matter.[72] At a time when a partial ban on atomic testing was sporadically under negotiation, Blackett continued to focus his interest on bilateral disarmament which would lead to a reduced number of atomic weapons and provide minimum mutual deterrence.

That the alleged Russian superiority in missiles was a fiction became a matter of public discussion in late September 1961 when Joe Alsop debunked the much publicised 'missile gap' in the Paris edition of the *New York Herald Tribune.* By November, Secretary of Defense Robert McNamara revealed figures for weaponry in the US armed forces: 1,700 intercontinental bombers and several dozen operational ICBMs, 80 Polaris missiles in nuclear-powered submarines, 300 carrier-borne aircraft armed with megaton warheads, and nearly 1,000 supersonic land-based fighters with nuclear warheads. Now it seemed ever more clear that the Soviets' motive in shooting down an American spy-plane, the U-2, in spring 1960, was to ensure the secrecy of locations of their many fewer land-based missiles that constituted the Soviet retaliatory threat. The aim of maintaining this secrecy was also a principal factor in Soviet resistance to inspections in a test-ban treaty.[73]

In autumn 1962, just following the Cuban missile crisis, Blackett's collection of military and public affairs essays written from the 1940s to the 1960s appeared under the title *Studies of War: Nuclear and Conventional.* Reaction to the book contrasts markedly with reaction in 1948 to *The Military and Political Consequences of Atomic Energy*, even though Blackett's arguments are strikingly consistent. But times had changed. Blackett's book appeared almost simultaneously with Kahn's *Thinking about the Unthinkable* and Edward Teller's *The Legacy of Hiroshima*, so that sometimes these books were reviewed together. The contrast with Kahn has already been noted. Teller, recently retired from directing the Lawrence-Livermore Laboratory for weapons research, argued the following:

> In a dangerous world we cannot have peace unless we are strong. We cannot be strong unless we are fully prepared to exploit the biggest modern power, nuclear explosives. Nuclear weapons can be used with moderation on all scales of serious conflict ... World War III would be much worse than anything we can remember. But it would not destroy mankind.[74]

As an anonymous reviewer wrote,

> A disenchanted observer of the strategic scene once suggested that Dr. Herman Kahn, the celebrated analyst of thermonuclear war, had been invented as some sort of cruel joke. No one with such views, it was implied, could possibly be real. *The Legacy of Hiroshima* will probably give rise to similar doubts about Dr Edward Teller ... Somewhere between the 'father of the bomb' and the unilateral disarmer stands Professor Blackett – cool, astringent, and objective.[75]

In contrast to their reaction to Teller's book, many prominent scientists praised Blackett's collection of essays, Freeman Dyson saying, for example, that Blackett 'writes with humor and grace and human wisdom, and with a deep sense of history',[76] and Nevill Mott noting that 'No review can do justice to the incisiveness of Blackett's arguments, their hard common sense and their basis in a lifetime's experience of science and war.'[77]

Some reviewers attributed to Blackett a practical effect on recent developments in nuclear policy, given that the US had substantially revised its pre-1961 policy and improved its non-nuclear resources in men and material. Nuclear weapons, for good or ill, had not made conventional weapons obsolete after all. But if Blackett was right in this result, it was land wars in Korea and Indochina that made the point, not his original arguments. A reviewer for the *Baltimore Sun* noted Blackett's disagreement with the development of small tactical nuclear weapons, adding that 'he has been right before'.[78] British historian A.J.P. Taylor wrote: 'Blackett is asking us to believe that he is sane and that most American experts are mad. That is easy to believe. But it is unlikely that his voice of sanity will drown out American experts and air generals.'[79]

One of the few thoroughly negative reviews came from Lewis Strauss, former chairman of the US Atomic Energy Commission, who ridiculed Blackett's 'remoteness from reality' for proposing that impediments to disarmament in the United States might be substantially economic, political and emotional in character rather than military.[80] To many, Blackett's position in this regard seemed common sense. In any case, his heretical views in 1948 had become familiar and debatable in the mainstream politics of 1962.

OUTSIDER AS INSIDER IN THE CORRIDORS OF POWER

While Blackett seems to have corresponded with few scientists in the US over these matters, he visited the US frequently, usually on scientific matters, and he began participating in the Pugwash Conferences on Science and World Affairs after the first Pugwash meeting in Nova Scotia in 1957. Organising members in the United States included Eugene Rabinowitch, Victor Weisskopf, Bentley Glass, Hans Bethe and Jerome Wiesner, who became President Kennedy's science adviser.[81] Blackett and Rabi both participated in the Pugwash Conferences at Stowe in 1961, Cambridge in 1962, and Dubrovnik in 1963.[82]

Blackett had influential contacts in the United States, among them Henry Kissinger, another Pugwash participant, whom Blackett met first in London in the summer of 1959. Upon his return to Harvard, Kissinger wrote to Blackett that he had found their views to be very close.[83] Before his meeting with Kissinger, Howard K. Smith, who first met Blackett while stationed with the CBS News bureau in London, reminded Blackett that Kissinger was one of the Harvard and MIT professors whom Senator Kennedy had gathered into his 'brain trust', as Kennedy prepared for the 1960 election.[84]

In the 1930s and 1940s, Blackett's political views were seen largely as persistently maverick, left-wing in character, even slightly mad. However, British scientists who were unsympathetic with Blackett's political views, or who disapproved of distinguished scientists espousing political views at all, usually saw no reason to doubt Blackett's personal integrity or dependability in scientific and professional matters. Typical was a remark by A.V. Hill, the biophysicist, MP for Cambridge University and Secretary for the Royal Society, who worked with Blackett during the war:

> Remember, that Haldane and Blackett, for all their queer political notions, are useful and cooperative members of the [Royal Society]

> Council: I am sure that Bernal and Hogben will be the same when their turn comes to serve ... We can keep them in order better by cooperating with them in scientific affairs than by formally setting up to oppose their political ideas in the name of science.[85]

Thus, while Blackett's political ideas were queer, he could be trusted in the inner circle of British scientists and gentlemen.

As mentioned above, Blackett was not Marxist and he explicitly identified his views with Fabian socialism. Yet when the Labour Party defeated the Conservative Party in July 1945, Blackett found himself in disfavour with Clement Attlee's Labour government on the question of the development of British nuclear weapons. The 1948 book provoked outrage. Blackett was accused of fostering communism and Soviet policies. Harold Wilson later recalled that his appointment of Blackett to the National Research and Development Corporation in 1949, while Clement Attlee's government was in power, provoked one of the most violent political reactions in Parliament that Wilson had known in 30 years of parliamentary turbulence.[86]

How effective was Blackett's voice in opposition to the proliferation of large arsenals of strategic nuclear weapons and the decline of conventional military forces? By the mid-1960s disarmament negotiations, as well as the limited test ban treaty, became part of mainstream international politics and conventional military capabilities were expanding. However, it is impossible to judge Blackett's precise role in global politics, even while noting the publication of his views in widely read American and British magazines and his conversations and correspondence with influential persons in government and military forces. Clearly his position had become a respectable one and his integrity rarely questioned by the mid-1960s. By then, even his argument about diplomatic motives for use of atomic bombs in Japan had become part of debates among historians of the Second World War.[87]

Blackett, who worked with Harold Wilson's Ministry of Technology in the Labour government of the late 1960s, ended his scientific career with election in 1965 to a five-year term as President of the Royal Society. He was elevated to the peerage in 1969, with the title Baron Blackett of Chelsea, by nomination of the Prime Minister to the Queen. Blackett was a member of the Athenaeum and a member of the Reform Club on Pall Mall. He and Lady Blackett lived in Dolphin Square overlooking the Thames.[88]

Blackett was at home in London, in contrast to Cambridge. He chose to leave the physics department at Manchester for the one at Imperial College in London in autumn 1953, knowing that he probably would be offered the directorship of the Cavendish Laboratory upon Bragg's retirement. When an inquiry came from Chadwick in summer 1953 about the Cavendish, Blackett declined.[89] He by no means had lost interest in scientific work, but his years in Whitehall during the war and his frequent visits to London only strengthened his attachment to London.

Following Blackett's death in 1974, *The Times* obituary essay carried the headline 'Lord Blackett: Radical Nobel-Prize Winning Physicist', noting that immediately after the war 'he was thought to be committed too far to the left for a Labour Government to employ with ease'.[90] Snow said of him that 'He had his enemies of course, because he was a committed, although perfectly respectable left-winger, and he made that totally clear.'[91] In describing Blackett's *alter ego* Frances Getliffe in the novel *Corridors of Power*, Snow wrote:

> The trouble with our major allies is that they methodically read every speech Francis Getliffe has ever made, and can't believe that any of us know anything about him. One of the few advantages of living in England, is that we do know just a little about one another, don't you agree?[92]

In speaking out on matters of international affairs, Blackett proved himself willing to take unpopular and principled positions, risking criticism and rebuke both from scientific colleagues and from politicians and military men who believed his only legitimate authority to lie in expert fields of science.

On policies for atomic weapons and military strategy, Blackett spoke as a man with strong credentials as an experimental physicist and as a founder of operational research, although Manhattan scientists did not consider him an 'atomic scientist' and military officers considered him principally a scientist.

Blackett spoke on public issues as a socialist, a member of the Labour Party and a government consultant who served on military, educational and ministerial committees from the 1930s to the 1970s. For Blackett, the battle to halt proliferation of atomic weapons was simultaneously a campaign to free capital resources and scientific expertise for improving the living and working conditions of impoverished classes in both the West and the East, including the Soviet Union. This had been a theme at the heart of his socialist views since at least the 1930s.[93]

Finally, as has been emphasised, Blackett's views on national policy and international affairs were the attitudes of an English gentleman and a Navy officer who had been trained in the customs of war in the last days of the Victorian and Edwardian eras. This identity probably helps explain the personal confidence (some said 'arrogance') and the sense of duty that led Blackett to take the unusual course among scientists of opposing his country's atomic weapons policy immediately after the Second World War. Blackett's status as an officer, a gentleman and a scientist in a small elite of Englishmen, who were well known to each other, ensured a hearing in the corridors of power, however controversial his views on war and politics.

NOTES

1. Quoted by P.M.S. Blackett in 'The Military Consequences of Atomic Energy', pp. 3–16, in *Studies of War: Nuclear and Conventional* (Edinburgh and London: Oliver & Boyd, 1962), on p. 4, originally published in M.L. Oliphant *et al.*, *The Atomic Age* (London: Allen & Unwin, 1949).
2. C.P. Snow, *Corridors of Power* (London: Macmillan, 1964; Penguin, 1966), pp. 42–3.
3. In an interview with John Halperin, Lord Snow explained that it was Blackett's politics that were given to Getliffe (p. 201). Another character, David Rubin, was based on I.I. Rabi (p. 192). In John Halperin, *C.P. Snow: An Oral Biography, Together with a Conversation with Lady Snow (Pamela Hansford Johnson)* (New York: St Martin's Press, 1983).
4. Ibid., pp. 17–18, 201. David Shusterman, *C.P. Snow* (Boston, MA: Twayne Publishers, 1991).
5. Blackett Papers, Royal Society Library, E24–E34. It was Lord Snow, along with Lord Chalfont of the Foreign Office, who formally introduced Blackett to the House of Lords on the occasion of his first sitting in 1969. Letter from Charles (C.P.) Snow to Blackett, 24 January 1969; and letter from Alun Chalfont to Blackett, 28 January 1969, Blackett Papers, A84.
6. See Alice K. Smith, *A Peril and a Hope: The Scientist's Movement in America, 1945-1947* (Chicago, IL: University of Chicago Press, 1968) and Robert Gilpin, *American Scientists and Nuclear Policy* (Princeton, NJ: Princeton University Press, 1962). More recently, Paul Forman, 'Behind Quantum Electrodynamics: National Security as a Basis for Physical Research in the United States, 1940–1960', *Historical Studies in the Physical and Biological Sciences*, 18 (1988), pp. 149–229; Barton J. Bernstein, 'Four Physicists and the Bomb: The Early Years, 1945–1950', *Historical Studies in the Physical and Biological Sciences*, 18 (1988), pp. 231–63; Lawrence Badash, *Scientists and the Development of Nuclear Weapons: From Fission to the Limited Test Ban Treaty 1939–1963* (New York: Humanities Press, 1995).

7. David Edgerton, 'British Scientific Intellectuals and the Relations of Science, Technology and War', in Paul Forman and J.M. Sánchez-Ron (eds), *National Military Establishments and the Advancement of Science and Technology, Boston Studies in the Philosophy of Science*, No. 180 (Dordrecht: Kluwer, 1996), pp. 1–35, esp. 16, 18, 25; and Greta Jones, 'The Mushroom-Shaped Cloud: British Scientists' Opposition to Nuclear Weapons Policy, 1945–1947', *Annals of Science*, 43 (1986), pp. 1–26, on pp. 5–6.
8. The best study is Thomas Hager, *Force of Nature: The Life of Linus Pauling* (New York: Simon & Schuster, 1995). Pauling, Nobel laureate in chemistry in 1954, received the 1962 Nobel peace prize in 1963 for his efforts toward a nuclear test ban treaty, which was signed as a limited ban in 1963.
9. On Blackett's family, Andrew Brown, 'Patrick Blackett: Sailor, Scientist, Socialist', *Physics World* (April 1998), pp. 35–8, on p. 35. Blackett told Brian Connell in an interview for Anglia TV that some people said he ran his departments like a captain runs a ship. Blackett thought there might be something in this and in the influence on his scientific work of his earlier career in the Navy. He preferred to delegate authority to younger or more junior people, he said, but, if things go wrong, the captain takes the blame. Blackett in interview with Brian Connell of Anglia Television, 4 October 1971, 14-page typescript, Blackett Papers, A32. The film is available as a non-viewable, preservation copy at the British Film Institute.
10. See [Sir] Bernard Lovell, 'Patrick Maynard Stuart Blackett, Baron Blackett, of Chelsea', *Biographical Memoirs of Fellows of the Royal Society*, 21 (1975), pp. 1–115, on p. 39; published separately as *P.M.S. Blackett: A Biographical Memoir* (London: Royal Society, 1976).
11. P.M.S. Blackett, 'The Birth of Nuclear Science', *Listener* (March 1954), pp. 380–1, one of three BBC talks, Blackett Papers, B116; and P.M.S. Blackett, 'The Ejection of Protons from Nitrogen Nuclei, Photographed by the Wilson Method', *Proceedings of the Royal Society*, A107 (1925), pp. 349–60.
12. Interview of P.M.S. Blackett with John L. Heilbron, Imperial College, 17 December 1962, Sources for the History of Quantum Physics, Niels Bohr Library, American Institute of Physics, p. 3. Of the Geiger counter, Blackett reminisced that, at that time, 'In order to make it work you had to spit on the wire on some Friday evening in Lent.'
13. Interview of Carl Anderson with Charles Weiner, Caltech, 30 June 1966, Sources for the History of Quantum Physics, Niels Bohr Library, American Institute of Physics, p. 16. P.M.S. Blackett and G.P.S. Occhialini, 'Photography of Penetrating Corpuscular Radiation', *Nature*, 130 (1933), p. 363. Also P.M.S. Blackett, J. Chadwick and G.P.S. Occhialini, 'New Evidence for the Positive Electron', *Nature*, 131 (1933), p. 473; and P.M.S. Blackett, 'The Positive Electron', *Nature*, 132 (1933), pp. 917–19.
14. In a letter from James Chadwick to Blackett, 18 November 1971, from Cambridge, Chadwick wrote of Rutherford's reluctance to develop nuclear physics in the 1930s, Blackett Papers, J18. Also see Jeffrey Hughes, 'Brains in their Fingertips: Physics at the Cavendish Laboratory, 1880–1940', in Richard Mason (ed.), *Cambridge Minds* (Cambridge: Cambridge University Press, 1995), pp. 160–76, on pp. 172–5.
15. Interview of Otto R. Frisch with Charles Weiner, in New York City at the American Institute of Physics, 3 May 1967, Sources for the History of Quantum Physics, Niels Bohr Library, American Institute of Physics, on pp. 19–25.
16. Materials that Blackett intended for an autobiography, including 'Interlude on

Politics', 2 pp., Blackett Papers, A10A; and letter from Alex Wood to Blackett, dated 5 February 1935, Blackett Papers, A26.

17. Julian Huxley, *Scientific Research and Social Needs* (London: Watts, 1934), p. x; and Blackett, 'The Frustration of Science', 13-page typescript based on 1934 BBC talk, for *The Government of Science in Britain* (1935), Chapter 7, Blackett Papers, H1.
18. *Government of Science in Britain*, Chapter 11: 'Pure Science: Discussion with Professor P.M.S. Blackett', pp. 203–24, on p. 224.
19. Note from Patrick Blackett to Michael Polanyi, from Penparc, 26 August 1939, Polanyi Papers, Regenstein Library, University of Chicago, 4:1. On Polanyi's naturalisation papers, Costanza Blackett to Michael Polanyi, from Penparc, 5 September 1939, Polanyi Papers, 4:1.
20. Tizard was the son of a Navy captain who had been navigator on the Challenger expedition. Tizard, a former pilot in the Royal Flying Corps during the Great War, studied mathematics and chemistry at Oxford and spent a year with Walther Nernst in Berlin. He was Rector at Imperial College from 1929 to 1942. Of Tizard, Blackett said: 'Of the individuals who have influenced me by their personality, I think Tizard comes next to Rutherford ... he seemed as genuinely interested in talking to a college porter, an aircraftsman or a young scientist as to a crack pilot, a professor or an air marshal. A visit with Tizard to an experimental establishment was an exhilarating experience: he left behind him a newer awareness of the tasks and a new keenness to get results.' P.M.S. Blackett, 'Tizard and the Science of War', Tizard Memorial Lecture delivered 11 February 1960 before the Institute for Strategic Studies. Reprinted from *Nature*, 185, No. 4714, 5 March (1960), pp. 647–53 in 16-page offprint (quotation on pp. 15–16).
21. Carbon copy of letter from Blackett to George P. Thomson, 28 July 1941; and Thomson's reply, 31 July 1941, Blackett Papers, J104. See Margaret Gowing, *Britain and Atomic Energy, 1939–1945* (London: Macmillan, 1964); and Margaret Gowing and Lorna Arnold, *Independence and Deterrence*, 2 vols (New York: St Martin's, 1974).
22. A letter, dated 17 August 1945, from the Office of the Prime Minister invited Blackett to join the Advisory Committee; a letter of 6 January 1948 signed by Clement Attlee dissolved the committee, Blackett Papers, D184. Other members of the Committee when it was first constituted were: Sir John Anderson, the MP for Scottish Universities; James Chadwick; Edward Appleton, secretary of the DSIR; Henry Dale, President of the Royal Society; George P. Thomson; Sir Alan Brooke, the Chief of the Imperial General Staff; Sir Alexander Cadogan, Under-Secretary of State at the Foreign Office; and Sir Alan Barlow, Second Secretary of the Treasury. See Andrew Brown, *The Neutron and the Bomb: A Biography of Sir James Chadwick* (Oxford: Oxford University Press, 1997), p. 304.
23. *Military and Political Consequences of Atomic Energy* (London: Turnstile Press, 1948) was published in a slightly revised and less caustic version, *Fear, War and the Bomb* (New York: Whittlesey House, 1949), for an American audience. It was distributed by the Book Find Club, the predecessor of Book of the Month Club. Paul Jarrico, chairman of the Film Division of the National Council of the Arts, Sciences, and Professions in Los Angeles, contacted Blackett about making a documentary film based on the book. He proposed including among the film technicians some of the men blacklisted from Hollywood film work and known as 'The Hollywood Ten'. Blackett declined, finding it hard to imagine how the subject could be properly tackled in a film. See letter from Paul Jarrico, Los

Angeles, to Blackett, 4 May 1949; letter from Michael Hodson to Blackett, 13 June 1949, Blackett Papers, H29. The chairman of the National Council of the Arts was Harlow Shapley and the regional chairman in California was Linus Pauling.

24. A nuclear research establishment was established at Harwell, south of Oxford, in 1946 with John Cockcroft as its first director. See Brown, *Neutron and the Bomb*, p. 305, note, p. 315. Gowing and Arnold note in *Independence and Deterrence* that a government memorandum circulated by Blackett in February 1947 shows no recognition that a decision to make bombs had already been made. Gowing and Arnold, Vol. I, p. 183.
25. Blackett was one of eight British scientists refused permission to visit the Soviet Academy of Sciences in mid-June 1945, on the grounds that they could not be spared from war work, although the German surrender had occurred in May. The eight were J.D. Bernal, P.M.S. Blackett, Sir Charles Darwin, P.A.M. Dirac, E.A. Milne, N.F. Mott, R.G.W. Norrish and E.K. Rideal. See typed press release from the Association of Scientific Workers, 16 June 1945, Blackett Papers, G91.
26. See Badash, *Scientists and the Development of Nuclear Weapons*, pp. 68–70.
27. During the period 1946–52 Blackett was Director of the Physical Laboratories, Dean of the Faculty of Sciences (1950–52) and Pro-Vice-Chancellor (1950–52) at the University of Manchester. He was instrumental in founding the Jodrell Bank observatory for radio astronomy, and he embarked upon a new research programme on the earth's magnetism. See M.J. Nye, 'Temptations of Theory, Strategies of Evidence: P.M.S. Blackett and the Earth's Magnetism, 1947–1952', *British Journal for the History of Science*, 32 (1999), pp. 69–92. On his role at Jodrell Bank, see Lovell, *The Story of Jodrell Bank* (Oxford: Oxford University Press, 1968); and interview of David Edge with Sir Bernard Lovell, 6 July 1971, at Jodrell Bank, Sources for the History of Modern Astrophysics, American Institute of Physics.
28. Blackett to Polanyi, 3 November 1941, Blackett Papers, J65. On Blackett and Polanyi, see Mary Jo Nye, 'Scientific Practice and Scientific Politics: A Preliminary Look at Blackett and Polanyi in Manchester', *Polanyiana: The Periodical of the Michael Polanyi Liberal Philosophical Association (Budapest)*, 5 (1996), pp. 21–35.
29. Blackett, 'Tizard and the Science of War', p. 8.
30. Carbon copy of unsigned paper, 15 August 1941, probably by Tizard, stamped 'Most Secret' and beginning, 'In these notes the effects of bombing on the morale of the civilian population of Germany are noted', 9 pp., Blackett Papers, D61. In a letter intended for publication in *The Times*, 27 April 1961, J.D. Bernal noted that a survey taken by two teams of about 40 workers each, who were studying effects of German bombing on Birmingham and Hull, concluded that the effects were small. Lindemann countered that if bombing on Birmingham had little effect, much heavier bombing of German cities must produce a decisive one. Carbon copy of letter, Blackett Papers, J44.
31. Blackett, *Military and Political Consequences*, pp. 9, 14–15.
32. Gowing and Arnold, *Independence and Deterrence*, Vol. I, p. 115.
33. Letter from Blackett to Nevill Mott, 14 November 1946, Blackett Papers, D175.
34. Blackett, *Military and Political Consequences*, p. 145.
35. Blackett, 'The First Real Chance for Disarmament', 37-page typescript for *Harper's* magazine, November (1962), on p. 29, Blackett Papers, F72.
36. Blackett, *Military and Political Consequences*, p. 120. Gar Alperowitz revived the argument in his dissertation and book of 1965. 'I think the only way you can understand why Nagasaki was tripped off, automatically, bing-bing, just like

that, with no consideration, is this tremendous rush to end the war – *not* just to end the war before an invasion, but *immediately*! … What was the rush? Well, P.M.S. Blackett, another Nobel prize winner, saw in 1945 that the only way you could explain that immediate, fast one-two punch, was the fact that the Russians were in fact scheduled to enter the war on August 9.' Quoted in Jerome R. Ravetz, *Scientific Knowledge and its Social Problems* (Oxford: Oxford University Press, 1979), note, p. 64. See Gar Alperovitz, *Atomic Diplomacy: Hiroshima and Potsdam: The Use of the Atomic Bomb and the American Confrontation with Soviet Power* (New York: Simon & Schuster, 1965) and, more recently, Alperovitz, *The Decision to Use the Atomic Bomb and the Architecture of an American Myth* (London: Harper-Collins, 1995).

37. 'Nobel Prizes: Professor Blackett and Mr. T.S. Eliot', *Manchester Guardian*, 5 November 1948, p. 5; and Edward Shils, 'The Atomic Problem: Professor Blackett's Book', ibid., p. 4.
38. For example, letter from H.T. Tizard to Blackett, 10 August 1948, who nonetheless thought it a thoughtful and well-written book manuscript, Blackett Papers, H37; and letter from George Thomson to Blackett, 16 October 1948, Blackett Papers, H37, who thought it an excellent book but that the Americans were fundamentally right.
39. Letter from Frederick Osborn, London, to Blackett, 26 November 1948; Frederick Osborn, 'The United Nations and Atomic Control', 15 December 1948, five-page carbon copy typescript; and Blackett's reply, six-page carbon copy typescript, Blackett Papers, H34.
40. Letter from Edward Mead Earle, Institute for Advanced Study, to Blackett, 1 July 1949, Blackett Papers, H36.
41. E.M. Friedwald, 'Blackett's Book Dissected', *Discovery*, 9 (November 1948), p. 352; Lord Cherwell, 'Atomic Bombing the Decisive Weapon – and Deterrent', *Daily Telegraph and Morning Post*, 9 December 1948, p. 4.
42. Waldemar Kaempffert, 'The Atom's Power in War and Peace: A Famous British Physicist Champions Russia's Side in the Momentous Debates', *New York Times Book Review*, Section 7, 13 February 1949, pp. 1, 32.
43. P.M.S. Blackett, 'Steps toward Disarmament', *Scientific American*, 206, 4 (April 1962), pp. 45–53, on p. 51.
44. Friedwald, 'Blackett's Book Dissected', p. 352.
45. Kaempffert, 'The Atom's Power', p. 32.
46. Carbon copy of letter from Blackett to J. Langdon-Davies, n.d., Blackett Papers, H37.
47. See letter from Edward Shils to Blackett, 17 December 1948, and carbon copy of Blackett to Shils, 23 December 1948, Blackett Papers, H41. Edward A. Shils, 'Blackett's Apologia for the Soviet Position', *Bulletin of Atomic Scientists*, 5 (February 1949), pp. 34–7; Philip Morrison, 'Blackett's Analysis of the Issue', pp. 37–40; Brien McMahon, 'Comment on Blackett's Book', pp. 40–3; and M. Marinin, 'An English Scientist Exposes Atomic Diplomacy' (translation from review in *Pravda*, 22 November 1948), pp. 43, 50. The editor of the *Bulletin*, H.H. Goldsmith, inquired of Blackett whether he would like to reply to Shils's review in the April issue (letter of 14 February 1949), but Blackett declined in a letter of 26 February 1949, Blackett Papers, H41.
48. Marinin, 'An English Scientist', p. 43.
49. Shils, 'Blackett's Apologia', p. 35; McMahon, 'Comment', p. 43.
50. Morrison, 'Blackett's Analysis', p. 40.
51. I.I. Rabi, 'Playing Down the Bomb: Blackett vs. the Atom', *Atlantic Monthly*, 183 (August 1949), pp. 21–4, on p. 21.

52. Ibid., pp. 21, 23, 24.
53. Formerly confidential document, 11 May 1951, No. 100-354451-5; formerly confidential document, 22 November 1952, No. 100-354451-6, Federal Bureau of Investigation File No. 100-354451. Thanks to Ronald E. Doel for copies of the copies.
54. Blackett had attended a cosmic ray conference in Guanajuato, Mexico. He and his wife were taken off the plane on the grounds that they had no visas, and they were questioned about their political views and possession of possibly subversive documents. In fact a suitcase was half-full of Russian reprints on cosmic rays, but their bags were not searched. See one-page typescript, 'Cosmic Ray Conference 1951', Blackett Papers, A10A.
55. Letter of 17 August 1960 to Blackett from Thomas H. Osgood, attaché at the American Embassy in London, Blackett Papers, A36.
56. Jeremy Bernstein, *Hitler's Uranium Club: The Secret Recordings at Farm Hall* (New York: American Institute of Physics, 1996), p. 79.
57. From a one-page typescript, 'German Scientists Brought to England after the War', Blackett Papers, A10A.
58. Six-page handwritten and unpublished 'Preface' for *Studies of War*, on p. 2, Blackett Papers, H93.
59. P.M.S. Blackett, 'British Policy and the H-Bomb', in *Studies of War*, pp. 27–46, on p. 27, originally published in *New Statesman and Nation*, 14, 21, 28 August 1954.
60. Blackett, 'Preface'.
61. Three-page typescript, 'Note on the Use of the Bomber Force', with Blackett's initials at the top in his hand. Follows unsigned note of 16 February 1942, Blackett Papers, D62.
62. P.M.S. Blackett, 'Thoughts on British Defense Policy', reprinted from *New Statesman*, 5 December 1959, 8 pp., on p. 6, Blackett Papers, D112. Blackett's opposition to a military strategy of destroying population centres was not unique. US Admiral William Leahy, Chief of Staff to Presidents Roosevelt and Truman, concluded his war memoirs by saying that 'These new concepts of "total war" are basically distasteful to the soldier and sailor of my generation'. William T. Leahy, *I Was There: The Personal Story of the Chief of Staff to Presidents Roosevelt and Truman Based on His Notes and Diaries Made at the Time* (London: Victor Gollancz, 1950), p. 514.
63. Barton Bernstein notes that Robert Oppenheimer and Enrico Fermi began to counsel the development of tactical nuclear weapons and preparations for limited nuclear war in late 1947. 'Four Physicists and the Bomb', p. 253.
64. P.M.S. Blackett, 'America's Atomic Dilemma', in *Studies of War*, pp. 17–26, on pp. 17–20 (originally published in *New Statesman*, 13 February 1954) and 'Nuclear Weapons and Defence: Comments on Kissinger, Kennan, and King-Hall', in *Studies of War*, pp. 54–72, on pp. 54–5 (originally published in *International Affairs*, October 1958). See David Rees, *The Age of Containment: The Cold War, 1945–1965* (London: St Martin's Press, 1967).
65. Blackett, 'Nuclear Weapons and Defence', p. 62.
66. Blackett, 'Operational Research and Nuclear Weapons', 22 March 1961, 17-page typescript, lecture given to the Royal United Services Institution, 22 March 1961, Blackett Papers, D109, and published in the *Journal* of the institution, as well as in *Encounter* and in Blackett's *Studies of War*. See especially p. 6 of typescript. Also, Blackett, 'Critique of Some Contemporary Defence Thinking', reprinted from *Endeavour* (April 1961), 9 pp., Blackett Papers, D112. On operations research, see M. Fortun and S.S. Schweber, 'Scientists and the

Legacy of World War II: The Case of Operations Research (OR)', *Social Studies of Science*, 23 (1993), pp. 595–642.
67. Blackett, 'Critique of Some Contemporary Defence Thinking', pp. 1, 2, 9.
68. Ibid., pp. 2, 4.
69. Oskar Morgenstern, *The Question of National Defense* (New York: Random House, 1959); Herman Kahn (ed.), *A Report on a Study of Non-Military Defense* (Santa Monica, CA: RAND Corporation, 1958); Herman Kahn, *On Thermonuclear War* (Princeton, NJ: Princeton University Press, 1960). See John Strachey, *On Prevention of War* (London: Macmillan, 1962), pp. 13–15.
70. Herman Kahn, *Thinking about the Unthinkable* (London: Weidenfeld & Nicolson, 1962), with an introduction by Raymond Aron who, like Kahn, defended this kind of thinking.
71. On RAND, see David Hounshell, 'The Cold War, RAND, and the Generation of Knowledge, 1946–1962', *Historical Studies in the Physical and Biological Sciences*, 27 (1997), pp. 237–67. In 1950 Blackett wrote a preface for the pamphlet 'Atomic Attack, Can Britain Be Defended?' which enraged John Anderson and others by arguing that civil defence in Britain against nuclear war was impracticable. In 1957 a government White Paper reached the same conclusion. See Jones, 'The Mushroom-Shaped Cloud', pp. 11–12.
72. Blackett, 'The Real Road to Disarmament', in *Studies of War*, pp. 147–66, on pp. 160–6; originally published in *New Statesman*, 2 March 1962, with shorter version under title 'Steps Toward Disarmament', *Scientific American*, 206 (April 1962), pp. 45–53.
73. On Alsop's article, see letter from Captain J.P. Wright, Ministry of Defence, to Blackett, dated 23 November 1961, on first- and second-strike doctrine, Blackett Papers, F84. Blackett, 'Steps Toward Disarmament', pp. 45, 49–50.
74. Edward Teller with Allen Brown, *The Legacy of Hiroshima* (London: Macmillan, 1962), p. viii.
75. Unsigned review, clipping with no source, entitled 'More Than One Approach to Thermonuclear Chauvinism', 6 December 1962, Blackett Papers, H95.
76. Freeman Dyson, review of Blackett's *Studies of War* and Ralph Lapp's *Kill and Overkill: The Strategy of Annihilation* (1962), photocopied review without attribution of source, Blackett Papers, H95.
77. Sir Nevill Mott, 'Nuclear Weapons: Playing It Cool', *New Scientist*, 25 October 1962, clipping, Blackett Papers, H95.
78. Mark S. Watson, 'Views on Military Trends', *Baltimore Sun*, 23 December 1962, clipping, Blackett Papers, H95.
79. A.J.P. Taylor, 'City of Destruction', *New Statesman*, 26 October 1962, clipping, Blackett Papers, H95.
80. Lewis Strauss, 'Lucid Essays on Disarmament, Not Entirely Realistic', *Chicago Sunday Tribune Magazine of Books*, 9 December 1962, clipping, Blackett Papers, H95.
81. Correspondence and Pugwash organisational materials in Blackett Papers, J66–J71. Active members in the UK included Edward (Teddy) Bullard, C.F. Powell, Joseph Rotblat, Nevill Mott, John Cockcroft, William Penney, Rudolph Peierls, Kathleen Lonsdale and C.H. Waddington. Rotblat, born in Warsaw in 1908, left the Manhattan Project at Los Alamos in winter 1944 when it became clear that Germany had not developed an atomic weapon. He later wrote that he heard General Leslie Groves say in March 1944 that the real purpose of the bomb would be to subdue the Soviet Union. Rotblat, who became a British citizen, was president of Pugwash when he and the Pugwash organisation shared the Nobel peace prize in 1995. Richard W. Stevenson, 'Peace Prize Goes

to A-Bomb Scientist Who Turned Critic', *New York Times*, 14 October 1995, p. 3.
82. J. Rotblat, *Pugwash – The First Ten Years: History of the Conferences of Science and World Affairs* (London: Heinemann, 1967).
83. Letter to Blackett from Henry A. Kissinger, Harvard University Center for International Affairs, 10 July 1959, Blackett Papers, F80.
84. Letter to Blackett from Howard K. Smith, Washington Bureau of CBS News, 3 April 1959, Blackett Papers, F82.
85. Quoted from letter from A.V. Hill to Tansley, 6 June 1941, in William McGucken, *Scientists, Society and the State: The Social Relations of Science Movement in Great Britain 1931–1947* (Columbus, OH: Ohio State University Press, 1984), p. 288; Hilary Rose and Steven Rose, *Science and Society* (London: Penguin, 1969), pp. 61, 63–4. Also see Robert Filner, 'The Roots of Political Activism in British Science', *Bulletin of Atomic Scientists*, 32 (1976), pp. 25–9; and Gary Werskey, *The Visible College: A Collective Biography of British Scientists of the 1930s* (London: Free Association Books, 1988).
86. Harold Wilson, 'The Blackett Memorial Lecture', Imperial College, 3 December 1975, 8 pages, Blackett Papers, A6.
87. See, for example, the use of Blackett's arguments in Louis Morton, 'The Decision to Use the Atomic Bomb', *Foreign Affairs*, 35 (January 1957), pp. 334–53; William Appleman Williams, *The Tragedy of American Diplomacy*, 2nd rev. edn (New York: Dell, 1972), 1st edn 1959, on p. 253.
88. Carbon copy of letter from Blackett to Peter Kapitza, n.d., but April 1973, Blackett Papers, J44.
89. Carbon copy of letter from Blackett to James Chadwick, 30 July 1953, Blackett Papers, A24.
90. 'Lord Blackett: Radical Nobel-Prize Winning Physicist', (unsigned), *The Times*, 15 July 1974, clipping, Blackett Papers, A1.
91. Quoted in Halperin, *C.P. Snow*, p. 204. Snow assumed that Blackett, like himself, had been subjected to security investigations by MI5 during the Cold War.
92. Snow, *Corridors of Power*, p. 229.
93. Robert R. Neild, 'Economic and Defence Policy in India', seven-page typescript, with note to Blackett dated 29 January 1962, Blackett Papers, F81.

15

The Scientific Context of Blackett's Achievements

Bernard Lovell

Blackett's scientific interests had been evident in his boyhood and throughout his naval career. Further, the emphasis on mathematics, engineering and science during his four years at Osborne and Dartmouth had suited him well. In the closing months of the First World War, as a lieutenant in the Royal Navy on active service in the Channel and North Sea, he had begun to study mathematics again, to read scientific textbooks; he also wrote to London University and to the instrument firm of Barr & Stroud seeking a post-war career.

In the event the decisive move had come in January 1919 from the Admiralty when, with other naval officers, Blackett was sent to Cambridge for a six-month course of general studies to compensate for the abrupt termination of their education when they had been hurriedly sent to sea in 1914. In later years Blackett reflected that he would no doubt have found a post-war career in some university but 'to be deposited, so to speak, on the shores of Cambridge just as the Cavendish laboratory was rising under Rutherford's inspired direction to great heights of eminence was luck indeed for me. I owe much to the Admiralty.'[1]

At the age of 22, three weeks after arriving in Cambridge, Blackett resigned from the Navy to become an undergraduate student. Fourteen years later he left as one of the world's famous scientists and as a Fellow of the Royal Society.

Blackett's Cambridge career was meteoric. After securing a second class in Part I of the mathematics tripos he was accepted as a student of physics and was awarded a first class in Part II in 1921. In the autumn of that year he became a research student under Rutherford, who had arrived at the Cavendish Laboratory two years earlier. Rutherford had been appointed the head of the Manchester physics department in 1907 and in the 12 years before he moved to Cambridge he had made two of his greatest discoveries. In 1911 he measured the deflection of the α-particles from a radioactive source when they passed through a sheet of mica and concluded that the mass of the atom was concentrated in a nucleus less than a thousandth of the size of the atom. Then in 1919 shortly before leaving Manchester, Rutherford discovered that by firing fast-particles into nitrogen he obtained hydrogen particles of greater energy than could be expected from elastic collisions and concluded that the nitrogen nucleus was being disintegrated in the impact.

The discovery was made by using a low-power microscope to observe the scintillations caused by the impact of the fast particles on a zinc sulphide screen. Rutherford wanted to obtain visual evidence of this disintegration and on arrival in Cambridge he had instructed a Japanese pupil, Shimizu, to use a Wilson cloud chamber to investigate what happened when α-particles hit the nucleus of a nitrogen atom. Shimizu soon departed for Japan but before doing so he had made an automatic cloud chamber and had secured a few thousand photographs of the tracks of α-particles in the cloud chamber. It was this problem that Rutherford handed over to Blackett.

Blackett modified the cloud chamber and within a few months he had taken 25,000 photographs. One of these yielded the clear evidence of the disintegration of the nitrogen nucleus. This photograph was soon to adorn every contemporary textbook of physics. In this work Blackett revealed his mastery and, indeed, his delight in experimental techniques. At this moment of triumph he decided to study the electronic structure of atoms with James Franck in Göttingen. Rutherford was annoyed with Blackett on two counts: first, that he wanted to leave the Cavendish for a year, and second, that he should be interested in anything but the nucleus of the atom.

After a year in Germany, Blackett returned to Cambridge and produced a series of papers on α-particle tracks in cloud chambers and on other topics that exemplified the elegance of his experimental technique, which, combined with his theoretical treatment of the systems and results, made him unique among the scientists of his age.

In 1932, although still in the Cavendish Laboratory and using the cloud chamber technique, Blackett's research underwent an important change. A few years earlier scientists in Germany, Paris and America had discovered tracks in the cloud chamber associated with cosmic rays – a penetrating corpuscular radiation incident on the Earth from outer space. Random expansions of the cloud chamber had been used for these observations. In 1932 an Italian student G.P.S. ('Beppe') Occhialini arrived in the Cavendish. He had worked in Italy with Bruno Rossi who had devised a coincidence system using Geiger counters for investigating the cosmic rays. In essence the system would respond only if an ionising particle passed through two or more Geiger counters. Occhialini introduced this scheme to Blackett who immediately grasped that the technique could be used to control the expansion of the cloud chamber. For example, with one Geiger counter above the cloud chamber and another below, the expansion could be triggered only if a cosmic ray particle passed through the cloud chamber. Formerly it required at least ten random expansions to photograph one track – and many of these were not of good quality. Of the first trial of the counter-controlled chamber, Occhialini said this at the Royal Society Memorial Meeting for Blackett in 1974:

> what not everyone had the chance to see was the passionate intensity in which he worked. I can still see him, that Saturday morning when we first ran the chamber, bursting out of the dark room with four dripping photographic plates held high and shouting for all the Cavendish to hear, 'One on each, Beppe, one on each.'

This technique, with the cloud chamber placed between the poles of a solenoid so that the curvature and thus the energy of the particles could be measured, dominated Blackett's research until the outbreak of the Second World War. In February 1933, the historic paper describing the evidence for the positive electron was published. Seven hundred automatic exposures yielded high-energy particles on more than 500 of the photographs. The interaction of the particles with matter was observed by placing a metal plate across the middle of the chamber and in the shower of tracks emanating from the plate they found 14 tracks which must have been caused by 'positively charged particles with a mass comparable with that of an electron'. In America, Anderson had already reached a similar conclusion. This independent discovery of the positive electron (or positron) marks a memorable event in Blackett's career – the second of two major discoveries in his years at the Cavendish for which he was ultimately to be awarded the Nobel prize for physics in 1948.

Blackett was soon to leave the Cavendish. He complained of the heavy teaching load and although he owed so much to Rutherford the two were not entirely compatible. Blackett, elected a Fellow of the Royal Society in 1933, wanted to run his own laboratory and be his own dictator. In 1933 he moved to Birkbeck where, at that time, teaching was confined to the evening and he had all the day for research.

At Birkbeck, Blackett became wholly concerned with cosmic rays. He secured money for the construction of a large electromagnet and cloud chamber system. He designed and built the 10-ton electromagnet giving a field of 14,000 gauss in a 15-cm gap between pole pieces 25 cm diameter. This equipment was a major departure in the nature of experimental physics of that epoch. Air-cooled, the magnet needed 25 kW and the whole counter-controlled cloud chamber exhibited Blackett's immense skill in the design of experimental apparatus. There was no chance of installing this system at Birkbeck so Blackett persuaded the college to erect a wooden hut (the Magnet House) in Malet Street.

In the years during which this equipment operated in Malet Street, Blackett investigated the energy spectrum of the cosmic rays. In these measurements he found some puzzling features which led him to conclude that 15 per cent of the primary particles were of protonic mass (that is, mass of the hydrogen nucleus). This was the beginning of an epic dispute in which Blackett maintained for some years that the behaviour of electrons and positrons of high energy could not be explained by existing theories. The essence of the problem was to explain how an electron of high-energy incident on the top of the atmosphere could penetrate to sea level with relatively little loss of energy. According to existing measurements of the absorption of cosmic rays the chance of this occurrence would be only about 10^{-5}. It is one of the oddities of Blackett's scientific career that he failed to recognise the significance of theoretical work in Cambridge published at that time which explained the apparent anomaly (the cascade theory of H. Bhabha and W. Heitler which showed that a particle of high energy traversing the atmosphere would give rise to a large shower of particles through successive collisions).

The year of 1937 proved to be one of much confusion for Blackett. After further measurements he concluded that the cascade theory was in principle correct, but that the theory must break down for particles of very high energy. In fact, he was being forced to the conclusion already reached by Neddermeyer and Anderson in America that other types of particle were present and that the great majority of the rays were 'probably not normal electrons'.

In the midst of these arguments about the nature of the penetrating cosmic rays Blackett moved to Manchester. The change in the nature of the physics department was cataclysmic. All the existing research vanished and the arrival of the 10-ton electromagnet from Birkbeck caused consternation in a university which was not then accustomed to 'big science'. With remarkable speed Blackett created a major research centre for cosmic rays. The laboratory became a haven for refugees fleeing from fascist Germany and Italy, and there were always visiting scientists of great distinction.

A few months after Blackett's arrival the coincidence of Werner Heisenberg and Homni Bhabha in the department led to a memorable weekend conference during which Blackett was finally convinced that relativistic quantum theory did not fail at high energies – that the cascade theory was correct and that particles heavier than electrons were in the primary cosmic ray beam at sea level – then called mesotrons or mesons. In an address to the British Association in 1938 Blackett cast aside all his previous doubts:

> the penetrating rays which are in a great majority at sea level, must consist of a new type of particle with a mass intermediate between that of an electron and that of a proton ... cloud chamber photographs have shown that the mass of the new particle is probably of the order of 150 times the mass of the electron.

During those first years in Manchester, Blackett was frequently absent from the laboratory. He gave many external lectures and in the summer of 1939 attended a major international cosmic ray conference in America. He always returned from these absences with a degree of impatience and would instantly pull a card from his pocket with a long list of jobs which he thought should have been done or with further instructions for action. His own technical skills were so great that he assumed others had similar abilities, be it to make Geiger counters or procure and erect a ton of lead blocks above the cloud chamber. He would then vanish and return days later with a similar list.

No doubt for the other young people on his staff there came a moment when they realised that factors other than cosmic rays were occupying Blackett's life. The present author's moment of realisation came abruptly one morning in early August 1939. About to complete packing the equipment in a van to be driven across France to the Pic du Midi in the Pyrenees in order to study cosmic rays at a higher altitude, there was an urgent summons to the telephone: 'On no account begin that journey – there is another job for you.'

Blackett's absence from the laboratory and his often terse behaviour and extravagant demands arose from his two lives – only one of which we knew. Indeed, the full extent of his other life, intimately involved with the Tizard Committee in the development of radar and the quarrels with Lindemann (later Cherwell), was not revealed until much later. The origin of Blackett's involvement in defence was the invitation in December 1934 from Lord Londonderry, the Secretary of State for Air, to serve on a committee under Sir Henry Tizard as chairman, to study possible means of destroying enemy aircraft. Blackett's name had been proposed by A.V. Hill as a naval officer before and during the war who had since proved himself by his work at Cambridge as one of the best of the younger scientific leaders of the day.

This was the beginning of Blackett's years when he used his scientific skills and instincts in the service of the armed forces – first in his development of the Mark XIV bomb sight at RAF Farnborough, then successively as scientific adviser to Anti-Aircraft Command and to RAF Coastal Command, and finally as Director of Naval Operational Research.

Blackett left the Admiralty at the end of the war and returned to Manchester. He was in his 48th year and with dynamic energy recreated his research department at a time of faith and hope in science and scientists. Simultaneously, his political activities occupied much of his time and thought. His wartime confrontations were as nothing compared with the bitterness of his political and scientific disagreements over atomic policy, which were to isolate him from the centres of power and influence for many years. His alignment with the Labour politicians in devising a scientific and technical policy for the UK and his increasing involvement with the generality of university problems, and later with India, led to a substantial diversion from his personal scientific research in the post-war years.

Nevertheless, and particularly after his membership of the Advisory Committee on Atomic Energy ended in 1947, he concentrated on the restoration of the physics department with great energy and determination. He expanded the cosmic ray researches in several directions and, in 1946 and 1947, G.D. Rochester and C.C. Butler made the major discovery of new fundamental particles – the V particles. Blackett's excitement and involvement in the discussions and arguments about these results did not deflect him from other investigations. He became interested in the Cerenkov effect and concluded that an extensive cosmic ray air shower should produce a flash of light, visible against a dark sky. He proceeded to carry out this investigation himself and stimulated further research of the phenomena.

Blackett's study of the Cerenkov effect was the effective end of his own research on cosmic rays. In the following years he continued to exert a great influence on the development of the cosmic ray research in Manchester and elsewhere, but his own interests underwent a remarkable diversion to the problem of the magnetic field. He became interested in the influence of stellar magnetic fields on cosmic ray phenomena. In these investigations he noticed that for the Earth and the Sun the magnetic moments were nearly proportional to the angular momentum. He studied the literature and, to his surprise, found that this general relationship had been known for some time and that a further test would be to make a measurement of the magnetic field of a star. At this moment he learned that astronomers in America had succeeded in making the first ever measurement of a stellar magnetic field and that the star, 78 Virginis, gave a polar field of 1,500 gauss. Blackett was highly excited and on 15 May 1947 read a paper to the Royal Society. He believed he had solved the problem of the origin of magnetic fields and that hitherto unknown principles of physics might be involved. Blackett had revived an idea first suggested by Schuster in 1911, that any massive body has a magnetic moment which exists in addition to and independent of any moment produced by ferromagnetic materials or electric current.

Blackett thought he could make a laboratory test of this law and began one of the most extraordinary experiments of his whole career. In order to test the theory that a rotating body should have a magnetic field he proceeded to build a magnetometer of great sensitivity with which he could detect a magnetic field of 10^{-8} gauss. In order to escape the local disturbance in the Manchester laboratory, he erected a copper-nailed wooden hut in a remote corner of a field at Jodrell Bank. The magnetometer case was carried on a massive concrete block supported on a 1-inch layer of soft rubber. The magnetometer was suspended on a quartz fibre, 25 cm long and 12–18 micrometres in diameter.

Blackett originally intended to spin a sphere beneath the magnetometer. Before attempting this difficult and hazardous task he decided to plan a simpler experiment based on the hypothesis that a field should exist near a massive body, at rest relative to the measuring instrument, due to the fact that both the body and the measuring instrument were rotating with the Earth. He used a gold cylinder 10 cm × 10 cm of mass 15.2 kg. He began observations during the spring of 1949 and continued for two years, by which time he had obtained a definite negative result. By that time other measurements had also cast doubt on the hypothesis.

Before Blackett decided to end these measurements his main interest had already shifted to another problem for which the magnetometer was admirably suited. He had seen a paper from the Department of Terrestrial Magnetism, Washington, on the pre-history of the Earth's magnetic field which claimed that the history of the Earth's field could be traced far beyond historic times by the measurement of the weak magnetism of certain sedimentary rocks. Blackett immediately visualised the possibility of extending the history of the Earth's field from the 400 years of the compass needle to over 500 million years of geological history for which reliable dating using fossils is possible. With his magnetometer he estimated that he could achieve ten times more sensitivity than the Americans. Blackett soon built up a research group to study rock magnetism and in the early months of 1953, shortly before the end of his Manchester period, his group had a major success. Measurements on samples of Triassic sandstones collected from two sites in Cheshire 35 miles apart showed that they were magnetised along an axis differing substantially from the present direction of the Earth's field. Measurements from more distant sites in England revealed that the landmass which is now Britain had rotated clockwise over 30 degrees and shifted from a position near the Equator. At this point Blackett and his rock-magnetic group left Manchester for Imperial College.

In the eight-year post-war period which Blackett spent in Manchester he was involved in many other activities apart from his cosmic ray and magnetic researches. There were two other scientific developments with which he became deeply involved. His association with F.C. Williams had stimulated his enthusiasm for computers. Before the war he had collaborated with Williams in devising a photoelectric curve follower for D.R. Hartree's mechanical differential analyser. By the standards of that time this was a remarkable device which followed the input curve more accurately than it was possible to do so by hand. This Blackett/Williams association became of great importance after the war. Williams believed that Blackett was entirely responsible for persuading the Ministry of Supply to place a £100,000 contract for the development of Williams's digital computer with Ferranti.

The other major development followed from the author's pre-war research in Blackett's laboratory on the high-energy region of the cosmic ray spectrum through the study of large cosmic ray air showers. This led through a most improbable series of events to the astronomical establishment now known as Jodrell Bank. Without Blackett's support and his political and tactical manipulations, both inside and outside the university, the large radio telescopes would never have been built. Indeed, it was his memory of the Battle of Jutland when he served on HMS *Barham* that led to his opinion that steering the 250-ft diameter telescope was similar to that of directing the 15-inch battleship guns. His direction to the breakers yard led to the procurement of the gun turret racks from HMS *Royal Sovereign* and HMS *Revenge* and 45 years later the elevation control of the telescope remains exactly as he had envisaged it – through those gun turret racks and analogous control system.

To the surprise of many, in 1953 Blackett decided to accept the invitation to succeed Sir George Thomson at Imperial College. He had never intended to spend the rest of his career in Manchester and at the age of 56 he felt this was the latest age he could make a worthwhile move to another place. The government had recently decided to double the size of Imperial College within ten years and this, no doubt, greatly influenced his decision.

Although Blackett was initially reluctant to become involved in the details of the new buildings he soon exerted his influence on the design, and when it was completed in 1960 his achievement was manifest. Typically during this period he had exerted a great influence on the staffing of the department. In an age when multi-professorial departments were rare he created seven new chairs.

From Manchester Blackett brought the core of his rock magnetic group and this remained his primary research interest. Twenty-five years had elapsed since the publication of Wegener's controversial work on the origin of continents and oceans. Blackett instantly realised the importance of the rock magnetic measurements to the continuing inconclusive debate. He initiated major investigations of the Triassic sandstones in Europe and set up a laboratory in Bombay to make a palaeomagnetic survey of the Indian subcontinent. The Royal Society discussion meeting on continental drift in March 1964 had been arranged by Blackett, and his rock magnetic measurements were a substantial influence in the changing attitudes in support of the theory of continental drift.

In the autumn of 1964 Blackett reached his 67th birthday – the age of his retirement from the chair of physics at Imperial College. His active research career had lasted for 43 years, interrupted by the six years of the Second World War. He achieved international renown in three fields of research – nuclear physics, cosmic rays and geomagnetism, and for his achievements in these subjects he will be remembered as one of the great scientists of the twentieth century. His influence outside the walls of his laboratory was immense. In the year of his retirement from Imperial College he was appointed chairman of the Advisory Council in the newly formed Ministry of Technology. This was the culmination of his work during the previous 14 years with the small group seeking to evolve a scientific and technological policy for a future Labour government. He was by Harold Wilson's side during the famous speech at the Labour Party Scarborough conference in 1963 when Wilson talked about the Britain that would be forged in the 'white heat of the technological revolution' to be initiated by a Labour government. After the Labour victory in the General Election of October 1964 the Ministry of Technology was created with Blackett as the adviser to the minister and the major influence in the new ministry.

Although Blackett had been one of the major architects of this ministry, his election as President of the Royal Society in November 1965 took precedence over all other activities. He exerted a great influence on the activities of the Society. The Royal Society emerged from the elitist body of scientists to attain the influence in international science and nationally in the support of engineering, technology and education which it holds today. His five years as president were a fitting climax to a career in science of the greatest distinction.

NOTE

1. Royal Society BLA/A11, a typescript of autobiographical reminiscences by Patrick Blackett (three versions of 'My Early Life').

16

The Reluctant Peer in Politics

Harold Wilson[1]

Pat Blackett was one of the most reluctant peers I have ever known and I will not refer to him as Lord Blackett: his career was long, distinguished and diverse, and his interests were in no way confined to science or confined directly to Britain.[2] Pat made distinguished contributions to fundamental theoretical work in several fields of physics, and the British and international scientific world is agreed about Pat Blackett's eminence in these fields, which led to the award of the Nobel prize for physics. Such pre-eminent excellence in one field would have sufficed for most men: not for Pat, who went on to show that he was able to make as outstanding a contribution to experimental and applied science as to theoretical physics, in war and in peace.

In war his great contribution came in the application of scientific techniques to the winning of the Second World War. Of particular importance was his determination to develop and to apply operational research techniques to the problems of warfare. War had moved out of the period when it was possible to depend only on the courage of the individual soldier, the tactical intelligence of the local commander and the hope that the quartermaster had brought up not only the bullets but the bully beef. The application of scientific techniques by Pat Blackett and his collaborators in the Second World War made a significant contribution to the war effort, in particular to the defeat of the U-boat offensive, which was threatening to bring this country to the edge of disaster.

In the winter of 1940 and spring of 1941 long-range German aircraft were taking a heavy toll of our shipping in an area, roughly 200 by 200 miles, west of Ireland. One of our fighters could be expected to sight an enemy aircraft at a distance of ten miles, and could therefore 'sweep' a lane 20 miles wide. It was therefore argued that the best tactic was to wait until ten fighters were serviceable and all there together and then sweep the entire area. The disadvantage was that when there were not ten fighters available none went out at all. His comment was this:

> The argument was that when 10 fighters were flown, the whole area was swept clean and the chance of sighting the enemy was 100 per cent; that meant that it was certain he would be sighted. When, however, any fewer number of fighters were flown, then the chance of sighting the enemy was less than 100 per cent; *in that case he might not be sighted at all.* The last statement is of course correct.

But, as Pat Blackett pointed out, the argument revealed 'a not-uncommon misconception about a problem in the theory of probability' and 'an exaggerated estimate of the actual probability (calculated by applying Poisson's Distribution) of the enemy not being sighted at all'. His analytical document of May 1943 set out the approaches that had had to be considered to this problem. It is quoted in the record of the Royal Society Memorial Meeting, and the extracts reveal a major contribution to the pioneering of operational research in this country. Comparing what he called the 'a priori', and the 'variational' methods, he went on:

> Another method of attack is to abandon the attempt to construct from 'first principles' a complete imaginary operation something like the real one under investigation, and to replace it by the attempt to find, by both experimental and analytical methods, how a real operation would be altered if certain of the variables, e.g. the tactics employed or properties of the weapons used, were varied

And of course the air marshals were vastly illuminated:

> Suppose the result of any operation of war is denoted by quantities Y_1, Y_2, etc. called the yields. Then these yields must be considered as functions of a larger number of operational parameters or variables X_1, X_2, … X, … Some of these can be given a quantitative measure but some can only be expressed qualitatively. An attempt to find the form of such a function … from first principles is, in general, of limited value, owing to the complexity of the problem and the non-quantitative nature of many of the variables. The

> common-sense procedure is to use the result Y of some past operation under known conditions to predict the result Y^1 of a future operation under new conditions.

In a tribute to the work of the scientific section of Coastal Command headed, until he moved on to naval operations, by Blackett, Air Chief Marshal Sir John Slessor said:

> A few years ago it would never have occurred to me – or I think to any officer of any fighting service – that what the RAF soon came to call a 'Boffin', a gentleman in grey flannel bags, whose occupation in life had previously been something markedly unmilitary such as biology or physiology, would be able to teach us a great deal about our business. Yet so it was.

Pat Blackett also made a significant contribution to the application of science and of scientific techniques to the problems of the peace. He would have readily echoed the words of Milton that 'Peace hath her victories, No less renowned than war.'

As President of the Board of Trade I had piloted through the House of Commons in 1948 the Development of Inventions Bill, which led to the creation of the National Research Development Corporation. Small though the bill was, and small the money voted for it, I believe it was one of the most brilliant, ingenious and – as it has turned out – rewarding concepts in our generation. I can say that without any loss of modesty because the idea was not mine but that of my predecessor, Sir Stafford Cripps. On the day he handed over to me, he mentioned three priorities he hoped I would follow with urgency and the setting up of the NRDC was one of these.

Cripps's qualifications were those of a scientist, a First World War factory manager before he became lawyer, long experience of patent work at the Bar followed by his Second World War experience as Minister of Aircraft Production. The consequence was an obsession with the extent to which one after another breakthrough by British scientists, particularly in universities and government research establishments, was picked up by some keen observer, most often not a British national, and then clothed with know-how on which ultimately we had to pay royalties. A whole generation of research – jets, radar, antibiotics – had been surrendered to the Americans virtually without payment: Cripps was determined that the work of the next generation, that is to say the early post-war generation, should be protected. NRDC was to be an essential means to this end. The key concept was 'Research Development', not, as so frequently misquoted, 'Research *and* Development', R & D.

When I came to set up NRDC in 1949, I appointed Pat Blackett to it. His appointment produced one of the most violent political reactions in Parliament I have known in 30 years there. The attacks on Pat Blackett which I had to meet make other Parliamentary turbulence like a gentle breeze in comparison. Pat Blackett was denounced and traduced mainly for the unorthodoxy of his views on world affairs, including nuclear questions and the need for co-operation with the Soviet Union and other countries, particularly if we were to avoid the division of the world into major nuclear power blocs, spreading to more and more smaller countries. It was his role as a missionary, not his role as a scientist, that some front-bench parliamentarians criticised.

He served on NRDC from its foundation in 1949 until 1964 when he came full time into the work of the new Ministry of Technology which I established. Over those 15 years he contributed a great deal to its development, and I believe he learned quite a lot from it, particularly on what would now be called the 'interface' between science and technology and productive industry.

All critics and some friends of NRDC thought that the £5 million with which it was endowed would not last long and might speedily go down the drain. That thought underlay the then Opposition attack on the whole concept. In the event, this forecast proved false. And, indeed, I would have been prepared to let it go down the drain if it did its job. From 1964, as the result of a lot of work Pat Blackett and I had done together just before entering government, we greatly expanded the provision and gave the corporation a new and more dynamic role.

The Development of Inventions Act 1965 raised NRDC's borrowing powers from £10 million to £25 million, and in 1963 the borrowing limit was raised to £50 million. But NRDC had been so successful in recent years that this last additional tranche of £25 million was not needed. Indeed, NRDC had required no government loans since 1971, and had been not only able to meet its outgoings from royalty and levy income but able to repay a considerable amount of its earlier borrowing.

Taking inventions and processes from universities, from government and other research establishments, nationalised industries, small and large firms in the private sector and private inventors, NRDC, by 1975, had assessed over 33,000 inventions in just over a quarter of a century. It had accepted about 6,300 for further development or exploitation, and it had successfully completed 1,660 licence agreements in Britain, and 224 foreign licence agreements. Its total number of income-earning inventions was 833. An organisation which was expected to lose money and still be worth having had been able to net a total licensing income from all sources of £39 million, of which £30 million had been earned from companies abroad. It had also undertaken joint projects with industrial partners and invested over £31 million, the greater part with industry on a pound-for-pound basis.

What Pat Blackett contributed and learned there I think made a powerful impact on his mind, and on his new thinking, in the late 1950s and early 1960s, about what an incoming Labour government might do in the field of industry and technology. It is, I think, no secret that his political views were more in sympathy with the Labour Party than with either of the other two main parties, though on a number of questions, particularly nuclear and certain international questions, he was highly critical of Labour establishment thinking, and was never afraid to make declarations which only tangentially approached some of the then current thinking of Labour's left.

In the years when Labour was out of office, he inevitably made less contribution to the work of government, though he still had his work on NRDC. But he was again able to devote his unbounding energies and resource to his scientific work, which enjoyed a second flowering both at Manchester and at Imperial College. After his move to Imperial College, Pat Blackett's major research interest was in rock magnetism, in which he did pioneering work of great importance even though he was intimately concerned with the great expansion of the college itself.

Towards the end of the 1950s, a group was formed to advise Labour Party leaders on the kind of things we should be thinking about on returning to government. The group was convened by a non-scientist, Marcus Brumwell, who hosted its meetings, and it provided a dining forum in which Labour frontbenchers joined with an unparalleled team of distinguished scientists and thinkers. Hugh Gaitskell attended it once or twice, and Alf Robens for a period was the main front-bench representative, though I later became a regular for a number of years up to and after becoming Leader of the Party. It was led by such men as Bernal,[3] Charles Snow,[4] Professor Bruce

Williams, Professor C.F. Carter, and Dr Bronowski.[5] Other distinguished scientists and technologists I prefer not to mention because of possible embarrassment to them.

On becoming Leader, I brought Dick Crossman from the backbenches and made him shadow spokesman on higher education and science, and he derived great inspiration and challenge from Pat Blackett and his colleagues. The then Conservative government were considering the future organisation of responsibility for science, higher education and technology. These were the years of the Trend Report, ending with the Hailsham–Boyle condominium at the new Department of Education and Science. But, as always, there was not enough thought given to technology, or the developments that were possible arising from technology.

I had told Pat Blackett that on forming a government I would set up a Ministry of Technology, separate from Education. (In passing, may I say that departmental reorganisation is always a choice of evils – if you decide that higher education must go with schools, and the whole range of education with science, then you have got either to separate technology from industry or to separate technology from science.) Very much influenced by Pat Blackett on these matters, I told him I would set up the Ministry of Technology which would begin as 'NRDC writ large' and then go on over a period to take over some of the main industrial functions – some of which were not being performed at all – from the Board of Trade, together with nuclear industry and research (other than military establishments), and the engineering functions from the Ministry of Aviation, together with shipbuilding.

Pat Blackett was delighted at the thought, and a few weeks before I was commissioned to form a government he handed me the first copy of his epoch-making paper entitled 'The Case for a Ministry of Technology'. During the weeks just before the general election of October 1964, he expressed anxieties about the possibility of maintaining in being an independent indigenous British computer industry, and said we should have to move very fast indeed on coming into office. When I formed the government and appointed Frank Cousins as the first Minister of Technology I told him of his remit, and my plans for the expansion of his ministry. I told him also that he had only a matter of weeks, perhaps not even beyond Christmas of that year, to save the British computer industry. I said, 'I don't know how you're going to do it, but you'd better get hold of Pat – he's the only one who can tell you how.'

This was done. Some of the methods were unorthodox to a degree. We found that an assortment of government departments were busy buying foreign products. I issued a directive saying that no department could buy a foreign product without making a case for so doing – in Cabinet itself. After two or three unsuccessful attempts to make cases, departments decided it was not worth the candle of subjecting their ministers to a period of hammering by Frank Cousins and myself. Looking back, I am not quite sure how this new form of protectionism fitted in with the requirements of GATT (General Agreement on Tariffs and Trade), the negotiation of which had been another of my 1948 preoccupations. But however that may be, it enabled me some time afterwards to interrupt a tirade from President de Gaulle about British subservience to the Americans, by reverently expressing my deep sympathy that the French government had not been able to prevent the take-over of their one substantial computer firm, Machine Bull, by General Electric.

Facing this and other urgent challenges, Pat Blackett, on the formation of the government, moved full time into his task – not only of saving computers, but of masterminding the creation of the new ministry, and helping Frank Cousins, and later Tony Benn, to instil an entirely new dynamic into Whitehall and indeed the wider field of British technology and industry. He was not a great admirer of advisory committees. Indeed, he made this clear in an article in the *New Statesman* just before the 1964 election.[6] He referred to advisory committees, 'so beloved of Whitehall, I suspect, just because of their relative ineffectiveness', and wrote that the Whitehall system 'seems almost designed to ensure the giving of advice without the responsibility of action and the taking of action without real knowledge'. He then compared advisory councils to the story of the FAO bull:

> Once upon a time, not long ago, the Food and Agricultural Organisation of the United Nations sent a prize bull to some developing country to improve the local breed of cattle. When the bull arrived it showed amiable interest but no more in the cows presented to him. When asked why he did not get on with his job, the bull replied: 'You forget that I am an FAO bull – so my role is solely advisory.'

In fact, Pat became deputy chairman of the Minister's Advisory Council on Technology (the Minister himself taking the chair) and also Scientific Adviser to the Ministry. But his influence and power far transcended the titles of these posts. I myself would have wished to bring him into the administration had he not been unwilling to go to the House of Lords at that time. He rejected the idea because he disliked anything smacking of inegalitarianism, but I felt that he could possibly have made an even greater contribution as a minister of state, had he felt able to accept it.

In the ministry he was responsible for attracting to the new department perhaps the most distinguished team of outstanding scientists ever engaged in such work, including John Adams.[7] Indeed, Pat Blackett, before he died, told a friend of mine who was doing Frank Cousins' biography that John Adams would not have joined the ministry if Pat Blackett had not been there. In July 1965, John Adams joined the Ministry of Technology as Controller.

Work on computers went beyond saving the British industry. Pat Blackett was responsible for the decision to set up a National Computer Centre at Manchester, to promote the effective use of computers through the dissemination of information and the provision of education and training in the use, programming and operation of computers. He was responsible also, with Ben Cant and Thomas Balogh, for one of the most important developments in the whole history of relations between government and industry, the Industrial Reorganisation Corporation, though he always regretted that this was taken over by the Department of Economic Affairs, who were responsible for the legislation. The bill to create IRC was the subject of the same shrill ideological battle as NRDC 18 years earlier, but, as soon as the corporation was established, it was wholeheartedly welcomed by industry, and the number of and distinction of top industrialists who joined this board probably excelled that of any industrial organisation ever set up in this country. Pat Blackett was later on record as saying that the decision of the incoming government in 1970 to change the nature of the ministry and to abandon IRC had cost the country at least two and a half years of 'crucial development time'.

Tony Benn, when he heard that I was to give this lecture, kindly wrote out several pages about Pat Blackett's role during the years when Tony Benn was a minister. 'It was on his shoulders', he wrote, 'that the main responsibility for formulating the objectives of the new Ministry of Technology rested when the Department was set up.' After referring to IRC and industrial restructuring, the Secretary of State for Energy goes on to say this:

> Another concern of his was the reorganization of Britain's research establishments, including the AEA, so that they could work with industry. For this reason Pat Blackett was keen to release more scientists and engineers into manufacturing industry, rather than entrench them in their laboratories with wider terms of reference. He therefore opposed a suggestion that the AEA should be converted into a British Technological Authority as had been proposed, believing that this would widen rather than narrow the Research/Industry gap. This issue continued to absorb a great deal of his time and interest, and he watched the manpower and research budgets of all the Government laboratories with a keen attention to this point.

Another nuclear project, since proved successful, with which the ministry was closely concerned was the development of the centrifuge project for the enrichment of uranium, in which Britain made a historic breakthrough and proceeded to finalise the process to full production in concert with the industry of Germany and the Netherlands.

When he became President of the Royal Society, in November 1965, Pat Blackett was able to give less of his time to the ministry, and had to give up his deputy chairmanship of the Advisory Council, but he continued as Chief Scientific Adviser, and was always ready to read the papers and give his advice to the minister.

Taking his entire contribution from 1964 to 1970, there can be no questioning of the central role Pat Blackett therefore played not only in the wedding of technology to government, and technology to industry, but also in stimulating and encouraging a development which was already proceeding in industry, in the 1960s and since – the development of a much more competent, professional corps of industrial management.

In April 1964, an article in *The Times* could summarise the sickness of British industry and management caused by this amateurism in these words:

> Money or a title alone still continues frequently to be the sole criterion for election of men (often holding a score or more similar appointments on other boards) who have but the vaguest idea of how the products of their firms are conceived, developed, made and sold. This is not denying the value of experienced men being

> brought in. But while the choice of the dilettante director remains a feature of company control, can this be claimed as anything but amateurism? On the executive side the trained director is the exception and not the rule. It is an acknowledged fact that the calibre of the lower echelons of managers still leaves a lot to be desired.

Six years later, in January 1970, I was asked to address the New York Foundation for Automation and Employment and, quoting what *The Times* had said in 1964, I followed it with a contemporary commentary, actually in the *Director*:

> on the brighter side, whole sectors of British industry have grown more efficient. British exporters have achieved staggering success and, despite all the strains imposed by Government and change, Britain goes into the 1970s still the most tolerant and democratic society in the world, with high hopes of industrial resurgence and new bonds with a united Europe. And from the boardroom view, perhaps the most significant achievement of the 1960s was the improvement in the expertise and knowledge, and the sustained enthusiasm, of the young British executive. Ask any international consultant where the best management lies, and he will put Britain high on the list.

No one would pretend that the Ministry of Technology, as Pat Blackett conceived it, solved all problems, even those which, looking back on those pre-oil prices days, now seem minuscule compared with those of today.

But Pat Blackett's message, the message that we have in the last resort only our wits to live on and we must make the very best of them, still stands, and is as true today as it ever was. If our industry is to be competitive and able to produce the wealth and prosperity on which all our social services and all the many other desirable things we want to do must depend, then we have to develop and apply the science and technology in which we can excel. If we could achieve only a small part of the excellence in all the skills which are necessary – marketing, finance, human relations, besides science and technology – that Pat Blackett brought to his many careers then we shall not fail to make our industry once again successful.

I would like to end on two points. Both of them are personally related to Pat Blackett. The first is the role of the universities, and indeed of the educational world as a whole, in developing the kind of relationships that are necessary between industry, science and government. Throughout almost all his working life, he had a university base. Despite his many and varied excursions into other fields, he always returned to the university. He recognised and fully understood the role which the universities – which are so widely represented here today – can make to our society. It is in the hands of so many here not only to teach and develop young men and women into critical and creative adults, but also to communicate to them the responsibility for developing the application of science and technology to the economy and to industry which was so dear to Pat Blackett's heart. As Chancellor of one of our great technological universities, Bradford, I welcomed the great support and impetus that Pat Blackett gave to the new technological universities, and particularly his doctrine of parity of esteem between them and older-established universities.

The second is that I welcomed too Blackett's emphasis on the interplay between science and technology. This reflected on his part a generation's work on trying to break down separatisms: separatism between research and industry, separatism – indeed class distinction – between different toilers in the same vineyard. For him, therefore, it was again a question of parity of esteem between a production engineer and a theoretical physicist.

Pat Blackett was concerned with one thing only and that was excellence. But he had the breadth of vision to see that excellence in the elimination of poverty and the creation of prosperity is as important as the development of the very frontiers of knowledge. Indeed, as Pat Blackett himself recognised, the two are interdependent. A society which is not materially prosperous will not be able to afford to do the fundamental scientific work which itself in turn will eventually stimulate and make possible the extension of that prosperity.

He was given endless formal recognition and marks of distinction, besides the Nobel prize, becoming President of the Royal Society, a member of the Order of Merit and a life peer. He received honorary degrees from many universities, from Chicago to New Delhi.[8] He was an internationalist with a passion for developing countries, and particularly all he learned about and did for India and other countries he visited.

As a man, his steadfastness of purpose and uprightness of view and total intellectual honesty throughout a long life underpinned all that he did, and those who worked with him through his life have always commented on his generosity. He was modest and firm in equal proportions and secured a personal relationship of trust and confidence with university administrators, staff and students, ministers, officials, scientists and industrialists, all of whom listened with the closest attention to everything he said. That was merely one reflection of one of the many merits of a truly remarkable man.

NOTES

1. This chapter is edited, by kind permission of Lady Wilson, from a speech given by Harold Wilson, later Baron Wilson of Rievaulx, at Imperial College, London when the laboratory there was named after Patrick Blackett.
2. In 1942, when nominated by the Prime Minister, Winston Churchill, Blackett had peremptorily turned down the award of a CBE.
3. (John) Desmond Bernal (1901–71), a polymath, a contemporary of Blackett's at Cambridge, where he joined the Communist Party, and Blackett's successor at Birkbeck College. Bernal played a leading role in the development of crystallography and in founding molecular biology. Before the Second World War he was a member of the Cambridge Scientists' Anti-War Group, but during the war he was scientific adviser successively to the Ministry of Home Security, Bomber Command and Combined Operations, where, with Solly Zuckerman, he was personal adviser to Mountbatten. One of his projects was 'Habakkuk', a proposal to use icebergs as aircraft carriers.
4. Lord Snow (1905–80), better known as the novelist C.P. Snow, whose character Getcliffe in *The Corridors of Power* is based on Blackett. He sided with Tizard, against Cherwell, in the controversy over bombing Germany.
5. Jacob Bronowski (1908–74), also a contemporary of Blackett's at Cambridge, mathematician, poet, humanist and broadcaster. During the Second World War he helped develop the science of operational research and after the war he applied the lessons learned in the National Coal Board. Well known for his 1970s television series *The Ascent of Man.*
6. Patrick Blackett, 'Wanted: A Wand over Whitehall', *New Statesman*, 68, 346 (1964).
7. John Bodkin Adams (1920–84), a self-educated man who helped to develop microwave radars during the Second World War, was appointed Controller at the Ministry of Technology in Harold Wilson's first government, and was executive director-general of CERN, 1976–81. CERN was the European Organisation for Nuclear Research, always known by the initials of its French name, Conseil Européen pour la Recherche Nucléaire; it is now – how Blackett would have approved! – the European Laboratory for Particle Physics.
8. According to Blackett's own notes, prepared for his intended autobiography, he had received 20 honorary doctorates.

Notes on Contributors

Robert Anderson has been Visiting Fellow at Corpus Christi College, Cambridge, and is now Professor of Communications, Simon Fraser University, Vancouver, Canada. He has been studying the modern history of science for 30 years and is currently completing a book on the national and international influences on the development of the Indian nuclear programme from 1944.

John Brooks studied natural and electrical sciences at St John's College, Cambridge, and in 1964 joined Elliott Automation to research computer memory technology. In 1973 he moved to Systems Reliability, where he has held a number of senior engineering and management posts as the firm developed its telephone network management products. In 1992 his first historical paper, on dividing engines, was published. He is now a part-time consultant and a postgraduate student at the Department of War Studies, King's College, London, where he is writing his doctoral thesis on Dreadnought gunnery instruments.

Andrew Brown's background is in medicine with particular expertise in radiology. His first degree was in psychology at the University of Bristol and his second degree was in medicine and surgery at the University of London. A member of the Royal College of Physicians and of the Royal College of Radiologists, he has published many articles on radiological topics and, more recently, on Sir James Chadwick, the discoverer of the neutron. Currently he is Radiation Oncology Associate, Elliot Regional Cancer Center, Manchester, New Hampshire.

Paul Crook is Emeritus Professor of History at the University of Queensland, Australia, from which he was granted an honours degree (1958) and a Doctor of Letters (1988). He holds a doctorate from London University (1961). His books include: *American Democracy in English Politics* (1965), *Diplomacy During the American Civil War* (1975), *Benjamin Kidd: Portrait of a Social Darwinist* (1984) and *Darwinism, War and History* (1994). He has published widely on Darwinian influence on British social thought, and is at present investigating the inter-war period in Britain, with attention to eugenics, the debate over sterilisation of mental defectives and the scientific response to Nazi race theory. He has spent a number of study leaves at Cambridge and is a life member of Clare Hall. His interest in the area bombing debate was sparked by a reading of Desmond Bernal's papers in Cambridge University Library.

Evan Davies describes himself modestly as a long-term student of naval, military and maritime history. In fact, he is well known to at least two generations of naval officers whom he taught while at the Britannia Royal Naval College, Dartmouth, in the History and English Department (latterly Strategic Studies and International Affairs Department). He now teaches maritime history in the Institute of Maritime Studies in Plymouth University.

Jock Gardner served in the Royal Navy for 30 years working as a practising anti-submarine specialist, in operational research appointments and as a member of the Defence Intelligence Staff. He now works as a historian in the Naval Historical Branch of the Ministry of Defence. In 1988–89 he studied at Cambridge, writing a thesis on Soviet missile-firing submarines. He has had many historical and strategic articles published, and reviews books for a wide range of periodicals including the *Historical Journal*. His *Anti-Submarine Warfare* was published in 1996 and *Decoding History: The Battle of the Atlantic and Ultra*, a re-evaluation of the significance of intelligence derived from code breaking in this important warfare area, was published in 1999.

Peter Hore, the Royal Navy's recently retired Head of Defence Studies, is originally a logistics officer who served at sea in frigates and destroyers, including exchange service in the United States Navy and two tours in the NATO Standing Naval Force. As a Captain he served in central appointments in the British Ministry of Defence, helping to define defence and naval strategy, and researching international relations and the effects of changing concepts, technology and geopolitics. As Head of Studies he was responsible for promoting a deeper awareness and knowledge of defence, especially maritime affairs, and for bringing the views of the defence academic community to the attention of defence and naval staffs. He has edited *Dimensions of Sea Power: The Strategy of Choice* and *Maritime Aviation: Light and Medium Aircraft Carriers into the Twentieth Century* and is the author of, among others, *Seapower Ashore: 200 Years of Royal Navy Operations on Land* and *HMAS Sydney: The Cruiser and the Controversy*, as well as several articles and reviews.

Malcolm Llewellyn-Jones retired five years ago from the Royal Navy after 26 years' service, mainly in the Fleet Air Arm. He was involved in the analysis of helicopter anti-submarine tactics and his flying career culminated in command of a naval air squadron, followed by six years in the Ministry of Defence sponsoring the requirement and operational analysis studies for the Merlin anti-submarine helicopter. Having gained an MA in war studies in 1997 he is now researching aspects of anti-submarine warfare between 1944 and 1954 for a PhD at King's College, London. He has published papers on the British preparations to defeat the Type XXI U-boat, the anti-submarine submarine, and training against the fast submarine. He has recently been appointed as a historian in the Naval Historical Branch of the Ministry of Defence.

Bernard Lovell was born in Gloucestershire in 1913. After graduating and carrying out research in physics at the University of Bristol, he was appointed Assistant Lecturer in Physics at the University of Manchester in 1936. Blackett succeeded W.L. Bragg as the Langworthy Professor of Physics in 1937 and Lovell worked in his cosmic ray group until he was sent to Bawdsey Manor (Suffolk) in August 1939 to be initiated in radar research. During the war Lovell first worked on the development of centimetre radar using the new cavity magnetron. At the end of 1941 he formed the group to develop the blind bombing H2S equipment for Bomber Command and the centimetre ASV for Coastal Command. After the end of the war Lovell returned with Blackett to Manchester and, with two army trailers of radar equipment, initiated research (based on a joint

Blackett–Lovell wartime paper), which led to the development of the Jodrell Bank Observatory in Cheshire, to the construction of the large radio telescope and to the development of the new science of radio astronomy. He retired as Director of Jodrell Bank and as Professor of Radio Astronomy at the University of Manchester in 1981.

Mary Jo Nye's research interests include the history of chemistry and physics since the eighteenth century in western Europe and North America, the social and cultural history of science, the history of higher education, and the political activities of scientists. She graduated from Vanderbilt University and completed her doctoral thesis at the University of Wisconsin. She has taught at Oklahoma, Harvard, Pittsburgh and Princeton in North America and at Cambridge in England. She is currently Thomas Hart and Mary Jones Horning Professor of the Humanities and Professor of History at Oregon State University.

Richard Ormerod has a background in industrial management, operational research, corporate strategy and management consultancy. He obtained his first degree in engineering at the Royal Military College of Science, Shrivenham, and his Master's degree in management science and operational research at the University of Warwick. Currently he is Professor of Management and Director of Executive Programmes at Warwick Business School. He is a consultant to large corporations such as Sainsbury's, Rio Tinto and PowerGen.

Geoff Sloan is Head of the Strategic Studies Department at Britannia Royal Naval College, Dartmouth. He received his doctorate in international relations from Keele University, and was a visiting professor at the US Naval Academy at Annapolis, 1991–92, and a Defence Fellow at St Antony's College, Oxford University, 1994–95. His main research interests are geopolitics, intelligence and international relations, and he is a leading expert on the theories of Mackinder. His three books so far are: *Geopolitics in United States Strategic Policy 1890–1987*, *Geopolitics of Anglo-Irish Relations in the Twentieth Century* and *Geopolitics Geography and Strategy* (with Colin Gray).

Philip Towle is the Director of the Centre of International Studies at

Cambridge University. He has previously worked for the Arms Control Department of the Foreign and Commonwealth Office, for Reuters News Agency, for the Royal Naval College, Dartmouth, and for the Australian National University in Canberra. He has written widely on arms control, air power and East Asian affairs. His most recent book, *Enforced Disarmament from the Napoleonic Campaigns to the Gulf War*, was published in 1997.

Harold Wilson (1915–95) was Prime Minister of Britain for eight years (1964–70 and 1974–76). He studied at Oxford and taught economics there before becoming Research Assistant to Lord Beveridge. During the Second World War he served in the civil service. Elected to Parliament in 1945, he was appointed President of the Board of Trade in 1947, becoming, at 31, Britain's youngest Cabinet minister since William Pitt the Younger in 1792. A consummate politician, Wilson won four out of five general elections, more than any other post-war British leader of any party. In 1976 Her Majesty the Queen appointed Wilson a Knight of the Garter, and in 1983 he was created a life peer. His many problems and achievements while in office included the nationalisation of the coal industry, the declaration of independence by the Rhodesian white minority government, Anglo-American relations during the Vietnam War, a referendum on British membership of the European Economic Community, the ban on capital punishment, a devaluation of the pound and the foundation of the Open University for continuing education.

David Zimmerman graduated from the University of Toronto in 1981. His PhD, written at the University of New Brunswick, was entitled 'Northern Waves: Science, Technology and the Royal Canadian Navy, 1939–45', since when he has become a recognised expert in military tactics and technology of the twentieth century, particularly of the Second World War, and author of numerous papers. He is currently Professor of Military History at the Department of History, University of Victoria, British Columbia.

Index